Mary Queen of Scots and the Babington plot. Edited from the original documents in the Public Record Office, the Yelverton MSS., and elsewhere - Primary Source Edition

John Hungerford Pollen

Nabu Public Domain Reprints:

You are holding a reproduction of an original work published before 1923 that is in the public domain in the United States of America, and possibly other countries. You may freely copy and distribute this work as no entity (individual or corporate) has a copyright on the body of the work. This book may contain prior copyright references, and library stamps (as most of these works were scanned from library copies). These have been scanned and retained as part of the historical artifact.

This book may have occasional imperfections such as missing or blurred pages, poor pictures, errant marks, etc. that were either part of the original artifact, or were introduced by the scanning process. We believe this work is culturally important, and despite the imperfections, have elected to bring it back into print as part of our continuing commitment to the preservation of printed works worldwide. We appreciate your understanding of the imperfections in the preservation process, and hope you enjoy this valuable book.

PUBLICATIONS

OF THE

SCOTTISH HISTORY SOCIETY

THIRD SERIES

VOL.
III

MARY QUEEN OF SCOTS AND THE BABINGTON PLOT

1922

MARY QUEEN OF SCOTS
AND
THE BABINGTON PLOT

Edited, from the original documents in the
Public Record Office, the Yelverton MSS.,
and elsewhere, by

JOHN HUNGERFORD POLLEN, S.J.

EDINBURGH
Printed at the University Press by T. and A. Constable Ltd.
for the Scottish History Society
1922

QA
787
A1P6

CONTENTS

	PAGE
INTRODUCTION—	
§ I. THE BAN AGAINST THE PRINCE OF ORANGE, 1579-1584 .	xiii
1. Loyalty to Queen Mary,	xiii
2. Enterprises, Leagues, and Excommunication Rumours,	xv
3. The Ban against the Prince of Orange, 25 August 1580,	xix
4. Consequences of the ban,	xx
5. Consequences of the murder, 1584,	xxiii
§ II. SPIES AND DUPES, 1584-1585,	xxx
1. Walsingham's political morality,	xxx
2. Thomas Morgan and Charles Paget,	xxxiii
3. Walsingham's spies,	xxxv
4. Dupes,	xliii
§ III. SETTING THE DEATH-TRAP — DECEMBER 1585-JANUARY 1586,	xlix
1. Gilbert Gifford's first steps,	xlix
2. Thomas Phelippes,	liii
3. The death-trap,	lvi
NOTE ON OLD AND NEW STYLE IN DATES,	lxiv
§ IV. JOHN BALLARD, 1584-1586,	lxv
1. The Previous History of Ballard and Tyrrell,	lxvi
2. What is the value of Tyrrell's evidence?	lxxii
3. A pilgrimage to Rome, March 1584-January 1585,	lxxiii

		PAGE
4. Ballard's character,	. . .	lxxviii
5. Ballard's first steps in politics, 1585,	.	lxxxi
6 Bernard Mawde,	. . . .	lxxxiv

§ V. PLOT AND COUNTER-PLOT, APRIL 1586, . . lxxxvii
    1. A Congress at Paris, ... lxxxvii
    2. Walsingham's agents, . . . xc
    3. Ballard's plotters, . . . xciii
    4 Gilbert's plottings, ... c
    5. The plotters disperse, . . . cii

§ VI. BABINGTON'S PLOT, MAY–JUNE 1586, . . civ
    1. Anthony Babington of Dethwick, . . civ
    2 Babington and Ballard, . . . cvii
    3. Consultations, ... cix
    4. John Savage, ... cx
    5. Gilbert Gifford and the conspirators, 7 June, cxi
    6. Counts in the indictment on the treasons committed on 7 June, . . . cxii
    7. Gilbert and Ballard leave London, . . cxvii
    8. Babington's activities, . . . cxx

§ VII. MARY WRITES TO BABINGTON, 25 JUNE–18 JULY, . cxxix
    1. Why she wrote, ... cxxix
    2. The letter in the post, . . . cxxxi
    3 Elizabeth's orders and Gilbert's solicitations, ... cxxxiii
    4. Mary's letter received and answered (? 4 to 6 July), ... cxxxvi
    5. Babington's answer on its way, . . cxxxviii
    6. Reading the letter, 10 July, . . cxl
    7. Mary decides, 11 July, . . . cxlii
    8. Writing her answer, 11 July, . . cxlvi

§ VIII. THE CATASTROPHE, 19 JULY–15 AUGUST, . . cl
    1. Ballard and Gifford. . . . cl
    2. Gilbert flies, 20 July, . . . clvii

CONTENTS

	PAGE
3. Poley and Babington,	clx
4. Babington's last letter to Mary, 19 July-3 August,	clxv
5. A little comedy,	clxvii
6. The end of the plot, 3 August-15 August,	clxviii
7. The conspirators disperse,	clxx
8. Gilbert and Mendoza (? 1-11 August),	clxxiii

§ IX. THE COUP DE GRÂCE, AUGUST 1586-FEBRUARY 1587, ... clxxviii
    1. Walsingham's task, ... clxxviii
    2. The secretaries confess, . . . clxxxiii
    3. Queen Mary's trial, . . . cxciii
    4. Mary's protests of innocence, . . cxcv
    5. The execution, ... cxcviii

§ X. EXEUNT OMNES, ... cc-ccxii

THE BABINGTON PLOT CORRESPONDENCE
SECTION I

Secret Correspondence of Thomas Barnes, Gilbert Curll, Queen Mary, and Anthony Babington.

Confession of Thomas Barnes. 17 March 1588,	3
1. Thomas Barnes to Gilbert Curll. London, 28 April 1586,	5
2. Gilbert Curll to Thomas Barnes. Chartley, 20 May 1586,	8
3. Thomas Barnes to Queen Mary. 10 June, ? N.S., 1586,	8
4. Barnaby to Curll. 'Lichfield,' really London, 6/16 June 1586,	10
5. Gilbert Curll to Barnaby. Chartley, 19/29 June 1586,	11
5A. Queen Mary to Barnaby. Chartley, 19/29 June 1586,	13
6. Gilbert Curll to Barnaby. Chartley, 25 June/5 July 1586,	14
7. Queen Mary to Anthony Babington. Chartley, 25 June/5 July 1586,	15

		PAGE
8.	Gilbert Curll to Barnaby. Chartley, 2/12 July 1586,	16
9.	Barnaby to Gilbert Curll. ? Chartley, 10/20 July 1586,	17
10.	Anthony Babington to Queen Mary. ? London, ? 6/16 July 1586,	18
11.	Gilbert Curll to Barnaby. Chartley, 12/22 July 1586,	23
12.	Claude Nau to Anthony Babington. Chartley, 13/23 July 1586,	24
13.	Gilbert Curll to Barnaby. Chartley, 17/27 July 1586,	25
14.	Queen Mary to Anthony Babington. Chartley, 17/27 July 1586,	26

Introduction; § 1 The authentic text, p. 26; § 2. The drafts, p. 27; § 3. The *Textus Receptus*, p. 29; § 4. Suspicions, p. 31; § 5. Reasons for acceptance, p. 32; § 6. While praising the enterprise in general, Mary refuses consent to the murder clauses, p. 33; § 7. An obscure passage, p. 34; § 8. Contemporaneous copies, p. 35; § 9. Linguistic peculiarities, p 37, The text, p, 38

15.	Anthony Babington to Queen Mary. London, 3/13 August 1586,	46
16.	Gilbert Curll to Barnaby. Chartley, Friday, 29 July/8 August 1586,	47

SECTION II

Confessions and Examinations of Anthony Babington

17.	Babington's First Confession Ely House, 18/20 August 1586,	49

§ 1. First acquaintance with Mary's party, p. 49; § 2. Ballard's arrival, p 52; § 3 Discussions, p. 54; § 4 Babington leader, p. 56; § 5 Surprise of the Queen's person, p 57; § 6. Other conspirators, p. 58; § 7. Poley, p 58; § 8. Lingering, p. 59, § 9. Gilbert revives the plot, p. 60; § 10. Details, p. 62; § 11. The correspondence, p. 63, § 12 Final plans, p 66.

18	Second Examination of Anthony Babington. Ely House, 20 August 1586,	67

CONTENTS

		PAGE
19.	Third Examination of Anthony Babington. No date,	76
20.	Fourth Examination of Anthony Babington. 20 and 21 August 1586,	77
21.	Fifth Examination of Anthony Babington. No date,	79
22.	Sixth Examination of Anthony Babington. No date,	88
23.	Seventh Examination of Anthony Babington. No date,	89
24.	Eighth Examination of Anthony Babington, 2 September 1586,	90
25.	Ninth Examination of Anthony Babington. 8 September 1586	96

SECTION III

Letters of Gilbert Gifford

		PAGE
26.	Gilbert Gifford to Gilbert Curll. London, 24 April 1586,	99
27.	Headings by Phelippes for letter from ? Gifford to Morgan. London, 24 May ? 1586,	101
28.	Gilbert Gifford to Thomas Phelippes. ? Near Chartley, 7 July 1586,	103
29.	Gilbert Gifford to Sir Francis Walsingham. London, 11 July 1586,	105
30.	Same to Same. London, 12 July 1586,	109
31.	Notes from three letters by Gilbert Gifford to Walsingham. London, ? 14, ? 15, ? 16 July 1586,	111
32.	Same to Same. London, ? 16 July 1586,	114
33.	Same to Same. London, ? 19 July 1586,	116
34.	Same to Same. London, 19 or 20 July 1586,	117

APPENDIX TO SECTION III

GILBERT GIFFORD'S LETTERS AFTER THE PLOT, 1586-1590,   118

§ 1. The new understanding, p. 118; § 2. Ordination, p. 122; § 3. Spy life in Paris, p. 123; § 4. In Prison, p. 126.

SECTION IV

Various Writers

I. Four Letters from Sir Francis Walsingham

		PAGE
35. Sir Francis Walsingham to Thomas Phelippes. ? Richmond, 2 August 1586,	.	131
36. Same to Same. ? Richmond, 3 August 1586,	.	132
37. Same to Same. Richmond, 3 August 1586,	.	134
38. Same to Same. Same day,	.	135

II. Extracts from the Official Record of the Trial — 136

39. Examination of John Ballard. 16 and 18 August 1586, . 137
40. Attestations of Babington, Nau, and Curll to Queen Mary's Letter III. [1], 5, and 6 September 1586, . 139
41. Headings for the Bloody Letter, . 140
42. Confession of Jacques Nau. 6 September 1586, . 141
43. Examination of Gilbert Curll. 23 September 1586, . 143
44. Examination of Jacques Nau. 21 September 1586, . 144
45. Examination of Gilbert Curll. 21 September 1586, . 146
46. Nau's Regrets and Curll's Dissuasions. 25 October 1586, . 148

III. An Order from Queen Elizabeth and Lord Burghley's Answer

47. Queen Elizabeth's Secretary to Lord Burghley. 15 October 1586, . 149
48. Lord Burghley to Sir Francis Walsingham. Burghley, 16 October 1586, . 150

IV. Father Crichton's Memoir, 1582-1587

49. De Missione Scotica Puncta quædam. Chambery, 1611, 151
    English Translation, . 162

CONTENTS

APPENDIX

GEORGE GIFFORD'S PLOT, 1583-1586, . . 169-175

Abstracts or extracts from the letters of the Nuncio Castelli, pp. 169, 170; John Baptist Taxis, pp. 169, 170; B. de Mendoza, p 170; The Nuncio Ragazzoni, p. 171; Father Heywood, S.J., p. 171; Confession of John Savage, p. 172; Examinations of Conspirators, p. 173; Articles by Young, p. 173; Gilbert Gifford, p. 174; Father Persons, S.J., p. 175.

INDEX, ... 176

REFERENCES.—This book was entirely compiled from the original documents at the Record Office and elsewhere (*below*, p. ccxii), and my references were made to them. Meantime, however, the great series of *Scottish* and *Foreign Calendars* were in progress and eventually covered the whole period under review. Then seeing how very useful these *Calendars* are, especially the *Calendar of Scottish Papers*, vol. viii., edited by Mr. W. Boyd, I freely and throughout added references to it, and even where a volume number is not repeated, this vol. viii. will always be understood.

Nevertheless, it would not have been scholarly to have removed the references to the manuscripts, even though for the purposes of the notes, the calendars may contain all the details required. Moreover, these references to MSS. may also be used as a secondary and practicable (though less expeditious) way of arriving at the calendared document.

INTRODUCTION

SECTION I

THE BAN AGAINST THE PRINCE OF ORANGE, 1579 TO 1584.

1. *Loyalty to Queen Mary.*

THE story is told that Queen Victoria, calling once on the late Sir John Millais, took his little boy, whose face is familiar to us in more than one of the great painter's pictures, and set him on her knee. But the child pouted, and would not be friendly, saying in explanation, 'You are wicked Queen Elizabeth, who cut off good Queen Mary's head.' Her Majesty laughingly kissed the child saying, 'No, dear, I am Queen of England, because I descend from good Queen Mary; and I have not a drop of wicked Queen Elizabeth's blood in my body.'

Queen Victoria's words illustrate vividly the principle, for the victory of which the Babington Plot was formed. Every English Sovereign who has claimed loyalty and allegiance since that time, has done so in virtue of his or her descent from Queen Mary. But at that time her hereditary claims, matters of vast import to the nation, were being tyrannically oppressed. In the year 1581 was passed the so-called 'Statute of Silence' (23 Eliz. c. 2), which made it punishable by death to discuss the rights of any heir. England was to expect Elizabeth's successor from a vote of her Privy Council.[1]

---

[1] *Statutes of the Realm*, 23 Elizabeth, cap. 2 § v. Though the bill was aimed nominally at the superstitious 'casting of nativities and setting of images,' it also enacts that 'any one who shall set forth by express wordes, deeds or writings, who shall raigne as King or Queen of this Realme after her Highnesse Decease ... every such offence shal be felonie ... and

Nor was this repressive policy confined to discussions of the succession. Who was ignorant of the many suspicions that attached to Elizabeth? Had she not been proclaimed a bastard by Cranmer, and by several acts of Parliament? Though no Pope had done this, still one of them had pronounced against her a never-to-be-forgotten sentence. No 'Statute of Silence' could make such things as though they were not. Every attempt to enforce silence proved that the tyranny of Elizabeth's government must needs cause, even among conservative minds, a vehement temptation to grasp at violent remedies.[1]

On the other hand, the hostility of Elizabeth's ministers will be found throughout this volume to dominate the situation. Unsatisfied with all they had done to weaken, humiliate and hold prisoner the second person in the realm, they were keen to deny her queenship altogether, and they were watching for the occasion to kill her. More than once had they offered to hand her over to her Scottish enemies for slaughter, and this 'great object' was only foiled by Elizabeth's refusal to pay the blood-money which the Scots required for putting away their Queen. Walsingham, with tell-tale frankness, familiarly called her 'the bosom serpent,' and the guardians he put over her repeatedly assured him that they would slay her, rather than let her escape.[2]

---

every offender shall suffer the payns of death and forfeyte ... without benefit of Cleargie.' The priest Thomas Alfield suffered death, 6 July 1585, under this act, though not for this clause. See his indictment, *Catholic Record Society*, v. 114.

[1] We shall find even her ministers in revolt against her capricious yet peremptory orders, p. 149. But Lord Burghley dexterously leads her to acquiesce in the ministerial plans, p. 151.

[2] In March 1585 one of Mary's custodians reported ' if any danger had been offered, *or doubt suspected*, the Queen's body should first have tasted of the gall.' In July following another wrote, ' I will never ask pardon, if she depart out of my hands.... If I be assaulted by force, *I will be assured by the grace of God that she shall die before me.*' Chalmers, *Mary Stuart*, ii. 142; J. Morris, *Sir Amias Poulet*, p. 49.

INTRODUCTION

Against the mighty powers and ferocious hearts of the English Council, the forces that supported the hopes of royal succession through the imprisoned Queen seem feeble, distant, and often quite misdirected. A cursory survey of the five years before the plot will make her position clearer.

2. *Enterprises, Leagues, and Excommunication Rumours.*

For almost a generation before the year 1581 the triumph of Elizabeth and of her religious revolution had seemed assured, both in England and in Scotland. By that year, however, the Catholic revival had become a considerable movement in England, especially since the landing of the two Jesuits Campion and Persons. By midsummer 1581 the revival reached even to Edinburgh, and it was then seen that the balance of power was not at all as stable as it had appeared to be. Since 1579 James had come under the influence of his catholic cousin Esmé Stuart, Sieur d'Aubigny, who had then returned from France. He procured the downfall of the Regent, the Earl of Morton, who was executed on the 1st of June 1581, while Esmé became Duke of Lennox on the 8th of August following. But as he was not remarkable either for courage or for conscience, his day of power was short. He had originally yielded to the Kirk, and he felt that even now he could not resist it, without a considerable foreign force behind him. So he applied to Spain, to the Pope, and to his cousin the Duke of Guise, and he made use of Father William Crichton, S.J., as his messenger. Crichton's bright and interesting memoir will somewhat cheer us after our research into this gloomy tragedy (pp. 151-168). We shall recognise in him the courage, coolness, and capacity which should characterise a loyal Scotsman. But during this first mission, 1582-3, his enthusiasm unfortunately outran his prudence. While it inspired the whole of Mary's party for the moment, the lack of caution afterwards led to great disillusionment.

Meanwhile the Duke of Guise discussed the subject at Paris with the Papal Nuncio, and with Juan Bautista de Taxis, the Spanish ambassador, on the 20th of May 1582, and within their council chamber all was favourable. It was agreed that messengers should be sent forthwith to Rome and to Madrid to urge the execution of the plans. Pope Gregory in turn heartily welcomed the idea, and promised such subsidies as he could, and Philip was also much inclined to join. He promised the services of his fleet, on its return from the Azores, whither it was starting to deal with the last resistance of the Portuguese in the war of succession. This it did victoriously in July 1582, but with its return to Lisbon in September, came bad news from Scotland. James had been captured by the Protestant party in 'the Raid of Ruthven,' and Lennox was in flight. The duke soon after died, and all his plans were abandoned. So ended the first 'Enterprise' (to use the word then most in vogue) for Mary's liberation and restoration to the crown.

Closely guarded as the captive Queen was, her name did not appear at all in the Spanish ambassador's first accounts of this undertaking. But Mendoza soon found that she must be reckoned with; and then he writes that that Queen 'virtually manages all these matters; and that the Scots are unwilling to conduct them otherwise than by her instructions and directions,'[1] a clear indication of her position, due partly to her birth, partly to her characteristic power of command.

In the following spring, 1583, James freed himself again, and again appeared to be as keen as ever on his mother's

---

[1] Mendoza to Phillip, *Spanish Calendar*, pp. 291, 323.

INTRODUCTION

side. But the death of Lennox, who had held several of the strongest castles of Scotland, had seriously altered the position of affairs. The negotiations were indeed taken up exactly at the point they had reached in 1582: but every one was more cautious. Philip, considering that a larger force would be needed than he could then supply, now refused to help. Indeed, much to Mary's regret, he never again agreed to the project.[1] He did not indeed exclude the possibility of war. Mendoza was instructed to use threatening language, and the Prince of Parma was not inactive in making remote preparations for the conflict. The long crisis reached its term at last, but only after Mary's death. The boldness of Drake and the English corsairs in 'singeing the King of Spain's beard,' finally convinced Philip that fight he must, if he would save his colonial empire. Babington and Mary were not mistaken in foreseeing that Elizabeth's policy must lead to war. But both, and especially Babington, erred greatly in believing, as he states categorically in his first letter to her, that the time was close at hand.

The fatal misconception of Babington and of his colleagues—that the catholic princes of Europe were ready to restore catholicism by force—was a popular, indeed an old misapprehension, of protestant origin. From the beginning of the Reformation, the Reformers had given wide credence to fables of a Grand Papal League for the extermination of heresy. It was a useful catch-word to keep all the new-religionists united; and the threats used by catholic dignitaries of excommunications to be executed by imperial power, were easily misrepresented as supporting these stories of papal leagues. In time, however, these illusory rumours began to die down in Germany, but only to reappear more boldly in the west. It was

---

[1] This we see in her long letter to Babington, *below*, p. 38.

impossible for catholic nations to enter into any new amity or entente, without giving occasion to reports of some aggressive alliance. In 1579, for instance, Philip, while preparing to enforce his claims to the succession of the throne in Portugal, was arduous in soliciting aid from the Grand Duke of Florence and from other Italian princes. This immediately caused a crop of papal league rumours, and, what is much to be regretted, John Lesley, Bishop of Ross, and Mary's faithful but imprudent advocate, was one of the propagandists of this very mischievous mistake. It had, we may believe, had an especially deep effect upon Babington, because it was rife in France just at the time he made his grand tour there, and was in an unusually receptive mood. We find him recurring to it even in his *Confessions*.[1]

There is no evidence that Mary fully accepted this figment, though dally with it perhaps she might. Elizabeth also would not accept the malevolent credulity of her ministers in these matters without some resistance. 'Her Majesty,' wrote Leicester, 'is slow to believe that the great increase of papists is of danger to the realm. The Lord of His mercy open her eyes!'[2] Eventually, however, she fully gave way to her entourage.

Connected with the fable of a papal league is that of alleged frequent renewals of the sentence of excommunication against Elizabeth. In fact, she was excommunicated once only, viz. in 1570. In 1583 indeed, during the preparation of the Empresa for that year, briefs were

---

[1] See *below*, pp. 84, 85, etc. I have told the story of this bogus league in the sixth chapter of *The English Catholics in the Reign of Queen Elizabeth*. Lesley wrote of it to the English ambassador at Paris in July 1580, *Foreign Calendar*, 1580, p. 372, etc. This rumoured league soon became part of the stock in trade of the persecutors; and was recounted at the trials of Campion and other martyrs. It still finds its place in our popular histories.

[2] Leicester to Walsingham, 5 Sept. 1582. *Domestic Calendar*, p. 69.

INTRODUCTION   xix

drafted for its renovation. But as war was at once negatived by King Philip, all the preparations were laid aside, and the matter lapsed into oblivion until our own days, when the document was published in *The Month*.[1] All the alleged republications are fictitious.

3. *The Ban against the Prince of Orange, 25 August* 1580.

It is hardly necessary to say that an excommunication is not a ban; it does not set a price on the head of the person under sentence, and the bull of Pope Pius did not even exhort Elizabeth's subjects to throw off her yoke. But there was in force at this very time a ban which was causing much discussion, and which had much greater influence on the Babington plot than the bull *Regnans in excelsis* against Elizabeth. This was the sentence pronounced by the Brussels government under Spanish influence against William the Silent, Prince of Orange, and Stadholder of the Netherlands.

The career of William was in many ways parallel to that of Elizabeth. As she had gradually protestantised the country and drawn it into hostility to Spain, so had William done with previously catholic Holland, over the administration of which Philip had at first given him much authority. But William not only led the people into change of religion, but also into open rebellion against Alva's disastrous misgovernment. After this Philip, his love and confidence having turned into detestation, began to cherish plans for William's assassination; and so did all the Spanish governors of the Netherlands, with the honourable exception of Don John.

When Alexander Farnese of Parma succeeded Don John

---

[1] *The Month*, April 1902, p. 395. Further details in Meyer's *Elizabeth and the Catholic Church*, p. 244. It is also alluded to in the *Spanish Calendar* (1596), p. 631, § 9.

in 1578, Philip ordered him to put a price on William's head, and in doing so, to follow exactly the precedents which had been set by Charles v., in pronouncing the ban of the Empire on earlier reforming princes. Farnese obeyed, though not very promptly. The ban was formulated on the 15th of March, and published on the 25th of August 1580; and we may say that public morality, not only in catholic but even in papal circles, then took a distinct step downwards on the subject of assassination.

Hitherto there had not been one charge of plotting against Elizabeth's life, brought by protestants against catholics, nor is any known to us from other sources.[1] But after this time, and for so long as the discussion of the ban on Orange continued, there is a distinct change. We do then find frequent charges of such plotting. Some catholics, moreover, then discuss regicide in a lax way, and we also find a reprehensible facility among some foreign ecclesiastics of high place in extenuating plans of assassination.[2] But a few years later still, after Orange had been murdered, and the ban had lapsed, the atmosphere cleared. Charges of murder plots again become very rare, and they are evidently fictitious. Catholics never discuss them, and we find the next Pope, Sixtus v., taking a strong position against any abuses in this matter.

4. *Consequences of the Ban.*

1. The first known instance of any discussion among the English catholics concerning the assassination of the Queen occurred at the end of 1580, not long after the ban

---

[1] I am speaking broadly. Of course, plots were (falsely) reported at times of excitement, such as followed the Rising of the North. But no formal charges were proffered, no evidence was proposed, there were no indictments found.

[2] The stories of Dr. Ely, of George Gifford and of Parry, which will be given immediately, illustrate these clauses.

was published. The subject had been mooted in England, but so little were the English able to settle the question, which the ban had placed in a new light, that 'they' (we do not know any names) requested Humphrey Ely, an Oxford Doctor of Laws, to go abroad and ask for further information from some ecclesiastic of high authority. So Ely went to Madrid, and questioned the Nuncio there, who was strongly inclined to approve, as one might have expected from an envoy in favour at Madrid. We learn this from the Nuncio's extant letter (14 November 1580) to the Cardinal of Como at Rome; and the Cardinal (alas!) wrote back giving a full consent. He had evidently entirely embraced the principles of the ban. In this case, however, the debate, plan, or plot, or whatever it was, came to nothing, and Ely never returned to England.[1]

2. Early in 1583 we find the plot of George Gifford, who offered the Duke of Guise that he would assassinate Elizabeth, if a certain large sum was sealed up and placed in security for him to receive in case of success. But before the negotiations had gone very far, information was received that Gifford was not to be relied upon, and

---

[1] I have discussed this case in *The Month*, June 1902, quoting the documents Dr A O Meyer, *England and the Catholic Church under Elizabeth*, 270, and Ap. xviii p 490, quotes still more extensively. Meyer accepts the statement of the nuncio, Mgr Sega, who says in error that Pius in his bull gave special licence to all Elizabeth's vassals 'enabling them to bear arms against her *impune*' Pius does not say this He calculated that the insurrection had begun, and trusted that it had succeeded, though in fact it had been crushed before he wrote He *does not so much as exhort catholics to throw off her yoke*, but declares that she has forfeited her rights, and is no longer to be obeyed

Sega's error was a natural one, and broadly speaking the bull supposes, what he mistakenly affirms that it states. The bull was not reprinted till 1586, so it must have been difficult to consult the text in 1581 Babington made the same mistake, *below*, p. 21, *n* 3 Being an easy error, the two are not necessarily connected But Sega had come from Flanders, and Babington also was inspired by news from thence. So it is not impossible that both errors were due to the discussions of the ban in that country

the affair dropped (pp. 169-175). We shall have to return to this later, because the Babington plot was in some sense a later development of this intrigue: meanwhile we proceed to Dr. William Parry, who began his treasonable practices about the same time.

3. William Parry was a ruined courtier, who had incurred the sentence of death for assaulting one of his creditors with violence. After some time in trouble, and occasionally even in prison, he resolved to seek his fortune abroad, for he was full of ambition and not altogether wanting in good qualities. So in August 1582 he went to Paris, and began to study law there. He also alleges that he then made a profession of catholicity; perhaps he made some necessary oath or profession preliminary to the degree in law, which he took next year. He now began to give himself the airs of a *politique* and a *philosophe*, and he also began to 'feel the minds' of priests in regard to regicide, which was then, in consequence of 'the ban,' a common subject of conversation. But the result of it all was that the other English catholic exiles became more and more suspicious of him. To escape ill consequences he made one journey to Venice, and afterwards another to Lyons, where he saw Father Crichton, S.J.[1] Thence he went to Milan, where he was favoured, perhaps, by that enthusiastic Welsh nationalist Dr. Owen Lewis, who may have commended him to Pope Gregory XIII. He would not, however, go to Rome, but returned to Paris in October, where he then found himself in better conceit with catholic Welshmen. He now began to discuss the above-mentioned questions with Thomas Morgan, and they were soon involved in plans for the Queen's murder. In December 1583

---

[1] In regard to his promised reception into the Church, Crichton reported favourably of his talents, but would not vouch for his intentions. To the Card. de Como, 5, 17, 18 July 1583, R O, *Roman Transcripts*, 80

Parry took his degree in Laws, styled himself Dr. Parry, and prepared to return.

One of the preliminaries was to write, 1st January 1584, and ask the Pope for an indulgence for a certain enterprise, which he had in hand tending to the 'liberation of the Queen of Scotland' and to other advantages for the catholic cause; but nothing definite was stated about the nature or about the details of the project. The Nuncio at Paris, who forwarded this petition, accompanied it, however, with repeated warnings against Parry as a spy. But Pope Gregory, and his secretary the Cardinal of Como, possibly relying on Lewis's commendations, very unwisely disregarded the Nuncio's warnings, and ordered him to send on a letter giving Parry the indulgence he requested. As he had not asked for any reward in money, they thought he might be relied upon!

Meanwhile Parry, having now returned, contrived to secure a personal interview with the Queen, and interested her with his flowery stories of the treasons he had discovered overseas. He assured her that he was expecting a letter of indulgence from the Pope, which would confirm all his statements; and in due course the letter came. Elizabeth was delighted, and now fully believed in Parry's ability and skill. He was rewarded, his debts remitted, and in the parliamentary elections of that autumn he was given the seat of Queenborough.

5. *Consequences of the Murder of Orange.* 1584.

Though the ban caused the bitterest indignation in England, this did not show itself openly till the beginning of 1584. The end of 1583 had been marked by a series of alarms. John Somerville, a weak-minded catholic gentleman of Warwickshire, declared that he would punish the Queen, ran into the street with his sword drawn, which gave the alarmists the chance they wanted for exciting the Queen and the public. There followed two similar cases, those of William Carter and Francis Throckmorton, which though not dangerous, were rather mystifying. A persistent plot-scare ensued. 'Les desfiances sont sy grandes à present pardeça, que lon a subson des ombres,' wrote Castelnau to France.¹ When the Prince of Orange was finally shot 30 June/10 July, the excitement became intense, and when this had begun to die down again in October, it was revived by the 'Band of Association for the Safety of the Queen,' which was devised by Cecil and Walsingham on a Dutch model.

This was taken with enthusiasm by whole counties and provinces, though the Queen never was nor would be for a moment in danger. The popular ardour would indeed have been laudable, had it not also been so extremely sectarian and bloodthirsty. On the first news of the assassination Francis Throckmorton was haled from prison, where he had lain under sentence for two months, and butchered in public (10/20 July 1584). Similarly when the Band of Association was about to be signed in Flintshire, Richard White, a catholic Welshman, incredible though this may seem to us, was quartered alive for his faith at Wrexham. We now know a further curious coincidence (which nowhere appears in the trial or acts of this martyrdom), viz. that White had written in Welsh an ode of triumph on hearing of the death of Orange.² When we remember that White was only a poor school-

---

[1] 1 January 1584, *Catholic Record Society*, xxi. 42.
[2] The translation begins, 'Thou, Orange, fat and tedious, Every one is glad when thou art enclosed in the grave: Thou drivedst yonder to sadden us; do thou thyself be silent now. When I under oppression heard a speech recited, which pleased me, I sang aloud (I did not wait) *Te Deum* twice well nigh.' It is a remarkably vigorous piece, printed by me in *Catholic Record Society*, v. 98, 99 For the Life of White see *Lives of the English Martyrs* (Series II. 1914, 1 127)

master in a remote country town, we can surmise how hot was the ferment everywhere, when news arrived that the protestant hero was no more. Inspired with enthusiasm White's carol bursts out with as much fierce joy as if the poet had been a soldier in the Spanish ranks. In words he was almost as ferocious as his persecutors were with knife and rope.

In this same excited mood the Band was everywhere taken in the protestant church, and it was soon supplemented by the bloody code called ' the laws of 27 Elizabeth ' under which catholic priests could be and would be put to death amid atrocious tortures, merely for their sacred character.[1] The gist of the Band of Association was this, that all who took it should persecute to the death that person *in whose favour* any plot should be formed against Elizabeth's life.

Any one can see what a threat this was to Mary. According to the letter of the Band, the plot might be unknown to Mary, or even a fictitious charge, and yet might have consequences fatal to her. For when the oath was taken, nothing had been said as to previous legal inquiries. Any of Mary's enemies might therefore, by concocting a plot, give occasion for her slaughter, especially as she was surrounded with guards, who yearned for her murder. Alas, what little difference there was, morally speaking, between the Ban and the Band. One barbarity of the latter, however, was to some extent remedied by Parliament, when it was redrafted in the form of an Act. It was then provided that legal proceedings should be taken before execution, and Mary eventually suffered under this law.

Thus was the Puritan party familiarised with the project

---

[1] The order of priesthood was supposed to make priests ' the Pope's men,' and therefore *ipso facto* traitors This law was potent for mischief during a century, then lapsed into desuetude, and was tardily repealed in 1844

of putting Mary to death, an idea in itself repugnant to the profound reverence which the English people as a whole cherished for royalty, as well to the reverence felt towards the legitimate heiress to the throne, with whom many sympathised much more deeply than they dared to show openly.

One of the first victims of the new blood-lust, to which the agitation had given rise, was Dr. Parry himself. He was fond of playing the philosopher, and in truth he was not without some humane and better feelings. He was not a mere brutal, man-hunting sleuth-hound, such as were so many others, whom we shall meet later on. Even in his correspondence with Burghley and Walsingham he endeavours to draw distinctions between catholic and catholic. He would play the traitor to papal agents, to the Jesuits and to most of the clergy, but he deprecated indiscriminate persecution, which as he knew to his cost made the name of England hateful throughout the Continent. In his interviews with Elizabeth he had touched on this same point, and she had in brave words assured him that 'never a catholic should be troubled for religion or supremacy, so long as they lived like good subjects.' Alas, that her laws and her practice so flatly belied her professions!

Her words, however, confirmed Parry in his endeavour to pose as a superior person. He thought he could take sides against the catholic leaders, while opposing the persecution of catholics merely as such. But such an affectation was not likely to be tolerated by the frenzied parliament of 1584-1585.

On 17 December 1584, the bloody code of laws against the catholics passed the Commons 'with little or no argument,' whereupon Parry declared that the measure 'savoured of treasons, and was full of confiscations, blood, danger, despair, and terror to the subjects of this realm;

. . . and that he would reserve his reasons for so saying for her Majesty.'

Though the inconstant philosopher was soon excusing himself on his knees for his speech, he was committed to the custody of the serjeant for his offence, but was freed next day by the Queen's orders. This, however, was the last time that she exerted herself in his favour. She was perhaps scared by the ensuing events; at all events she soon became altogether changed, as irritable and bloodthirsty as the most intolerant Puritan. 'Never,' wrote Walsingham, 'have I seen her Majesty so much commoved.'

Parry's strange career had in fact reached its term. He was in money difficulties, and thought he saw a way out of them by playing anew his old trade of informer. He talked treason with one Edmund Neville, the titular Lord Latimer, a returned exile, whom Elizabeth's government was treating harshly. Each schemer probably wanted to betray the other, but Neville was the more successful, laying an information on 9 February 1585, which caused Parry's arrest and eventually his sacrifice at Tyburn not merely for the words spoken to Neville,[1] but for the whole intrigue with Morgan and the Cardinal of Como. There was, of course, the difficulty that Parry had but lately been rewarded for the very same 'treasons,' for which he was now to be executed. But this was got over by invoking the name of the Queen, against whom no reproach could be openly levelled. During Parry's trial Sir Christopher Hatton said that the Queen was so 'magnanimous, that, after thou haddest opened those traitorous practices (with Morgan) in sort as thou hast laid it down in thy confession, she would not so much as acquaint any one of her High-

---

[1] We shall see below that, according to the procedure in Elizabeth's court, a *provocateur* had not only to obtain a general approval (such as Parry might have claimed to hold), but also a specific permit for each new treason, if he wished to keep safe. This Parry had confessedly not obtained.

ness's Privy Council with it. . . . No not till this enterprise [with Neville] was discovered and made manifest.'

This was a cryptic way of saying that the Queen had changed her mind and would defend him no longer; so Parry underwent, in Palace Yard, Westminster, the appalling sentence for high treason on the 2nd of March 1585. Though his conspiracy was a bogus one from first to last, it was, of course, highly criminal in itself. One cannot affect sympathy with the victim, though he was perhaps no worse than many another courtier of that day.

The incident of Dr. Parry is important on many accounts. Keeping, however, the circumstances of the Babington plot in view we may notice that Parry tried thrice, but in vain, to elicit from priests opinions in favour of regicide.

He consulted Father William Crichton about it at Lyons, probably early in 1583, but the Scotsman repeatedly answered, *Omnino non licet*, 'It is altogether forbidden,' and explained that if priests cause bloodshed they become irregular; that is, unable to exercise their sacerdotal functions.[1]

When leaving France, early in 1584, Parry met William Watts, or Waytes,[2] a secular priest, and began to talk to him of his plans, altering, however, the names of those concerned. Watts pronounced this case 'utterly unlawful, and with him many English Priests did agree, as I have heard.' Christopher Driland, a priest in England, consulted by Parry, also dissuaded him. But because he did not denounce him, he was afterwards kept in prison till the end of Elizabeth's long reign.[3]

But against this united feeling of English and Scottish

---

[1] Holinshed, *Chronicle*, iv. 572. R.O., *France*, xiii., under 1 March 1585, a letter from Crichton, who says, 'Whosoever was consenting to the conspiration of any death, was to be degraded and deprived [? of the use of] his order of priesthood, and to be punished with extremity.'

[2] Parry's *Declaration*, § 3. In *State Trials*, Holinshed, etc.

[3] Law, *Jesuits and Seculars*, 1889, p. 135.

priests, we have to set the blameworthy and extremely stupid letter of the Cardinal of Como, giving Parry an indulgence. I call it stupid, because he insisted on its being forwarded by the Nuncio at Paris, who had repeatedly assured him that Parry was a rascal. The case against the Cardinal (who has also appeared in the story of Ely, and of George Gifford) is clearly a strong one. Though he never pronounced in favour of assassination, there seems no doubt that he was for the time infected by the 'Ban-fever,' which had taken a firm hold on many of his contemporaries.

1. The events described in this section show us certain changes in the circumstances of the Scottish Queen, which made the Babington plot a possibility. Chief among these was the Spanish ban against the Prince of Orange, which familiarised catholics with the defence of regicide, and caused a distinct lowering of moral standards on this subject, even among catholic churchmen in high places. It also occasioned various bogus plots, which caused much bitter feeling. The actual murder of the Prince led to the Band of Association and to the acts of Parliament which eventually regulated Mary's trial. It familiarised not only the Puritans, but many others, who had hitherto regarded the blood royal as sacrosanct and inviolable, with the idea of the Scottish Queen's murder.

2. The Catholic revival of 1581 had also had a subtle but deep effect. It indirectly encouraged all those of the ancient faith to regard their co-religionists abroad, as possible, or even probable allies. It filled them with courage and ambition to free themselves from the insufferable persecution, with which they were oppressed.

3. The permanent factors in the situation were, on the one hand, the power which Mary possessed over all conservative minds, in virtue of her being the legitimate heir

to the throne, and, on the other, the hatred with which she was followed by Walsingham and his party, for ever thirsting for her blood. Elizabeth was not bent on Mary's death, but she was intensely interested in the spy system, and we see her in the case of Parry easily won over to a course of horrible cruelty.

SECTION II

Spies and Dupes, 1584-1585.

The present section may at first seem not only gloomy but also disconnected and incoherent. But these unfortunate qualities are, alas! also germane to the story we are following. Our drama originated among men far removed from being great characters. Its first beginnings must be sought among minds unbalanced and depraved by the controversies over the ban. Rascals of varying degrees of infamy are at work endeavouring to give a downward turn to tendencies which are already reprehensible. There is nothing for it but to watch these unpleasant gentlemen, and their hardly less repellent dupes. It is amongst them that the situation will take form and shape.

1. *Walsingham's Political Morality.*

As soon as Elizabeth heard of the accusations brought by Dr. Parry against Thomas Morgan, she passionately vowed to be revenged upon him, and ordered her ambassador in Paris to present an urgent request to the King of France for his arrest and extradition.[1] The King had many reasons for wishing to stand well with her, and

---

[1] R.O., Foreign, Elizabeth, France, xiii., under February 1585.

complied so far as to throw the man into the Bastille (1 March 1585), and to put his correspondence under lock and key; but he was slow to go further. The English Queen was naturally detested by the French people, and the officials, of course, arranged that nothing compromising should be found among Morgan's papers when the time came for giving them up. As for handing over Mary's servant to be tortured into a confession of guilt, the French King, despicable as his general policy was, would not consent to make himself guilty of so dishonourable a breach of the law of nations.

In her deep vexation Elizabeth wrote to the King a characteristic letter, which began by saying she was ' enragée' at receiving his note, and concluded with the words: 'I swear to you that if he is denied me, I shall conclude that I have joined a league not with a King but with a Papal Legate or the President of a seminary. I shall be as much ashamed at yours as I should at their bad company.'[1]

No wonder that Morgan was rather better than worse treated after such an outburst of spleen. But for all that the Welshman was kept in the Bastille, more keen than ever to be revenged on his enemies, who on their side were more than ever alert to entrap the rash, quarrelsome man in some intrigue that might ruin both him and his mistress.

We must not, of course, go so far as to think that Walsingham planned beforehand every step subsequently taken by his spies and employés; nor has any evidence been brought to support the allegation that he even had some of the principal conspirators in his pay. There was a rumour at the time that he had employed Ballard; and Queen Mary alluded to it at her trial, whereupon

---

[1] R O, Foreign, Elizabeth, France, xiii f 127, under 10 March 1585

Walsingham arose and made a protest, which is worthy of attention:

> My mind is far from malice. I call God to record that as a private person I have done nothing unbeseeming an honest man. Nor, as I bear the place of a public man, have I done anything unworthy of my place. I confess that, being very careful for the safety of the Queen and realm, I have curiously searched out practices against the same. If Ballard had offered me his help, I would not have refused it. Yea, I would have recompensed the pains he had taken. If I have practised anything with him, why did he not utter it to save his life?[1]

Walsingham therefore 'calls God to record' that he has done as a private person 'nothing unbeseeming an honest man,' nor as a public man, 'anything unworthy of my place.' We notice the significant distinction between private and public honesty, and the low standard claimed for the latter, and we see that he maintains that the worst he had done even in his public capacity is 'curiously to search out practices,' and to encourage, 'yea, recompense,' informers who offered him their services.

This acknowledgment is probably true to this extent, that Walsingham did not as a rule assume in person the part of tempter, nor prescribe to his spies and agents the exact line they were to take. But to say this and no more would be to understate his responsibility for the plots, which he gloried in bringing to light and which, his admirers believe, would have been the ruin of England but for his patriotic services.

These admirers forget that there would have been no conspirators, but for the multitude of injured men then in England who had no remedy for their wrongs; and that their wrongs and sufferings were the result of the cruel and tyrannical persecution of which Walsingham was the chief upholder. Long before the Babington plot, he had

---

[1] *State Trials*, 1730, p 145.

no doubt banished from his mind his responsibility for the cruelties with which he was familiar; and he could appeal with a calm conscience to the All-Knowing to record his innocence. 'My mind is free from malice.' That is to say he saw nothing amiss in the system of violence, cant, and fraud in which he was the principal agent. He encouraged, assisted, and 'recompensed the pains' of his informers, and by so doing he clearly made himself, in the sight of Him whom he invoked, responsible for the treachery and lies, and wickedness of their multiplied and prolonged plotting against the life of his victim.

2. *Thomas Morgan and Charles Paget.*

The efforts of these spies were favoured by many circumstances, above all by the venturesome and pugnacious character of Thomas Morgan. He had acquired Mary's favour by his activity in finding messengers for her correspondence, and in dunning the French government for the payment of her dowry, and she had rewarded him by giving him her confidence, and the control over a large part of her income, which was a great source of power among the poor catholic exiles. Amongst these there had arisen a quarrel between the 'Welsh' and the 'English' party; and Morgan, as the leader of the 'Welsh,' had undertaken a fierce *vendetta* against Dr. Allen, Father Persons, and the other leaders of the 'English,' and, as will presently be seen, he even troubled the discipline of the college at Rheims. Whatever the merits of the quarrel, it could eventually only tell in Mary's disfavour.

The restraints of the Bastille contributed to the same result. Had Morgan been free, and able to make personal inquiries into the credentials of those whom we shall see palming themselves off upon him as friends and sympathisers, he would not, I feel sure, have been befooled as grossly as he was, time after time. His detention was at once sufficiently lax to allow the adventurous to have access to him, yet sufficiently strict to exclude ordinary friends, and withal to excite continually his desire for revenge.

Unable to attend personally to the important negotiations confided to him by his mistress, Morgan now made use of Mr. Charles Paget as his lieutenant, a man who in his turn proved as unreliable as his chief. To say nothing of certain quarrels which preceded his leaving England,[1] we find him at first begging Elizabeth for pardon (1582). When his prayer was refused, he flew to the opposite extreme, and encouraged Elizabeth's foreign enemies and conspirators against her life. When Mary was dead, and his pension from her had ceased, he returned (1596-1598) to his old prayer for mercy from England, and attacked the Jesuits with the utmost virulence, charging Persons, for instance, with having given that encouragement to Parry and Savage, of which he himself had been guilty. His prayers were again spurned, the English agents describing him as 'an unconstant fellow, full of practices, true to no side' (June 1599).[2] Eventually, however, after King James's accession, he obtained pardon, and so made his exit with better fortune, surely, than he deserved. But whatever be said about his quarrels and changes of side, one thing at least seems clear, that he was not the right man to help Morgan through a difficult crisis, when great prudence and great self-restraint were imperatively required.

It was perhaps the weakest point in Mary's otherwise wonderful character that she was a bad judge of men. All

---

[1] *Catholic Record Society*, ii. p. 183.
[2] The article on Paget in the *Dictionary of National Biography* is rather incomplete. For the quarrel with the Jesuits, see his articles and their answers, Stonyhurst, *Anglia*, ii. n. 46; also *Catholic Record Society*, ii. p. 183, *Domestic Calendars* for 1598, 1599, pp. 68, 234. Strype, iv. 1 389, Tierney-Dodd, iii. p. xcv., and Winwood's *Negociations*, i. 52, 71, 89, 112, etc., and my *Institution of the Archpriest Blackwell*, 1916.

her calamities may be said to have come from her inability to distinguish between men who, though shallow and imprudent, were attractive, pushful, self-assertive, and those who, though in reality more capable, steadfast and estimable, did not make so brave a show. She was not, I think, deceived (though some opponents have said she was) in believing Morgan and Paget to have been at heart faithful to her. But their good intentions were not likely to counterbalance the ill results, which were morally sure to follow from leaving the guidance of her fortunes to persons so unscrupulous, so quarrelsome, so reckless as they. It was the opinion of Cardinal Allen at the time that Mary was 'ruinated' by her servants' 'unfortunate proceedings,' and Dr. Lingard arrived at the same conclusion upon a mature consideration of the papers published subsequently.[1]

3. *Walsingham's Spies.*

(1) The first to offer Walsingham his services against Morgan was one Robert Bruce, a Scotch gentleman of good family, the younger brother of the Laird of Binnie. His treachery was not suspected by our older historians, but now his career has been briefly but well described by the late T. G. Law in the Appendix to the *Dictionary of National Biography*, though even this writer was not aware that Bruce's bad faith began in 1585. Just before Morgan's arrest Bruce was on the one hand procuring from him ample letters of credence and information about all the plans of the party, while on the other he was proffering these secrets to the English Secretary through the ambassador at Paris, but on the condition *that he must be well paid.* Sir Edward Stafford thereupon wrote home:

'He promiseth and offereth great things, but plainly he sayeth—that "a working man is worthy of his hire," and will

---

[1] Knox, *Letters of Cardinal Allen*, p 328, and Lingard's *History*, vi pp 405, 569, 640.

not put himself in danger without certainty of a reward (both standing for his life) as long as he serveth well : and now also presently, for, as he sayeth, he is in debt almost two hundred crowns here. Because it is an extraordinary reward, I thought good to advertise you, that her Majesty's pleasure may be known; as also what he shall trust to have, while he doth service to deserve it. . . .

'The man is a great papist, and you may be sure that it is either spite or gain or both, that maketh him to do it. I leave all things to your honour's judgment. But in my judgment two hundred crowns were well ventured to get such an service, for I think that he will be able and willing to discover matter of importance.

'Although there be no trust to a knave, that will deceive them that trust him ; yet such as he is must be entertained. For if there were no knaves, honest men should hardly come by the truth of any enterprise against them.'[1]

The last sentence is a good example of the political morality of Walsingham and his subordinates. ' Knaves must be entertained that honest men may come by the truth ! ' Elizabeth's parsimony seems to have saved her on this occasion from having directly encouraged Bruce's knavery. But the only reason for thinking so, is because we find him a year later still offering to sacrifice his honour for English gold, and Stafford still urging the advantage of employing him.

(2) Robert Pooley, or Poley, was a much worse sort of intriguer. He was in Walsingham's confidence at the same time that he was hailed as ' Sweet Robin ' by Babington and his friends. When the plot was approaching maturity it was his rôle to keep the plotters within the reach of Walsingham's arm until everything was ready for their destruction.

On this occasion he came direct from England to the

---

[1] Stafford to Walsingham. R.O., Foreign, Elizabeth, France, xiii. 25 January 1585.

Bastille, bringing with him letters from Christopher (afterwards Sir Christopher) Blount, a gentleman in Leicester's retinue. Morgan had most imprudently asked Blount to correspond with himself and Mary, and Blount's answer was to send Poley, who played his part so well that both Morgan and Paget wrote in July 1585 commending him to their mistress.

A week later, however, Morgan heard that Poley's letter had been intercepted. His means of conveyance should be avoided therefore until the mischance were explained.[1] Later on Morgan returned to his praises, while Mary warned Babington against him.

(3) George (afterwards Sir George) Gifford of Itchell, Hants, and Weston-under-Hill, Gloucester, has been mentioned above. He was born of a family which long remained catholic, and his brother, Dr. William Gifford, eventually became Archbishop of Rheims. George lost his father when he was quite young. In 1578, when a mere youth, he was drawn into Elizabeth's court, and made a Gentleman Pensioner, but he soon wasted his patrimony by extravagance, and became involved in disreputable and criminal enterprises. In 1586, when he had been arrested on suspicion of complicity in Babington's plot,[2] it was found that he was 'wanted' for a whole series of misdemeanours, receiving stolen goods, assisting burglars, and profit-sharing with robbers of many sorts.[3] Still, he did not lose his place, or the royal favour, was eventually knighted for service against Spain, married a wife from

---

[1] Morgan's letter of 20 July 1585, printed in full in Murdin, *State Papers*, 1759, p. 446, and in the *Hatfield Calendar*, iii. p. 101. See also R.O., *Mary Queen of Scots*, xvi. 7, 8, 15, 17, 70. Phelippes was jealous of Poley, as the adherent of a rival courtier.

[2] He then carved his name and arms in the Beauchamp Tower.

[3] R.O., *Domestic Elizabeth*, cxcv. 58 (13 Dec. 1586). 'Articles against Gifford.' For the charges of April 1583, see *ibid.* clx. 29.

the all-powerful Cecil family, and died a successful and an honoured man, in this world's estimate.[1]

In April 1583, however, as in 1586, he was in difficulties with the police. One Nix, a noted highwayman of those days, had broken prison, and Gifford was implicated in the affair. He therefore found it advisable to cross over to the Continent, where he occupied himself in a bold speculation. He applied at the beginning of May, to the Duke of Guise, for a large sum of money, which he asked to have locked up, and the key delivered into his possession, until he should assassinate Elizabeth.

Before many days had passed, the worthlessness of Gifford became known, and his project was rejected. But at first, alas! it was tolerated; such was the demoralisation which I attribute to the Ban, and to the wars of religion. The Duke's father had been assassinated by the Protestants, and this murder had exercised an evil influence over the son, a brilliant soldier, who might in better times have been a national hero. His first impulse was to accept, and he communicated the plan to the ambassador of Spain and to the Papal Nuncio, and both, it must be confessed, gave ear to the proposal with the most reprehensible calmness. They were not asked to approve the project, only to take advantage of it, and to be ready for the *débâcle* which it was hoped would follow. They had the decency to appear a little ashamed of the project, but in effect they raised no objection. They communicated the plans, not indeed to their masters, but to their respective Secretaries of State, who in their turns took the news as calmly as Cecil did, when he read that of the impending murder of Rizzio; as quietly as Elizabeth when suggesting to Poulet the advantage of ridding her of

---

[1] See *The Giffards*, by Major-Gen. the Hon. George Wrottesley, 1902, who however shows little grasp of the Babington plot period.

Mary. But murder by State trial was so well understood in Elizabeth's court, that the use of poison or of the stiletto was little needed, and little practised.[1]

The letters about the conspiracy of George Gifford have been printed more than once, and an abstract of them will be found *below* at p. 169. They throw a strong light on the temper of mind which made the Babington plot a possibility. The age of which we write, perfectly understood that assassination could never be actually allowed, but it had not yet appreciated how much harm the least condonation of such crime could do to the body politic. The sequel to our story will show but too sadly and surely how many miserable calamities might have been averted from the catholic cause, but for those unworthy answers to George Gifford's vile offers. The answers became known (in an inaccurate version) to the *provocateur* Gilbert Gifford, who used them to tempt Savage, Ballard, Babington, and his friends. Alas! they formed one of the chief snares by which those poor fellows were brought to their doom, and thereby Mary to hers.

To return to George Gifford: his intrigue in Paris was carried on during the month of May 1583, at the end of which month the Nuncio writes that it will come to nothing. Before midsummer George was back at Elizabeth's court acting as Gentleman Pensioner, and drew his half a crown a day, as 'bourdwagis,' for 'four score and seventeen dayes,' that is, for the whole summer quarter, 24 June to 28 September 1583.[2] He said nothing that we can trace about his bogus plot. If he ever gave it up is unknown,

---

[1] 'Trial for high treason seems in this reign to have been a formal but certain means of destroying an obnoxious man. Nobody was, nor does it appear how anyone possibly could be acquitted.' J. Reeves, *History of English Law*, ed. Finlason, 1869, iii. 810.

[2] R.O., Exchequer of Receipt, Gentlemen Pensioners' Rolls, no. 14. The rolls for the three previous quarters are unfortunately wanting. He continued to receive his pension while in the Tower, in 1586. Roll 17.

and seems unlikely. He was arrested, however, with the Babington conspirators in September 1586; through the use which Gilbert Gifford had made of his name. He then denied the evidence brought against him, and escaped.[1]

This escape and his subsequent prosperity, when so much against him was known, raises a strong suspicion that he was acting a double part, for most, if not for all the time.

(4) At this point an account of Parry's intercourse with Morgan would have been in place, had there not been an occasion to give it in the previous section. There can be no question that this was a clear case of provocation.

(5) The next tempter to proffer his services to Morgan was Nicholas Berden, whose real name seems to have been Thomas Rogers. We know nothing definite about his early history. Roger, or Rogers, was a name taken by more than one spy; so that caution must be used in classifying references.[2] Berden was employed not only against Morgan, but still more against Philip, Earl of Arundel. In the Earl's correspondence, printed by the Catholic Record Society,[3] twenty-six of Berden's letters will be found, which give many details of his dishonesty, craft, and low morality.

So far as the history of Mary Stuart is concerned, Berden, as he is henceforth called, enters it in July 1585. He was then arrested, doubtless by prearrangement with

---

[1] Phelippes inquired by letter from Gilbert Gifford (then in Paris), what the truth against him really was; *Mary Queen of Scots*, xviii. 25; Boyd, viii. 489; Gilbert's slippery answer, *M.Q.S.*, xx. 45; Boyd, ix. 222, is printed below at p. 174, and at least rebuts his own previous story.

[2] I have myself mistakenly identified this Thomas Rogers, *alias* Berden, with Roger Yardley in *Catholic Record Society*, iv. 54, etc. Both were called Roger, or Rogers, and they sometimes lived in much the same circle. Roger Yardley, however, remained a good catholic, and was a prisoner in the Tower at the time we meet Nicholas Berden as one of Phelippes's assistants in 1587-8.

[3] *Catholic Record Society*, xxi. no. 20.

Walsingham, and thrown into prison in company with the priest and future martyr, Edward Strancham. Then having got out of prison (ostensibly through the mediation of a protestant relative), he betook himself to Paris, with letters, etc., of Strancham in his possession, which he used as tokens to Strancham's friends in Paris, and through them he was ere long introduced to Morgan.

A fair number of his letters to Walsingham at this date are extant, and from them we can watch the progress of his intrigues.[1] He did not attempt to initiate conspiracies of his own. That would in any case have been premature. Moreover, he was a mean villain, whose ambitions were of a lower order: to steal letters, to betray confidences, to inform against priests, and, above all, to become the messenger between Morgan and Mary's friends in England. Time was needed for him to ingratiate himself with the leaders of the various factions, but by the end of the year he had attained this object; for on 28 December he announces that they (that is, Morgan and Paget) wish him to go over and try to open up correspondence with Mary. But when he thus seemed to have been on the point of complete success, his next letter showed that his services were after all not likely to be required; for he sent word that Morgan had received the news that Gilbert Gifford, after some adventures, was likely to accomplish all that could have been expected from himself. Berden's services therefore were now not likely to be wanted in Paris, so he returned to England, where we shall soon meet him again.

(6) The appearance upon the scene of Gilbert Gifford, to whose provocation the Babington plot owed its existence, marks the opening of a new scene in the tragedy. Gilbert

---

[1] R.O., *Domestic Elizabeth, Additional*, xxix. nn. 38, 42, 45, 47, 52, 55, 62, 85; in *Catholic Record Society*, xxi. no. 20.

was the son of John Gifford, of Chillington, whose family was noted for its firm adhesion to the ancient faith. A couple of generations later (by which time the family name had taken the form Giffard) they won themselves an honoured place in the history of the country by their heroism in helping to save Charles II. after the Battle of Worcester.[1] Gilbert was a somewhat distant cousin of the George Gifford of whom we have spoken above, the Hampshire branch having, as it seems, migrated from Staffordshire when William de Gifford (*d.* 1129) became Bishop of Winchester. The Doctor William Gifford, whom we shall meet with further on, was of this Hampshire branch, and brother to George. It will be our misfortune to see little else here but the weak side of this William, though in later life, when the unfortunate ascendancy which Gilbert won over him during their college career had passed away, his career became much more honourable. A great preacher, a man of learning, a distinguished member of the Benedictine Order, he rose to be Archbishop of Rheims and Primate of France, perhaps the only Englishman who ever occupied that post.

Gilbert Gifford seems to have gone abroad about 1577, and after a stay at Paris, to have reached the English College at Rome, where he took the college oath on the 23rd of April 1579, being then nineteen years of age. Six months later he was joined by his cousin William, who was two years his senior in age, but over whom he soon gained an unfortunate predominance. Gilbert had been at college during the disturbances which were occasioned by the inefficiency of the first Rector, Maurice Clenog, an old Welsh churchman. But when the Welsh Rector had been removed, Gilbert became more unmanageable than ever.

[1] G. Wrottesley, *The Giffards*, 1902. At pp. 143-159 numerous extracts about Gilbert Gifford.

Before September 1580, it was found necessary to expel him, but an allowance was given him for a year and a half in order to continue his studies outside the college. His cousin William having then completed his college course, they both set out northwards. Instead of settling down at Rheims, however, there ensued fifteen months of vagabond life spent in roaming over England and the Continent, during which time his friends frankly gave him up for lost. At last he turned up in rags at Rheims, crying and showing every sign of repentance. Though at first Allen would not receive him, he afterwards, with too great facility, which one cannot quite excuse, admitted him to the Seminary (October 1583), and to the preparation for the priesthood.

As we have no bad news of him during the next two years, we might naturally have supposed that they had been well spent. But at the end of that time we find him quite calmly occupied on a work of startling wickedness. He was hatching a plot against Elizabeth's life in the college itself.

4. *Dupes.*

(1) From the *Douay Diaries*, we learn that one John Savage was living at Rheims in 1581, having received Confirmation on Lady Day, and he left on the 1st of December. We know nothing of his parentage. The *Douay Diary* happens on two occasions to describe his companions as *nobiles*, i.e. of gentle birth, from which an inference might be made that he belonged to the yeoman class. At his arrest and trial he was reported as having no goods, except a horse, which was given as a reward to the pursuivant who captured him. Yet he seems to have consorted on equal terms with other gentlemen of birth and property, and Gilbert Gifford [1] calls him 'one of the best companions, and best conditioned, besides a very good scholar and

---

[1] Morris, *Sir Amias Poulet*, p. 381 ; Boyd, x. 221.

practical, and as pliant and pleasant in company as ever I knew.' His companion, Charnock, who was with him at Barnard's Inn, as well as in the Spanish camp, said, ' I knew he was an excellent soldier, a man skilful in languages, and learned besides. When I met him in England, I was glad to renew old acquaintance.' [1]

What Savage did when he left the college in December 1581 does not appear. It was then, very possibly, that he enlisted under the Prince of Parma. The Queen's Counsel at his trial seemed to believe that he was there almost up to the time when the conspiracy was hatched. But the *Diary* informs us that he returned as early as the 10th of May 1583, and the next thing noted concerning him is his departure on the 16th of August 1585. If (as is likely) he remained at college all that time, we must presume that he was studying for the priesthood, and should have to consider him a *prêtre manqué*, a somewhat unbalanced pietist, rather than a dare-devil soldier ready for any violence, as the Crown lawyers tried to represent him. However this may be, the sum-total of our information about him produces the impression of an intelligent but harmless, simple, cheery fellow, over whom Gilbert Gifford had won complete ascendancy and could make him call black, white. In his examination of 14 August, Savage said, ' He [Gilbert] told me that an English Treatise was being made at the Rheims College to be sent over hither, inveighing against such as would seek her Majesty's death; but that the same was but a device to blind the eyes of the Privy Council to have less fear for her Majesty's person.' [2]

Like all English Catholics, Savage no doubt had the most profound respect for Allen and the English College. But now, on Gilbert's unsupported word, he reverses all

---

[1] *State Trials*, p. 132.   [2] Boyd, p. 681.

his previous standards, and takes for pure good what Allen's college 'inveighs against' as evil. He even presses this view on others!

Let us pause before we pass a severe sentence on this simplicity. We shall find high names in plenty as we proceed, protestant no less than catholic, of men who were inveigled into giving confidence to Gilbert, and afterwards regretted what they had done. Savage sinned indeed, but amid influential company.

(2) To return to the college of Rheims in 1585. A college friend of both Gilbert and Savage was Christopher Hodgson, a priest of the English College, Rome, and now, like Gilbert, a reader, or tutor as we might say, in philosophy at Rheims. Like Gilbert he was also miserably factious, and though he did not fall so low as his companions, he afterwards became a restless wanderer, a sacerdotal failure.[1]

One day, about midsummer, 1585, Hodgson and Savage were talking about 'exploits,' when they were joined by Dr. William and also by Gilbert Gifford. The conversation turned to the assassination of Elizabeth, and Savage believed that he was solicited to kill her. Eventually, after thinking the matter over for three weeks, Savage agreed and took a vow he would do so, being, it would seem, distinctly under the impression that Dr. William Gifford considered this as praiseworthy and meritorious. I do not myself believe that this was Dr. Gifford's opinion,[2] nor in truth do I feel certain even of the leading facts above summarised, the evidence for which is liable to very grave exceptions.

---

[1] *Catholic Record Society*, ii. pp. 134, 205, and notes. The last we hear of Hodgson in the correspondence of Gilbert Gifford is that he had possessed himself of £2000, belonging to the Earl of Westmorland. R.O., *Domestic Elizabeth*, ccxix. 13.

[2] Charles Paget says that Dr. Gifford eventually wrote to Walsingham to protest against Savage's story.

For not only is there no confirmation at all of the story from either of the two Giffords or from Hodgson, but the confession of Savage, the only evidence which we have, has come to us in an intentionally mangled form. In the *State Trials*[1] it was manipulated on purpose to produce the impression that Dr. Gifford was the only tempter, Gilbert's name being omitted entirely. In the Record Office there is a less emasculated form of this passage,[2] which shows that Gilbert played some part in the seduction of Savage. But this Record Office paper is itself only a supplement to Savage's original story; and this, into which it should be dovetailed, is missing. If we could get still fuller documents, we should probably find that Gilbert acted the principal part, and that Dr. William's share in the matter was that of giving answers to questions skilfully proposed to him by Gilbert; questions and answers the bearing of which the doctor may not have appreciated. Upon a broad consideration of the whole story this is the hypothesis which I favour, though I do not in any way build upon it.[3]

In the August following Savage left the Seminary; and it is probable that he was dismissed by Allen, because of some rumour of the above transactions getting abroad. But we only hear this obscurely from Gilbert in a later and very suspicious letter.[4] The *Diarium* of the college suggests nothing untoward. *Discessit* we read, the same being used for missionaries and friends. There does not seem to have been any external pronouncement.

Savage then entered at Barnard's Inn, and studied law,

---

[1] *State Trials* (1730), ii. p 121

[2] Boyd, viii. 611, cf. 681 and ix. 14, from R O., *Mary Queen of Scots*, xix. n. 38, dated 11 August; The British Museum copy, Cotton, *Caligula*, C ix 290, is dated 15 August

[3] More about *Dr William Gifford in 1586*, in *The Month* for April 1904.

[4] Boyd, ix. 222, Dr Allen—'caused Savage as it were to be expelled the house for a colour.'

remaining about London, still resolved (so his 'confession' states) to strike a blow, if the chance should offer, and still of a mind that such a blow would be justifiable. Gilbert, meantime, continued his studies for the priesthood, entirely unconcerned for Elizabeth's danger, either then, or later, when he was in close and constant intercourse with Walsingham. Indeed, it was exactly then that he tried his best to excite Savage to action!

The conclusion must surely be, that danger from Savage was at least remote. Gilbert, when present, could talk him into any frame of mind that might be desired. When the tempter was absent, Savage's natural simplicity preserved him from doing harm.

To what extent Savage belonged to George Gifford's plot cannot yet be definitely proved. But no doubt the probabilities are very strongly in favour of his having been suborned by Gilbert on purpose to help George, and that he was directed to him in London. Babington believed this, for he used these words, 'those who set Mr. Gifford, Savage, and Ballard first in hand,'[1] as if all three were in the same case. Moreover, Babington elsewhere speaks of Ballard, Savage, Gifford, having been in the plot before his own.[2] Again, in the confession of Savage, according to the form read in court, Savage is said to have thought that by joining the plot he would please 'all the Giffords.'[3]

If there still remains some obscurity about the relations of Savage with George Gifford, this will be due to the government having kept the name of the latter out of the legal proceedings, as he was now a protestant and in court favour.

---

[1] *Confessions*, iii. § 5. Babington also speaks of 'the plot of Savage and Gifford' in Boyd, viii. 685, and here Tichborne seems to hold the same opinion.
[2] *Confessions*, i. § 2, end.
[3] *State Trials*, 121; Boyd, ix. 14.

It does not indeed follow that, if Gilbert and George worked together in 1585, they also worked together at an earlier date. Still we cannot but suspect that so it was. The conjecture is evidently suggested that Gilbert was acting the part of *provocateur* all through, in collusion with his cousin George.

It will also be noted hereafter, as an indication of Gilbert's habit of mind, that no sooner had he got to work in England, than he bethought himself of his Rheims achievement, and wanted to bring Dr. William over, in order to inveigle him into acting once more the part which he had played with Savage.

Savage having left the college at Rheims in August 1585, Gilbert remained on there quietly while his cousin, Dr. William, was summoned by Morgan to Paris in September. Berden has told us that Morgan's object was to send him to England, probably in order that he might act as a sort of figure-head for the so-called 'Welsh' faction. For as the persecution had killed off all the leading laymen among the catholics, they had come to look for leadership to clerics like Allen and Persons, and these were all on the so-called 'English' side. Morgan was therefore endeavouring to get a clergyman of repute to represent him, and we see from his letters and from those of Charles Paget, that they endeavoured to push Christopher Bagshaw, Alban Dolman, Meredith Hanmer and others, into the foreground, and next spring they renewed the attempt with Dr. Gifford. Yet such was the rashness of Morgan and his friends, that all their clerical allies were either betrayed by their letters, or fared the worse for their patronage.

Dr. Gifford, however, refused Morgan's offer, and returned to Rheims accompanied by Edward Grately, a clever young priest and a fellow-student with the Giffords, but who, alas! was, like them, entirely bewitched by Morgan's wretched feuds. Grately begged Gilbert, though not yet a priest, to come and take the place which Dr. William had refused. Gilbert consented, left the college on 8 October 1585, and was warmly welcomed by Morgan, who wrote a very lengthy letter in his favour to Queen Mary.[1]

It is far too long to quote here, but it is worthy of remark as showing how little real skill Morgan had in correspondence of this kind. It abounds in minute instructions, which were probably impracticable, and in unnecessary details, as to which he could form no safe judgment under his circumstances, and which would do great harm if the letter were intercepted, as in fact it was.

For us, however, the main thing is that Gilbert was now officially connected with Mary's correspondence. Having previously known of Savage's resolution against Elizabeth, and presumably having even enticed him to that course, it will be strange if Gilbert does not manage to link Savage, or some kindred spirit, with the correspondence; and then Mary's life, under the Association law, will be forfeit.

SECTION III

Setting the Death-trap—December 1585-January 1586.

1. *Gilbert Gifford's First Steps.*

Gilbert Gifford left Rheims on the 8th of October 1585, and on the 15th Morgan wrote for him the necessary letters of introduction. Yet he was in no hurry to be off from Paris, and it seems to have been about the 10th of December before he landed at Rye, where he was 'apprehended' and sent up to London. Whether this was prearranged or not we do not know, but in due course he appeared before

---

[1] Murdin, *State Papers*, p 454.

Walsingham, and then, at least (whatever may have happened before), the compact between them was soon settled.

What their contract exactly was is, of course, not on record. But the numerous letters of Gilbert, both to Walsingham and to his servant Phelippes, leave no doubt that Gilbert was taken on as a *provocateur*. Yet one caution on this point may be necessary for us. According to our ideas, such an *agent* would presumably be encouraged at once to foment plots, and perhaps the more the merrier. But that was not in the least Elizabeth's view. Her ideal was that every one should be kneeling in obedience before her. That any subject should show resentment and much more hostility, was a crime of inconceivable gravity. So, while she allowed Walsingham to dabble in a little vague plot-mongering, if he assured her that this was a necessary precaution, and practised by other princes; yet no general permission would be a valid safeguard, if the plotting were real and serious, unless her licence had been specifically obtained for each case. The example of Parry illustrates this; and when Gilbert eventually sought safety in flight, the explanation he gave to Walsingham was—You can imagine how fearful a thing it was—' to deal with such treacherous companions *without any warrant or discharge*' (p. 120).

As we proceed, we shall find that even Poulet and Walsingham himself have to get leave 'from on high,' when a new development in their game has to be begun. It was quite unlikely therefore that a mere tool like Gilbert should have received a really free licence to conspire. His flight, when he saw the crash coming, shows how clearly he perceived this; and the indictment, followed by a death sentence on him, which Walsingham at once ordered evidently confirms it.

So Gilbert had to walk warily in his mischief-making. Yet being a born master of the art, he knew how to dare, as well as how to wait. He knew that, if he waited too long, his opportunities would pass. So he dared. His words about the permit, just quoted, show it, and other proofs will appear as we proceed; his interview with Mendoza just after the discovery of the plot (p. clxxiii), being perhaps the most striking instance of his craft that we know. Bearing this in mind, we may be sure that, if at first he went quietly, he would miss few if any opportunities that presented themselves.

At a much later period, when Gilbert wanted to throw all the blame on Morgan, he alleged that 'he had at once informed Morgan' of Walsingham's readiness to help him in his agitation 'against Allen and the Jesuits.' There can, however, be no question that what he really said was that he had 'easily escaped Walsingham's hands,' and that he had already taken steps to pass letters to Mary. The first phrase was immediately reported back to Walsingham by Berden in Paris, who must have heard it from Morgan; while Morgan himself soon after wrote to Mary to say that he hears that his letters to her have been 'sent on.' The date of the dealings with Walsingham was probably about December the 20th, for on that day Richard Daniel, a searcher at Rye, was paid for bringing up a prisoner to Court from thence. Daniel was not unfrequently rewarded in those inquisitorial days for the same thing, but at dates which do not at all fit in, as this does, with other definite landmarks of our story.[1]

---

[1] Berden wrote from Paris on December 18/28 that 'Thomas Fitzherbert did make Gifford acquainted with the French convoy for letters' At the end he adds, 'Here is news of his apprehension on the coast, whereof there is great sorrow' On Jan 2/12 he writes, 'Here is great joy that Gilbert Gifford escaped your Honour's hands so easily' (*Additional Calendar*, pp 162, 167) Morgan's letter of 18/28 January is in Murdin's *State Papers*, p. 470, *Hatfield Calendar*, iii p 129

Daniel was paid by the Treasurer of the Chamber. He had brought his prisoner first to Lord Cobham, Warden of the Cinque Ports, then to the Court at Greenwich. R.O., *Declared Accounts*, 542, r. 78.

It has often been said, and that by writers who profess to be favourable to Walsingham, that Queen Mary was brought from Tutbury to Chartley at this time on purpose that her correspondence might be watched, according to the plan afterwards carried out. This may be so, though her removal was in appearance due to her own representations during the earlier part of the year. Elizabeth professed that in such indifferent things she was 'very careful to yield that lady any reasonable contentment.' Chartley had been selected as early as September, and the remove would have been made then, but for the protests of the Earl of Essex, to whom the house belonged. So other plans had to be made tentatively, until the final order to move there could be given on the 23rd of November. The packing up necessarily took some time, and Queen Mary made the journey on Christmas Eve 1585.[1]

Thus there was plenty of time for Gilbert to look about him before going down to Chartley, and we should for many reasons have expected that the first place at which he would present himself would be the French embassy, for Berden in his letter of 18/28 December says that Gifford was 'made acquainted with the French convoy for letters.' This phrase signified that Morgan was secretly allowed to send his letters in the ambassador's bag as far as London, thereby escaping the danger of their being captured at the ports, the place where they were in the greatest danger. In London, one of the subordinates in the ambassador's house might get into communication with some friend of Mary's, and by their means Morgan's letters might eventually find their way in. The French ambassador at that time was Guillaume de l'Aubespine, baron de Chateauneuf, who wrote a memoir on the plot. A large part of this paper is preserved to us, and it is frequently cited

---

[1] Morris, *Sir Amias Poulet*, pp. 94 and 112.

INTRODUCTION

as an authority of the first importance. It should be remembered, however, that it was written a year or more after the events described, during which time any one's memory for small details is liable to become a little confused; moreover, there is an element of self-defence about the composition which may detract a trifle from its value here and there. There can, however, be no reason for not accepting the following account of Gilbert's advent to London:

In the month of December 1585, Gifford came to England with letters from the Archbishop of Glasgow, Morgan, and Paget, which testified to his catholicity and fidelity to the Queen of Scotland. The French ambassador had then appointed Cordaillot, one of his secretaries, to attend to the affairs of that Queen, and he, on seeing Gifford's letters, asked him the reason of his journey. Gifford said that he had been entrusted with secret letters for the Queen of Scotland, and that as she was now confined in a house not far from his father's home, he hoped to be able to accomplish the task. Cordaillot, nevertheless, answered little, for he knew that Walsingham was endeavouring to find out whether he corresponded secretly with the Queen. Gilbert urged that having been ten or twelve years away from England he would easily pass unknown, and would probably not be recognised even by his father and sisters. Again, he looked so young, without any beard, that his real age, and consequently his identity, would not be suspected. Still he was not yet trusted, and eventually withdrew. It was afterwards discovered that he was lodging with Phelippes, a servant of Walsingham.[1]

2. *Thomas Phelippes.*

As Gifford had already taken up his abode with Phelippes, it may be well to introduce this personage, who from now onwards plays such a large part in our story. Thomas Phelippes was the son of William Phillips,[2] 'Customer of

---

[1] A. de Labanoff, *Lettres de Marie Stuart*, 1844, vi. 281-2 slightly abbreviated. Renewed search should be made for the missing portion.

[2] Note the difference of spelling in the surname. It was a custom of the time for various members of a family to differentiate their signatures

London,' then, as now, a post of importance, to which Thomas afterwards succeeded. In appearance he must have been forbidding, and have formed somewhat of a contrast to the young and innocent-looking Gifford. Queen Mary herself describes Phelippes as ' of low stature, slender every way, eated in the face with small pocks, of short sight, thirty years of age by appearance.' However unprepossessing in appearance, he was a splendid correspondent, wrote a beautiful hand, and was evidently untiring with his pen, as witness the innumerable deciphers, copies, and letters, which he wrote off with astonishing facility. He must have been well educated, though we know not where he was schooled. Latin, French, and Italian were so familiar to him that he could read ciphers written in those tongues, but in Spanish he was less proficient. He shows a fair acquaintance with literary allusions and classical quotations.

This skill he no doubt acquired in great measure by travel. I first hear of him in Paris about 1578 where Walsingham has lent him to Sir Amias Poulet, then ambassador there, to help in deciphering intercepted letters. In 1580 I find mention of a ' Mr. Philipps, an English papist, at Rouen.' If this be our man, he was pretending to be a catholic for the time; and we know that Morgan afterwards told Mary he had great hopes of ' recovering ' Phelippes to her service, which seems as though he had at least dallied with her cause about this time. After this he travelled a great deal in France, presumably as an intermediary between Walsingham and other spies. Sometimes the still more delicate task was assigned to him of conveying to French Huguenots the money with which Elizabeth

---

by adopting various spellings of the family name, so long as its pronunciation was more or less faithfully observed, and these individual name-forms were generally adhered to. But of course all spelling was then in a more fluid state that it is now.

supplied them in their rebellions. Walsingham trusted him so much that he sent over to him in France various intercepted cipher dispatches, of which no one in England could make head or tail. For some little time before our story begins he had come home again, and would seem to have lived in Leadenhall Market. On 3rd May 1586, his income was increased by Elizabeth's order.[1] This might look like a retaining fee for the great work of his life on which he was so soon to launch. It may be that Walsingham's plans were by then arranged. It would seem more probable, however, that Phelippes had fallen into debt, as he so often did later on, and that the Queen's *largesse* was a way of salving his credit.

Be this as it may, Phelippes comes before us as a past-master in all branches of letter stealing, and a man with a real genius for deciphering. Yet even here exaggerations have been made. In point of fact, the deciphering of Mary's correspondence was easy work in the present case, because at its recommencement all the old ciphers had been changed, and a new alphabet sent to each correspondent. Phelippes took copies of all these keys as they passed, and after that his work was relatively simple.

We have already used, and shall be constantly using the evidence of letters, which come to us proximately from him. The question is often asked, Can we credit his alleged deciphers, as honestly reflecting the originals? He was certainly not invariably honest, and his profession was one which exposed him to strong temptations. But after carefully going over and re-deciphering many of his deciphers, I have come to the conclusion that in all essential matters he was faithful to Walsingham, and that wherever we find a cipher *sent in to his master*, with the decipher attached, the work may, broadly speaking, be trusted.

---

[1] Morris, *Sir Amias Poulet*, p. 115.

This is already a great deal, and enables us to make use with confidence of an enormous number of letters on an intelligible principle, which will prepare us to carry our criticism further when need arises.

Such a man was Gilbert's new patron and host,[1] and it does not surprise us to learn that as soon as Mary had settled down at Chartley, Phelippes betook himself thither, doubtless to prepare the ground, and to inform Sir Amias Poulet, Mary's keeper, and his old master in Paris, of the plans that were being made. Gifford, too, went down, and it will be remembered that, whereas he had told Secretary Cordaillot 'that his father and sisters would not recognise him,' yet he went down with his father's commission to look after some business. At all events it is a fair inference that the father knew of his going, seeing that he subsequently summoned him back to town.[2] These little indications show the extreme care taken by Walsingham's *employés* to have an ostensible explanation of their movements, which would not betray their real motives.

3. *The Death-trap.*

Phelippes, as we have seen, had already made all the necessary arrangements with Poulet. All Mary's household, even the laundry-maids, had been carefully cut off from intercourse with the outer world, so that it seemed

---

[1] That Phelippes estimated Gilbert's talents highly is clear from his exertions on his behalf and the commendations to Walsingham. See *below*, p. 118, and Morris, pp. 156 and 226, where he protects Gilbert against Justice Young.

[2] His father, John Gifford of Chillington, Staffordshire, was a staunch catholic, condemned as a recusant convict to live in partial confinement in London. He was thus unable to watch his son's doings; on the other hand, it was represented to him that an occasional service done to Phelippes by Gilbert might lead to a relaxation of his restraint. (Cf. Morris, pp. 153, 390.) In March he was allowed to visit baths for his health. *Acts of Privy Council*, xiv. 19. Mary's letter to him, Boyd, viii. 560.

INTRODUCTION lvii

to be, and really was, absolutely impossible to pass out a letter by any of the means which had hitherto proved successful. On the other hand, Gifford's method of communication was to be winked at, and his *modus operandi* will be fully explained later. His plan was put to the proof on the long winter's evening of 16 January, and that night Mary had the intense delight of receiving the letter from Morgan which commended Gilbert. With it there was a note from Gifford himself offering to open up a regular course of communication with her friends abroad.

The pleasure which such a missive would have brought to Mary was extraordinarily keen. She had always rejoiced in receiving letters from home or from those to whom she was attached, or about those in whom she was interested. This was noted by ambassadors and others from her youth upwards. But of late Poulet's inflexible severity and ceaseless vigilance had cut off all private communication with those abroad, and all she could hear came in the *open* letters sent her by the French ambassador. These Poulet read before they were delivered, or did not deliver them at all when they seemed to him inconvenient.[1] On the other hand, he was not sorry to tell her reports unfavourable to her own friends, reports which, as he says, were as grateful to her ' as salt to her eyes.' For almost a year she had been thus deprived of intelligence about current events drawn from friendly sources, and this long fast had of course greatly enhanced the fascination which news from home would always have had on a heart so generous and so loyal. Now she suspected no harm. The only fear which crossed her mind was lest the brave man who (as she imagined) had risked so much to bring her news should fall a victim to his daring, as so many others had already done.

---

[1] He sent one back, for instance, 7 July 1586, because to him it seemed to reflect on the English in general. Morris, p. 216.

This was the burden of the answer she wrote to Morgan next day, 17 January, 'conforme to the ancient computation,' by the same means that she had received the missive.

After condoling with Morgan on the misfortunes which had 'undeservedly, I doubt not,' befallen him, she gave orders that he was to receive an increased subsidy from her much-reduced income, and sent him two letters to forward. She also bade him 'keep himself from meddling with anything that might redound to his hurt, or increase the suspicion already conceived against you in these parts, being sure that you are able to clear yourselfe of all dealing for my service hithertill.' This was an allusion to the charge of his having plotted treason against Elizabeth with Dr. Parry, of which we see that she held him guiltless, though he still needed to be cautioned. In conclusion she added that while she fully trusted the bearer's honesty, she feared he might be discovered, so great was Poulet's vigilance.[1]

This letter, having been delivered by the Burton brewer to Gifford, would have been brought by him during the evening to Poulet. If Phelippes was still at Chartley, it would be opened and deciphered at once, and the decipher would be sent up to Walsingham. If Phelippes had already returned to town, the original packet would be sent up by express riders, and the decipherment would be done there. Walsingham would then have made up his mind about it; and given the original to Arthur Gregory,[2] his special expert for resealing opened packets. Meanwhile Gilbert rode up to town at his ease, and found the packet

---

[1] Labanoff, vi. 204

[2] Arthur Gregory seems also to have been used to imitate handwritings, and to write with invisible inks (See R O, *Domestic James I*, xxiv 38, *Domestic Elizabeth*, cclx 49) He is mentioned in this correspondence by the name of 'Arthur.' Morris, p 278. If Phelippes had already left London, as is not impossible (Morris, p 126), the process of decipherment will have been as described *below*, p cxlix

ready to be conveyed to the French ambassador in London; by him it was forwarded to Paris, and reached Morgan on 15 March. Two months from Chartley to Paris! It is necessary to note the extreme slowness, even under the most favourable circumstances, for the conveyance of letters which had to pass secretly. The extra delay caused by opening, reading, and reclosing was by comparison trifling. This was one of the circumstances which enabled Gifford's plan to be worked out without arousing suspicions.

When Gifford showed Mary's packet at the French embassy, he again requested to be entrusted with such letters as were waiting to be carried to her. Though this was not yet granted, his reception was much more cordial than at his first visit. He now received a special letter to take back to Mary, which, says Chateauneuf's memoir, was still kept purposely vague and unimportant in order to test still more thoroughly the reliability of the 'convoy.'

On the 25th of January, Sir Amias writes to Phelippes that he is 'looking daily to hear from *your friend*,' this being the disguise under which Gilbert was always mentioned in the correspondence of Poulet and Walsingham; Phelippes, on the other hand, designating Gilbert as 'the secret party.' This was another of the many precautions used by Walsingham's orders, in order to keep all as secret as possible.

On the 30th, Mary's keeper writes again to Walsingham, 'to trouble him with this abstract here enclosed of the French ambassador's letters to this Queen, finding nothing else in the packet worth advertisement.' The enclosed 'abstract' is now missing, but the tone of the above extract shows that the letters were unimportant. If the French ambassador's letter was the same as that carried by Gilbert, Poulet's note will confirm Chateauneuf's memoir. But the ambassador's letter may only be the ordinary *open* letter sent by post. The letter carried by

Gifford must have been passed in to Mary about the 28th or 29th, for on the 31st her answer was written and passed out again. Mary was now quite convinced of the safety and practicability of the channel of communication, and, so far as she was concerned, Gifford's plans were already successful.

But just at this moment a cloud passed over the relationships of Sir Amias and 'your friend.' Instead of bringing the letters back to Chartley after dusk,[1] Gifford sent a note to the Knight, asking him to appoint a trusty messenger to whom he might deliver them. The suspicious Puritan at once took alarm. He answered that he ' had learned not to trust two, where it sufficed to trust one.' So Gifford came ' late in the night, the 5th of this present ' February, and handed him all that he had received. Yet he did not altogether satisfy Mary's keeper. He let out that he knew that the letter to the French ambassador had a cipher in it, which showed that he had been prying to some purpose. Moreover, he ' doubled in his speech once or twice.' In short, the rigid but sharp Sir Amias felt that he was dealing with a trickster, in whom he felt no confidence. Still, he did not like to press hardly on Walsingham's ' friend,' so he contented himself with warning his chief. His diffidence melted away but slowly, as the correspondence proceeded so successfully from his point of view.

Mary's letter, as we have said, contained her full assent to the continuation of the correspondence. This assent was conveyed in the following words, which need a slight explanation: 'Send me by this bearer all the packets, which you and Cherelles have in hand for me, but enclose them in a small box or bag of strong leather.' The clause

---

[1] The secret letters seem always to have come in before dawn or after dusk.

INTRODUCTION

about giving Gifford all the packets is clear enough. It is what he had been aiming at from the beginning, and enabled him now to pick and choose what he liked or thought most convenient for his purpose, or as Phelippes might instruct. We even find him using this order, as a warrant for opening thick packets and making them lighter, and, *vice versa*, for putting more into thin packets. The object of this move was, of course, to have a free hand in breaking seals without going to the trouble of closing them, and pretending that they had not been opened.

Even more significant was the little phrase about the box, or leather bag. It may be remembered that Sir Amias had managed so well at Chartley, that the imprisoned Queen had practically no chance of sending out letters even by the laundry-maids.[1] Yet there was still one, and only one, uncontrolled outlet.

The brewery was small, and it was necessary to employ a brewer who lived at Burton, and brought in his beer in barrels, which he fetched away again when empty. Sir Amias's guards watched the casks closely, both going and coming, but never thought of looking *inside* them. Gilbert or Phelippes had the idea of bringing the letters within the barrels; fitting them, it would seem, into a corked tube which would slip through the bung-hole.[2]

In the curious cant adopted by Poulet, this brewer is called 'the honest man,' his dishonesty to both sides being such that it is positively amusing, and gives a slight interlude of comedy in a tragedy otherwise sufficiently sad and sordid. 'The honest man' (we do not know his real name) had previously supplied Tutbury with beer, so that he was

---

[1] ' I cannot imagine how it may be possible for them to convey a piece of paper as big as my finger.' (Poulet to Walsingham, Morris, p. 126.)

[2] This is Chateauneuf's contemporary account, Labanoff, vi. 284. But Camden (1607) writes as though the letters were left behind a brick in the wall. *Annales* (ed. 1625), p. 438. *English Translation*, p. 305.

well known to both sides from the beginning. He was at first, in appearance, secured by Gifford by a handsome bribe to be paid by Mary, and he afterwards demanded and received quite considerable sums at her hands, for the risks he was supposed to be running for her. Having received the letters, he first showed them to Poulet (for which he was also well rewarded), who, after a comparatively short examination, sent them back again to the brewer at his house in Burton. After this he was visited by Gifford, or Gifford's 'substitute,'[1] whom *he imagined to be a genuine servant of Mary*, and to them he delivered his packets. Thus he was led to believe that he was the only traitor, that his treason to Mary was not, after all, so very serious, for Poulet did not keep the packets long. When once he had given them to Gifford they were, he thought, in the hands of Mary's servants, and no more harm (from Mary's point of view) would come to them.

We know that Poulet's real object in inspecting the packet at once was to keep a check on 'the honest man.' If the same letters did not come back to him through Gifford again, it would be evident that 'the honest man' was forwarding them by another channel; whereas if they did come back through Gifford in right order, there was little doubt that he was playing 'honestly' his part of the double game. Poulet was constantly on tenter-hooks, when any delay occurred, lest 'the honest man' should play 'the very knave.' But in the end the regular receipt of all the correspondence in the order agreed upon calmed Sir Amias's anxieties on this head.

---

[1] 'The Substitute.' His name does not transpire in any of the plot papers. Phelippes says, 10 March 1586, 'Choice is made of *a substitute* of honest credit, good wealth, good understanding, and servant to the Earl of Leicester.' Morris, p. 154. Eighteen months later (7 September 1587) Phelippes wrote to Gilbert that, 'Sir Amias with Hoby protest they took the letter from an honest man.' *Domestic Elizabeth*, cciii. 36. This sounds as if Hoby was the intermediary between Sir Amias and *the honest man*.

INTRODUCTION lxiii

Yet there was another source of annoyance, which, though petty in itself, was galling to Poulet, whom Elizabeth had bound to the greatest economy. The 'honest man,' finding that his services were wellnigh indispensable to both sides, began to assume grotesque airs of superiority, and settle the times for meetings to fit in with his arrangements, making others hurry or wait simply to suit his real or even perhaps pretended convenience. Finally and hardest of all, as Mr. Froude well puts it, 'like a true English scoundrel, he used the possession of a State secret to exact a higher price for his beer,' [1] and this in peremptory tones, to which the hard-hearted Puritan was forced, however reluctantly, to agree.

But in spite of these drawbacks 'the honest man,' as has been said, did his part of the knavery without really failing. He gave the packets to Gifford, who reconveyed them secretly to Poulet, and they were either read then and there, if Phelippes was on the spot; or if he was not there, they were sent up to London by express riders, and were deciphered there by Phelippes. Meanwhile Gifford was riding leisurely to town, where he found the packet resealed and ready for him to carry to the French ambassador, who in due time conveyed it abroad to Morgan, to whom it was always addressed.

The letters to Mary came in exactly the reverse order. Morgan sent them to Chateauneuf, whose secretary gave them to Gifford. Gifford took them to Phelippes, and while the latter was deciphering them in London and making the packet up again, the former rode quietly and leisurely on. An express conveyed the re-made-up packet to Poulet, who gave it to Gifford, who gave it to the 'honest man.' The 'honest man' showed it once more to Poulet, and, when Poulet had returned it to him again,

---

[1] Quoted by Morris, p. 191, see also pp 192, 195, 196, 210, 211.

he put it into the corked tube, and slipped this through the bung-hole of the beer barrel, which he delivered at Mary's side of the house. There the tube was taken out and carried into Mary's little chancery. Then the covering letter from Gilbert Gifford, or Barnes, was at once opened and read, and a few lines of answer were sent out, while the brewer rested his horses after their long journey, some eighteen miles, from Burton. The covering letters which survive show vividly the working of the secret post. (*Below*, pp. 1-48.)

No sooner was the new post going regularly, and in appearance safely, than Elizabeth made a mysterious speech to the French ambassador (April 1586).

'Monsieur Ambassador,' she said, 'you have much secret intelligence with the Queen of Scotland. But, believe me, *I know everything that is done in my kingdom.* Besides, since I was a prisoner in the time of the Queen my sister, I know what artifices prisoners use to gain over servants, and to have secret information.'

Chateauneuf was full of suspicion at this; but could not believe that Elizabeth was for once talking truth. It was a pity he did not tell Mary.[1]

Note on Old and New Style in Dates.

In the correspondence which will follow, it is necessary to take account of the different styles of reckoning time. Since January 1584 France had adopted the more correct calendar introduced by Pope Gregory XIII. (hence called 'Gregorian Calendar'), while England still kept to the older reckoning which was ten days behind the other (hence called 'Old Style'). Russia still follows Old Style, which is now thirteen days behind New Style, which we in England have meanwhile adopted. Hence the date, Petrograd, 10/23 January 1920, means the day called 10 January in Russia, 23 January in London. Similarly Paris, 1/11 January 1585, means the day

---

[1] Labanoff, vi. 291.

of 1585 called 1 January by English time and style, 11 January by French time and style.

This then is the rule for reading a date expressed like a fraction. The upper figure means English time, the lower continental time.

Notice that the double figure does *not express any doubt* between two times. If there was a doubt, one might write, ? 1-11 January 1585. But the fractional form refers to *one and the same day*, differently numbered in different styles.

When the whole passage refers to England *only*, or to the Continent *only*, then if only one number is used, it will obviously mean the local time in the place under discussion.

In the case of letters written to and from Chartley, it is generally necessary to notice both styles. The English date was used there for all domestic purposes, for instance in the Journal of Bourgoing. But the letters from France, which comprised so large a part of Mary's correspondence, having been written in New Style, were also answered by her in New Style. Moreover Phelippes, in the notes that came with the secret correspondence, arranged to use it in his covering note of 6/16 June, R.O., *M.Q.S.*, xviii. 6; Boyd, viii. 440; and *below*, p. 10. What his reason was we do not know. Perhaps, from having deciphered some of her letters to Paris, he knew she sometimes used that style; perhaps he craftily thought that its assumption would help to create the impression that he was a catholic, and so contribute in its way to her undoing.

SECTION IV

JOHN BALLARD, 1584-1586.

The snare which was to cost Mary her life having been set, the next move would be to invite conspirators to make use of its apparent advantages. It will not be hard to see that the first steps in this treacherous proceeding would have been taken in deep secrecy, and that little or no record of them should survive. In the later stages of the plot, when the die was cast, and the conspirators on both sides had grown accustomed to their parts, a good many letters were written which have been preserved; and we shall then be able to follow the story in the very words of the principal agents.

To be frank, we do not know precisely when the plot did begin. We know that in the months of January, February, March 1586, the various conspirators and *provocateurs* approached each other, and that intrigues began, which, with certain modifications, afterwards developed into the plot. But the circumstances of the first meetings never transpired, and our attention must in this chapter be concentrated on the movements of the suspects; for if we follow them closely, we shall pick up clues, that will leave little doubt as to the objects they have in mind.

First then as to Gilbert Gifford, we find from Barnes's confession [1] that these two were lodging together about the beginning of March, and that Gilbert then had a cipher to correspond with Savage; and from this we infer that he did not relax his hold on his college friend. Of George Gifford himself we hear nothing, but from the confessions of the Babington conspirators, we know that Savage's conspiracy (*i.e.* the later phase of George Gifford's plot) was strengthened about this time by the accession of Thomas Salisbury, and also of Ballard, and as the latter becomes from that time onwards its most active member, it will be well to go back, and to put together such information as we possess about his previous career.

1. *The Previous History of Ballard and Tyrrell.*

John Ballard, according to the *Douay Diaries*, was born in the diocese of Ely. He was educated at Cambridge, where he had, on 14 June 1574, taken the degree of

---

[1] *Below*, p. 3.

INTRODUCTION lxvii

Master of Arts.[1] He arrived at Rheims on 29 November 1579,[2] and was eventually ordained priest at Châlons 4 March 1581, and returned to England on the 29th of the same month. Savage, it may be noted, had arrived before Ballard had left; but Gilbert Gifford was then studying in Rome, so that they could not have met at this period.

Of Ballard's work in England during this first nine months, no details seem to be known. At the end of this time he was a prisoner in the Gatehouse at Westminster, and amongst other priests, who were his companions there, he met for the first time Anthony Tyrrell, with whom he was destined to be in closer connection during the next few years than was at all usual, considering the circumstances under which priests in England had to live at that time. To begin with, they were fortunate enough to break prison together and to get clear away, just before the end of the year 1581. They separated, but met again not long after in Norfolk, Ballard then going under the name of Turner. After this for more than two years they saw nothing of each other, Tyrrell probably keeping near London, Ballard going farther west.

Early in the summer of 1584 they met again in London. They were both feeling in want of a holiday, and had raised £100 and £60 respectively for that purpose. Ballard had the larger sum for a journey to Rome, and it was provided by friends, on whose behalf he was to have obtained certain dispensations and faculties. Tyrrell had originally only meant to go beyond seas and live quietly; in order to

---

[1] B M., Cole MSS., Add. 5885, p. 28 John Venn, Sc.D., and J. A. Venn, M A, *Matriculations and Degrees in the University of Cambridge, 1544 to 1659*, 1913, p 35, give his career as follows (contractions expanded) 'St Catharine's, sizar, Michaelmas term, 1569, migrated to Caius College, Lent term, 1569-70, A B King's College, 1574-5'

[2] 29° Novembris 1579, Huc venerunt .. duo Cantabrigienses, Englishus et Ballardus: hic artium magister est, etc T F. Knox, *Douay Diaries*, 1878, p 158, cf 173-8

continue his theological studies, which had been, as Father Morris says, 'dangerously short,' having lasted only two years. Embarking from near 'Southampton House,' they were carried over by one Bray in company with six others, their fares being five shillings a head.

For the episode which will now follow we have a minute account by Anthony Tyrrell. But his story, though so often taken as good evidence, loses most of its power to convince, when we consider the singular circumstances of its composition, of which a short account must be premised.

On the 4th of July 1586, Tyrrell was arrested for the third time and sent to prison for his faith. He wrote begging Lord Burghley for mercy in somewhat ample terms, but nothing in particular occurred until after the arrest of Ballard (4 August), which terrified Tyrrell lest he should be involved in the mad schemes of his former friend. Hereupon he lapsed into a sort of delirium that he must betray everything. Hysterical symptoms had not been wanting before. He had lately assisted at the so-called 'exorcisms' of certain neurotic young people, and had written an exaggerated account of the phenomena in *The Book of Miracles*,[1] which proves that he was already

---

[1] This MS is lost, but Samuel Harsnett, *Egregious Popish Impostures*, 1603, quotes Tyrrell's own statement about it, p 254. The episode of exorcisms, though it lies outside the Babington plot, is so near akin to it that further references to the topic must be added here. At the reformation epidemics for witch-hunting, devil-finding, exorcisms, and the like became prevalent from time to time both among protestants and among catholics. In 1585-6 it spread to the English catholics, reaching its maximum in Lent 1586, when perhaps a score of priests practised exorcisms, and some hundreds of converts were made. The apostle of the movement was Father Weston, S J, and its lay patron was Edmund, son of Sir George Peckham, whose large mansion, Denham Hall, Bucks, provided a refuge for the exorcists. The ground of the movement appears to have been hysteria to some extent, and otherwise nothing else but the childish simplicity of the age. Before Easter 1586, common sense began to declare against the exorcisms, which were often a little cruel, as well as

then in an over-wrought, untrustworthy mood. After the 27th of August, however, he completely surrendered to Lord Burghley and Justice Young. He accused Ballard and any catholic of every charge of which he thought the inquisitors wanted to find them guilty; and he carried out any sacrilege, villainy, or betrayal they suggested. He bore false, but fatal, evidence against three or four priests, who suffered martyrdom; and, at the instigation of Lord Burghley and Justice Young, he had also said mass and heard confessions in order to maintain his reputation (*Fall* i.).

Early in 1587 a good old priest, William Barlow, had the courage to speak to him frankly and lovingly, at which the poor wretch's heart was changed and he promised entire conversion. But he had not the courage to fly his surroundings, and he soon relapsed into all his old malpractices, and offered to become a protestant preacher (*Fall* ii.). For this purpose he was freed, 2 March 1587, when his catholic friends again prevailed on him to return to the fold, and they collected £40 or £50 to get him abroad. He went, but did not persevere long. By Midsummer 1587, he was back again, and had placed himself in the hands of the government (*Fall* iii.). It was during that last short lucid interval that he wrote a full account of his previous falls in which he embodied many useful documents. This was eventually published in our own day.[1] His own

---

very dangerous because of the persecution. One of the last exorcisms is fully described in Boyd, viii. 698-701, ix. 11.

Edmund Peckham fell ill and died in July, and the movement was buried in his grave. Denham was searched by pursuivants and afterwards sold. Father Weston and other exorcists were imprisoned; several were martyred. For reference and extracts see my *Supposed Cases of Diabolical Possession in* 1585-6, in *The Month*, May 1911; *also* T. G. Law, in *XIXth Century*, March 1894, and his more critical article on Tyrrell, in *D.N.B.*

[1] *The Fall of Anthony Tyrrell*, prepared for publication by Father Persons, published by John Morris, S.J., in the *Troubles of our Catholic Forefathers*, ii. 1875

subsequent changes of creed made it inopportune for catholics of those times to do so.

Having now fallen thrice, his imprisonment was rather devised to obstruct the influence of his catholic friends, than thought necessary to prevent his escape. Indeed, there was talk of a comfortable living, on condition of his publicly revoking what he had lately written. He agreed to the terms, and the date for the recantation sermon was fixed for 21 January 1588, the third Sunday after Epiphany.

But as that day drew near, Tyrrell's mind began to change once more, and while he was thought to be writing a recantation sermon, he was really writing several fresh declarations of his own infamy in having betrayed innocent blood. These he kept secret, clearly foreseeing how the matter was likely to fall out.

When the day arrived 'there wanted not concourse of people from all parts, and of all sorts, and many of the Council and nobility were also present, to hear so rare a comedy. And first of all a preacher of their own was set up to make the prologue, which was very long, containing an earnest exhortation to be attentive to what the other would say, and to believe him. Immediately after him Anthony Tyrrell was brought up with much honour to the pulpit, and then, after that he had commended himself upon his knees to God, he began his speech.'

After three minutes, as might be imagined, there was a mighty uproar, and a rush to tear down the preacher who was 'uttering the plain contrary of that which they expected.' Yet before he was dislodged he had, with a sweep of the hand, thrown out among the crowd those copies of his speech which he had made before in writing, and though instant proclamation was made for them to be brought in and burnt, one copy fell into catholic hands, and has been preserved.

'Tyrrell was carried away on men's shoulders to the gaol of Newgate and then to the Counter, the Protestants crying vengeance upon him, and he weeping bitterly, knocking his breast, and affirming that he had done nothing that day but upon mere force and compulsion of his conscience.' In the Counter he was comforted for three months by a Scotch catholic, Alexander Hamilton, who managed to speak to him through a chink in the wall, but after this neighbour had gone, his resolution again failed. Again he promised to preach a recantation sermon, and this time, on the feast of the Immaculate Conception, 8 December 1588, he actually did so, and received as his reward, two small livings and a wife (*Fall* iv.).

But not even this kept him quiescent. At the end of 1593 he was found to have been abroad, and it was rumoured that he had changed his faith once more. An enquiry was ordered, but evaded. It seems that some negotiation had been going on with a sister, who was a Bridgettine nun of Sion. They had lately been migrating from Rouen, and Anthony declared that he wanted to bring her home. But there were other very ugly features about this escapade. Tyrrell had to confess that, while staying in London, he had been leading a very immoral life. The end of this adventure is not known in detail.

On 15 June 1602, he repeated before Bancroft the statement that the exorcisms had been dishonest, and after that he fades from sight, though more than one contemporary assures us that, *Mortuus est poenitens*.[1]

---

[1] Besides Morris quoted above, and the biography of Tyrrell in *D N B*, his *Confessions* at R O have lately appeared in Boyd, and his *Recantation*, of January 1588, is printed in Bridgewater's *Concertatio Ecclesiae Anglicanae*

2. *What is the Value of Tyrrell's Evidence.*

After reading this extraordinary record of mutability in matters where men are generally more firm, the question will arise, What of his evidence concerning the plot? Tyrrell had no real connection with it. He had been imprisoned before Babington communicated with Mary. He is not named by any of the genuine conspirators (except to reject some stray statement quoted to them from his confessions), nor does he mention (either truly or falsely) any detail of the genuine conspiracy. But he had long been intimate with Ballard, and that agitator had asked him 'to persuade all the friends he could to be ready'[1] for an invasion; and he had perhaps complied to some extent. In abject terror lest he should suffer for this, he had sought to propitiate Lord Burghley by turning Queen's evidence, and saying everything he possibly could against his former friend. Mr. Froude and his followers accept these accusations in full, discarding his subsequent recantations with the sneer that they were written when Tyrrell had 'fallen into the hands of the priests.'[2] As if the testimony given out of fear of death, or torture, or for the receipt of money or other advantages were of more value than that offered in spite of personal inconvenience or danger, and without hope of reward!

But the real difficulty lies deeper. We are here dealing with a man who was suffering from hysteria or intense nervous strain. When terrified, he became quite unreliable, and fell at once, like a bird before a snake; he was no longer responsible for his words. This must influence the credence we give to him.

Yet he was not always under the spell of fear, and we

---

[1] Boyd, p. 655.
[2] *History* (1870), xi. p. 45, *n.*

need not reject everything that he says. He will be rational enough when not afraid. We can also assist ourselves by comparing his charges and his recantations, though we must remember that the latter also may be subject to some exaggeration.

Though Tyrrell's libels are sometimes gross, as those against the Pope, Dr. Allen, and the Earl of Arundel (evidently because they occupied high positions), his more usual fault is that of adopting a bitter, exaggerated, or melodramatic tone, while recounting the experiences of a catholic missionary of those days. Even when he is not lying, he is a bad witness, making minor misrepresentations in order to curry favour with his protestant masters.[1]

With these cautions for and against Tyrrell's evidence, we may now go over his story.

3. *A Pilgrimage to Rome, March 1584 to January 1585.*

Tyrrell's story[2] then informs us that Foscue, as he always calls Ballard, with the rest of their party landed at Dives, Normandy, and went on to Rouen, where Tyrrell had a sister, Gertrude, a Bridgettine nun. Thence to Eu, and they meant to have spent some time in the neighbourhood, when they were summoned by Dr. Allen to the Seminary of Rheims, where they arrived during the Easter holidays. In his *Confessions* he says that they here heard many heinous treasons against the Queen, of which he gives

---

[1] Examples of this may be found by comparing his account of Mr. Bold (Boyd, p. 653) with Bold's own account (*Ibid.*, pp. 697, 698). See also *below*, Babington, Examinations, viii. §§ 12 to 16, and the parallel passages there noted. Also *Catholic Record Society*, v. 107, some tests for his account of the martyr priest, Thomas Alfield. The retraction of nine charges against the Earl and Countess of Arundel in *Hatfield Calendar*, iii. 222.

[2] This he told several times: in his *Confessions* of 30 and 31 August (Boyd, pp. 641, 643), also in a memoir, printed in the *Fall of A. Tyrell*, in Morris, *Troubles*, ii. 325, etc.

details, incriminating both Allen and William Gifford. But in his retractions he specifically withdraws this, 'whereof, God forgive me, no one word was true.' Allen and the Seminarists looked rather askance at them, as though they were shirking the dangers of England,[1] but Allen, on their explaining their intention to study, approved and sent them to the Jesuit College at Pont-à-Mousson, where they would find the facilities which they came to seek. Here they stayed till the end of July, and then started for Milan on their way to Rome.

It was while they were at Pont-à-Mousson that the Prince of Orange was assassinated, 10 July 1584, and the debates which then followed doubtless had their influence on some of the incidents of which we shall now hear.

At Milan they found that St. Charles Borromeo was absent, but Dr. Owen Lewis, the Cardinal's Vicar-General, received them hospitably. It was in his interviews with the Welsh churchman that Foscue at length began 'to speak plain English.' 'We shall never be able to plant religion soundly,' he said, 'unless the Queen be made away.' 'You speak like a Phineas,' was Dr. Lewis's answer, '*sed caute loquendum*.' After this Foscue would occasionally mention the subject of killing the Queen to Tyrrell, who strongly opposed any violence to 'God's holy anointed.' Foscue's answer was, 'I am resolved to be satisfied fully in Rome.' 'All which,' said Tyrrell afterwards in his retraction, 'from the beginning to the last period, I protest before God, to have been most untrue, and a mere invention of my own pernicious brain, to get credit with my Lord Treasurer.'

Having arrived in Rome 'at the latter end of August,'

---

[1] This is not reflected in Barret's letter to Agazario at Rome, from Rheims, 6 April 1584, 'Tyrrell and two others have come here as a rest from England.' Stonyhurst, *Anglia*, i. 18.

they went to the English Hospice and stayed there till the beginning of October.¹

Tyrrell, as the climax of his story approaches, becomes more and more artificial in his style. They get into conversation first with the Rector, then with the General of the Jesuits, then with Pope Gregory himself about the assassination of the Queen; and their approbations of her murder are given with an increasing clearness and force, and a rising scale of applause and of promised reward. Father Agazario the Rector listens with pleasure, will not give an answer himself, but offers to procure one shortly. In a day or two the General of the Jesuits appears; he hums and haws, says it is a matter only to be discussed by men of tried security, but eventually gives leave for Father Agazario to take them to the Pope, and obtain an authoritative solution. So they go to the Pope, the Jesuit explains their doubts, and then the Pope delivers a handsome and well-turned approbation of the murder of the Queen. 'Children, beloved in Our Lord, we have always loved you in the bowels of Christ. . . . For your various requests, we will consult and you shall have answer, but as touching the taking away of that impious Jezabel, I would be loth you should attempt anything unto your own destruction, and we know not how our censure in that point would be taken among her subjects, who profess themselves our subjects. But if you can wisely give such counsel, as may be without scandal to the party or to us, know ye that we do not only approve of the act, but think the doer, if he suffer death simply for it, to be worthy of canonisation. And so with our Apostolic Benediction we dismiss you.' When

---

¹ The dates are given almost exactly. The *Pilgrim Book*, still preserved at the English College, Rome, bears witness that they arrived on 7 September (which would be 29 August, Old Style) and left on 2 October (New Style). Foley, *Records S.J.*, vi. 555.

they got home the Jesuits insisted that the Pope's words should be kept very secret, and if necessary even forsworn. Tyrrell concludes by saying that the Pope's words were the first thing which unsettled his adherence to catholicism. Nevertheless, he adds, 'Notwithstanding the Pope his censure, and Dr. Lewis his persuasion, I imagined for all that, that Foscue's words had been but speeches of vanout (vanity), knowing the man vainglorious, and desirous of his own praise, and to be meddling in things above his own reach.' If he had not put in this he would have been guilty of ' concealing ' high treason.

Coming back to Rheims they told all to Allen, who 'bit his lip at the Pope his resolution, but affirmed, notwithstanding that the deed was *in itself good*, but must never be preached, taught or persuaded. When I am asked, I have always answered with a *non-licet* and so I exhort you to do.'

In his retraction he calls the whole of this Roman episode 'a long and monstrous tale, and most untrue. Neither was there ever any such speech or negociations with the persons in any of the places named, neither would we ever have durst to have proposed any such thing unto them, if Ballard or I had been so wicked to conceive it, as I thank God we never were.'[1]

A further circumstance about Tyrrell at this time is now known to us, which shows how far from truthful his words were, 'Since I heard the Pope's censure pronounced, I began to settle my mind to try out some better religion.'[2] Far from meditating on a secession to protestantism, he was in reality asking to be received into the Society of Jesus. 'But as there are difficulties,' wrote Father General Aquaviva, after he had gone, to Father Persons, then in France, 'which are known to your Reverence. Our answer

---

[1] Morris, *Troubles*, ii. 370. [2] Boyd, p. 648

was that we would commend this thing to you. So, if you think him fit, you may in our name receive him; otherwise you should console him as well as you can, and advise him to adapt himself to the Divine will.'[1] We do not know what the obstacle to his reception was; but Father Persons seems to have considered it a sufficient one; at all events there is no more talk of his joining the Jesuits. Tyrrell says that Ballard made friends with Christopher Bagshaw, the future Appellant, who became his guide to Rome.

When they left Rheims, Tyrrell went to Rouen, while Ballard proceeded to Paris, where he became acquainted with Morgan, Charles Paget, and others of his faction. Eventually they started from Rouen on Christmas Eve (New Style) 1584, and 'after a little expecting were landed by Southampton upon St. Stephen's day, as it fell out in England' (26 December/5 January) and gradually travelled from one friend to another till they got to Suffolk, and parted at Mr. Nicholas Tymperley's. Tyrrell returned to London, and Ballard joined him there; and thenceforward they lodged together as a rule, but they often changed their residences, as priests were then obliged to do. In 1585 they made three long rounds among catholics, whose names and houses he now betrays. The most important was the second circuit in which, after they had travelled to Leicestershire, Ballard 'slippeth into Yorkshire, where he repaired unto Typpings,' and thence visited the Borders. In a third journey they again rode as far as Typpings, and towards the end of the year apparently 'Foscue became acquainted with Babington, C. Tylney, "Jacques" (Jacomo Francisci) Sir Christopher Hatton's man, and divers others.'

This brings Tyrrell's accusations of Ballard down to March 1586, the time of the latter's departure for France,

---

[1] *Epistolæ Galliæ*, f. 60 v. 22 October 1584.

and the limit of the present section. His pages are now principally filled with accusations of the catholic gentlemen who had known or helped him during his ministry, and whom Burghley of course wished above all things to plunder and ruin.

4. *Ballard's Character.*

Tyrrell's most valuable pages are probably those which describe Ballard's peculiar character. Even to Burghley he portrays him, not as a murderer, but only as ' a man vainglorious and desirous of his own praise, and to be meddling in things above his reach.' His descriptions of the feasting in company with young soldiers and gentlemen of means have character strokes. ' We had . . . such suppers, dinners, banquets as it cost myself in one year 100 *li.* and where I spent one pennie, Foscue spent three.' ' Ballard's acquaintance increased daily, and out went we in countenance and credit.' . . . ' About Bartholomew-tide, we met together in London, when Foscue had his attendants as thick as might be, every gentleman calling him Captain : insomuch that in every tavern and inn in London he was called Captain Foscue ; and every man thought, that knew him, that he with a great band should have gone over with my Lord of Leicester.' . . . ' He was always so bold with gentlemen, that apparel should cost him nothing.'

Here we probably have a true, if somewhat spiteful, description of those weaknesses and minor faults, which were eventually to lead Ballard to ruin.

Ballard was far from being a man of bad life. Babington at first described him to Queen Mary in high-flown terms as ' a man of virtue and learning and of singular zeal to the catholic cause and your Majesty's service.' Making fair allowance for Babington's youthful enthusiasm and desire to make a good impression on the Queen,[1] we may

---

[1] Babington's *Confessions*, viii. § 1.

accept the statement as true, noting that no mention is made of the man's prudence. In ordinary circumstances an ecclesiastical superior would probably have been well able to keep him to the business of his profession, in which his zeal and his popular manners would no doubt have led to considerable success. But persecution had made it impossible for an ecclesiastical superior to live in England; and Morgan was keeping up a feud with Allen, which was extremely prejudicial to church discipline. The consequence was that Ballard, coming under Morgan's influence,[1] gradually became obsessed with the idea that he was a statesman with a special mission to fulfil.

Like so many priestly politicians, he was deficient in practical common sense, and the victim of theorists and of extremists. In the impressionable years that followed his conversion, he had been in France and Flanders while civil wars of religion were raging, and all sorts of extreme theories were being propounded. It is to be feared that the formalism or laxity of such catholic churchmen as tolerated the ban and the assassination of the Prince of Orange, further contributed to the weakening of those moral restraints, which needed as much strengthening as possible in England, in the midst of all the irritation to be borne there.

Another matter, which will require watching, is Ballard's accuracy and reliability in reporting on a political situation. It will appear as we proceed that, partly through sanguine temperament, partly through inability to take the measure of the weakness of Spain and of the other friends of Mary Stuart, he habitually gives to all he approaches an exaggerated idea of the alliances which he proposes, and of the assistance which he is able to promise. At the critical

---

[1] Writing some years later James Younger told Lord Burghley that he had heard Allen say he had always dissuaded Ballard, who, however, was ruled by Morgan (*Domestic Calendar*, 1592, p. 258).

moment after his return from the North in July 1586, this weakness will show itself very clearly, and is probably the reason why the conspirators, when once they were in difficulties, 'quickly disliked Ballard's discretion.'

We must also distinguish between Ballard before the conspiracy, when he seems to have been a gay, pushful, active, popular fellow, and after he had entangled himself in his wide, ill-knit, all-risking conspiracy, the anxieties for which oppressed and distracted him. He then comes before us as a man incapable of measured judgment, of facing the truth, of sober thought. He has become a restless monomaniac, distracted between hopes and fears, sure to bring ruin on any side he inspires.

The injury which Ballard did to the catholic cause was enormous, almost incalculable. It was only natural that those who suffered for his misdeeds should have been furious at his evil offices. He was accused by Mary Stuart of being or of having been a spy of Walsingham, and this error, having been accepted by Chateauneuf, has been copied even by some modern apologists of Mary.

Babington reproached him bitterly (even at the time of his death) for having 'abused his zeal in religion,' and there is little doubt that he at one time really meant to have betrayed the priest to Walsingham. But Ballard's silence, though he wavered at first under his tortures,[1] and his self-control at death, show that the man did not lack a certain distinction and generosity.[2] His social gifts were clearly of a high order.

---

[1] See *Crichton's Memoir, below,* pp. 160, 167.

[2] I cannot quite endorse Simpson's words (*Campion*, p. 336) : 'Not only was the treason of a Ballard or a Robert Catesby in its insulated effect, almost as pernicious as the martyrdom of a Campion was beneficent, but also through them, in the old protestant language rebellion was turned into religion, and faith into faction.'

In protestant language, that had been done in England years before Ballard's treasons, and it was also done in many other countries in which

INTRODUCTION lxxxi

5. *Ballard's First Steps in Politics*, 1585.

Ballard's meddling in politics had been very very slight before the year 1586. Perhaps the only serious cause for suspicion is offered by his visit to Morgan and Paget at the end of 1584. But even if he did then begin to co-operate with them, it is probable that he did not as yet do more than send them news of the same class that we now read in our daily papers. After his return to England, in January 1585, he made a short tour among the catholic gentry of East Anglia, and another (perhaps two) between Whitsuntide and Bartilmas (June to August). The latter journey, we know, was made with a political object, but not a very serious one. During these journeys Ballard probably sought out such catholic gentlemen as were likely to favour forcible measures. He came into communication with Mr. David Ingleby, brother of Sir William Ingleby of Ripley, who had married Lady Margaret Neville, daughter of the Earl of Westmorland. Ingleby, though now a fugitive, was perhaps the most earnest and extreme supporter of the *ancien régime* who still remained in England. Another friend was Edward Windsor, brother of Lord Windsor, and afterwards one of the conspirators. The first definitely political act, with which we can connect Ballard's name, was to procure for these gentlemen news of the plans of the Scottish catholics. This he did through John Boste, another priest and afterwards a martyr. Though the matter is a small one, it may be worth quoting the abstract of Ballard's examination of 5 September 1586, in which he is reported to have confessed as follows:

'Ballard saith that the last year [1585] in summer he was sent by David Ingleby and Edward Windsor into the North to

---

Ballard's name was never heard. It is, however, no exaggeration to say that his treasons were among the greatest calamities which catholicism in England has had to endure.

f

understand if the Lords of Scotland meant to stand out; and he understood by Boste that, if the Lords of Scotland had not aid, they were not able to hold out, and that the Lords of Scotland found great fault with the English Catholics, that they did not hold out as they did. For if they did, and joined together, they might the better attain to liberty of religion. And the Scottish Lords looked for aid out of France, but they were prevented by the broils. And this answer of Boste the said Ballard returned to Edward Windsor and David Ingleby.'[1]

Even here there is nothing really reprehensible, perhaps nothing of any importance whatever. But 'in the end of Christmas 1585,' or, as we should say, early in 1586, Ballard undertook a negotiation which involved politics of an emphatic type. He went to Scotland to consult with Lord Claude Hamilton 'about aid for an invasion of England.' We learn this from Dunne's confession.

'Dunne confesseth that Ballard in the end of Christmas last, told him he would go into Scotland; and at his return thence before Lent, he told him, he had been with the Lord Claude, about aid for an invasion against England.'[2]

Lord Claude Hamilton was the most important of 'the Queen's Lords' in Scotland. He had led the van of her army at Langside, and was in many ways one of her ablest supporters. He was also, next after his brother John, the nearest heir to the throne of Scotland. He had just returned home after exile, and had been well received by King James. We do not know what passed between Lord Claude and the English priest. Lord Claude had no great power, and probably could not give Ballard promises of any value. In any case Ballard was not discouraged. He returned to London 'before Lent' (Ash Wednesday in that year fell on the 16th of February) and he then became acquainted with Savage's plot, and thereupon

---

[1] *Scottish Calendar*, Boyd, p. 695.   [2] *Ibid.* p. 692.

resolved to go over again and to consult with Morgan and Paget.

It is evident that a good deal more happened in London in February and March than yet meets the eye. We should give much for an authentic account of the way in which Ballard was admitted to the conspiracy of Savage and George Gifford. We should also much like to know, whether Gilbert was aware of what was going on. There is no question that he was in touch with Savage, and keeping him to his impossible 'vow.' Indeed, this was the time when Phelippes wrote to Walsingham, that Gilbert could soon find out anything going on among the catholics.[1] Yet it will appear later that Gilbert, though so near to the persons concerned, did not as yet know much about Ballard's plans. On the other hand, for reasons which will presently appear, we know that Walsingham must by this have heard a good deal about that busy person.

During this same stay in London Ballard told Edward Windsor and Tilney that there would be an invasion, and promised with his usual boldness of statement, 'places and entertainment' if they would go abroad to join the invading force.[2] We have heard from Tyrrell that Ballard was by this time acquainted with Babington and the rest, and that before starting for France his friends and he met for dinner at the Plough without Temple Bar.

Of this meeting Tyrrell gives the following account:

'Fortescue's last going into France was in Lent last about the middle thereof. All his friends and acquaintances about

---

[1] Writing of a letter addressed to Scotland, Phelippes says: 'My secret friend shall know what becomes of it.' 19 March 1586; Boyd, viii. 253.

[2] 'Ballard half a year past told Edward Windsor and Tilney that there would be an invasion shortly, and persuaded them to go beyond the seas, promising to provide places and entertainment for them.' Tilney's examination of 21 August. Ballard according to this spoke to them 'half a year ago'—that would be about 21 March; Boyd, p. 686.

London were privy thereto. Divers dined with him in Fish Street, at the King's Head, the day of his departure from London.'¹

Babington, being cross-examined over this, gave the following slightly different account:

'In the last Lent this examinate took his leave with Ballard at the Plough without Temple Bar, the night before Ballard's going. At which time there was in this examinate's companie Mr. Tichborne and Mr. Barnewell. With Barnewell there was Anthony Tunstall, Mawde, Dunne, and one Donnington, whom this examinate knew not.' (*Below*, p. 95.)

Mawde was an emissary of Walsingham. At this feast, which was meant to throw the secretary off the scent, his representative has found a place at the board!

6. *Bernard Mawde.*

Ballard started off for France, it being then about the middle of Lent (about 13th to the 21st of March, O.S.), and arrived at Rouen, where he took up his lodgings near the Church of St. Nicaise, in company with the same Mawde, whom Babington has just enumerated among the guests at the Plough. This was the man whom Walsingham says he 'used towards Ballard.'² Evidently, therefore, the secretary even at this early date knew that 'the grand practitioner,' as Gilbert afterwards styled him, was a source of danger, and had already gone so far as to place a special spy at his side. We must therefore describe Mawde's *modus operandi*, and seek for some explanation of his present from his previous history.

Bernard Mawde had once been a 'gentleman in the household' of Edwin Sandys, Protestant Archbishop of York,

---

¹ Tyrrell's *Confession*, R.O., *Mary Queen of Scots*, xix. 69. 15; Boyd, viii. 653. On the last line of the page last mentioned, for Wade read Mawde.
² Boyd, viii. 589.

and had afterwards implicated his Grace in a certain false charge of incontinency, of which (so far as we can now see) the Archbishop was certainly not guilty, though he weakly consented to pay Mawde and his confederates hush-money to prevent the affair being made public. Nevertheless, it leaked out; and Sandys was then obliged to defend himself before the Privy Council. He did so, however, to such good purpose that Bernard Mawde, 'gentleman,' and the rest, were found guilty on the 8th of May 1583. Of him the Court of Inquiry stated that he 'had lately served the said Archbishop, and upon sundry misbehaviours and abuses by him committed, was put out of his service, in respect whereof he was become a malicious enemy against the said Archbishop,' and had been the prime-mover in fabricating the false charge. His sentence was to give back to the Archbishop all the money obtained by fraud, to pay to the Queen £300, and to be imprisoned in the Fleet for three years. Had he not 'humbly submitted himself and confessed his offence,' his ears would have been slit 'as he had well deserved.'[1]

Three years' imprisonment to run from the 8th of May 1583 should have kept this mischief-maker out of the way of doing harm until the middle of May 1586. But already in the middle of March he is sitting at table with Ballard in the Plough Inn without Temple Bar; and it was surely not the first day that he had sat in that company. The conclusion is obvious, that he had been let out in order to spy upon the catholics. Walsingham knew there was mischief afoot.

Mawde was eventually the only one of the *agents provocateurs*, whose treachery the conspirators discovered. It is mentioned by Babington in his last letter to Mary, and

---

[1] John Le Neve, *Protestant Bishops of the Church of England*, ii. 42, prints the above decree, etc.

was denounced openly during the trial of Edward Windsor, who having at first escaped capture, was tried later. Though of course sentenced, he escaped death through the intercession of his mother. He afterwards wrote to Hatton (30 May 1587) explaining his pleas. He says that Mawde, and Jacques [1] (Jacomo Francisci) earnestly persuaded him not to give up Ballard (as Windsor was about to do). They were, he said, 'the chief workers of this conspiracy, and wholly employed by Ballard. . . . I call upon them to appear at the King's Bench.' [2]

I have found only one of Mawde's letters to Walsingham, 1 August 1586, written after Ballard had given him the slip and had returned to London. He writes as we might expect at that time, confessing that for the moment he has no news. On the 5th of August, Walsingham writes to Elizabeth that Mawde had never got thoroughly into Ballard's confidence, so that it seemed useless to employ him any further.[3] That he was a very odious traitor is clear enough; though perhaps not a very effective one.

We hear of Mawde again in 1592, when having gone to Spanish Flanders, in order to continue his trade of spying,

---

[1] Jacomo Francisci, commonly called Captain Jacques, was a soldier of fortune, born in Antwerp of a Venetian father. He was now in the following of Hatton; later, 1589, he entered the service of the Duke of Parma, and from that time was constantly accused by English spies of encouraging others to attack Elizabeth. This must greatly strengthen the suspicions which arise from charges such as the above. It does not seem that he was admitted to Babington's conspiracy, which was formed in June; and the reason for this may be that he was then in Ireland. He was in prison in the Fleet before he went over to Parma, but we know not why. Tyrrell in his *Confessions* charged him with being Ballard's constant companion, and a participator in all his plottings; but in his *retractions* he recalled some six times all charges of disloyalty.

[2] R.O., *Domestic Elizabeth*, cci. *n.* 50, 30 May 1587. Typping also declared that 'Ballard and Mawde told him about the invasion.'

[3] Boyd, viii. 579, 589; the latter is also printed, Tytler, iv. 130. The letter of 1 August is written under the *alias* Montalto. The MS. is R.O., *Scotland*, xli. *n.* 4.

he was arrested. A deposition against him survives,[1] which was then made by Mr. John Pauncefote, of Pauncefote-Hasfield, Gloucester, an exile for his faith. As he had married Dorothy, the sister of Edward Windsor of Bradenham, Bucks., mentioned above, he was likely to know about Windsor's charges made in court against the spy. He was also, as it happened, at Rouen at the time of Ballard's visit in 1586. He says of Mawde: 'Il se faisoit nommer alors Montalto, et se faignoit de vouloir estre catholique, estant héréticq.' Later on, he says, he betrayed Ballard and the rest to their deaths. As to this 'tous ceulx qui le cognoissent, afferment le dict Bernard Mawde estre cause de telle exécution,' and then he mentions Edward Windsor's protest mentioned above.[2]

With this section closes for us the period of greatest dimness and uncertainty. We have discerned various dark figures, engaged in mischief, which we cannot at first fully fathom; and Walsingham's *agents* are mixed up with them. Now they will all gradually come further into the open.

SECTION V

Plot and Counter-plot, April 1586.

1. *A Congress at Paris.*

It has been well said by Dr. Lingard that the Babington plot was in reality a double conspiracy, that of Walsingham himself against Mary, and that of Morgan and Babington against Elizabeth. Each depended on the other. Without Walsingham's aid to carry letters, Morgan and his asso-

---

[1] *Bulletins de la Commission Royale d'Histoire de Belgique*, par Alphonse Goovaerts, 1896. 3me série, vi. no. 1.

[2] Mawde escaped this time. In 1596 a spy, called Williamson, stated that if either he or Poley returned to Flanders, they would be executed (*Domestic Calendar*, 1596, p. 29).

ciates could not even have begun to plot : while, but for Morgan's plottings, Walsingham would have lost his chief title to popular glory. Whether the English statesman had already begun actively to foment plots through Gilbert Gifford, Mawde, or others, is not yet proven. But at all events the English gold with which he avowedly baited his snares had already seduced many ; and now he was prepared to go further.

The scene of the following intrigues is Paris, and Ballard is on his way there attended by his treacherous companion. They reached Rouen about the end of March, according to the new style in use there ; and they were shortly after followed, or perhaps even preceded, by another of Walsingham's emissaries, Solomon Aldred, who was to carry out a suggestion of singular malignity, which had been made by Gilbert Gifford. To understand this we must go back. When Gilbert first came over, he told Walsingham, at Morgan's suggestion—

'That he had waged perpetual hostilities with the Fathers of the Society, that he was resolved to continue. That he hoped to get many to join him, and that he was minded to essay and try anything whatsoever against them. . . . This pleased Walsingham exceedingly, who freed me and gave me £20. All this, as it occurred, I let Morgan know, adding, in a letter which passed under Walsingham's eye, that I had undertaken to call over Dr. William Gifford ; but I wrote at the same time by the French post, to prevent his coming.' [1]

The confession here quoted was written at a much later date, 14 August 1588, when Gilbert was in the prison of the Archbishop of Paris. He was then excusing himself with the plea that Morgan had been his leader, and was responsible for him from the first ; and by these arts he successfully concealed his machinations against Mary.

A man so factious as Morgan was easily deceived. To

---

[1] *Hatfield Calendar*, iii. 347, 14 August 1588. See *below*, p. 128.

him it seemed perfectly natural that a young catholic cleric should go over and hob-nob with the fanatical persecutor Walsingham, if he declared he did so out of hatred of the Jesuits. It aroused no suspicion that Walsingham should appear to be so amused by this, as to allow Gilbert all the liberty, leisure, and money he needed. By such simple excuses Gilbert kept Morgan completely hoodwinked. He never had a suspicion until the catastrophe was over. His was folly so egregious, that many thought it must have been malicious. This conclusion, however, was exaggerated: Morgan's main intention was good. He was entirely devoted to carrying on correspondence for his mistress; and whilst that went well, his prison walls and his attention to petty feuds prevented his noting what went amiss.

I will not attempt to sound the mind of Dr. William Gifford, or of Edward Grately, who was classed with him. They also suffered from factiousness: but I think their chief fault was an overmastering desire to return to England and enjoy such liberty as they saw Gilbert had won, they knew not how.

In the above confession Gilbert represented himself as having but once desired the calling over of Dr. William, and of having then put an obstacle in the way. But this, as we shall see both now and later, is a very imperfect representation of the story. Solomon Aldred, once tailor at the English College, Rome, and now in Walsingham's secret service, had in fact come over on purpose to bring Dr. William back. At Rouen Aldred had met Edward Grately, a priest who had at first done remarkably well on the mission, but had latterly fallen into Morgan's faction. Aldred fastened on him at once, and warmly urged him to turn protestant; and to these instances the priest answered so weakly that the ex-tailor thought that he was on the point of giving up his faith. This, however, was

Aldred's error; and Grately's letters make it seem likely that the mistake was due chiefly to the apostate's fanaticism. Nevertheless, the priest wrote to Dr. William at Rheims to come to Paris, and the Doctor gave up his lectures and came. Here he met both Aldred and Grately as well. The latter had made the journey as a guide to Ballard, and they had left Mawde behind.

Thus plotters on both sides were in Paris about the 14th or 15th of April, and both parties at once went to work, each conspiring in their own way. Let us follow Walsingham's agents first.

2. *Walsingham's Agents.*

As we already know, the object of Walsingham is to procure conspirators, and the man he now wants is Dr. William Gifford. Aldred has already made progress towards his capture, for he has withdrawn him from the College, and has now got him into his lodgings, and is forcing Walsingham's summons upon him, with Grately, and even the English ambassador, to assist. William was weak,[1] and already wavering, and Aldred was vexed at his want of enterprise, 'He is very willing to inveigh against them' (*i.e.* Allen and his party), 'yet loth to put his credit in hazard, fearing lest he should be known.'[2]

The Doctor clearly does not suspect the terrible purpose for which Walsingham wants him; that of a stalking-horse, by which he may destroy Queen Mary, and with her as many of her party as he can. As to this, his treacherous cousin Gilbert was using words like these, 'Dr. Gifford's coming is most necessary. He is sure to be greatly employed. . . . Morgan and Paget with the rest will impart all things to him, which I am too assured I shall

---

[1] In March 1583, Dr. Allen had described him as 'valde labilis et infirmi animi.' Knox, *Letters of Cardinal Allen,* p. 186.

[2] *Calendar Domestic Addenda,* 1580, p. 174.

INTRODUCTION   xci

know, for he can hide nothing from me. Therefore the sooner he were sent for, the better leisure we shall have to provide for their devilish desire.'[1]

The last words admit of no doubt. Dr. William was to become the spiritual leader of the participators in the conspiracy which Walsingham was preparing, which was to end in the destruction of Mary and the ruin of her followers. If, even as it was, Dr. William was indicted and did not avoid the verdict of *Guilty,* he would surely not have escaped with life, had he placed himself within the power of the man who was now beckoning him over with such unprincipled hypocrisy.

Fortunately indeed for himself the Doctor eventually refused to go to England; even though Sir Edward Stafford, the English ambassador, came to urge him. We have Gifford's paper of reasons of refusal; not a very glorious document[2] seeing that he promises to advance still further the faction of Morgan, just at the time when it was so supremely necessary that all should support Allen, and avoid the party quarrels which threatened the cause of Mary with ruin. It is surely disappointing that this eloquent, good, and able man, though he well knew so much of Walsingham's malevolence and wickedness, should not have done anything to frustrate his plots, or to hinder the evil influence of the apostate Aldred, whom he had known before as a catholic in Rome. Had Dr. William but given the alarm, Ballard, Babington, and others might have been

---

[1] B M., Harleian, 286, f 136; see *below,* p 111. There are two letters almost identical, of 11 and 12 July. Though this date was three months later than that at which we now stand (15 April), there is no question that the intentions of Gilbert and of Walsingham were the same all through. An example of 'imparting all things' to a theological authority may be found in Babington's *Confessions,* 1 § 9, where Babington tells Gilbert, 'he should assure us from beyond seas by authority that this action was directly lawful in every part'

[2] R O., *Domestic Elizabeth,* cxcix *n* 95, cf *Addenda Calendar,* p. 174. Stafford's letter of 15/25 April is R O , France, xv. f 176

put upon their guard, or at least made more cautious. On the other hand, Gilbert's reflection was, 'How necessary it is *to entertain* Doctor Gifford and Grately, otherwise it were impossible but I should be suspected' (*below*, p. 118).

Morgan soon learnt about this interview, but he was easily persuaded there was no harm in it. Fearing, however, lest Mary should get to hear from Allen's party something sinister about so great a departure from clerical conventions, he wrote to reassure her on the 24th of April. He praised Dr. William and Grately, 'who without all doubt will overtake the Secretary' [*i.e.* Walsingham]. They act 'indeed to profit their country, and not to serve Secretary Walsingham's turn, whatsoever they may promise him.'[1]

These words describe truly enough the estimate of Morgan in regard to Walsingham's plot. He had entirely misconceived and disregarded its danger, when some knowledge about it was not very far from him.

But he must not be taken as an adequate witness for William Gifford or for Grately. So far as our papers go, they are playing the parts of waverers; but if we knew their minds better, we should probably find that what they really wanted was toleration on the same terms as Gilbert Gifford had (they thought) obtained it; that is by separating from Dr. Allen and the Jesuits. But Allen's name stood so high that they did not dare to break with him openly, and so they lingered on. Grately eventually fell, while the doctor, attending to his college work, came through safely.[2]

---

[1] Morgan's letter is printed in full in Murdin's *State Papers*, p. 511. The abstracts in Boyd, p. 332, and *Hatfield Calendar*, iii. 139, are too brief. Walsingham, of course, saw this letter, which presumably caused the indictment of Dr. William. See Morris, p. 278.

[2] For the incident regarding Dr. Gifford, see *The Month*, March-April 1904, *Dr. Gifford in* 1586. Most of the documents quoted here are there printed. See also Boyd, p. 500, where D. A. is Dr. Allen.

3. *Ballard's Plotters*.

We may now contrast the somewhat inglorious intrigue of Aldred to ensnare William Gifford and Grately, with the daring and unscrupulous projects of Ballard. Both meetings probably took place about the same time, and possibly at no great distance one from another.

Don Bernardino de Mendoza, Captain of light horse, and Knight of Santiago, at the time of Ballard's visit, had been Spanish ambassador in Paris since the beginning of 1585, and he had been sent there on purpose to pursue a vigorous policy in regard to England. For this he was a very fit agent. A retired soldier, full of energy and of confidence in the greatness and resourcefulness of his country, he had moreover suffered much from Queen Elizabeth, to whom he had been ambassador before. Her government had taken every opportunity of thwarting and irritating him; and had finally driven him out of the country, with ostentatious disregard for diplomatic courtesy, on the discovery of an alleged plot by Francis Throckmorton. Don Bernardino had left breathing threats of vengeance, and Philip II., convinced of his rectitude and ability, had made him ambassador at Paris. It was a good bold move, yet not without some drawbacks. It led, in the first place, to a violent quarrel with the outgoing ambassador, Don Juan Bautista de Taxis and his supporters, Don Bernardino's now over-wrought temper giving rise to much friction. He had, for instance, while in England, been a warm supporter of Father Robert Persons. But when Persons, during his exile, was taken up by Taxis, Mendoza took the side of Morgan, and from henceforward strongly opposed the friends of the English Jesuit. Similar cases soon multiplied. Irritation and desire of revenge was making his policy precipitate and unbalanced.

Such was the man to whom Ballard was now led by

Charles Paget, instead of by Morgan, who was still in the Bastille. As we might have expected, the Spaniard welcomed the priest warmly, and Captain Foscue, extremely susceptible as he always was to the influence of men of station, fell completely under the spell of so redoubtable a politician. Here is the account of the interview, given by Mendoza to his master, followed by the report of Charles Paget to Mary written two weeks later. Paget descends to many more details than Mendoza, and is far more indiscreet.

Mendoza to King Philip II., 11 and 12 May 1586, N.S. (Spanish Calendar, 1580-1586, p. 576. The original is Paris, Archives Nationales, K. 1564, now n. 58; kindly verified by Père J. de Joannis, S.J.).

The French . . . [try to influence the English catholics to distrust your Majesty]. . . . It is believed, however, that the latter will take no notice of this, as they have sent a priest to me, on behalf of the principal catholics, to say that God has infused more courage than ever into them, and has opened their eyes to the fact that no time is so opportune as the present, to shake off the oppression of the Queen and the yoke of heresy, that weighs upon them, since most of the strongest heretics are now absent in Zeeland. They say that as I have never yet deceived them, they beg me to tell them whether your Majesty had determined to help them to take up arms, when they decide to do so. I replied in general terms, speaking of your Majesty's good-will towards them and encouraging them in their good intentions; and I sent the priest back well posted in what I thought necessary, and told him to return to me with full details, as in so important a matter we must have more than generalities. Paris, 11 May 1586.

A separate cipher addressed to Secretary Idiaquez himself follows (Spanish Calendar, p. 579. Spanish text, Paris, Archives, K. 1564, now n. 65; kindly collated by Père de Joannis, S.J., printed Teulet, v. 348).

I beg you to have the following very carefully deciphered and put into his Majesty's own hands. It is written and ciphered by me personally:

I am advised from England by four men of position who have

the entry into the Queen's house, that they have discussed for at least three months the intention of killing her. They have at last agreed, and the four have mutually sworn to do it. They will, on the first opportunity, advise me when it is to be done : and whether by poison or steel, in order that I may send the intelligence to your Majesty, supplicating you to be pleased to help them after the business is effected. They say that they will not divulge the intention to another soul but me, to whom they are under great obligations, and in whose secrecy they have confidence. Paris, 12 May 1586.

Charles Paget to the Queen of Scots, 19/29 *May* 1586 (printed in Murdin, *State Papers,* p 517 Boyd, p. 386, but this version is somewhat abbreviated).

It may please your Majesty. . . . Since the writing of my last to your Majesty, there came hither out of England a priest called Ballard, one that is very honest and discreet, and is entirely acquainted with all the best catholics of England, and with some of Scotland where he hath been. He told me how he was sent hither to declare the minds and readiness that the most part of catholics and schismatics [1] were in, to take arms so as they might be assured of foreign help. I brought him to the Spanish ambassador and made him to signify his knowledge therein. And so he declared in general how many of the principal Noblemen and knights in the North parts, in Lancashire, the west country, and divers other shires besides, were willing to take arms. What number they would make armed and unarmed, and that many of them had given their promise by oath, and received the sacrament of performance And that now the Earl of Leicester having all the best of the protestants, captains, and soldiers with him, and the people grieved, were much discontented with the oppression used towards them by reason of the wars in the Low Countries, the time were now very fit and proper to give them relief.

The Spanish ambassador heard him very well, and made him set down in number how many in every shire would be contented to take arms, and what number of men armed and

---

[1] It was usual at this period for the catholics to term any of their co-religionists who through fear went to the established churches 'Schismatics' It was a popular, not a theologically accurate term.

unarmed, they could provide.[1] He (Ballard) said he might not name the persons, because he had engaged the contrary upon his priesthood. He likewise gave him information of the ports with many other things fit to be known.

Howbeit, because he came with so general resolution, the Spanish ambassador hath given him further instructions, in what sort he would have him to proceed in more particular, and with secrecy enough, and after satisfaction given him in these points, from some of the principallest and wisest, he doth assure him that the king his master, the King of Spain, will be brought to give them reasonable speedy relief. The principallest point given him in charge is, that the safety of your person may be well continued; and, if it be possible, that your Majesty be taken out of your keeper's hands. Also what port were best to land in, which port I think will fall out to be Newcastle, Hartlepool, or Scarborough, or some port town in the North. The aid which should be given shall be by the Prince of Parma with such expedition and so much beside the expectation of the Queen of England, as it will wonderfully vex her, for that she will never so much as dream of that course, but think whatsoever is intended will be performed from Spain.

This Ballard will be here again, God willing, after my return from the Spaw. What then falleth out to the purpose, your Majesty shall be advertised thereof with diligence. The ambassador hath already advertised the King of Spain in general terms what Ballard came for. He wisheth me not to write to your Majesty till things be brought to a better resolution and more certainty; but hereof he is to pardon me. For though to content him, I said I would not, yet I know my duty and obedience ever command me to declare to your Majesty what importeth you; and specially such a matter of importance as this is: and therefore am I humbly to beseech your Majesty to direct me in what sort you will have me to proceed further, and especially for your liberty, wherein many be to be considered, and that will I do.

Postponing for a moment what we have to say about the light here thrown on the plot in England, we will first

---

[1] 'How many in every shire, etc.' See *below*, p. clxxvi.

INTRODUCTION

conclude our account of the meeting in Paris. It is perfectly clear then that both Paget and Mendoza regarded this conference as the opening of intercourse with a new power, that of the body of the English catholics. Ballard's proposals, they thought, are the first, vague, indeterminate expressions of those who had hitherto lain altogether motionless, silent, purposeless. Until they became vocal and purposeful, no plot, no plan could have any success. Ballard is sent back to them to begin again on new lines; to make the English offers clear, definite, secure. 'We must have more than generalities,' says Mendoza. It is only when this new beginning has been made, that negotiations, properly so called, will begin.

But Paget strikes a different note. Not only does he write to Mary against Mendoza's advice—an unwise breach of discipline—but he is evidently straining throughout, in order to make Ballard's plans appear more attractive. While Mendoza called them 'generalities,' and though they were, as we shall see in the event, mostly mere fancies, Paget is endeavouring to produce the impression of definite numbers, and sworn confederates. He dwells on the different localities that are assured—the north parts, Lancashire, the West country, and 'the numbers set down in every shire, who would be contented to take arms,' etc.

But Paget's exaggerations are but child's-play compared with those of Ballard. He returned to England, and handed on his message; but in so doing we find him making, according to Babington, the following surprising changes, (*below*, p. 52).

'Ballard told me that, being with Mendoza in Paris, he was informed that—in regard to the injuries done by our State to the greatest christian princes, it was resolved by the Catholic League to seek redress, and to perform this summer without further delay, having in readiness such forces, and all warlike preparations, the like of which was never seen in these parts of Christendom. The Pope was the chief disposer. The Kings of France and Spain concurred. . . . The Duke of Guise, or the Duke of Maine would conduct the enterprise for France. For the Italian and Spanish forces, the Prince of Parma. The number would be about 60,000 men.

'And hereupon he came over to inform thus much, to sound the catholics for assisting, and for the preservation of their possessions, upon which the stranger would enter by right of conquest without sparing any, in case they did not declare themselves performers.'

The alteration is indeed complete. The sum of Mendoza's message had been this. 'Bring to us before September definite numbers, attestations, and plans, and we will surely help you.' The sum of Ballard's message is 'The invasion is fixed for September in any case. Come and assist. That will be the way to keep your estates in safety.' According to Mendoza the time would be decided by the English catholics; the assistance would come from the Spaniards: no mention is made of the French. According to Ballard the time is September, the attacking force is the mythical catholic League,[1] with the Pope supreme, and the kings of Spain and of France taking leading parts! The foreign army of 60,000 men seems also suspicious. Talking to Savage, Ballard used that figure for the army of English insurgents who had promised to rise.

Perhaps some friend of Ballard may here object that I am blaming him on inadequate evidence for these exaggerated statements, which do not come to us from Ballard directly, but through Babington. May it not be that the blame for them should rather attach to the latter? The answer is, first, that Babington does not stand alone; Savage, Gifford, and others tell the same story, though briefly and without details. Moreover, as evidence accumulates, we find Babington a distinctly good witness, while Ballard

---

[1] See *above*, p. xvii.

is as constantly a bad one. (See p. 105.) He now evidently lets his imagination run riot: and the wish is father to his thought. On the other hand, Babington's confessions will show that the layman had an excellent memory, and is able to give by heart, without again consulting the originals, quite long summaries of letters, often in the words of the original.

As we cannot believe that Ballard intended to deceive his companions, we must conclude that he thought his account of Mendoza's plan was broadly the same as that which Mendoza would give of it. In other words, he was practically beside himself. Woe to those who, henceforward, trusted to his teaching, or confided in his information. The same phenomenon is afterwards to be remarked in the other conspirators. Once men of firmness and good conscience, they became *exaltés* to the point of mental aberration, passed their time in talking crime, and bewildered themselves with the morality of the ' ban.' [1]

It also follows that Paget and Mendoza were entirely deceived as to their messenger. They thought they were dealing with a prudent man, and taking a non-committal first move; in reality they were filling the head of this enthusiast with the most exaggerated dreams. This was not to be a preliminary overture, but the final declaration. They would never see Ballard again. Nothing could now prevent his urging on his intrigues till they burst into public notice. The die was cast. A lunatic was at the helm. Shipwreck was certain.

Before we leave Mendoza and his letter, we ask ourselves, what is its value in regard to the rising and to the plot, of which it speaks in a vague, grandiose way. We shall find as we proceed, that there is no real basis for the talk of the English catholics dealing *as a body* with Mendoza

---

[1] Babington's *Confessions*, viii. pp. 94, 95.

through Ballard, with a view to an extensive rising. On the other hand, the confessions subsequently taken show that there was a good foundation for saying that a conspiracy had begun, and that it comprised George Gifford, Savage, and also, presumably, Thomas Salisbury, Tichborne, and Edward Windsor. But even here we have very little evidence to rely upon. When Babington commenced his plot, his first condition was that this preliminary machination should cease, and, for some reason or other, the government showed no anxiety to go back upon it. To us, therefore, it remains something definite indeed, but obscure and intangible as to its details. It would certainly not have been better organised than Babington's plot, which took its place: nor would George Gifford (from what we heard about him above) have inspired more enthusiasm than Babington. Gilbert's efforts to keep Savage up to the mark, one of which was made at this very time, also suggest the idea that the older conspiracy was really moribund (*below*, pp. 169-175).

4. *Gilbert's Plottings.*

Hardly were the intrigues at Paris over, than who should come over to France but Gilbert Gifford. In his later confessions he says that he soon got tired of his work in England and came over for a change. The truth, however, probably is that he went over to carry on the intrigue for getting Dr. William Gifford to come to England. Grately had written on the 10/20 April, to ask Walsingham to let him come. Gilbert Gifford knew well the advantage of keeping his friends in France deceived, 'Otherwise it were impossible but I should be suspected.'[1]

---

[1] Gilbert to Walsingham, 11 July (*below*, p. 108). Grately's letter of 20 April, from Paris (R.O., *Domestic Elizabeth, Addenda*, xxix. *n.* 100) says, 'If Mr. Colderin [Gilbert Gifford] come to Rouen at once, he may deliver your pleasure to me.'

Walsingham consented, and on Sunday, 24 April/4 May (*below*, p. 99), Gilbert wrote to tell Curll that he was going abroad during the ensuing week, and that he had appointed a ' second substitute ' who would take letters down, whilst he was away. This ' second substitute' was Thomas Barnes, of whom we shall hear more (*below*, pp. 1-5). Ten days later, 3/13 May, we find Walsingham telling Phelippes that ' some warning is to be given to G.,' *i.e.* Gifford, and this prepares us for his prompt return.

Whether, while in France, Gilbert went to Paris in May seems unlikely. At all events if he visited Morgan, he did not visit Mendoza. He had, however, some communication with Grately, praised Walsingham's kind intentions and so forth, in order to maintain the deception that his intercourse with the persecutor was due to some honourable causes.[1]

The only matter connected with the conspiracy with which we knew that Gilbert concerned himself during this stay abroad, was to receive and bring back a letter to Savage, urging him to persevere with the plot. This may have been important, but we know very little about it. Savage confessed that he had, just before Babington joined the conspiracy, received three letters, from Morgan, from Dr. William, and from Gilbert Gifford, to confirm him in the plot.[2] That is all.

That Morgan should have written asking Savage to support Ballard, was natural under the circumstances. Also it was natural for Gilbert Gifford to have communicated by letter, before he could return in person. So the fact of these treasonable letters may be accepted, but the inferences to be drawn from them are not yet certain.

---

[1] Grately to Walsingham, R.O., *Domestic Elizabeth, Addenda*, xxix. 100 ; dated ' this 28 May ' (=18 May O.S.). It begins, ' The sincere relation which *our friend* upon his arrival did make of your honour,' etc.

[2] Boyd, viii. 681, ix. 14 ; *State Trials*, 1730, p. 122.

5. *The Plotters disperse.*

Ballard returned in May to Rouen, where he rejoined Mawde. Then they gave out that they were going to go to Milan, but they really went off in the opposite direction to England.[1] Ballard, before leaving, gave out with his usual rashness, 'que en dedans six sepmains aprez son partement, on oiroit grandes nouvelles d'eulx,' and Pauncefote, who tells us this, remarks that the time corresponded with his arrest, and that of his companions. The date of Ballard's return was Whitsuntide, 22 May 1586.

It is possible, though not likely, that Gilbert Gifford came back together with Ballard. They both returned about the same time; but Chateauneuf is mistaken in his memoir, where he says that Gilbert sent Ballard over from Paris.

Ballard on his arrival at once began the construction of the new plot, which the indictment dates the 30th and 31st of May, while Gilbert pushed on to Chartley and reached his rendezvous on the 1st of June. Though it is possible that he may on these travels have picked up news of Ballard's fresh conspiracies, still it is safer not to assume this. Gilbert's recall was certainly due to Poulet's uneasy fears lest Mary should send out letters by some fresh means. During April and May there were no letters out at all, though so many were coming in. Might not that portend some trickery in the 'honest man,' whose doings often seemed suspicious?[2] Really there were no reasons for alarm. Mary's silence really signified that, having received

---

[1] So Pauncefote, *Bulletins de la Commission royale d'histoire*, vi. 1, Brussels, 1896.

[2] 'The honest man playeth the harlot with this people egregiously,' Morris, p. 191. 'I am of opinion it shall be well done to assure the honest man, thereby to know if he have any other vent for his letters,' *Ibid.*, p. 195; both letters undated. It was Gilbert's function 'to assure' the brewer.

the posts of about two years all at one time, several weeks were necessary to decipher and digest the news which they contained. Gifford on his return went down to Chartley, yet did not go to the house, but took up his lodging as before with Mr. Newport, steward to the Earl of Essex, and from thence interviewed the brewer and the substitute. He communicated with Mary's jailor by letter, which Poulet considered ' more safe, than if he had come in person during these short, light nights, especially considering that many of this Queen's family are stirring all night, by reason of her infirmity at present.' [1]

Gilbert had arrived on the 1st of June, and on the 3rd all Poulet's anxieties were set at rest by the receipt, through the ' honest man,' of a packet whose size explained by itself the unusual silence which had preceded. Moreover the brewer obtained a special tip of £10, which, Poulet thought, showed that ' this people make good account of this packet.'

Poulet now changes his tone entirely, for the plot against Mary is clearly prospering, ' All is now well, thanks be to God . . . I think myself very happy.' In this good humour he also praises Gilbert, whom he had so severely blamed when he was in a bad temper not long before. His misgiving then was that Gilbert had ' played the wanton ' in begging too freely for money from Mary, and in particular for a pension. It was not, of course, that the knight minded Mary being robbed ; but he feared that some little misfortune might perhaps intervene ; and then this quasi-robbery might be looked at with different eyes.[2] However, this mood is now past, and he praises ' your friend ' warmly. He is ' very careful in this service, and professeth to have vowed himself wholly to your devotion, as one bound thereto by your singular benefits.'

---

[1] Morris, p. 196.   [2] *Ibid.*, pp. 193, 197, 198.

Still even so a secret grudge yet remained. Writing on easier terms to Phelippes, that day or the next, Poulet said, '*Your Friend* had committed two or three great and gross faults in this country, which moved me the rather to expect the worst, but I trust the last dispatch from hence [evidently Mary's large post-packet] was so effectual as will suffice to salve all sores.' (Morris, p. 198.)

This is rather mysterious. Sir Amias is so fond of strong terms that we may well suspect that he is overstating. Gilbert's crime may perhaps have been renewed insistence for money: but we cannot forget the 'great and gross fault' of his life, which was so soon to bring him to prison in Paris until his death. It could not surprise us to find that he was already guilty of falls the same in kind.

SECTION VI

Babington's Plot, May-June 1586.

1. *Anthony Babington of Dethwick.*

Anthony Babington, to whom Ballard now presented himself, was clearly a man who deserved a better fate. He belonged to an ancient family, originally settled at Babington or Bavington in Northumberland, whence it migrated to Dethwick (or Dethick) in Derbyshire. Here Anthony was born to considerable wealth in October 1561. He was brought up a catholic, and at eighteen he married Margaret Draycot. He now had one child, a daughter.[1]

---

[1] There is a notice of Babington by W. Durrant Cooper in *The Reliquary* for April 1862, pp. 177-200. Some valuable State papers are there printed in full, viz. R.O., State Papers, *Domestic Elizabeth*, cxcii. 17, 18, 22, 34, 39, 40, 41, 42, 47, 49; cxciii. 45, 62. *Miscellanea of the Exchequer*, T.G., no. 10,657 [*sic*], *Inquisition* into his goods in Nottinghamshire, 9 January 1587: also in Derbyshire, 18 January. *Ibid.*, 10,591 [*sic*], Goods in London. British Museum, MS. *Lansdowne*, no. 50, art. 77, Babington's Books. All that belonged to Babington in fee

INTRODUCTION

According to Chateauneuf's memoir he had once been a page to the Earl of Shrewsbury when keeper of the Scottish Queen. This has been improved upon by our romanticists,[1] who make him a page to the Queen and her 'infatuated admirer.' With the same want of accuracy they describe him as having joined a secret society for the protection of Jesuit missionaries, when no such society existed. In 1580 he had gone to France for six months, and on his return rendered service (the details of which are not known) to various priests and missionaries. He also, at Morgan's request, forwarded five different packets of letters to Mary Stuart during two years (probably 1583, 1584), but then refused to continue (p. 50). Nevertheless Morgan had by then established a hold over him, which was to end fatally.

Father William Weston, S.J., a pious man but somewhat wooden in character, who came to England in 1585, has given in his memoirs [2] an interesting and sympathetic account of our Anthony.

---

was given to Raleigh, 17 March 1587, Exch. Misc., J.E.G., no. 14,229 [*sic*]. The settled estates went to his brothers Francis and George (B.M., Add. 6697, f. 444). R.O., *Domestic Elizabeth*, cxcii. 39, 40, are also in *London and Middlesex Archaeological Collections*, i. p. 289. The notice in the *Dictionary of National Biography* gives many useful facts and references, though without much grasp of the plot itself.

[1] Labanoff, vi. 288, and the *D.N.B.* under Babington.

Simpson's theory of a 'Catholic Secret Society' will not stand historical investigation. Babington and his friends helped Jesuit missionaries in secret, it is true, but that does not make a Secret Society. See *The Month*, June 1905, p. 592.

[2] Morris, *Troubles of our Catholic Forefathers*, ii. pp. 181-7.

Father Weston did not write until nearly thirty years later, by which time his memory was getting faulty. Several errors will be named, and others might be added. His chief authority, he says, was Father R. Southwell's *Supplication*, written at the end of 1591, which Weston had read in MS. at the time, and quotes 'as well as I can remember it.' Nevertheless he makes many mistakes. He introduces, for instance, a long episode about some one feigning to be the Duke of Guise, which is neither in the printed edition of the *Supplication*, 1601, pp. 30-40, nor in the MS. of the book among the Petyt MSS. (Inner Temple Library, 538,

'Anthony Babington was a man of good family and good property; he was well off for money and valuables of all sorts. Young, scarce thirty years of age,[1] he was attractive in face and form, quick of intelligence, agreeable and facetious; he had a turn for literature unusual among men of the world. He had spent some time at Paris and elsewhere, and on his return gathered round him, by force of his gifts and moral superiority, other young men of his own rank, zealous and adventurous catholics, bold in danger, earnest for the protection of the catholic faith, or for any enterprise intended to promote the catholic cause. . . .

As he was inclined to the idea of foreign travel, it was a pleasure for him to hear me describe various localities which I had seen and known. Once when his coach and horses were ready to take him to his distant home, he begged me to accompany him, hinting that he hoped to have something to accomplish.'

But the retiring padre refused, partly shy of Babington's lavish expenditure, partly (he hints but does not openly say) because he was not sure what the business might be, in which he would be involved.

Babington was not a hero, much less a great conspirator. Young and philosophic, pious and friendly, he was not a man of action, nor of decision. He had not enough of the cunning of the serpent to judge securely of men like Gifford, Poley, and Ballard. He yielded too easily to their advances, was slow in perceiving the danger which those advances implied, and he was not vigorous enough to adopt heroic remedies in the last resort. He could never make up his mind whether he should conspire or betray the

---

xxxvi. ff 56-77) Like most catholics of his day, he believed that the conspirators did *not* intend 'the death of Elizabeth, as the heretic declare falsely, but the release of the Queen of Scots, and the conveying her into France' (p. 183) He was in prison *before* the plot was disclosed, and had no opportunity for revising his impressions in the light of the disclosures then made. I have occasionally condensed or revised the translation from the original Latin text.

[1] In reality he was only twenty-five.

INTRODUCTION

conspirators. He accepted the leadership at the request of others, and his idea of leading was to insist on 'lingering.' In the end he showed an undignified resentment against Ballard for having induced him to undertake the part of a traitor.

There is no trace of his having been infatuated with Mary Stuart. It was love of religion and of country which inspired him. But youth, wealth, inexperience, and over-confidence in his considerable gifts, made him the sort of prey on whom Morgan and Walsingham, with their respective adherents, were only too anxious to fasten their talons.

2. *Babington and Ballard.*

Here is Babington's account of Ballard's visit to him, some sentences of which were quoted in the last chapter:

'About the end of May last, as I remember, there came unto me at London, at my lodgings in Herne's Rents, one Ballard a man whom I had known before his departure into France. He told me he was returned on this occasion. Being with Mendoza he was informed that in regard of the injuries done by our State unto the greatest Christian Princes—by the nourishing of sedition and division in their provinces [that is in France and Flanders], by withholding violently the lawful possession of some [as in Zeeland] by the invasion of the [Western] Indies, by piracy and robbery of treasure, and other wrongs, intolerable for so great and mighty princes to endure—it was resolved by the Catholic League to seek redress and satisfaction. This they had vowed to perform this summer without further delay, having in readiness such forces and warlike preparations, the like was never seen in these parts of Christendom.

'The Pope was the chief disposer, the Most Christian King, and the King Catholic, with all other Princes of the League, concurred as instruments for the righting of their wrongs, and for the reformation of religion.'

[Later on Babington says that 'Ballard from the mouth of

Mendoza swore that September would not pass without an invasion.']

'The conductors of this enterprise, for the French nation would be the Duke of Guise or his brother the Duke of Maine. For the Italian and Hispanish forces, the Prince of Parma; the whole number about 60,000.

'And hereupon he had come over to inform thus much and to sound the catholics of the land, for the assisting in this enterprise and for the preservation of their possessions, upon which the stranger would enter by right of conquest, without sparing any, in case they did not declare themselves with the performers' (*below*, p. 52).

We have already commented, in the last chapter, on the extraordinary changes which had passed over Mendoza's message, as it passed through Ballard's fanatic brain; changes of which Babington too felt a certain suspicion, which is reflected in his story, and more plainly still in his answer. On the whole, nevertheless, he accepted Ballard's message, and even in his last confessions we find him repeatedly returning to it. Like a child he believed it good as well as true.

To Ballard's grandiose proposition, this was Babington's philosophic answer:

'I told him, I held the Princes so busy with home affairs, as I thought they would not intend the invasion of this country until their own were settled, whereof there was little expectation as yet. And if they would invade, I could not conceive from whence they would have so many men, or means to transport them. Further, that I held their assistance on this side small, notwithstanding the excommunication (which either was or should be revived)[1] so long as her Majesty doth live, the State being so well settled.'

Then at last came the sting in the tail.

'He answered, that difficulty would be taken away by means already laid: and that her life would be no hindrance herein.

---

[1] A popular error (see *above*, Section I. § 2).

He told me the instrument was Savage, who had vowed the performance, and some others, whose names he told not, neither was I inquisitive. As I guess [George] Gifford, and one in court near Sir Walter Raleigh. And so we departed for that time' (*below*, p. 54).

The infamous temptation had found an entrance. Babington was a lost man.

3. *Consultations.*

Babington had not yet consented; but he had listened, hesitated, and begun to believe. His old happy easy-going days were over. He became restless and care-worn, and in this he was not alone. Babington's story continues:

'Soon after Mr. Salisbury, Mr. Tichburn, and Mr. Barnewell inquired what I thought therein.'

Evidently Ballard had approached them, as he had approached their friend Babington, and the four proceeded to debate the whole subject in approved academic forms. Babington began:

'I told them that we seemed to stand in a dilemma. On the one side lest the magistrates here might take away our lives by massacre (as has reasonably enough been feared) or by the laws already made, by means whereof, there is no catholic whose life is not in their hands. On the other side lest the stranger should invade and sack our country, and bring it into subjection. Betwixt which two dangers hanging, we discoursed much of both.

'In the reformation (*i.e.* revolution) we found conclusion (termination) of our dishonour and of the desolation of our country: in the delay thereof—extreme hazard.

'Books had lately been imprinted to show, that all Catholics were traitors, that it was not possible for a papist to be a good subject: which opinion holden, must needs ensure us of their desire of our extirpation.

Any man may judge what spurs desperate perils be, to prick forward men to perpetrate anything, to adventure their delivery from such extreme terms, or at least to free their country and their fellows in faith by deaths holden honourable. And likewise (any may see) in what danger the state doth stand, in which remain an infinite number of men in the same terms, and by consequence of the same minds. Whom either utterly to root out, or by some easy toleration to hold better content—seemed to be expedient for the security of the State. That any toleration would ever be admitted, was despaired. Extirpation, therefore, was to be looked for upon the first assurance of any occasion, as might seem sufficient to excuse the fact somewhat abroad, and to hold satisfied the multitude at home.

'Thus we discoursed: in fine for a conclusion I told Mr. Salisbury I thought it the best course to depart the realm, with licence, if it were possible; if not, without.

'This also because of the danger of civil war or invasion among the many competitors, who might arise if the Queen's Majesty were taken away. As for the Queen of Scots, she was in great danger at that day, and being old and sickly must soon be succeeded by her son, whom we distrusted. Which sorrowful considerations moved a conclusion to depart the realm, in which intention we left each other for that time' (*below*, p. 56).

4. *John Savage.*

The next to be drawn in was John Savage, whose earlier career has already been sketched. It will be remembered that at the persuasion of Gilbert, and perhaps of William Gifford, he had joined in George Gifford's conspiracy in the year 1585, and had admitted Ballard to his secrets about March 1586.

According to the speech of the Queen's Counsel at Savage's trial, 'Ballard sent to Savage to speak to him on Lambeth side. He then told Savage of Babington's practice, and brought him to Babington, who was not friends with Savage before.'[1]

The original indictment gives the same story, but with different details. Here Savage goes to conspire with

---

[1] *State Trials* (1730), i. 125.

Ballard on the 30th of May, and on the 31st he receives three letters of encouragement in his plot from Morgan, Dr. William, and from Gilbert Gifford.

From Savage's subsequent statements,[1] it seems that in these letters (if not earlier) he was told that Allen highly approved of his plot; and he was also told that Persons had praised George Gifford's plot. But in any case the statements of these three correspondents, who were all in the faction *against* Allen and Persons, was insufficient evidence, and we also know from other sources,[2] that Allen strongly condemned the plot.

Savage, probably quite ignorant of Allen's real mind, at once consented to join Babington, and, as we shall see, gave up his own plans to adopt those of Babington, which, however, were so far very vague indeed.

All this, be it observed, is quite in Savage's manner. He will undertake any plotting put before him with the most obliging promptitude: but he never does anything. These three letters must have passed through Phelippes's hands, but he also does nothing. Gilbert Gifford was actually one of the writers. If then both he and Phelippes knew, we may be certain that Walsingham knew also. And still nothing happens! We must therefore conclude that they considered the danger to Elizabeth as altogether negligible. The way for the conspirators was still being made comfortable and easy for them.

5. *Gilbert Gifford and the Conspirators, 7 June.*

It has been mentioned that Gilbert was to have received a packet of letters from the 'honest man' at Burton on the 4th of June. He may then have started for town on

---

[1] The Record Office copy, *Mary Queen of Scots*, xix 38, gives 11 or 15 August. The British Museum copy, *Caligula*, C. ix f. 29, has 17 August. See Boyd, pp. 611, 681.

[2] R O, *Domestic Elizabeth*, ccxlii p 258, statement by James Younger

the 5th, and have been there on the 7th. The government story of what happened on that day is told in the Indictment. This must be cited in full, yet not without a caution. To say nothing of popular errors about the Papal League, there is also here (it seems) an error of fact, that Gilbert and Ballard plotted *in company*, whereas in fact, as will presently appear, they did not meet till July. The truth is that they were plotting *simultaneously but separately*.

6. *Counts in the Indictment on the treasons committed on 7 June.*

'ALSO the aforesaid John Ballard and Gilbert Gifford for the fulfilling and accomplishment of their most wicked and unspeakable betrayals and treasons, imaginations, compassings, intentions, and proposals, afterwards that is on the seventh day of June, in the present year of the said Lady now Queen, the 28th, at St. Giles aforesaid, treasonably convened, met and came together in order traitorously to confer, treat and hold colloquy with the said Anthony Babington, by which ways, modes and means they might fulfil and complete their treacherous intentions and proposals.

'AND on the same seventh day at Saint Giles aforesaid, and on divers other days and times, before and after, both at St. Giles aforesaid as elsewhere in the same county of Middlesex, they treacherously held colloquy with the same Anthony, about a certain invasion in the realm of England intended and prepared by the then Bishop of Rome, with the help of Philip, king of the Spains, and of other foreign princes, to be made and executed in this present summer.

'AND they traitorously recounted and declared to the said Anthony Babington, that through the aforesaid Bernardine de Mendoza and Charles Paget they were required and asked that some provision, some course and method should be taken and begun within this realm of England to procure help, adherence and assistance for the said foreigners and aliens, who were to invade this realm. Moreover for procuring some means by which the said Mary, late Queen of Scots, could be delivered from custody and set free.

INTRODUCTION cxiii

'Upon this the said John Ballard, Gilbert Gifford and Anthony Babington afterwards on the seventh day of the said June, in the aforesaid twenty-eighth year of our said lady the Queen now, at St. Giles aforesaid, treasonably, feloniously, and wickedly, fixed, concluded, and absolutely resolved, mutually, one to the other, that they could not effectuate and complete this except by the killing and final destruction of our said lady the now Queen, their supreme and natural lady.

'Upon this the said Anthony Babington on the same seventh day of June at St. Giles aforesaid, and at divers other days and times before and after, both at St. Giles aforesaid, as elsewhere in the said county of Middlesex, feloniously, wickedly, and treasonably devised, consented, and concluded, with the said John Ballard and Gilbert Gifford that our aforesaid lady Elizabeth, now Queen of England, their supreme and natural lady, should be most wickedly, unspeakably and treacherously killed, and that the said Mary late Queen of Scots, treasonably and by force should be torn away and delivered from the aforesaid custody, and that the auxiliaries, and assistencies and reliefs, both for the deliverance of the said Mary, late Queen of Scots, as for the said foreigners and aliens enemies of our said lady the present Queen and as it is said, about to invade this realm of England as enemies, should be received, and provided for. And that all these things should be done and effected simultaneously, as it were in the same instant time, and together.'[1]

Extraordinarily cumbersome as the legal style is, it was necessary to quote the passage in full, in order that it may clearly appear that the government originally wished it to be believed, that Gilbert was among the plotters from the first. But later on Gilbert's name was entirely omitted from the corresponding passage published in the

---

[1] The original Latin is written in words so much abbreviated, that the five paragraphs above occupy less than seven lines, which however are very long. There are no paragraphs, and no punctuation in the MS. The official summary is given immediately. The original is membrane 18, in Pouch xlviii. of the *Baga de Secretis*, for Elizabeth, at the Record Office. It was found 'a true bill,' on 7 September, but proceedings had begun on the 5th.

cxiv MARY STUART AND THE BABINGTON PLOT

State Trials. The two following parallel passages tell their own story.

Abstract of the original indictment quoted above, printed in the 'Fourth Report of the Deputy Keeper of the Public Records,' 1843, p. 276; References to Gifford are *here* italicised.	*Declaration of the Indictment by Sandys, Clerk of the Crown, from* 'State Trials' (1730, i. p. 123).
AND that Ballard and *Gilbert Gifford* afterwards, to wit, 7 June, 28 Elizabeth at St. Giles', had a discourse with Babington how they should fulfil their treacherous intentions, and conferred with him concerning the invasion intended and prepared by the then Bishop of Rome, with the aid of Philip, king of Spain, and other foreign Princes:	AND Thou, the said John Ballard, the 7th day of June in the 28th year at St Giles, didst go to have speech and confer with the said Anthony Babington, by what means and ways your false, traitorous, imagined practices might be brought to pass.
AND that *they* treacherously told and declared to Babington that . . Mendoza and Paget had required aid and assistance to the invaders, as also for the delivery of Mary late Queen of Scots.	AND that Thou the said John Ballard didst oftentimes declare of an Army of the Pope and the king of Spain for to invade this realm, and didst also declare that Paget and Mendoza required them the said Babington, Savage, etc, to procure means how this realm of England might be invaded.
WHEREUPON Ballard, *Gilbert Gifford* and Babington, 7 June, 28 Elizabeth, at St. Giles'; resolved that this could not be done except by the destruction of the Queen.	AND that there Thou, the said Anthony Babington didst say the same could not be brought to pass without the murder of the Queen's most excellent Majesty.
AND Babington on the same day traitorously *agreed with the other two*, that the Queen should be slain, the late Queen of Scots delivered by force, from her imprisonment, and help raised . . . and that all things should be done simultaneously.	AND afterwards, that is to say the seventh day of June at St Giles, Thou the said Anthony Babington didst falsely, horribly, and traitorously and devilishly conspire to kill the Queen's most excellent Majesty, and for to deliver the said Mary Queen of Scots, out of the custody wherein she was, and how to bring foreign enemies for to invade the realm.

What can be clearer from these two columns, both inspired by the same government, than that it at first wished to emphasise this charge against Gilbert, but afterwards deliberately omitted his name. This will be found to agree exactly with the story we have to tell. Whilst the indictment was being drawn up, Gilbert had fled the country, and the government had reason enough to dread lest he should turn upon them. Then his letters, protesting fidelity to his principals, came in; and Walsingham recognised that he might still be confided in. So Mr. Secretary took up a middle position. He would not alter the indictment (which would have caused comment), but he sent word (28 August) to Gilbert to 'be content that we *speak* evil of him'—and the Queen's counsel were evidently instructed not to urge the charges against him (*below*, p. 119). Keeping these facts in view, there is no mystery in the double form of these papers.

Of the two government statements, the second, which deliberately omits Gilbert's name, is plainly political and valueless. But is the first reliable? To some extent it is supported by other evidence. Babington's statements show that Gilbert had conspired with him, before he left, about the 20th of July, for France.[1] Savage's confessions show that Gilbert had also conspired with him, sending him three letters of encouragement,[2] and all the conspirators, including Ballard, seem to have felt quite sure of his privity and co-operation.[3] With this evidence before them the government might well enough indict their *agent provocateur*, and they obtained a verdict as a matter of course.

---

[1] See *below*, p 116

[2] Savage describes these letters in his confessions of 15 and of 17 August. He gives 31 May as the date of their receipt (*i.e* less than a week from 7 June) Of their bearing he says, 'All which letters were to encourage Savage to proceed in that action as honourable and meritorious.' Boyd, viii. 612, 681.

[3] See *below*, p 106

Yet none of these three heads actually proves that Gilbert did sit in conclave with the whole band on the 7th of June, and in particular we shall hear him tell Walsingham on the 11th of July that he had never met Ballard before that day.[1] As it is not so likely that he would then have lied to Walsingham, we must assume as our working hypothesis, that they had not met before. Though he was already in the confidence of Babington and of Savage, he had not apparently gained knowledge of their whole project, nor of all their associates. Nor is there any ground for wonder in this; for no definite plans had yet been formed by Babington, and the enrolling of conspirators was only beginning.

As to the conspirators, there is no authentic roll of them. But by the 7th of June, at the meetings in Babington's rooms—when the general resolution was taken of putting Mary on the throne with the aid of the So-called Catholic League—they counted, according to the government list, thirteen, including Gilbert. This list may be given here in full, though most of those who joined later were not conspirators in any usual sense of the word.

1. John Ballard, late of London, clerk.
2. Edward Wyndsore, late of Brandenham, Bucks., Esquire.
3. Anthony Babyngton, late of Dethycke, in the county of Derby, Esquire.
4. John Savage, late of London, Gentleman.
5. Thomas Salysburye, late of Llewenny, Denbigh, Esquire.
6. Edward Abyngton, late of Henlyppe, Worcester, Esquire.
7. Chidiock Tychborne, late of Porchester, county Southampton, Gentleman.
8. Charles Tylney, late of London, Esquire.
9. Robert Barnewell, late of London, Gentleman.
10. Edward Jones, late of Cadogan, Denbigh, Esquire.
11. John Traves, late of Prescott, Lancashire, Gentleman.
12. Henry Dunne, late of London, Gentleman.

---

[1] See *below*, p 105.

INTRODUCTION cxvii

 13. Gilbert Gifford, late of London, Gentleman.
On the 27th of July two more joined—
 14. Sir Thomas Gerrard, late of Wynwicke, Lancs., Knight.
 15. John Charnock, late of London, Gentleman.
On the 12th of August—
 16. Elizabeth (*sic*) Bellamy, late of Harrow on the Hyll, widow. (A second indictment follows calling her 'Katherine').
 17. Jerome Bellamy, of Harrow on the Hyll, Gentleman.
 18. Robert Gage, late of London, Gentleman.[1]

Of these some had consented or 'vowed'[2] to take part; but no definite plans were yet formed. Savage indeed affected to consider his original plans valid until their place was taken by others; but nobody ever seemed to think of reducing his proposals to practice.

6. *Gilbert and Ballard leave London, 6 or 7 June.*

The two conspirators who were more deeply in earnest, Gilbert and Ballard, now left town. The reasons for Ballard's departure are perfectly clear. Mendoza and Paget had treated his previous plottings as mere 'generalities.' They told him to find out definitely who would rise and who would not. So he started off immediately on this quest. The traitorous Bernard Mawde still rode at his side. Father Robert Southwell in his *Supplication to the Queen* gives us an incident or two of this journey. For instance, that Mawde had procured (doubtless through Walsingham) 'a commission to take horses' Presumably

---

[1] *Fourth Report of the Deputy Keeper*, p 276.
[2] Babington's *Confessions*, viii p 92, 'denied that he was sworn unto the Scottish Queen, but vowed his service by his letter (and never before), but limited and restrained with his dutie and allegiance to the Queen's Majestie' On the other hand, on p 93, he wrote, 'Such of the gentlemen aforenamed, as were to undertake the action against her Majesty, did vow and promise to perform it After signification of assurance from the Scottish Queen, this examinate meant they should have received the sacrament upon it'

that was a privilege granted to those who 'rode post,' to commandeer a change of horses, when their own beasts were tired. This would have given Mawde a certain authority, and might well make Ballard glad of his company. The second incident is that Mawde had procured a letter to the 'Lord Admiral of Scotland.' This might act as a sort of passport with English searchers and constables.

In spite of his advantages, however, Mawde does not seem to have made any discoveries of importance. But he undoubtedly fomented the plot. Edward Windsor afterwards said that at a time when he had resolved to break with Ballard and all his works, Mawde talked him round again and persuaded him to continue.[1] Similar things were no doubt done elsewhere.

On the whole then we are not justified in suspecting that Mawde was responsible for much in the development of the plot. Nevertheless his presence in the company of Ballard served as safeguard, and this helps to explain why nobody, except Elizabeth, was alarmed about the conspiracy. Her own officials were helping it on with vigour.

Gilbert Gifford almost immediately after the meetings of the 5th and 7th of June went back to Paris,[2] and on the 10th Barnes took down Mary's post to Chartley. We have no written explanation of Gilbert's journey, but it fits in well enough with what went before. It was quite natural, from Walsingham's point of view, to send him to Paris. For there the plot had been first laid, there too Morgan lived, and Mendoza, from whom the most valuable secrets might be elicited. On the other hand, from Babington's point of view the journey to Paris would have entirely

---

[1] R O, *Domestic Elizabeth*, cci no 50, 30 May 1587.
[2] Gilbert is said to have written to Phelippes on the 11th, but nothing is now known about this letter. It subsequently fell into the hands of Gilbert's enemies (*Addenda Calendar*, p. 227, below, p 127)

commended itself, because he desired to know the opinion of catholic divines upon the lawfulness of their project. When Gilbert returned without any such opinion, Babington was vexed, and sent him back again to get it. Thus, though one might have imagined that Gilbert's first task would have been to procure all the information possible from the conspirators in England, the reasons for going to Paris were also strong.

In point of fact, though Gilbert haunted Morgan, and got money out of him, he seems to have obtained little news. Morgan was inclined to be prudent, and would not open up about 'the matter in question'; though he 'promised that in time he should know all.'[1] In regard to Ballard, however, Morgan distinctly warned Gilbert to be 'discreet,' and 'to give him as little honour as may be in the face of the world,' though 'his credit should be preserved for many causes, as you know.' This is exactly the same line that Morgan was taking at this period with Mary herself.[2]

Gilbert's countermove was to spend his week in Paris (about 14 to 21 June) working with Grately in the hurried production of a MS. book against the Jesuits. It had nothing directly to do with the plot, but it was a veil to prevent his (Gilbert's) part in the plot from becoming too clear to Grately and Morgan. It will be remembered that Gifford had explained his favourable reception by Walsingham, by saying that the Secretary was won over by Gilbert's declaration of hostility to the Jesuits. So also Grately, consumed with the desire of obtaining a favour like Gilbert's, now offered their common work as a token which Walsingham would perhaps highly prize. The real reason for Gilbert's going and coming was entirely shrouded

---

[1] These are Gilbert's phrases Morris, p. 220, or Boyd, p. 517
[2] Compare Morgan to Mary, 24 June/4 July, and to Gifford, 9/19 July; in Boyd, pp. 467, 515.

from the eyes of his intimates by this ruse. To carry a libel like this was important enough in the minds of Morgan and Gratcly to explain anything.

The book is lost; it was never published, and it did no great harm to those against whom it was composed. But against those who wrote it, it reacted very unfavourably indeed, as the sequel will show.

The most striking epitome of this journey of Gilbert's, to Paris and back, is in his confession of 1588:

'In truth, for my part, all this was done, that I might bring to a conclusion that business about the assassination of the Queen of England, which was then in hand, and many gentlemen had conspired for that purpose.'[1]

Gilbert was soon back. On the 26th of June/6 July, the French ambassador wrote to Mary that 'the gentleman who serves you' (*i.e.* Gilbert) is back in London, and so he sends this letter. She answered that he had promised to be back at Chartley before the end of June.[2] On the 29th Poulet speaks of 'your friend at his coming,' as if he were expected immediately.[3]

8. *Babington's Activities.*

After Gifford started for Paris, Babington's principal undertakings had been the following. On the 8th of June he had sworn Salisbury to raise a revolt in Denbigh, while on the 9th and 10th he discussed with Savage further particulars of the assassination. On the 10th Barnewell,

---

[1] 'Consensimus omnes ut (liber) traderetur, erat enim ille praetextus ultimi mei redditus in Angliam. Revera autem ex parte mea totum hoc ideo erat factum, ut negotium illud de interficienda Regina conficerem, quod tunc agebatur, et nobiles complurimi in id conjurassent' *Hatfield Calendar*, iii. 348.

[2] Compare Boyd, p 472, and Labanoff, vi. 428.

[3] Morris, p. 213

INTRODUCTION cxxi

Tichborne, and Tilney were in conference, on the 13th Salisbury and Jones discussed plans for the Welsh rising. On the 22nd, Windsor, Abington and Dunne met with Babington and Ballard.[1]

Without laying too much stress on the accuracy of these dates from the indictment, we may assume that they represent roughly the chief meetings of the conspirators. Babington we see acting as leader, though he had not yet definitely accepted the post. It may be that Ballard was still to visit some person of title, and ask him to lead. This matter was not settled until his return. The only subject agreed upon was the acceptance of the visionary foreign aid. No one of them doubted that it was allowable to use such aid, for the 'reformation' of the ills they laboured under. Then there was the difficult question of how they should deal with Elizabeth. Savage, as has been explained, had, under Gilbert's persuasions, undertaken or 'vowed' to assassinate her. This plan had been rejected by Babington 'at the first knowledge thereof' (p. 57). But the suggestion put forward in its place, had also (it seems) been one of assassination, with this difference, that it was to be carried out by six instead of by one. But this proposal also was only tentative. Even the names of 'the six' were never settled. The plan was not agreed to by all, nor was it even known by every one of the conspirators. Then Abington, on the 22nd perhaps, proposed 'the surprise of the Queen's person,' and to carry her off to some 'strength,' apparently to Kenilworth Castle, and to appoint catholic ministers.

The discussion of such plans was exactly suited to Babington's temperament, and the debates were long continued. The other conspirators grew impatient, but

---

[1] Ballard's name seems wrongly inserted here, as he did not complete his northern tour till about 8 July.

Babington kept to 'lingering' as a sort of policy.¹ 'They still cried out of my delays, as a thing tending to discovery. I excused it with the expectation of Gilbert's return, whereupon I did affirm something to be done.' ²

As a practical measure Babington proposed the obtaining of a licence to travel abroad. At first sight this may seem like mere cowardice, but it is not to be so interpreted. The petition gave him an excuse for keeping in town, for having his friends about him, for raising money and the like. If the plan offered a good way of retreat, it might also be of use in providing an occasion of attack.

The necessary licence to travel had to be granted by the Queen herself, and Babington had applied for one, at an earlier date, through Sir Edward Fitton.³ He now had recourse to Robert Poley. We have already heard of Poley in the year 1585, when he was in the service of Christopher Blount, and had come over to Paris to get the confidence of Morgan. Since then he had entered the service of Lady Sidney, Sir Philip's wife and Walsingham's daughter, and he was in the position to gain favours of many sorts. 'Father Weston has left us a good picture of the man.

'He (Poley) held one of the smaller offices in court, and had obtained some familiarity with Secretary Walsingham, whom he served in the quality of a spy, being quick-witted by nature and ingenious in deceiving, and he had, according to report, received large sums from the Secretary. Having contrived to insinuate himself into the intimate acquaintance of the chief catholics, who resided about London, he would often receive them in his own house, and at a table handsomely

---

[1] Tilney during the trial said, 'Babington forsooth will be a statesman; when, God knows, he is a man of no gravity.' *State Trials*, 130, ii

[2] Babington's *Confessions*, 1. § 8, p 60 The last words again prove that Gilbert must have been in the plot *before* he crossed the sea

[3] Babington's *Confessions*, 1. § 1 For Sir Edward Fitton see *D N B*. Also the trial of the conspirators

supplied. Through this familiarity, he gained the reputation of a worthy man, both honourable and devout, and he was often admitted to be present at Mass, the Sacraments and exhortations. He knew exactly how to behave himself and came to them without a shadow of suspicion.

'Having by his catholic demeanour and friendship with good men acquired a high character, he tried to avail himself of it to fasten himself upon me, and to obtain more familiarity than I was anxious for. In short, he made me so many promises and was so obsequious in his manner, that it made me sniff, as at something that did not please. For instance, his house, his room, his keys, his coffers would all be open to me, and might be used by me. Whether he were at home or absent, he would make arrangements, that in any time of peril or difficulty whatever, I should always find a refuge in his house. If I desired to send letters or money to any place beyond the seas, he never had any doubt but that he could help on my purpose, and send them from any harbour or any port of the sea-coast.

'Now I knew that the possibility of any such promises was beyond the reach of good or sincere catholics. It is not possible for them to venture to make such offers, or to give such aid, where all around was so disturbed and hostile. I began therefore to avoid him by degrees and to see as little of him as possible. Even this did not appear absolutely safe; for I could not long escape him, and his expostulation on account of my altered behaviour. It became clear to me, that he felt himself offended in no small degree. The marks of his affection began to cool. I am not able to state what he afterwards attempted against me, but rumour reported that he was the man who betrayed me.'[1]

Babington knew in general that Poley was a man distrusted by catholics,[2] but he did not know him personally,

---

[1] Morris, *Troubles*, ii 169. Weston's arrest was really due to accident.
[2] 'Master Poley' is mentioned in *Leicester's Commonwealth*, written in 1584 (ed 1642, p 86) in a way that is meant to be uncomplimentary, viz as one of the Leicester faction, but no specific charge is advanced against him. Babington even told his new friend that 'All men in England being catholics had me [Poley] in general in vehement suspicion' (*Poley's Confession*, Boyd, p 597.)

until he approached him 'about the middle of June last,' to obtain a licence for travelling. Poley procured him an interview with Walsingham at Greenwich towards the end of June; Babington made 'general offers of service' to which Walsingham replied with 'many honourable speeches.'[1] Walsingham knew well from Gilbert, perhaps also from Mawde and from Mary's letter bags,[2] that Babington was conspiring against the government, and his 'honourable speeches' therefore were only a diplomatic mask. Yet it was not his main object to lure the luckless youth to ruin. It would have suited him far better to have made Babington confess. Mary's death, not Babington's, was his prime object.

As the matter remained unsettled, Poley saw Walsingham at Barn Elms in the beginning of July, and asked for a second interview. When granting this favour Walsingham changed his tone a little, complaining to Poley that Babington, though 'offering service,' was 'close and spare in opening himself, and the means of his offered service,' and that perhaps he had better see the Queen herself and speak openly to her.

When he heard this Babington seemed 'most glad,' says Poley. He came to Walsingham (about 3 July),[3] but after all 'opened himself no further than before.' Walsingham 'did not discourage him at all,' and told him 'he would procure his access to her Majesty.' But in private he told Poley that 'he had more and more reason to suspect him,' because of his closeness. A third interview followed about the 13th of July.

---

[1] Babington's *Confessions*, and Boyd, p 595.

[2] At all events Walsingham had forwarded to her Morgan's letter of 29 April/9 May, recommending correspondence with Babington. In fact, Mary answered that letter on 25 June, which was also probably the day of Babington's interview. But this note had not yet reached the secretary.

[3] Poley at first *described* this as having taken place on 13 July In the margin he adds that this is eight or ten days too late. Boyd, p 596.

INTRODUCTION

It would seem that Babington was now perhaps buoying himself up with hopes. Walsingham had questioned him twice, without (so Babington thought) guessing his real mind. And again he fancied that Poley's obsequiousness was true friendship; in other words, he imagined that he had won over this rusé old courtier. So he began to indulge with him in philosophic debates, such as those which we have heard him carry on with Salisbury and his other intimates (*below*, p. 58).

'I conferred with Robin Poley, concerning this action, who I presume hath discovered that part long since. I proposed unto him three courses, in any of which he vowed to follow me before he knew what they were.

'I told him I disliked of the course holden with Mr. Secretary both by him and me, for we stood indifferent [1] betwixt the two states and not very sincere unto either.

'Methought it was better either:

'(1) To dedicate ourselves to the preservation of this from all practices dangerous to the Queen's person or the state: and this I presumed, by reason of my credit with the catholics here and elsewhere, did lie expressly in my power;

'(2) or otherwise to the subversion of the present;

'(3) or lastly, to leave the service of both, and to dedicate ourselves to a contemplative life, leaving the practice of all matter of estate.

'He, with an indifferent conscience swore upon his salvation to follow me and my fortunes in any of these direct contrary courses that I should undertake, and asked me which I liked best.

'I told him the contemplative life. So should we bear no blame of any or either party, and spend our time there [abroad] in security, with profit in study, whilst this state stood. And after, if it pleased God to send a good world, we might take the fruit of other men's labours, exempted from the danger accompanying the change.

'He held the course to depart the realm best for any particular [*i.e.* for our personal advantages], but added withal that he

---

[1] *I.e.* evenly balanced

had ever found me to reckon little of my particular, in question of any common good. No doubt either of the two courses were better (if it could be advised) than the preservation of the present estate with the hazard of the other: this he allowed not. It rested then to embrace of necessity the last [of these two], which he did willingly, in appearance.

'And hereupon I persevered therein, who otherwise, if he had so advised, had departed the realm with these other gentlemen my adherents. But being by extreme fortune denied means to travel, and persuaded by this man and Ballard that this course was best, I still entertained the practice, but with such extreme delays as might well betray the repugnance which was in my nature, and the dislike which I had of this fact, by means whereof no doubt her Majesty's life was preserved.

'Ballard oftentimes reproved my slowness, and told Henry Dunne that he doubted I would discover it to the Queen herself, unto whom he heard I should be brought. And this no doubt I had done, if I might have had assured hope or pardon for the rest, whom I loved so much, that I could not endure to discover it to their overthrow.

'Thus lingering, as no man of resolved malice could have done in a case so extreme dangerous; we debated *obiter* (to entertain the time and their expectations) of many practices. They still cried out of my delay, as a thing tending to the discovery thereof. I excused it with the expectation of Gilbert Gifford's return, upon which I did affirm something to be done.

Here again Babington is describing himself to the life; a lover of his friends, a philosopher, a man whose ideals lay rather in the realm of thought than in the active life. The hypocritical Poley too is vividly pictured. He is ready to swear fidelity, before he knows what the alternatives are: and then adroitly argues in favour of conspiracy.

There is yet another contemporary account of those days, well worth comparing with that of Babington—that contained in the memoirs of Father Weston, who looks on the whole affair in a very different light.[1]

---

[1] Morris, *Troubles*, ii. 184. In these memoirs Father Weston makes two mistakes. The initiative in arranging the meetings may possibly have

INTRODUCTION cxxvii

'In the course of a few days (Babington) was sent for to pay a visit to Walsingham, who put him many questions concerning the Queen of Scots, and after a severe expostulation, informed him that he was himself aware of his most secret designs, and that it was in his power to disclose many secrets if he chose. He said that he knew as a certain fact that letters had passed and repassed between him and the Queen; and after divers threatening words, he charged him to cultivate affection for his own country, and the fidelity of a subject towards his own sovereign.

'How the other defended himself, I cannot tell, but he did so as well as he was able. Finally Walsingham dismissed him full of trouble, as I conceive, and very thoughtful and -disturbed with fear as to the result.

'After an interval of a few days he was sent for again. Walsingham once more went over his former discourse, but with greater gentleness and words calculated to soften his feelings . . . saying for his part, he was ready to bring him under the notice of the Queen and to obtain for him a personal interview. Then stretching out his hand he added: "Come now; act with confidence, and do not fear to speak out freely."

'All these particulars Babington narrated to me with his own lips, and profound was my sorrow when I heard him. I knew full well what a master in the art of deception this Walsingham was, and how powerful to accomplish what his mind was set upon. I therefore answered that he (Babington) might as well put out of his mind all idea of travel. "It will not be soon or easily that this affair will be brought to an issue. I cannot tell you in what manner you can escape out of his snares. If you yield, you give up your religion; if you decline his offers,

---

come from Walsingham *indirectly*, but Weston's precise statement that Babington was 'sent for,' cannot be supported.

Again Walsingham cannot at once have told Babington that he knew of his correspondence with Mary, because Babington did not write to her till after his second interview. But Walsingham may have so spoken at the third interview, 13 July. He may also have warned Babington against plotting.

It is pertinent to refer here again to Elizabeth's words spoken to the French ambassador, when the secret correspondence first began, that *she knew everything that took place in England.* That hint, too, was not understood (above, p. lxiv.)

you inevitably incur the peril of death. If you waver between the two, you will still risk your life, and lose your reputation among catholics."

'Babington replied, "No one who has ever known me will suspect my catholicism, even if I do use a little liberty in speaking and acting."

'I answered: "No one doubts that you are a catholic and will always be one. But if ever you say words or attempt actions, which catholics would be ashamed to suggest even to their most trusted and intimate friends, you will find it impossible to escape suspicion or to avoid disgrace."

'This was my last conversation with Anthony Babington. I never saw him more.

'Even if I had had the opportunity of seeing him I should have abstained. Not that I feared for himself or for anything he might do, for in his religion he was always the best and bravest of young men. Nor did I imagine that Walsingham would ever be able to lead him astray in any matter that would be dishonourable to a catholic.[1] But it was clear to my mind that I could not preserve intimacy with men of his description, and still maintain the principles of our Institute in their purity. It requires us to partake in such matters only as may concern religion, withholding ourselves from political affairs. This would be in the present case impossible, for he would be driven to consult me frequently and to impart to me much information.'

Father Weston here takes a view of his duties which may seem formal and strained, when judged by ordinary modern practice. It must be remembered, however, that he was writing for his fellow-religious, to whom his ascetical principles and rules were familiar. Babington evidently had secrets, and Weston saw danger. He did not see how he could help; so he held off and thereby saved life and reputation. His words are in any case instructive as a contrast to those of Gilbert Gifford, who was perpetually asking Walsingham to induce Dr. William, his cousin, to

---

[1] Weston, we see, did not imagine the power for evil of clerics like Ballard and Gilbert Gifford.

INTRODUCTION

come over, on the score 'that he would be very much employed [*i.e.* in advising whether this or that course or measure were morally right] and that the Doctor could keep no secret from him.'

To sum up a most critical chapter.

1. The plot was commenced by Ballard coming from abroad, commended by Morgan to Babington, whom he makes acquainted with Savage. The conspiracy, *i.e.* the resolution to put Mary on the throne, was formed 7 June, and Gilbert heard in general of these still undeveloped proposals about the same time. He then went abroad to get all the information he could from Morgan, and then, 14/24 June, returned to bring the plot to a head, and was back in London 26 June/6 July.

2. Babington, after admitting conspirators up to the number of thirteen, arranged some method in their plans, *e.g.* the murder by the six gentlemen was settled, though the names of the six were never agreed upon. But he soon tired of this, adopted a more or less deliberate policy of 'lingering,' and confined his efforts to obtaining a licence to travel. For this purpose he had three interviews, 25 June, 3 and 13 July, with Walsingham, who endeavoured to win him over in order to ruin Mary. But Babington did not betray his knowledge of the conspiracy, and he did not suspect the meaning of Walsingham's hints.

SECTION VII

MARY WRITES TO BABINGTON, 25 JUNE–18 JULY.

1. *Why she wrote.*

During the months of March, April, and May, Mary acknowledged the receipt of 'an infinite number of old packets, being the mass which had been accumulating at the French embassy for the last two or more years. Amongst these arrived a letter from M. de Fontenay, dated conjecturally 1 August 1585, which still lies among her letters at the Record Office.[1] In this de Fontenay informs her that he had sent her a despatch from Scotland with the news of what he had done, in January 1585. This had been carried by 'le Sieur Anthony Rolston,' to within two leagues of Wingfield, where Mary was then confined, and had been left at the house of 'le Sieur Anthonie Babington.' Babington was then at London, 'en parlement' (*i.e.* at the law-courts); but his servant had promised 'that the master would cause it to be delivered to her Majesty as soon as he returned from town.'

The suggestion which this letter gave, that Mary should communicate with Babington, was not long after enforced by another old letter, written by Morgan in July 1585, which reached Mary on the 10/20 of May 1586.[2] Morgan was then endeavouring, though rather despairingly, to move Babington to enter anew into the Queen of Scot's service, and 'put his helping hand to further her intelligence, which he is well able to do, having many friends and kinsfolk in the parts where her Majesty liveth.'

These two letters having lain on her table for over a month (20 May to 25 June) seem to be quite sufficient to account for the following letter from Mary to Babington on the 25th of June.[3]

---

[1] R.O., *Mary Queen of Scots*, xvi. 24a, 25. Another copy at Hatfield, printed almost in full, *Calendar*, p. 117. In passing it may be mentioned that this letter contains strong evidence of the divisions among Mary's followers.

[2] *Hatfield Calendar*, iii. p. 103. In extenso in Murdin, p. 453. These give the day as the 25th. But Curll in the postscript to Mary's letter of '20 May' (Labanoff, vii. p. 328; Boyd, p. 392) gives the day as 6 July. The letters, which arrived '20 May,' were carried by Barnes.

[3] *Below*, p. 15. The text is a re-decipher of Phelippes's copy of the original cipher. In this sense the text is a new one.

Morgan had sent to Mary a long draft letter, to be used in writing to Babington (R.O., *Mary Queen of Scots*, xix. 58, in Boyd, p. 345), dated

'I have understood that, upon the ceasing of our intelligence, there were addressed unto you from France [*i.e.* from Morgan] and Scotland [*i.e.* from de Fontenay] some packets for me. I pray you, if any have come to your hands, and be yet in place, to deliver them unto the bearer hereof, who will make them to be safe convoyed to me.'

2. *The Letter in the Post.*

There is no sort of mystery here, great though the consequences of the letter were to be. It was, in the ordinary course, put into cipher by Curll on the 25th of June (O.S.), which style was used in Mary's household, and also in her correspondence when she was writing to those who followed that computation. An accompanying note from Curll to the bearer Barnes was written at the same time. The main object was to warn him to be ready to receive what I have called 'The Second Post' on Sunday, July 3/13. Then it went on (*below*, p. 14):

'In the mean season, her Majesty prayeth you to send your foot-boy as closely [*i.e.* secretly] as you can with these two little enclosed bills; the one to Master Anthonie Babington dwelling most in Derbyshire, at a house of his within two miles of Winkfield; as I doubt not but you know, for that in this shire he hath many friends and kinsmen.

'The other bill, without any mark or *superscription*, to one Richard Hurt, mercer, dwelling in Nottingham Towne.

'Unto neither of the two foresaid personages your said boy needeth not to declare whose he is (unless he be already known by them with whom he shall have to do), but only to ask answer; and what is given him to bring it to your hands: which her Majesty assureth herself you will [do] with all convenient diligence.'

On the 25th of June the three tiny letters were enclosed in the box, slipped into the beer keg, and consigned

---

29 April/9 May. This, however, was late in arrival. Nau, however, the French Secretary, mistakenly thought that Mary followed Morgan's draft (Labanoff, vii. 208), and this has led some students astray.

to the 'honest man,' who having conveyed the keg to a convenient spot, took out the packet, brought it back, and gave it to Sir Amias, according to the method with which the reader is familiar. Sir Amias did not think much of it, 'being so little, as could be nothing answerable to that which you expect.' Still he gave it back *de more* to the brewer, who gave it to 'the substitute,' who again brought it to Sir Amias, who thereupon sent it by post to Walsingham, with his letter of the 29th of June,[1] and it should have been in Walsingham's hands on Thursday the 30th.

This letter of Sir Amias's is chiefly concerned with the rewarding and paying off of intermediaries, especially 'the Substitute' (? = Hoby), and eventually also of Thomas Barnes, the 'second messenger.' This would much simplify the cumbrous series of checks, so often described. When Barnes had been paid off, Phelippes would go on using his name, when writing to Curll.

So far as our immediate purpose is concerned, Phelippes already does this. Barnes exerts no personal influence whatever on events. He is a mere agent, a name. His letters are handed on to Phelippes, who deciphers them, and composes answers to them. On the other hand, Mary was told quite a long romance about him, viz. that 'Barnaby' was a cousin of Gilbert Gifford, that he lived in Lichfield and had a brother in London, and as both used the same cipher the one might be taken as representing the other. This is clearly the theory on which Curll wrote from this time forwards. Mary, as will be seen from the letters on her side, was evidently quite touched by this new idea of two brothers acting with one soul in her service. But it was all deceit. Phelippes had really been the outside correspondent from the first, and from now onwards he would keep all in his own hands. On the 7th of July Gilbert

---

[1] Morris, p. 212.

pledged himself to ' cut him [Barnes] clear off this course,'[1] and this he seems to have done.

When Phelippes received the packet, having opened and deciphered the accompanying note to Barnes, for which he had the key ready, he then proceeded to copy the cipher to Babington, upon the back of the decipher, where it may still be read. And when he did this, we may take it, either that he had not got the key to Babington's cipher in his pocket, or that he wanted to keep a copy of the cipher for caution's sake, or else he desired to pass on the note as quickly as possible, leaving the deciphering to be done at leisure.

This then looks like desire of speed. Yet the letter did not reach Babington till Wednesday the 6th of July (O.S.).[2] It had therefore remained in Walsingham's office for a week. There must have been some strong reason for this delay, though we are unable to say definitely what it was.

3. *Elizabeth's Orders and Gilbert's Solicitations.*

Perhaps time was needed to take Elizabeth's orders as to what should be done next. There is no doubt that she was kept informed of Walsingham's various moves. We have heard her tell the French ambassador significantly that she knew everything that was being done in England. That was in April, when the secret correspondence had begun. In June matters were moving much faster. If this letter from Mary were given to Babington, it would almost certainly bring matters to a head. On such a matter Elizabeth's orders would have to be taken afresh: and it may well have taken some days to reassure her, and to obtain her consent to the continuation of the plot.

---

[1] Morris, p. 217.
[2] According to the indictment it did not reach him until the 8th, but the answer of Babington was in Phelippes's hands before 7 July. *Mary Queen of Scots*, xviii. 32. Labanoff, vii. 191.

The departure of her court from Greenwich to Richmond, which took three days, July 11 to 13, may well be connected with this discovery, which was by no means a pleasant one for the pleasure-loving Queen.[1]

Another reason for delay *may* have been to allow time for Gilbert Gifford to galvanise the conspiracy into fresh life. We know that, while Gifford was away, the plot had languished: that Babington was deliberately 'lingering,' and that he ' excused this ' with the expectation of Gilbert's return, ' upon which he did affirm somewhat to be done.' Nay, Babington even entertained the thought (though half-heartedly) of giving up the whole conspiracy, or at least of going abroad. More important still, Babington was not without repugnance and doubts as to the lawfulness of their plan on various points, and so were others of his companions.

Deeply interested as Walsingham was in helping the conspirators over all their difficulties, he had his agent ready to assist them here as elsewhere. Gilbert Gifford aimed at no half measures. ' Really on my part all [*i.e.* all that concerned the book against the Jesuits and my return in June] was done for this, that I might bring to completion the business of the assassination of the Queen of England.' [2]

As to this Babington says, ' Gilbert Gifford was before this [*i.e.* before 26 June] come over to Savage, much discontented that he left off to execute what he had vowed, and that he could not be discharged in conscience upon

---

[1] Tytler, iv. 130, following Camden, places the communication of the secret to Elizabeth a month later. But this is not tenable. Walsingham on 3 August wrote, ' I doubt greatly her Majesty hath not used that secrecy that appertaineth' (*below*, p. 133) This shows that she must have known for some time. Since the publication of Poulet's letters, it is clear that Elizabeth was constantly informed on all topics.

[2] ' Revera autem ex parte mea totum hoc ideo erat factum, ut negotium illud de interficienda Regina Angliæ conficerem.' *Hatfield Calendar*, iii. 348.

the pretences [allegations], which I made of [for] his discontinuance from persecuting the same: all which he heard as mere delays.'¹

Babington added later, ' Ballard from the mouth of Mendoza swore that September could not pass without an invasion, Charles Paget confirmed as much, *and since Gilbert Gifford confirmed the same.*'²

It is important to take Savage's words together with those of Babington.

'It was said *by Gilbert Gifford* that the Pope did levy great number of men in Italy . . . to enter this island.

'Farther, *the said Gilbert Gifford informed me* that there was an Englishman with the Prince of Parma, who is to inform the Earl of Leicester. . . . But all is as well to cut the throats of my Lord's forces as his own. . . .

'Touching the intended invasion of the Spanish and the French aforesaid, it is certain, *as well by the speeches of Gilbert Gifford*, as also by the letters of Morgan, that the French would not attempt to invade, before such time as either the Catholics had taken away her Majesty, or else might be almost certainly assured that the Queen of Scots could be and should be delivered. . . . But for the Spaniard . . . if none of these beforementioned things chance, they shall be in England, *said Gifford*, before Michaelmas day.'³

Babington describes himself as annoyed at Gilbert's considering that such wild and unsupported statements as the above were a sufficient justification for the revival of Savage's old plans. This discontent became vocal a little later.

It is clear, therefore, that provocation to conspire was exerted by Walsingham's agents in the strongest way

---

¹ Babington's *Confessions*, p. 60. Savage is here again represented as a good-natured lump, who can be turned any way.

² *Below*, p. 84. A letter from Paget of this tenor is at p. xcv. *above*. It would have arrived early in June. Gilbert may have confirmed it on 7 June, but much more probably after the 26th.

³ Savage's *Confession*, 15 August 1586, B.M., *Caligula*, C. ix. 290 ; R.O., *Mary Queen of Scots*, xix. 41 ; Boyd, p. 611.

just at this crisis: and the delay before handing in Mary's letter, all things considered, made that provocation much more effective. About the 4th to the 6th of July, Gilbert went down to Chartley, and about the same time Mary's letter was handed to Babington (though the indictment, it would seem mistakenly, put this on the 8th).

4. *Mary's Letter received and answered (? 4 to 6 July).*

Here is Babington's full and frank confession of its receipt and of his answer:

'§ 1. I received by a boy unknown to me, letters in cipher, signifying her Majesty's discontentment for the breach of intelligence, and requiring me to send by that bearer, as I did, certain letters which I had received from Thomas Morgan in April (as I remember) last past, directed unto her. These letters I was earnestly entreated to convey unto her, but did not seek the means, only I kept them in safety. . . .

'§ 9. Having means to send to the Queen of Scots by the boy that came with her pacquet, I writ unto her touching every particular of this plot. . . . § 11. The tenour of it was that Ballard coming from Mendoza had informed me of the purpose of the Christian princes touching this country.

'That I was desirous to do her some service therein for her delivery. If there were assurance on the other side of such things as were necessary to this exploit, that there would not fail of correspondence on this side. [*Ibid.*, § 3.]

'That there were six would undertake somewhat upon the Queen's person. [*Ibid.*, § 8. Wording differs.]

'That myself with six [*sic* for ten] others would undertake her delivery. [*Ibid.*, § 7.]

'That there were ports to be sounded [*sic* for appointed] for the landing of forces, and assistance sufficient within to join those without. [*Ibid.*, § 4, c. d.]

'That rewards were necessary to be promised to the chief actors for their better encouragement, and to be given to their posterities, if they miscarry in the execution.'[1] [*Ibid.*, § 9.]

---

[1] See Babington's *Confessions, below*, pp. 51-64, the full text of Babington's letter at pp. 18-22. As it is important to notice the accuracy with

INTRODUCTION

The chief point to be considered in this letter is, of course, the intimation, which it gives to Queen Mary, of the proposed dispatch of Elizabeth. Whatever doubts may have in the past been raised by Lingard and others regarding Babington's letter, this evidence from his own *Confessions* is alone sufficient to establish the main course of our narrative. A discussion of other views, which have been put forward about possible interpolations, is given *below* at pp. 31-33.

Next let us notice that Babington's letter to Mary has no intrinsic connection with the letter from her. She had asked him to forward letters. He sends her a full plan of campaign.

It is indeed strange that a man, not very much used to writing in cipher, could have got this whole letter written, ciphered, and sent off during one day, having previously deciphered the letter from Mary. This lends a certain verisimilitude to a conjecture of Nau's[1] that Babington had written to Mary *before* she wrote to him. And so it may well have been. Babington had long ago received both from Mary and from Morgan an invitation to forward letters to her, as well as a cipher code, in which to write himself. What wonder if, when his difficulties became serious, he had sketched out a letter, and had already put it into cipher, when, by good or evil fortune, Phelippes's 'unknown boy' arrived with Mary's note.

In a postscript at the end of his letter Babington added a question to Nau asking Mary's opinion of Poley.

---

which Babington quotes, about 18 August, the letters written about 6 July, cross-references have been added to Babington's letter. Babington's condensation of the text will be found to be very well done, but the tone has been very very much modified. For the 'round and ready' tone of the original, see Babington's *Confessions*, p. 91.

[1] Labanoff, vii. 209 ; Boyd, ix 6.

5. *Babington's Answer on its Way.*

The note was now handed to the 'unknown boy,' who after we know not what devices, to make sure he was not followed, delivered the letter at Phelippes's house, and it was soon deciphered, and discussed with Walsingham. The Secretary's orders were at once given, though we know but one particular of them, that Phelippes was himself to take down Babington's letter to Chartley. For Babington had thrown out the hint that he would be at Lichfield on the 12th of July to receive Mary's answer. Now if that answer had to be taken to London and back, 280 to 300 miles, the delay in transit might have created suspicion, for it was only about fifteen miles from Chartley to Lichfield. By going down, however, Phelippes could copy or decipher the answer, which Mary would send to Babington, as soon as it reached Sir Amias's hands. Phelippes therefore left London on the 7th of July, as usual under the cover of night.[1]

Before this, Gilbert Gifford, having revived the conspiracy, as above seen, had been down to Chartley, from the 4th to the 6th of July. His object was the old one, to see if his dishonest intermediaries were faithful to their employers, and also (probably) to prepare the way for the paying off of as many of them as possible. Meantime he picked up 'Post II.' of 2/12 July, which would probably have been carried out from Chartley by the brewer on the 3rd, and which may have got to Gilbert's hands by the 6th. At the same time [2] he heard that Barnes had returned to town the week before. Hereupon Gilbert resolved to follow him on the 7th, giving the packet to Sir Amias for transportation.

---

[1] Phelippes to Walsingham, 7 July, Labanoff, vii. 191; also July 8, Morris, p. 218.

[2] Morris, p. 217.

INTRODUCTION cxxxix

Next day Sir Amias's courier, riding up to town, met Phelippes on his way down, between Stanford and Shilton. Phelippes thereupon stopped the courier, and took from him Mary's packet, which he carried back to Chartley next day. For there he would have had leisure to decipher the secret letters, and to seal up the packet again, while he awaited the writing of Mary's answer.[1]

Phelippes arrived at Chartley on the 9th, and as the brewer came next day, the 10th of July, Phelippes wrote the deceitful covering note to Curll,[2] saying that 'his brother' had received this packet, which Babington said 'required great haste,' and therefore 'the boy returned without staying for any dispatch from the French ambassador.' This was now sent in with Babington's note.

On the 14th Phelippes and Poulet wrote to give accounts of its passage in. 'It was thankfully [!] received with such answer given by writing as the shortness of the time would permit, and with promise to answer more at length, at the return of the *honest man*, which will be within three days.'[3] During these days Phelippes had copied out the ciphers, which were in 'Post II.,' and had deciphered one of them. He had also deciphered the billet from Nau to Babington. This first acknowledged the arrival of the packet, and then prudently refused to give credit to Poley, of whom the Queen of Scots had indeed *heard* praise, but had seen nothing to warrant her recommending him.

Phelippes's note of the 14th of July contained the expressive words : ' We attend her very heart at the next,'

---

[1] The stretch of road from Stanford to Shilton runs not far from the L N W. railway line after leaving Rugby, a little over 90 miles from London. It had taken Phelippes 24 hours to ride this, and he was vexed with his bad progress. He had hoped to have done the whole 141 miles to Chartley in that time. Morris, p. 218, erroneously read the two local names as Stilton and Stamford

[2] Barnaby to Curll, 10/20 July, *below*, p 17

[3] Morris, pp. 223-5.

that is, We expect an answer before our deceptions can be dispelled.

Ah, if she could but have had in attendance such councillors as a queen would normally have had! If she had but been free from the exasperating annoyances of imprisonment! If she had but known the truth!

6. *Reading the Letter*, 10 *July*.

Meantime what was taking place within Mary's apartments? Striking indeed was the contrast between the knight's hall and the deposed Queen's little cabinet. In the one sat the knight and the decipherer, congratulating one another on the good success of their half year of prolonged and laborious deception, and eagerly counting the minutes before the answer to Babington is finished. In another part of the house was a little study, where, under an old canopy, the sickly but great-hearted woman sat at the head of the table, at which Nau and Curll, her secretaries, are busy deciphering the little billets just received. Curll, grave old Scotsman that he is, becomes more and more animated and uneasy as he gradually draws out into plain writing Babington's extraordinary offer. He hands it to Nau, who reads it, also with signs of disapproval. Nau passes it on to the Queen, who goes through it with the closest attention.

Evidently a crisis is at hand. One thing, they think clear. The catholics of England, powerless though they might be to upset heretical tyranny, were most certainly able to bring about a crisis, the consequences of which were not easy to foresee. 'If this attempt be made and fails,' said the Queen—the words find their place in her final letter—'it were sufficient cause given to that Queen, to enclose me for ever in some hole, forth of which I should never escape, if she did use me no worse; and to pursue with all extremity those that had assisted me, which would grieve me more than all the unhap that might fall upon myself.'

Nau advised her to leave the letter unanswered.[1] It was Mary's general policy to decline with thanks the plans occasionally made for her liberation by private individuals. The Master of Gray and Hugh Owen had both received civil but distinct refusals within the last few months. But this case was evidently not that of a single private individual, and Mary's heart was at that moment yearning with more than ordinary vehemence for rights and liberty. She had till lately hoped that her son would procure her some measure of freedom. But he too had failed her. He had pusillanimously surrendered to the English faction, and for a miserable pension had accepted dependence, and surrounded himself with her foes. The coming years, all-important for the formation of his character, seemed black even to despair. Mary would not agree to put aside the letter, and the matter was left for further consideration.

So well aware was Mary of danger from Poulet, that she recognised that no locks of hers were safe from his violence; and she was therefore accustomed to hide the more important ciphers she received upon her own person.[2] Did she put Babington's letter into her bosom. when her conference with her secretaries ended ? Whether she did or not, its specious offer had already won entrance into her heart.

When Poulet retired to bless the Almighty for prospering the work against the woman he hated, to his prejudiced mind right and wrong had changed places.

The soul of Phelippes is harder to read. Facile, sharp,

---

[1] Nau to Elizabeth, 10 September 1586 Labanoff, vii 205 R O, *Mary Queen of Scots*, xix

[2] So Nau, Memorial of 1605, B·M , *Caligula*, B v 233

and unscrupulous was this child of bourgeois parents. Trickery and deception now came to him naturally. He met Mary in her drive, and immediately put on a smiling countenance, but said in his heart, '*sicut ab hoste cave.*'[1] Mary was disquieted. What did that 'slender-figured man, eated in the face with small-pockes, of short-sight, with dark yellow hair and light yellow beard' portend? She endeavoured by her servants, and even by herself, to sound his mind, but all in vain. Morgan had assured her he was a friend whom she might trust. He disappeared the day before the 'honest man' was to carry off her 'third post.' Still she did not suspect, and actually wrote to Morgan to ask him if he could explain!

Poulet's sternness melted towards the skimpy, pock-marked plebeian. He had used him as a decipherer years before; and in the sacred work of bringing his prisoner to the block he became quite maudlin over this 'old good friend.' He 'cannot thank (Walsingham) enough' for sending him down. Together they passed the three days not unhappily, with little doubt of the result. They were not mistaken.

7. *Mary decides*, 11 *July.*

If Mary hesitated for the first moment, her mind was firm by the next day. 'Elle s'est laissée aller, à l'accepter,' says Nau.[2] She had decided to accept the situation offered by Babington. Not that there was ever any indication that she distinctly or formally desired the assassination of the English Queen. Mary's person had been thrice

---

[1] R.O., *Mary Queen of Scots*, xviii. 48, Morris, p. 223, Boyd, p. 523. In Mr. Thorpe's *Calendar*, we find: 'He (Phelippes) had a smiling countenance from her.' The editor should have explained that the two last words were *his own addition*. One must not say that this meaning is *impossible*, but it is not the obvious meaning of the words.

[2] Labanoff, vii. 205.

restrained of liberty; her son James had been as often seized upon by force. Babington's followers, moreover, at all events a number of them, understood the plan to be for the restraint of the English Queen, and not for her death. If Mary should have taken the same view, that cannot be considered at all wonderful.

However, even if she thought Babington's words spelt assassination and nothing else, there is no word of hers to show that she approves of political murder. The contrast between her letter and Babington's is marked.

Babington had conjured her to use *her authority* to assure the conspirators honourable reward. We know from Ballard's words to Gifford that this was one of the vital points of the letter.[1] After stating that six gentlemen would make an attempt on the Queen's person, Babington wrote in his letter (§ ix.). 'It rests that, according to their infinite good deserts and Your Majesty's bounty, their heroical attempts may be honourably *rewarded* in them (if they escape with life) or in their posterity, and that so much I may be able, *by your Majesty's authority* to assure them.'

Mary's answer does not confirm this request. Though she is asked to pledge ' her *authority* to assure them that they shall be *rewarded*' for the attempt on Queen Elizabeth (and the promise of future reward certainly involves an approbation of the deed which is to be rewarded), Mary's answer is:

(*a*) '*To yourself in particular* I refer, to assure the gentlemen above mentioned [and she has been speaking both of the six and of others] (*b*) of all that shall be requisite *on my part* for the entire execution of their good wills.' And again at the end (§ xvii.): 'I do and will think myself obliged, as long as I live, towards you (*c*) for the

---

[1] *Below,* p 107

offers you make to hazard yourself as you do *for my delivery*, and by any means that ever I may have, (*d*) I shall do my endeavour to recompense by effects your deserts *herein*.'

Or we may put it in this way.

(*a*) Asked to give her Royal authority — she tells Babington to use his own.

(*b*) Asked to reward, after the event, the six gentlemen for the attempt on life, she always avoids this: but in a parallel passage she promises—that she will not be wanting in *her part* of the enterprise, and her part had nothing to do with assassination.

(*c*) Finally that she will reward all those who assist as much as she can; (yet not for assassination), but for helping her *to escape*.[1]

But whatever force we attach to this formal withholding of assent to the assassination in detail, she nevertheless materially does consent to the plan as a whole.

The whole tone of her answer is that of gratitude and approval. The clauses in which she holds back or evades, are so blended with those in which she fully agrees, that excited and impatient readers would not wait to weigh her restrictions. Babington was not expected to do so, nor did he.

If the assassination was a crime, Mary was not free from guilt. If it was not a crime, but an inevitable incident in the struggle for liberty, Mary was free from blame. That was the reason uppermost in her mind. She considered herself an independent sovereign: with every right to recover her liberty, if necessary by an act of war; and not bound to interfere between the English Queen and her subjects. This, without doubt, was for her the determining factor in the situation.

Let us take the similar case of Mendoza after the dis-

---

[1] This matter is discussed in greater detail *below*, at pp. 33-35.

covery of the plot. He had been told by Ballard of the intentions of Savage and George Gifford, and of this he had actually sent word to Idiaquez, and to Philip. He had also heard from Gilbert about the Babington plot; and had wished (though too late) to encourage the conspirators. Later, when the plot had been discovered, and while he was being angrily charged by the English ministers with having encouraged and indeed with having 'conducted' the conspiracy, he wrote again (10 September).[1] He declared that 'of course he would omit no act of war against those who had begun war against Spain : but that, as to assassination, he had never advised any of her subjects to conspire against her life, she being their sovereign and a woman.'

It is not my object here to defend Mendoza. I am dealing with his point of view only, with his describing himself as having 'never advised any of her subjects to conspire against her life.' If Mendoza is sure that Philip will see that view, and be satisfied with it, can we wonder that Mary should have taken an almost exactly similar view of her duty and of her execution of it?

Liberty and her rights were the objects for which Mary strove. She was ready to lose her life in that struggle. Why should she forbear lest Elizabeth should lose hers? She would accept Babington's offer, and do all in her power to make it a success.

The chief need was that of foreign help. Without that any attempt would be madness. It was of the first necessity therefore that some one should go abroad and bargain with Mendoza for the most exact and faithful engagements of help. When the day of its proximate arrival drew near, the attempt on the Queen's person

---

[1] *Spanish Calendar*, p. 623 The original Spanish, which is not in *Documentos Inéditos*, is much to be desired.

should be made, and of this instant word was to be sent to Chartley, before warning could come to her keeper. The house should be attacked, and she carried off to some strong place of momentary safety, until foreign forces could interpose, and give such encouragement and assistance to the English catholics as would hearten them to seize the direction of the kingdom.

8. *Writing her Answer*, 11 *July*.

Mary came down to the second day's conference with her secretaries, having some headings on these topics already sketched out in her own hand.[1] Mary made Nau read Babington's letter aloud again, in the presence of Curll, and 'then the Scottish Queen directed Nau to draw up an answer to the same letter, the which Nau drew in French.'[2] Nau explains that it was Mary's habit to take her letters 'de point en point,' and to explain the answer to be made to each, Nau writing down, making notes 'aussi particulièrement et amplement que je puis faire.' Then he read his notes aloud, or showed them, and next he threw these notes into the form of a connected letter, after which he again showed and delivered them for her to decide upon. 'Her Majesty does not allow any letters of importance or secret notes to be written outside her "Cabinet," nor is any letter sealed except in her presence, and she always reads the letters anew before they are put

---

[1] Nau wrote on 3 September of Mary giving him 'une minute de la lettre escripte de sa main pour la polir et mectre au net' (*Mary Queen of Scots*, xix. 77, 78; Boyd, p. 665). On 5 September he speaks first of, 'une minute de la main de sa Maiesté, comme j'ai déposé': and later on he says it was 'pour la plus part escripte de sa main' (*Mary Queen of Scots*, xix. 89, 90; Boyd, p. 680). This minute, however, appears not to have been found later. It would have been of supreme value to establish the text of Mary's letter of 17 July. But bullied and fed-up with false information, Nau and Curll at last became confused and unreliable. *Below*, p. cxc.

[2] B.M., *Caligula*, C. ix. 378, *below*, p. 142.

into cipher, or translated, which was Curll's department, and the same is true of her letter to Babington.'

Curll's examination states, that when Nau had read to the Queen the French minute, ' the Scottish Queen willed this examinate to put it in English, which this examinate did accordingly. And when he had so done, this examinate did read the same so Englished unto Mr. Nau. Which done the Scottish Queen willed this examinate to put the same letter so Englished into cipher, which this examinate did.' [1]

Mary's plan depended chiefly on help from Spain, and she at once decided to write by the same post (though in the event the letters went a few days later) to her representatives at Paris to approach Mendoza, and learn for certain when the Spanish auxiliaries might be expected. So she would at once have communicated with Charles Paget, who had first written to her about Ballard, as well as with Mendoza and her ambassador the Archbishop of Glasgow. To ensure consistency in these letters Nau wrote a few headings:

Secours de dehors.
Forces dans le pays.
Armée d'Espagne au retour des Indes
Armée de France en mesme temps, si la paix se fait.
Guise, s'il ne passe, tiendra la France occupée.
De Flandre, de [? le] mesme.
Escosse au mesme temps.
Irlande ainsy.
Coup.
Sortie.[2]

---

[1] Nau especially notes (5 September, *Mary Queen of Scots*, xix 90) that the suggestion about firing barns was hers; also the order of the plan, beginning with the application to the Spanish ambassador in France, to ask for support, and going on to her liberation from Chartley as soon as support was at hand

[2] See p 140

Nau says that he composed letters to the Archbishop of Glasgow, to Mendoza, and to Charles Paget with these headings before him. But, as Lingard says, this cannot be considered an adequate explanation of them, for none of the letters indicated are written strictly on these lines, though they all have recollections of them.

'Curll delivered the letters first written in French by the Scottish Queen unto the same Queen again, and did put that which himself had Englished into cipher by the Scottish Queen's commandment, and that which was Englished [*i.e.* his English translation] this examinate did put into a trunk that was in the Scottish Queen's cabinet under lock and key.'[1]

Thus was the fatal packet completed. The letters to Paget, Englefield, and Mendoza were all intended to assist in procuring aid from abroad, without which Mary recognised that the attempt for freedom must be in vain. Had not her yearning for liberty impaired the balance of her mind; had not her long retirement, and her recent entire estrangement from politics weakened her otherwise strong powers of judgment, she might have known beforehand how altogether vain and illusory was the support, on which she now leant. There seems little doubt that she actually

---

[1] B.M., *Caligula*, C. ix. 382. It appears from Nau's later paper (B.M., *Caligula*, B. v. 233) that Mrs. Curll kept the key, and that Nau thought too much was preserved. He thought Mary trusted too much to her friends about the court, believing that they would warn her in case her coffers were to be searched.

In the *Hardwicke Papers*, ii. p. 237-50, there is a paper entitled, *Evidence against the Queen of Scots*. It is a popular 'report,' a vulgarised statement, not copied precisely from documents, and in this the official document, just quoted, is misrepresented as follows: 'He saith also, she willed him to *burn* the English copy of the letters sent to Babington.' This alteration is made in order to make this deposition agree with the erroneous account there given at pp. 249-50 of the proceedings on 24 October, in which Curll is said to have affirmed that 'as well the letter which B[abington] did write as the drafts of her answer to the same were both burnt at her command.' See p. 147 *below*.

INTRODUCTION

gave some credence to Babington's wild representations 'of great preparations by the Christian princes for the deliverance of our people'; an idea which that unsophisticated philosopher had first accepted from the fanatically sanguine Ballard; and had then seriously vouched for to her, relying on the fraudulent representation of Gilbert Gifford.

If allowance can be made for these fatal misconceptions, Mary's letters are otherwise admirable state papers; sane and well arranged, conciliatory, inspiring, confident.

To Paget she writes that he and the emissary from Babington are to urge Mendoza to espouse the new enterprise, while Mendoza and Englefield are urged with simple but very telling arguments to bring the Spanish king to the point of immediate action.

Everything a woman in her position could do was done. On Sunday the 17/27th of July the fatal letter was sent out with a note to 'Barnaby' (really Phelippes).[1]

'To make this enclosed surely delivered in the hands of Anthony Babington, if he be come down to you in the country. Otherwise that it be kept still in your or your brother's keeping until Babington his arrival, or for an ten days, within which time her Majesty intendeth to have a packet ready to be sent unto the French ambassador by your boy.'

In effect, for some reasons not mentioned, Post III., *i.e.* the packet of letters to go abroad, was retained another ten days. But on Monday (18/28 July) in the short darkness of a midsummer night the letter to Babington was lodged in Phelippes's hands, and by the Tuesday Phelippes had copied and sent it up to Walsingham, with ⌐⌐ (the gallow's mark) on the outside.[2]

Pious Poulet 'was wonderfully comforted by these

---

[1] *Below*, p 25
[2] Walsingham to Phelippes, 22 July, Morris, p 245.

discoveries'; [1] but Mary was fast in the snare. It was now only a question of policy, how and when the *coup de grâce* should be given.

SECTION VIII

The Catastrophe, 19 July–15 August.

1. *Ballard and Gifford.*

Phelippes on the 2nd of August wrote to ask **Walsingham** 'whether Babington is to be apprehended, or otherwise played with.'

'Or otherwise played with.' These words really sum up the section that now opens. Not that Walsingham wished to spend a month playing like a cat with a mouse. His object was to discover whether there were any more confederates, and to leave time for an answer to Mary's letter. When this had been done, and Chateauneuf had written his letter of 5/15 August, the signal was given for a general arrest; and then only at Elizabeth's orders. Walsingham was not alarmed. He knew there was no danger. It was only a question of securing victims and evidence. Phelippes was much more excited and would have struck sooner. Elizabeth was genuinely afraid, but still left Walsingham a fairly free hand.

Even our oldest historians argued from Walsingham's preparations, that he must have been pre-informed; though they never knew how. Early in June he had begun new measures for clearing the prisons, and in July something even more novel and drastic was attempted. The apostate spy Berden, whom we met above in section II., was made a sort of commissioner for advising what degree of severity, and what of mercy should be meted out to each

---

[1] Morris, p. 235.

imprisoned catholic—a proceeding thoroughly characteristic of the Tudor tyranny.¹

The poet, Father Southwell, in his *Supplication to Her Majesty*, 1591, tells this story, probably about Martin Aray, a priest who was to have been banished at this time.

'How privy Sir Francis was . . . to the certain period of the time wherein all his endeavours would come to the full point, may be gathered by this. Being by a priest, that was to be banished, sued unto for 20 days' respite to despatch his business—first repeating the number and then pausing a while with himself—"No," saith he, "you shall have but 14. For if I should grant you any more, it would be to your hindrance; as you shall hear hereafter." Herein he said true: for much about that time was public notice taken of Babington's matter, . . . infinite houses searched, and all men's eyes filled with such a smoke, as though the whole realm had been on fire; whereas in truth it was but the hissing of a few green twigs, of their own kindling; which they might without any such uproars have quenched with a handful of water '²

The clue to the conduct of the conspirators at this crisis is, that they never knew or suspected their real danger, viz. that Gilbert had been a traitor before they began to plot: so that Walsingham had known everything from the first. We shall find Babington gradually nerving himself for a partial revelation, which he regarded as a sure means of escape, at least for himself, and Ballard too had similar dreams. But Walsingham would not even see them.

The position at the time Mary posted her fatal letter (17 July) was this. All the conspirators were in London and in great suspense. Their leaders felt they had gone

---

¹ The papers are printed in *Catholic Record Society*, ii. 241-56
² Southwell, Robert, S J , *An Humble Supplication to Her Majesty*, 1595. Really printed in 1602 B M., 3935, aa, 33 Of course it does not follow that the plot was due to Walsingham's 'endeavours,' merely because he knew that Babington's intrigue must come to a head in a fortnight. But it does show that Walsingham knew more than he was willing to divulge

very far, and now that so many people knew their secret, it would be impossible to stop. Babington was falling more and more under the sway of Robert Poley, while Ballard, who is said at the trial to have returned to town shortly after Babington's note to Mary of the 6th July, came under the observation of Gilbert Gifford.

We left Ballard in the North accompanied by the spy Mawde. His business was to find the exact number of those who could be counted upon to rise; and the results of his inquiries are only known to us through the reports of conversations given in the next section. From the conspirator's point of view, the results were most disappointing. After passing through Lancashire, and possibly even Northumberland, they parted. Ballard turned South, meaning eventually to go on and report to Mendoza. Mawde crossed into Scotland to deliver his letter to the Lord Admiral. At Edinburgh, however, he found that he was short of money, and that Father Holt was gone; so he turned, and went back to his native Yorkshire, from whence he wrote under his old *alias*, Montalto, to Burghley or Walsingham on the 1st of August.[1]

By that time the conspirators knew of his treason, and this makes us turn to his letter with interest, which is, however, soon disappointed. Though cringing, and offering himself for any work, it contains no news beyond the details of his journey given above. Curiously enough there is a letter from Walsingham to Elizabeth written the day before which explains this lack of news. He tells her that Mawde 'seemeth not to stand *in any sound concert* with him [Ballard], though he was content for the serving of his turn to use him.' That is, Ballard had been ready

---

[1] R.O., *Scotland*, xli. 2. B. Montalte (not 'Bontalte' as in Thorpe's *Calendar*), 1 August, Boyd, viii. p. 579. The hand is the same as that of Mawde's autograph of 1581, in *Domestic Elizabeth*, clv. 102, allowance being made for travel, misfortunes, and perhaps the practice of false hands.

to use the advantages of Mawde as a riding-companion, as Babington had used the comfortable refuge of Poley's garden. But real intimacy had followed in the latter case, while 'no sound concert' had ensued in the former. Whence we may infer that but few details about the conspiracy reached Walsingham through this spy. Still there is evidence from John Tipping, and especially from Edward Windsor, that Mawde was active in persuading waverers to follow Ballard's courses.[1] When Mawde's treachery was discovered, as it was later in July, we can understand that the conspirators were much alarmed.

By the 9th of July Ballard has returned to London, having made the discovery that the English catholics were very far indeed from being ready to rise. But being a fanatic, he is unable to look this truth steadily in the face, and speaks about it in contradictory terms to persons whom he wishes to impress in different ways. To Savage, 'best of companions'[2] and a simple soul, whom everybody imposed upon, Ballard said:

'That he was almost assured of three-score thousand, ready to assist him in these parts, only that the greatest part of them were altogether unprovided of armour,[3] the which defect was promised to be provided out of France.'

To more discerning conspirators like Gilbert he spoke (10 July) very differently:

'(They) must needs obtain the Queen her hand and seal to allow of all that should be practised for her, without which we labour in vain; and these men will not hear us. . . . He

---

[1] Walsingham to Elizabeth, 5 August, 1586, in Tytler, iv. 130; and less precisely in Boyd, p. 589. Edward Windsor to Hatton, 30 May 1587, *Domestic Elizabeth*, cci. 50. Tipping's *Examination*, Boyd, p. 696.

[2] Morris, p. 381.

[3] That Ballard said this during this crisis of July is proved by Savage adding, 'This going into France had been determined, had he not been prevented [*i.e.* arrested].' Savage, *Confession* of 15 August, also called 11 August, Boyd, p. 611.

complained much of Sir Thomas Tresham, of my cousin [Mr. John] Talbot [of Grafton] for not only would they not hear him, but threatened to discover him. "And," saith he, " unless we obtain that from the Queen, all is but wind."'[1]

To Babington he said :

'Those who should be most forward were most slow, and .... the older the colder.'[2]

To Dunne and others he said he had heard of 500 more then he knew before. This is possibly true, but it probably meant but little.[3]

This meeting of Ballard with Gilbert was on Sunday the 10th of July.[4] On the 12th they met again for the same purpose. Gilbert reported to Walsingham that evening that Ballard was very angry with Morgan and Paget, because they had not yet written; and that he was half inclined to go over to France at once; but finally he agreed to await communications from them. 'It is certain he hath determined no certain course'; he knew, however, that Phelippes had gone down to Chartley, 'with commission to open and read all letters and packets he met with by the way,' also that he had spoken with confidence of the beheading of Queen Mary. In fine 'the great practitioner' begged Gilbert once more, to get 'approbation for all his actions' from the imprisoned Queen, and Gilbert promised 'to presume what I could.'[5]

About the 16th there was a third meeting. Letters from Morgan had now arrived (written about the 3rd or

---

[1] *Below*, p. 107.

[2] Babington's *Confessions, below*, p. 56.

[3] Boyd, p. 683.

[4] In reporting this meeting to Walsingham, Gilbert represents that this is the first time he has seen Ballard. Ballard, on the other hand, was already aware of Gilbert's privity to the plot. Morris, p. 220; Hosack, ii. p. 602.

[5] B.M., Harleian MSS., 286, f. 136. Gilbert Gifford to Walsingham, autograph, some words in cipher, unpublished. See *below*, p. 109.

4th O.S.) which threw Ballard into feelings akin to despair. The conspirator had done his best to move his friends to rise, representing that the mobilisation of the invading army would be ready as soon as the rising could take place. Now he found this *impasse*. On the one hand, the men whom he relied upon refused absolutely to move; there was no chance of their acting the parts he had assigned to them without Mary's personal command. On the other hand, Morgan (3, 4 July) wanted to prevent *all* communication of catholics with the Queen. Instead of invoking her authority, they should rely on his (Morgan's) promises. He undertook indeed to bring their needs to the Queen in due time; but he had a poor reputation in the country, and his word was hardly more trusted than that of Ballard.[1]

Poor Ballard! 'With weeping he said he was utterly discredited: that thousands would be undone for his sake. For he had dealt with many, trusting upon Mendoza and Paget. That they sought all honour for themselves, and gave him but words.'

Had he been less excitable, Ballard would surely have seen that Morgan had something to say for himself; and that his message was at all events dictated by sincere attachment to his mistress.

Still the Welshman was clearly quite on the wrong line, because he conceived the assassination as something separate or separable from the rest of the conspiracy: while nothing was clearer than that invasion, escape, and assassination, or seizure, must be as nearly as possible simultaneous. Mary must therefore have some warning, and it was ridiculous for Morgan to think that he could wield Mary's authority.

If Ballard's idea of 'getting Mary's' approbation of 'all his actions' was wildly impracticable, Morgan's idea

---

[1] B.M., Harleian MS., 360, *n.* 27. A copy, endorsed 10 September. See *below*, p. 112.

of warning Mary by means of blood-curdling hints, dropped in postscripts to her secretaries, was equally fantastic. That, however, was his plan. On the 24th of June, after warning Mary that Ballard was employed on something so dangerous that she must not know anything about it, he added a note to her secretaries: 'There are many means in hand to remove the beast that troubleth all the world.' Again, on June 29th O.S. (9 July N.S.), he wrote to Mary's secretaries: 'There are some good members that attend opportunity to do the Queen of England a piece of service, which I trust will quiet many things, if it shall please God to lay his assistance to the course, for which I pray daily.'[1]

In truth such letters would seem to be not a whit less dangerous than those of Babington, without being of any *certain* use. It is true that less was eventually said about Morgan's letters; but this was because the Babington letters were answered, and so formed part of a *sequence* of singular completeness and force. For us, however, Morgan's letters must be considered as containing clear evidence of his guilt.

We now return to Gilbert Gifford, whom we left picking the brains of the excited Ballard. Eventually the pair went off to Babington, who is represented as having

'Declared the many dangers and difficulties touching a chief man for a head and for authority in this cause. For the noblemen would do nothing before they saw some certainty: and the rest being all equal, would bring confusion. Morgan sought for nothing but honour for himself, but Babington would seek honour for them that better deserved it. He himself would go [? to Mendoza] and solicit these matters' (*below*, p. 113).

From all this Gifford gathered that Babington wanted

---

[1] Morgan to Mary, June 24/4 July, Boyd, p. 469; June 29/9 July, *ibid.*, p. 480.

INTRODUCTION clvii

to be chief himself; and that Ballard backed him in this ambition. Finally Ballard wrote back to Morgan:

'That his demand was far unreasonable, to request the naming of the personages. So too it was to seek all to his own hand, being but a servant to the Queen; no more than they' (*below*, p. 113).

2. *Gilbert flies*, 20 *July*.

So for all his brave words to Savage, Ballard was evidently in the utmost uncertainty, and almost in despair about the rising, and thereupon the question arose, should he go across and report to Mendoza, as he had promised to do; or should he stay and keep the side together? He prepared for the one eventuality by getting Mr. Knight, a gentleman of Mr. Vice Chamberlain (Hatton), to procure him (about 17 July) a licence to travel abroad, under the name of Mr. Thoroughgood, of the Temple, who, it was pretended, was 'touched by the death of Best,' and wanted to escape the wrath of Sir Christopher Hatton.[1]

Then Ballard changed his mind again; and two undated notes from Gilbert to Walsingham carry on the story. The one note says:

'Ballard hath changed his opinion in going down with me. So, if your Honour list to take him, I desire to understand by this bearer' (*below*, p. 118).

The other says:

'I purpose immediately after the receipt of your Honour's letters, to go down to the country and withal to leave such

---

[1] Boyd, p. 592, *n.* 11, and p. 532; Morris, p. 235. Some blood feud between the followers of Hatton and of Walsingham seems here insinuated; but no explanation is at hand. This news about Ballard seems to have been sent down by Gilbert to Walsingham and Phelippes about 17 July, and Phelippes sent it back to Walsingham on 19 July. Ballard had in the meantime obtained the pass.

means with this bearer for the taking of Ballard that easily he shall compass it without any suspicion on my part.

'He [Ballard] told me this day of his dealing with Rowe concerning your Honour. He asked my advice therein. He knoweth not what to conceive.

'I told him that your Honour has showed great courtesy of late to Catholics, and that it might be your Honour meant friendly, and so he is persuaded.

'But what your Honour will appoint concerning the man, I can execute it' (*below*, p. 116).

In the meantime a certain reaction was setting in against the solicitations which Gifford had made at the beginning of the month, in order to revive the plot. Babington declares that he commissioned him to obtain ' from beyond the seas' answers on the following topics from some convenient ' authority.'

'I told him that I would he should assure us from beyond the seas by authority—

'1. That this action was directly lawful in every part.

'2. That there might be assurance given of the readiness of all such provision as was required.

'3. That some authority were granted for the (advancement) of men to dignities and some offices.

'4. And to have rewards granted for such as should undertake any dangerous attempt.

'Until all which were done, I advised him to withhold such as were employed against the Queen's person, which then were Savage, Gifford, and one (as I remember) said to be near Sir Walter Raleigh. If he did not, I protested and swore I would discover it unto the Queen.

'This he much disallowed, as Savage told me. He went over disliking much my courses. He said he was to pass by means of the French ambassador, as a Frenchman' (*below*, p. 61).

So Babington in his confession. When further interrogated, he said that the 'authority' for the third and fourth question would have been Queen Mary (*below*,

p. 70). The assurance, asked for in the second heading, was clearly meant to come from Mendoza. That asked for in the first heading should probably have come from the Nuncio at Paris, or from Dr. Allen. But to what an extraordinary pitch of confusion had not the plans of the conspirators come, when Babington at the very last hour wants reassurance, and that even as to the lawfulness of their undertaking; and actually asks Gilbert Gifford to obtain it! What more unpractical? What more certain to lead to calamity?

We have Gilbert's letter to Walsingham asking permission to go over and carry out the commission alone (see *below*, p. 114). But how characteristic is that note of a restless, traitorous mind! No names, no dates, no definite facts; and three out of the four quærenda mentioned above are left out. Now that we know the issue, we can see that what Gilbert really wants is to get away. So he omits references to Babington's question about the permissibility of the enterprise; and confines himself to the second heading, ' Whether the King of Spain intendeth anything or not.' May he go, and find out the answer to that?

For some reason unknown to us, Walsingham never answered this. It was perhaps sent by mistake to Phelippes at Chartley, and news of it only came round to Walsingham too late to be of any importance. The commission, however, remained, and so did Gilbert's desire to fly, before the catastrophe took place. As to this, Chateauneuf's memoir [1] has something to tell us.

On the 20th of July Gilbert, accompanied by Savage and one other, perhaps Ballard, came to ask at the French embassy, if they might send a man with letters to France, who might pass as servant to the next special messenger

---

[1] Labanoff, *Lettres de Marie Stuart*, vi. 275, end.

to Paris. As Dujardin was just back from Scotland, they were told that their man might ride with him next evening.

On the 21st Gilbert turned up alone, and said that he would go. At this Chateauneuf became suspicious, for he regarded the young man as Queen Mary's special servant, who ought not to be employed in other business. What was the reason of these frequent journeys abroad? Especially let him beware of that busy Mendoza.

Just at this point, alas! Chateauneuf's memoir ends abruptly, without telling us how the unscrupulous Gifford parried the French jealousy of Spain. But the true reason for his departure was confided to Phelippes later on. 'The greatest cause of my going away was that I feared to be brought to witness some matters concerning the Scottish Queen, face to face' (Boyd, ix. 221).[1]

And why had the fear of Mary's face gripped him at that particular moment? It was because on the 19th of July Phelippes had sent up the copy of Mary's fatal letter to Babington with the little 'gallows-mark,' ⌐ on the outside. The postman noted it, however, and the news came to the conspirators, which, says Walsingham to Phelippes on the 22nd of July, 'hath greatly increased their suspicion. My friend (*i.e.* Gilbert) remains still here.'[2] But unknown to Mr. Secretary, 'friend' Gifford had fled with Dujardin on the night before.

3. *Poley and Babington.*

Just as there could be no anxiety about Ballard, so long as Gifford kept sending in his notes, so there was nothing to fear about Babington whilst he was being shadowed by Poley. Poley afterwards wrote out a long account of

---

[1] R.O., *Mary Queen of Scots*, xx. *n.* 45. Gifford to Phelippes, no date, perhaps October 1586. See also *below*, p. 121.

[2] Morris, p. 245.

the way he had done this,¹ and some details of his manœuvres must now be given. The confession is not a very exciting or inspiriting document. It tells us little that is Machiavellian about Poley, but much about the youthful Babington's easy-going, plastic character, with his marked love of comforts and of prolonged discussions. In a previous section the commencement of their intimacy in June has been described, also the assurances of Poley, that he would procure the licence to travel. He was also ready to swear secrecy and fidelity to Babington and his projects before he knew what these might be, though he was in general aware that negotiations were in progress between Mary on the one side and Morgan on the other. On Saturday the 9th of July, he had reported to Mr. Secretary the contents of Morgan's letter to Babington, of the 16th of May,² and Walsingham, having Babington's letter to Mary of the 6th of July in his keeping, was only urgent that Babington should again come to court, and make suit not, as he had hitherto done, in general terms only, but explain in detail the services which he would render, if he received the licence to travel.

Accordingly, on the 13th of July, Babington saw the Secretary for the third and last time. Walsingham urged the young man with great instance to say all he could, telling that he had been 'especially warned against him.' Indeed, it is said that he even told him, that he knew he had corresponded with the Scottish Queen.³

Babington, who had so far flattered himself he was getting the best of the interviews, was much frightened, and asked Poley afterwards, whether it would not really

---

[1] R O , *Mary Queen of Scots*, xix n 26. Boyd, pp 595-602.
[2] Boyd, p 596
[3] So Weston, writing twenty years later, Morris, *Troubles*, ii 185, cited above

l

be better to open out to Mr. Secretary. Poley's answer is only known through his own version of it to Walsingham, to whom he of course said that he had told Babington he need fear no dishonourable treatment at Walsingham's hands.

At this Babington asked him how he came to know so much about the Secretary, and Poley coolly said, because he had performed what he (Babington) was offering to perform—that is, he had given Walsingham 'intelligence' derived from catholics.

'Impossible!' answered Babington. 'All men of note, being catholics, hold you in suspicion.' [*I.e.* you cannot have knowledge from them.]

Poley answered that he gave in news he had derived from Morgan.

'How is that possible, considering how suspicious Morgan is?'

Poley laughed, 'Such points are better imagined, than questioned or resolved.'[1]

Poley's policy in reporting this interview was, of course, to represent his conduct in a light as pleasing to Walsingham as possible. He wanted to leave the impression that Babington deceived himself. Babington's version of the conversation would doubtless have been different, but his 'confessions' throw no light on the subject. Still there can be no possible question that Babington must have been at least as obtuse and foolish as he is here represented. For he continued to trust more and more to a man whom he knew, or at least must have suspected, to be playing a double game.

Walsingham had told Babington to set down in writing precise particulars of the 'services' he proposed to render, when abroad; but Poley, who fell ill for several days at

---

[1] Poley's *Confession*, Boyd, p. 597.

INTRODUCTION

this juncture, says nothing of the dispatch of the letter, and it seems never to have been written.

But when Poley next reported to Walsingham (about the 25th of July) he told him, the Secretary, that there was a plot against the Queen's life. Walsingham, however, did not show any surprise at this, but put him off with talk of an alleged plot in a very different quarter. Four suspicious men had sailed from Boulogne, and also one Douglas a Scottish Jesuit, and one Yardley a suspect. If Babington would give information to lead to their arrest, the service would be sincerely appreciated.

Babington, when he heard this, professed all zeal for the work assigned him, and next day told Poley that, though he could find nothing about the supposed Scottish Jesuit, the suspicious men who left Boulogne were really two Jesuit Fathers, Garnet and Southwell, who were already in London.[1] Being under suspicion, he, Babington, did not like to approach them without Walsingham's formal permission. Poley having brought this to Walsingham came back with leave for Babington to visit the Jesuits. This was Friday the 29th of July.

It is remarkable that Father Southwell, in his first letter after reaching London, dated the 25th of July, says, 'At the court there is said to be a matter in hand, which, if it prove successful, bodes extremity of suffering to us: if unsuccessful, all will be well.'[2] A Delphic utterance, no doubt; but one that points clearly to his having been in communication at least remotely with people who knew a good deal.

---

[1] Walsingham had probably heard of these Jesuits through Morgan's garrulous letters of 3 and 14 July (N.S., *i.e.* 23 June and 4 July O.S.). Boyd, p. 499.

[2] *Catholic Record Society*, v. 308. Later on (*ibid.*, p. 314) Southwell blames strongly 'the wicked and ill-fated conspiracy.' But when writing his *Supplication*, pp. 30-40, he knew more about the circumstances, and his blame is more discriminating. See *The Month*, March 1912.

But to return to Poley and Babington. It was Friday the 29th of July that Poley brought back the message that Babington should shadow and betray the newly arrived Jesuits, Garnet and Southwell. 'What,' asked Babington, 'before it is surely understood that they were practising against the State?' The two began to argue, and eventually, Poley having once more given him his hand and the promise of secrecy, Babington began that evening and the two next days to tell him about the plot. Not indeed that he betrayed his companions (except Ballard); what he revealed was, in reality, the plot of George Gifford, Mawde, and the rest at the time *before* he joined it. But more recent events were also mentioned, especially Queen Mary's second letter, which Babington was then answering. Poley saw this; indeed, when Babington came in from a walk, he found his new friend coolly making a copy of it. Poley thereupon tore up his notes, while Babington said he would take the letter itself to Walsingham. Poley remembered the letter well enough to give a good account of it in his confessions. After three days of confidences like this, Babington bade him go and prepare Walsingham for a (more or less) full disclosure next day.

On Wednesday morning, the 3rd of August, Poley rode down to Richmond, where Walsingham then was, bursting with his secret. But Walsingham received him quite coolly, and put off the interview with Babington till the Saturday following, having previously told Phelippes that he did not mean to see his victim until he was a prisoner (*below*, p. 134). When Poley returned and told his story, both men were filled with fear.

Nevertheless Poley had done Walsingham a very good turn by keeping Babington quiet and comfortable in his garden. Walsingham himself confessed it, 'I do not find but that Poley hath dealt honestly with me' (*below*, p. 135), and indeed but for the enchantments which the old intriguant had thrown over the boyish leader of the conspirators, persuading him that he would be 'in great favour with the Queen' as soon as he made his discovery, 'he would not have tarried so long upon so extreme points of danger.'[1]

Another event of these final days, not often mentioned, is that Ballard (perhaps in imitation of Babington) also wrote to Walsingham, offering to turn Queen's evidence. John Charnock was sent to court with the letter, but again Walsingham would not see him. The facts were mentioned in court during Charnock's trial, but excited no comment.[2]

4. *Babington's Last Letter to Mary*, 19 July-3 August.

We now go back to Mary's letter, a copy of which Phelippes had sped up from Chartley in Staffordshire to London on Tuesday, the 19th of July. A special post should have done the distance, about 150 miles, in 24 hours.[3] Walsingham, on the receipt of the news, probably took orders from 'on high,' that is from the Queen; and it was not until Friday the 22nd that he wrote and told Phelippes to return and bring up Mary's original letter with him.[4] But Phelippes was then anxious to pick up Mary's promised letter to Mendoza, which (he hoped) might show Babington's influence, and so he stayed on. For some unknown reason that letter was delayed until 29 July/8 August.

On the 25th Phelippes sent in a letter (now lost) to Mary, keeping up his usual deceptions; but the game was now very nearly over. Phelippes left Chartley on the afternoon of Wednesday the 27th of July, and Poulet

---

[1] For the incidents of this section, see Poley's *Confession*, Boyd, viii. 600.
[2] See *State Trials*. Trial of Charnock.
[3] Morris, p. 224. But 36 hours (p. 246) was not infrequent.
[4] Morris, p. 245.

made sure he would have been with Walsingham by Friday the 29th.[1] The postscript to Mary's letter was probably added later in the day.

At night on this same Friday the 29th, Babington received Mary's answer, written on the 17th; and there can be no question that, when it reached Babington's hands, it had appended to it a postscript, asking Babington to name 'the six gentlemen.' This is clear from the recollection of the letter given in the confessions both of Babington and of Dunne.[2] It is also owned, in language that cannot be misunderstood, by Walsingham (*below*, p. 133). A draft by Phelippes is extant and endorsed as such by him (p. 46); and the fact is affirmed by Camden.[3] It was also a very easy task to add a few more dashes and dots at the end of other dashes and dots, and to an expert penman like Arthur Gregory, or Phelippes, a very simple operation. The object of the postscript was, not to encourage the plot, but to get Babington to set down the names of the 'six' chief conspirators. Those who would not believe Walsingham guilty of inciting to assassination directly, will perhaps see little improbability in his having sanctioned a postscript such as this. But whether one admits this probability or not, the evidence for the existence of the postscript is overwhelming.

'"I received" says Babington, "a letter [on the 29th of July] in the same cipher by which I wrote unto her, but by another messenger, which was a homely serving man in a blue coat. He also brought me a letter from his master [really from Phelippes] unto me, by which he promised to discover himself by the next dispatch unto me, subscribed no name, and willed me not to be curious or inquisitive until

---

[1] Morris, p. 246.
[2] Babington, *Confessions*, p. 65; Dunne's *Examination*, Boyd, p. 692.
[3] Camden, *Annales* (under 1586), p. 438. See also Conyers Read, *The Bardon Papers* (Camden Soc. III. xvii.), p. 133.

his own coming. The letter enclosed, he said, came from the Queen of Scots." '[1]

Babington told the man to return for his answer in a day or two.

Indolent and excited, Babington had not the patience to work out the cipher by himself. 'Mr. Tichborne did assist in the deciphering, for that I could not endure the pain [fatigue].' When done, Babington showed the copy to Ballard, and afterwards even to Poley.

The answer he eventually drew up was not ready till the 3rd of August. It stated that they had all been in great alarm, as to which he will only say, for the present, that it originated in Mawde, ' who came out of France with Ballard. Ballard acquainted him with the cause, and employed him of late into Scotland. By his treachery we and the whole plot have been brought into extreme danger. . . . By what means we have in part prevented this . . . with our final determinations, my next letter shall discover.'

What those ' means ' were, what ' our final determinations,' we do not know. It must be remembered that Mawde was so far the only danger suspected. As he had joined Ballard at the time of the previous plot (that of George Gifford), Babington may have thought that by denouncing it, he would be safeguarding everything. But this is only conjecture. In reality the searchers were now close on the tracks of the whole party.

5. *A Little Comedy*.

Then ensued a little comedy. While Poley was carefully keeping Babington in his own house to prevent his bolting, Phelippes, Berden, and Milles were hunting for him in vain

---

[1] Babington, *Confessions*, p. 64. The covering note was, of course, from Phelippes, and the accuracy which Babington remembered it, shows that it had awakened suspicions.

at his accustomed lodgings. First a messenger was sent to ask Babington for his answer to Mary. But he could not be found. Phelippes thought he might have slipped down towards Chartley, and Ballard also disappeared about the same time. Great were the lamentations for the unexplained absence of Gilbert. 'Sorry I am,' wrote Walsingham, 'that G. G. is absent. I marvel greatly how this humour of estranging himself cometh upon him.'

That night, 2 August, Walsingham was quite put out. Next morning, 3 August, he wrote to Phelippes (*below*, p. 133).

'You will not believe how much I am grieved at the event of this case. I fear the addition of the postscript hath bred jealousy [suspicion], and praying God to send us better success, I commit you to His protection. Your loving friend,

FRA: WALSINGHAM.'

A second note to Phelippes on the same day approved of his plans for the arrest of Ballard,' but with no other course of proceeding than with an ordinarye Iesueste.' That is to say the warrant and the searchers were only to describe him as a priest. Moreover, so great was Walsingham's love for secrecy, that the warrant for Ballard's arrest was to be signed, not by himself, but by the Lord Admiral. As for Babington, if Phelippes thought that an answer to Mary's letter might yet be got from him, he might wait till Friday (5 August), but not longer; for in any case 'better to lack the answer, than to lack the man.'

6. *The End of the Plot, 3-15 August.*

On the evening of the same day, the 3rd of August, Phelippes 'abridged his honour's anxiety' with the happy news that he had discovered that Babington was still in town, at Poley's garden.[1] Next day, Thursday, August the

---

[1] R.O., *Mary Queen of Scots*, xix. *n.* 6. Boyd, p. 584.

4th, Poley's house was surrounded, and Ballard arrested there between 11 and 12 o'clock, perhaps before the eyes of Babington, who was still lying in bed.[1]

Babington was naturally startled, if not terrified, by this stroke. But second thoughts were more reassuring, seeing that he was not touched, while Ballard was seized for the honourable cause of his priesthood. What shall he do next? What did Poley, so practised in court procedure, advise?

Poley of course assured him, that if he would remain quiet, all would go well. He himself would go to court and arrange matters with Walsingham. He would plead that the arrest would prove most injurious to those promised services, which Walsingham had welcomed. If Ballard might at least be removed from public prison for a week, as taken under a wrong name, people would think he had been discharged, and Babington would not lose his reputation. Such was the story told in Poley's memoir; which having lost the last page, now ends abruptly with the words, 'In this unlikely hope I left him assured, and went to court.' On his arrival Poley himself was put under arrest. The reason for Poley's arrest, however, probably was not (as older writers on Mary's side used to think) merely that it might serve as a blind to deceive the catholics. It was, in the first instance, presumably due to the jealousy of Walsingham's followers against a new-comer from Blount's or Sidney's household. Milles had written on the 4th 'P[oley] is a notable knave with no trust in him' (Boyd, p. 588). But after his arrest, Walsingham, who had never been against him, appears to have been quite satisfied by his confession. He was kept for a while in the Tower, but afterwards set free, to continue his old trade.

---

[1] Milles to Walsingham, Boyd, p. 588: Poley's *Confession*, R.O., *Mary Queen of Scots*, xix. 26. Boyd, p. 602.

7. *The Conspirators disperse.*

Poley being thus unexpectedly, and in appearance inexplicably under arrest, Babington was again the prey to conflicting emotions, now swayed by anger and resentment, now again by fear, anguish, and yearning. Inspired by these feelings, he wrote to Poley a letter [1] which is quite a remarkable production from a literary point of view, as Babington's utterances so often were.

'ROBYN,

'*Sollicitæ non possunt curæ mutare aranei stamina fusi.*[2] I am ready to endure whatsoever shall be inflicted. *Et facere et pati Romanorum est.*[3] What my course hath been towards Mr. Secretary, you can witness, what my love towards you, yourself can best tell. Proceedings at my lodgings have been very strange. I am the same I allwayes pretended. I pray God you be, and ever so remayne towards me. Take hede to your own part, least of these my misfortunes you beare the blame. *Est exilium inter malos vivere.*[4]

'Farewell, sweete Robyn, if, as I take thee, true to me. If not, Adieu, *omnium bipedum nequissimus.*[5]

'Retorne me thine answere for my satisfaction, and my diamond, and what else thou wilt. The furnace is prepared, wherein our faithe must be tryed. Farewell till we mete, which God knows when.

'Thyne, how farre thou knowest,

'ANTHONY BABINGTON.'

At another of these moments of excitement, Babington suddenly resolved to put the plot against the Queen's person into instant execution (4 August). 'Forced by the

---

[1] B.M., *Lansdowne*, 49. n. 25. Contemporary copy, no date. The MS. has several careless readings, especially 'rati' for 'aranei' in the first line. See Boyd, p. 658; Lingard, *note* R, vi. 423, 695, gives 4 August as date.

[2] Nor care nor cautel ever mends; of spider's threads the broken ends.

[3] Both to do and to bear [this is worthy] of Romans.

[4] To live amidst the wicked; what an exile!

[5] Of all two-footed things, the wickedest.

extreme danger, and no hope of any pardon for so hateful an offence, the attempt upon the Queen's person was then, and never till then, resolved on my part.' He met some of the conspirators in 'Paul's Walk,' and urged Savage to undertake the deed at once. Savage, who always mechanically undertook whatever he was urged to do, consented. He was furnished with arms and money by Babington, and Charnock was appointed to support him in his desperate enterprise. But, as before, nothing whatsoever came of his promises.

Meanwhile, in Poley's absence, the task of 'playing' with Babington was entrusted to an agent more in touch with the Secretary's staff. This was his man Scudamore, to whom Babington should have given money before, in order to obtain the travelling licence.[1] A letter was therefore brought by him to Babington from Walsingham, saying that the arrest of Ballard had been due not to him, but to that officious magistrate [and notorious persecutor of catholics] Mr. Richard Young. Walsingham could not indeed openly stop Young; but if Babington wanted to escape him, he had better keep in the company of Scudamore.[2]

Walsingham's kindly note restored Babington's confidence; he took off Scudamore and Scudamore's man to dine at a neighbouring hostel: but during the meal a note had come to Scudamore from the court, and Babington, sitting at his side, detected that it gave orders for his arrest. This nerved him for action. Without betraying the least anxiety and leaving his rich cloak and sword on the back of his chair, he stepped towards the bar, saying he would 'pay the shot.' Then slipping out he ran on foot to Westminster, where he met Gage and Charnock, and they

---

[1] Boyd, p. 595.
[2] Camden, *Annales*, 1625, p. 439, *translation* of 1635, p 306

fled northwards to St. John's Wood (5 August). In its now vanished glades they were joined by Dunne and Barnwell, and lay hidden there nearly ten days, until at last hunger forced them to approach Harrow, where (in spite of a proclamation for their arrest) they begged and obtained some food from a catholic family called Bellamy, living in the old, moated house of Uxendon.[1] The family eventually had to atone for their perhaps excusable charity by the executions of two of the younger sons, Bartholomew and Jeremy, and the death in prison of their venerable grandmother Catherine Page.[2]

Near Uxendon Babington and his companions were arrested on the 14th of August, and were brought up in triumph to the Tower on the 15th. Tilney, Charnock, and Gage, with the two Bellamies, were at once imprisoned there. Ballard, who had been examined before, was now probably to be tortured. Tilney, Savage, and Tichborne had attempted to escape southwards, but had been already arrested in the London suburbs. Salisbury got away to the west, and after some fortunate escapes, was arrested

---

[1] Only the moat now remains. The family was finally ruined by Topcliff, who arrested here the poet Southwell in 1591. For the sad story of the fall of the Bellamies, see Simpson in *Rambler*, 1857, i. 98-115. Morris, *Troubles*, ii. 44-66. The latter does not advert to that ruin having taken place in two stages.

[2] According to the catholics (*e.g.* Father Weston, *apud* Morris, *Troubles*, ii. 187), Bartholomew Bellamy died under or in consequence of torture: according to protestants he ' hanged himself in the Tower ' (*Catholic Record Society*, ii. 257). Oddly enough the Tower Bills (September 1586) do not mention Bartholomew at all (*Catholic Record Society*, iii. 24). See also Morris, *Troubles*, ii. p. 49.

While at or near Uxendon the conspirators received the sacraments for the last time from Mr. Davis, a priest who had just escaped imprisonment. In later years Davis wrote about the plot, ' Of that tragedy Sir Francis Walsingham was the chief actor and contriver, as I gathered by Mr. Babington himself, who was with me the night before he was apprehended ' (quoted by Challoner, *Missionary Priests*, i. no. 55). Such was the verdict on Walsingham, which catholics of that day were almost sure to arrive at, on hearing Babington's story.

with Jones in Cheshire. Edward Abington managed to avoid the pursuivants in his native country, Worcestershire, for a month; and Edward Windsor kept free in the same way for half a year, and then through interest escaped with his life. Babington and the other prisoners, after being examined at Ely House, the London residence of Sir Christopher Hatton, were sent to the Tower on the 24th and 25th of August.

8. *Gilbert and Mendoza (? 1-11 August).*

Though the plot was now dead, we must, before we close this section, return once more to Gilbert Gifford.

We have heard Babington's answer to Gilbert's last attempts to galvanise the plot into life. He should go abroad again, said Babington, and bring back new decisions from catholic authorities that the plot was praiseworthy in all details, and that the Spanish auxiliaries were in readiness. He may even have given him formal letters of credence for the purpose, or Gilbert may have forged them. At all events, leaving London as we have seen on the 20th/30th or 21st/31st of July, he would have been in Paris about the 25th July/4th August, and a few days later he had an interview with Mendoza, of which the ambassador gives a long and interesting account on the 3rd/13th August.

Mendoza had no knowledge of the antecedents of the young man with whom he was talking, when Gilbert produced his 'proper' credentials, and spoke glibly of his commissions and of his honoured family. The ambassador was so impressed by this, that he adopted the word 'el gentilhombre' as his sobriquet.

Instead, however, of treating of the commissions, which Babington had entrusted to him (and Babington's statement has all the appearance of verisimilitude), he played his part of *provocateur* with the utmost boldness and consummate art. Instead of inquiring whether Spain was ready, and showing that the English catholics could not rise till this was assured, he tells the Spaniard that troops are *not* required, that the English are *sure to rise*, and inflames him by every art to write to England in favour of the assassination. The letters, he knew, would be intercepted, and he, Gilbert, would secure a new triumph.[1]

He began, therefore, with a long recital of the names of the English nobility and gentry, and of the soldiers and sailors, who were pledged to rise. Then comes a description of the Babington plot (p. 605), which is only delayed until they have Mendoza's approval.

Babington had in truth insisted that Spanish troops were indispensable. Gilbert says, 'They will *not* ask for troops to be sent.' 'If I,' wrote Mendoza, 'will give them my word, that they shall have help from the Netherlands in case they need it . . . they will at once put into execution the plan to kill the Queen . . . and they . . . beg me most earnestly for God's sake to send them an instant answer.'

Flop! went Mendoza into the trap, with even less discernment than Savage, Babington, or Mary had shown.

'I received "the gentleman," wrote the befooled veteran, 'in a way which the importance of his proposal deserved, as it was so christian, just, and advantageous to the Holy Catholic Faith and your Majesty's service.'

Alack! alack! for the political morality of the sixteenth century, when strained by adverse circumstances!

'I wrote them two letters by different routes, one in Italian and the other in Latin, encouraging them in the enterprise.

---

[1] *Spanish Calendar*, pp. 603-4. The Spanish text is in A. Teulet, *Relations politiques*, v. 371; the original is in Paris, Archives Nationals, 1564, 135 (olim 150), collated for me by R. P. de Joannis. It will be remembered that what Babington had asked for was the declaration 'by authority,' presumably by Allen or the Nuncio, that this assassination was lawful.

If they succeed in killing the Queen [Note which action is *now* to come first], they should have the assistance they required from the Netherlands. Troops would not be needed at once, and afterwards (it seems) only in relatively small numbers' (p. 608).

'And so he went on—"I promised," "I urged," "I thanked," and in the end "I advised that they should either kill or seize Cecil, Walsingham, Lord Hunsdon, Knollys, and Beale of the Council."'

It is quite likely that Gilbert had suggested all this to Mendoza. It corresponds to the 'Star-Chamber practice,' of which he had probably often talked with Savage.

Then the ambassador went on to reassure his master:

'This is the most serious plot which has been heard of from the English Catholics. They have never before proposed to take away the Queen, which is now the first step they intend to take. . . .'

Finally comes what was, of course, to him the real point:

'If the Queen falls, the country will submit without effusion of blood, and the war in the Netherlands will be at an end, which will result in infinite advantage to your Majesty's interests and to those of your dominions.'

Sad indeed it is to see the representative of a great power fall to the profession of principles so unworthy, principles which, however, were not unacceptable to his master, as the King's 'postille' (marginal notes) unmistakably show.[1] And the religious cant, though less sanctimonious than that of Poulet, is equally detestable. Only in its perfect frankness is the Spanish immorality somewhat less repulsive than the English.

With this Mendoza sent 'a statement of the Counties of England, and their present position'; it contains surmises as to the numbers of catholics, according to counties,

---

[1] *Spanish Calendar*, p. 608. King Philip noted in the margin against these words of Mendoza's, 'That was well done.'

capable of bearing arms in the whole of England, which was estimated at 30,200 in all.

We are naturally curious to know whether this was Ballard's old report, or one brought over by Gilbert Gifford. Mendoza, though indefinite, seems to mean the former. He says it was drawn up by '*un*' *clerigo*, whom he had sent to England. This corresponds with Ballard and his mission; and, moreover, Mendoza uses 'el clerigo' as Ballard's *sobriquet* in this very letter. It is true that he here speaks of 'un' (not 'el') clerigo, but small inexactitudes were common in those days, and in Mendoza's letters not at all unfrequent. In any case, the paper was not made primarily for the Spaniards, who are never mentioned in it—but for Queen Mary's party. Loyalty to her has inspired the writer, who probably was Ballard.[1]

Whether Gilbert had anything to say in the construction of the paper is a matter of conjecture; and even if it was altogether Ballard's, its authority would be next to nothing.

Regarded exclusively as a work of art, Gilbert's dexterity and diplomacy at this interview surely deserves our unqualified admiration; and it is almost a disappointment to add that the astute plan fell absolutely flat. The letters were not intercepted, they never reached England at all. In the turmoil and excitement which resulted from the arrest of the conspirators, all ways of communication were cut; Morgan recovered the letters from the French post, and Gilbert's magnificent stroke fell harmless, except that in later times Mendoza's letter has come to light, and exposed him to the severe strictures, which he richly deserves.[2]

---

[1] See *above*, pp. xcv, xcvi.

[2] Indeed, even at that time, something transpired. Mendoza had employed Grately to cipher his letters, and Grately told Gilbert later that the Spanish message was, 'Ammazzate la Bastarda excommunicata heretica.' Gilbert sent this on in his cipher of about January 1587, too

Had such trumps fallen into Walsingham's hands at that moment, it is hard to estimate how terrible might have been the consequences for Mary, for the catholics of England, and indeed for the cause of catholicism in the North, for an enthusiastic protestant crusade might easily have been started. Mendoza's previous letters to Ballard had, as Gilbert knew, been carried to England in the French ambassador's bags, and he had doubtless made, or hoped to make, preparations for their interception. In fact, the French dispatches were seized, though nothing was found in them: but this violation of the law of nations was probably not due to Gilbert.

A noticeable feature about this solicitation is that Gilbert seems to have acted throughout on his own initiative. Walsingham and Phelippes did not then know that he was in Paris, and they were not a little vexed at his being away from his usual post in London. Nor when he began to correspond again can I find any allusion to his part in this exploit, though he did mention the part played by Grately (Boyd, ix. 220).

From this one infers that he did not himself know how deep an impression he had made on Mendoza. The ambassador's diplomatic bearing and Spanish dignity probably concealed from the Englishman the depth to which he had been affected. The letters were entrusted to other channels, and Mendoza insisted on Gilbert remaining in Paris for a time, to avoid the suspicion which would be aroused by frequent coming and going. It was conceivably this precaution which upset Gilbert's plans. Anyhow, we see that he acted on his own responsibility in these matters, without waiting for Walsingham's orders.

---

late for Walsingham's use (now, *Mary Queen of Scots*, xx. 45; printed Boyd, ix. 220). As Grately was in the pay of the English ambassador, we may be sure that he had also been told. But the question again arises, can we believe these slippery rogues implicitly?

The same thing had doubtless happened before. There had been egging on of Savage and Babington, about which Walsingham knew in general, but did not want to know in detail. We are not to assume that the extant letters of Gilbert to his master told him everything he said and did. They probably only conveyed such a minimum as was necessary (after fuller conferences by word of mouth with Phelippes and himself) for receiving further directions.

SECTION IX

The Coup de Grâce, August 1586-February 1587.

1. *Walsingham's Task.*

For some time back we have known that Mary was in the toils; we have now to see how the final blow was given. It is a mournful, sordid scene, in which Mary comes out a heroine by the exercise of the highest moral courage. These events, however, may be given on a briefer scale; partly because they are more widely known, partly because they contain so many issues irrelevant to our main object, which is to ascertain the truth about the Babington plot.

That Elizabeth's government would avoid giving the secrets of the plot to the public followed at once from the way in which the conspiracy had been instigated, nursed, and exposed. The part which Walsingham and his agents had played must be kept quiet at all costs. If public attention had been directed to the fact that Elizabeth's ministers had conspired against the heiress to the throne, it would have caused an outcry in that day as it would in ours; so great was the respect then paid to royalty, so easily might the dormant sympathy with the Scottish Queen have been aroused.

This then is to be the first condition of the inquiry—

that it must conceal the origin of the conspiracy, and the methods by which it had been carried on. Before the 5th of August Elizabeth had commanded Walsingham ' to keep to himself the depth and manner of the discovery.' This order he carried out perfectly, not only concealing everything that he had done, but also all the activities of his agents; and where was it that they had not given encouragement and assistance.[1]

Still, on the whole this was easy work. No one who glances at the *State Trials* of those days, especially at the trials of those whose treason was in reality their religion, can fail to be struck by the facility with which the State got its way, however weak its case. And so it fell out here.

Though the seizure of Mary's secretaries and of her papers was one of the first steps in the prosecution of the plot, no further steps against her were taken for several weeks. The letters were carried to Windsor, and Phellipes went down with them, to explain to the Queen their significance, and ' understood from her Majesty's self how well she accepted his service.'[2]

I do not suppose that Phelippes told the Queen everything about Gilbert's provocation, nor about Poley and Mawde's shadowing of the conspirators. Had she known how unreal and fictitious the whole plot had been, she could hardly have been so very much alarmed, as she undoubtedly was. In fact, her fits of terror now became one of the determining features of the situation. The frightening feature was that Savage and Barnwell had been to her court, and that three of the gentlemen of her guard,

---

[1] Walsingham to Elizabeth, Tytler, iv. 130; Boyd, p. 589, undated, but must be after 4 August. The letter also shows that Elizabeth was interested in the tricks of the detective system, in *provocateurs*, ciphers, etc., and gave advice as to their application.

[2] Morris, p. 245.

viz. Tilney, Abington, and Windsor, were implicated as participators, while George Gifford was also charged. These defections in her very entourage were naturally calculated to arouse both anxiety and suspicion, in a lady accustomed to live with great openness before her people. We cannot wonder at Elizabeth's letter to Sir Amias,[1] written in the first burst of her indignation, and full of reproach for the 'vile murderess.'

It was natural that the conspirators should have been taken in hand first. They all confessed in full, as soon as they were arrested, or after a very short delay. Ballard, Savage, and Tichborne were the first captured, and their recorded confessions began on the 8th, 10th, and 11th of August respectively. Those of Babington, Barnwell, and Tilney began on the 20th and 21st. The confessions of all were finished by the 5th of September.[2]

Whether any were tortured except Ballard is uncertain; probably some were, and of course they all knew that the rack was waiting for them in case they were obdurate. The reason why so much severity was shown to Ballard will probably have been to obtain from him the names of those who had made him promises of aid in case of an invasion. For a moment he wavered, but he was chivalrously assisted in the Tower itself by Father Crichton, an adventuresome Scottish Jesuit,[3] and after this he stood firm. We do not know that any beyond the conspirators were named by him, except casually or by inadvertence. Upon the whole he bore himself with a courage worthy of a better cause.

Babington confessed very fully, and, as was his wont, with eloquence and good reasoning. Perhaps the most

---

[1] Morris, p. 267.

[2] All that remains of them is a set of extracts on points needed for their trials. A full summary of these is in Boyd, viii. 680, etc.

[3] See Crichton's *Memoir*, below, p. 151.

regrettable feature in his confessions was his endeavour to intimidate the Queen by declarations of the certainty of a Spanish invasion, and of further attempts against her life. Deceived as he was on those points, there was perhaps no great wonder in his speaking as he did. Nevertheless in his inexperience, he was playing foolishly into the hands of the persecutors.[1]

On the 13th, 14th, and 15th of September the conspirators were tried in two batches, and of course condemned. The proceedings would have shocked our modern ideas of justice. The indictment having been read, the prisoners (except Babington) all pleaded *Not Guilty* to the charge of intending to murder the Queen, though they admitted the other counts of the indictment. But on being pressed they all pleaded *Guilty* to the whole indictment. No explanation of this change was asked for, nor can any be given definitely now; but to judge from their confessions we may surmise that their meaning was, not that they never imagined assassination, but that they had not arrived at any final conclusion about it. They had no idea at all how they had been betrayed.

On the second day the defence was much more spirited, and there was a strong though vain appeal that lawful witnesses should be produced. To which the Queen's solicitor, Thomas Egerton, pointed out that they had been indicted under a statute of 25 King Edward III., by which *imagining* treason was made a capital offence. 'How then,' asked the solicitor, 'can the secret cogitations, which lie in the minds of traitors, be proved by honest men?'[2] A brief but vivid summary of the judicial procedure throughout this case.

Nothing at all came out in the evidence regarding the

---

[1] See *below*, p. 86, n. 3.   [2] *State Trials*, 1730, p. 129.

way in which the plot had been commenced, carried on, or detected; nothing about the Queen of Scots; and we now know that Elizabeth gave orders that this was to be so, because she feared that some friend of Mary might be so irritated thereby as to murder her forthwith.[1] She was still under the spell of fear, which Walsingham had cast over her.

For the same reason she insisted to Lord Burghley that 'for more terror' some extra torment should be added to the already appalling sentence of quartering alive.[2] The execution was therefore conducted slowly; but the public was shocked, and next day the culprits were allowed to hang till they were dead. Yet the printed account of the executions attributes this clemency to Elizabeth. 'The Queen being informed of the severity used in the executions the day before, and detesting such cruelty, gave express orders that these should be used more favourably.'[3]

It is an open question whether we should regard this as a mere flourish of flattery, or as a sober record of yet another *volte face* on Elizabeth's part, during this period of excitement.

As soon as the conspirators had suffered, the question of Mary's execution began to be agitated. As we have heard, Walsingham was keeping in the background, and Lord Burghley was given the lead. And now was felt the ill effect of the references to Burghley's friendliness in the secret correspondence. They had been begun by Morgan, and Walsingham had (3 May) 'Salved that packet that toucheth "the great person" (*i.e* Burghley), as neither he nor the cause shall take lack.'[4] That is to say, while showing Elizabeth the intercepted letters, he had kept back that particular letter lest her jealousy should

---

[1] *Bardon Papers*, p. 45. [2] *Ibid.*, and p. 47.
[3] *State Trials*, p. 135. [4] Morris, p. 189.

be excited. But, if Walsingham told Phelippes of his manœuvre, he probably also told Burghley, when the opportune moment to do so arrived. For this Walsingham may have waited, for Mary in July asked her ambassador to make some of her grievances known to Burghley, hoping that he might remedy them; and Phelippes, while sending on a decipher of her words, writes, 'She is very bold to make way to the "great personage" (*i.e.* Lord Burghley), and I fear he will be forward in satisfying her, till he see Babington's treason.'[1]

From these words of Walsingham's underling we infer without doubt that Cecil was by comparison friendly to Mary, but that Walsingham had in his hands the means of making him her enemy, by showing him her correspondence. Walsingham no doubt did so, as soon as the trial of the Queen was resolved upon. For from thence onward Burghley and Hatton, the leaders of the moderates, were pushed to the fore, and Burghley wrote to Elizabeth's private secretary, Davison (15 October, Boyd, ix. 102), boasting of his activity against the Scottish Queen.

2. *The Secretaries confess.*

We do not know precisely at what date it was resolved to try Mary for her life. Phelippes, a very well-informed outsider, at first, 19 July, reckoned only on the execution of Nau and Curll.[2] Walsingham, in his answer, 22 July,[3] 'hoped a good course would be held in this cause.' Everything depended on Elizabeth.

Throughout the month of August dealings with the conspirators, and the study of the papers captured at Chartley, had occupied every one's attention. Nau and

---

[1] Morris, p. 235. Phelippes adds, 'I doubt not your Honour hath care enough not to discover which way the wind comes in,' *i.e.* not even Burghley was to know how the plot had been worked.

[2] Morris, p. 235.   [3] Morris, p. 245.

Curll were confined in Milles's house, and we hear of their having little disputes on philosophic and religious questions.

The secretaries knew that Mary's papers had been captured; but they did not suspect that Phelippes was thoroughly familiar with the whole correspondence: he had all the original ciphers with the deciphers of all the papers sent to Mary, and copies by himself of all the letters which had come from her. In this collection, however, one indispensable document was still wanting. There was as yet no copy of Mary's all-important letter to Babington, the very face of which would not awaken serious suspicion. For if a copy of the letter, in the form familiar to us, had been given to Babington and his friends, without preface or preparation, they would at once have noticed the absence of the postscript, which he, Dunne, and Poley all described quite clearly. On the other hand, if the secretaries or Mary had been shown a copy with the postscript, they would at once have perceived the forger's hand. Whether it was Phelippes, Walsingham, or some other who planned the clever fraud which was now practised on the confiding young Babington, we cannot say; but the extant papers show us pretty clearly the stages in which the deceit was worked out.

Even in his earliest confessions, now lost, Babington had said everything he remembered about the letters, and in the first surviving examination (18 August), he says, first, that he will now pass over the letter, as he has already said all that he could call to mind. Then, being told to write down his recollection again, he does so at the end of his paper, and upon the whole very fully, accurately, and he mentions the postscript (*below*, p. 65). On the 20th we find that his memory was refreshed by having further clauses laid before him; and he is asked if he remembers them. Yes, he does; and then he rewrites them, in improved order and language. Evidently he was in a mood to oblige the government as far as he could. But his attention having been fixed on the earlier parts of the letter, he *now passes the postscript* unmentioned (*below,* pp. 77-9).

Eventually he attested all the letters and the cipher-key mechanically in almost exactly the same terms.[1] The eight councillors who were conducting his examination immediately countersigned his signature to each letter: and this sham authentication has established the text without the postscript, as we now know it. In his readiness to oblige, Babington had been gradually led to overlook an omission of grave importance for the authenticity of the evidence.

To give greater éclat to their copy the government report states that Babington, before subscribing, had corrected 'two or three words mistakenly copied,' and also that he had signed 'every page' of the letters, whereas all the available copies of that day show that he only subscribed each letter.[2] In this way was Babington's engaging frankness made to shroud the dark treasons of Walsingham and his scoundrels.

Early in September Lord Burghley began to examine the secretaries on the captured papers. At first an attempt was made to frighten them. From the point of view of Elizabeth's councillors (as we have heard Phelippes say) their lives were certainly forfeit, and this was constantly dinned into their ears. But to threats they would not yield.

Before the 4th of September, however, we see from a note of Lord Burghley's that another method had been tried

---

[1] The cipher-key is now, *Domestic Elizabeth,* cxciii. 54, attested 1 September. The other attestations are not dated; but they were shown to Curll and Nau, 2 September. The cipher-key may be the copy kept by Curll; if not, it is the copy made by Phelippes. For Babington's authentications, see pp. 23, 30, 46.

[2] R.O., *Mary Queen of Scots,* xviii. 51; xix. 9; Yelverton, xxxi. 206, etc.; *Caligula,* C. ix. 238; *Caligula,* B. v. 164; Boyd, viii. 587; Labanoff, vi. 394; *Hardwicke State Papers,* i. 233.

clxxxvi MARY STUART AND THE BABINGTON PLOT

to shake their constancy, and with greater avail: 'Writings to touch both Nau, Curll and Pasquier' had been produced; and if more might be brought forward, 'it shall serve us (Lord Burghley is speaking) and spare our threatenings.'[1]

The 'writings to touch Nau' and the rest, were the drafts, in their own handwriting, of the letters to Morgan, Paget, and others, which treated of the invasion of the realm. Nau says[2] that he at first denied everything, even his own handwriting, which so enraged Walsingham, that he ran at him, and shook his fist in the Frenchman's face until Lord Burghley 'doulcement' persuaded him to sit down. Nau's autograph draft in question may have been that at the Record Office (*Mary Queen of Scots*, xviii. *n.* 44), which still bears the attestation, 'Cecy est de ma main. NAU. 2 Sept. 1586.'

On that same day Curll too was shown the Babington-Mary correspondence, and he attested the altogether innocent 'first letter' of Mary to Babington, written on the 25th of June; and he also admitted his own draft of Mary's letters to Englefield and Charles Paget.[3]

Nevertheless next day (3 September) Walsingham reported that neither Curll nor Nau would confess knowledge of the really important Letters II. and III., in which Babington had disclosed the conspiracy, and Mary (saying nothing at all about the murder plot) had given directions to deal with Mendoza and others about the invasion.[4]

That night's post, however, brought news that both secretaries were weakening. Walsingham was more satisfied with Curll: while Nau sent in his 'first answer in

---

[1] Conyers Read, *Bardon Papers* (Camden Society, 1909), p. 43.

[2] Nau's defence of 2 March 1605, *Caligula*, B. v. 233. Another draft letter acknowledged by Nau in Labanoff, vi. 81.

[3] Morris, p. 284; Boyd, p. 666. Next year, 16 August 1587, Curll admitted his decipherments of Letters II. and III., *Caligula*, D. i. 90. See *below*, p. cxc.

[4] *Mary Queen of Scots*, xix. 80, printed in Morris, p. 283.

confessing the writing of the letters by a minute of the Queen of Scots,' as Lord Burghley has endorsed it.

He stated that Mary had heard of plans for her escape two months before, and that she had then handed him an autograph minute, ' une minute de lettre escripte par sa main pour la polir et mectre au net.' Then he went on to say that ' this is clear to your Honours, for you have both the one [Mary's minute] and the other [Nau's own draft] in your hands.'[1]

This, of course, led to orders for a search to be made for Mary's minute, and for Nau's draft; but neither could be found.

We must pause here to appreciate the issues involved, and must begin by removing the false impression caused by a faulty passage in the *Hardwicke Papers*.[2] There we read, ' She (Mary) willed him (Curll) to burn the English copy of the letter sent to Babington.' This is proved to be fictitious by reference to the official record printed *below*, p. 147, and note. In place of the above quotation, we there find the words, ' the letter which was Englished this examinate (Curll) put into a trunk, that was in the Scottish Queen's cabinet, under lock and key.'

Evidently we have here before us a plain falsification of evidence, which perhaps took place when it was desired to lay a case before the French or the Scots. Government in those days treated evidence with the same violence with which they oppressed individual liberty. ' These fine councillors of England,' wrote the French ambassador a little later, ' never produce the original pieces, but only copies, to or from which they add or subtract what

---

[1] R.O., *Mary Queen of Scots*, xix. 78; Boyd, viii. 665.
[2] *Miscellaneous State Papers from . . . Lord Hardwicke . . . etc.*, 1778, i. 237. See *below*, p. 147.

they like.'¹ It may also be added, that the Hardwicke document does not profess to be a copy of the official evidence, though it does claim to be a 'report' of its substance.

Phelippes, having been asked to find the two French drafts mentioned by Nau, sent instead an argument of his own, which may be represented as an effort to show that the papers desired were not necessary. Phelippes no doubt had a motive for destroying the minutes, because they did not support the postscript. But Walsingham wrote so feelingly to Phelippes himself about their loss, that he cannot have suspected that Phelippes had destroyed them,² and I question whether the servant would have done this without orders. On the other hand, later on, when the record of the preservation of Curll's English minute was tampered with, the minute itself will probably have been destroyed, unless indeed Phelippes or some one else had done so before, lest it should betray the postscript. Nau's words of the French drafts by Mary and himself I take to have been uttered under the influence of false information, such as we shall hear of immediately. We must also remember Mary's words at her trial, that she was well assured ' that neither her words nor her writing could be shown against her.' ³

On the 4th of September both Burghley and Walsingham wrote independently to Hatton and to Phelippes, who were at Windsor, begging them to press Elizabeth for a slight change of policy.

---

¹ Ces beaux conseillers d'Angleterre . . . jamais ne produisent les mesmes pieces originaulx des procedures, mais seulement des copies, esquelles ils adjoutent ou diminuent ce qu'il leur plait. F. H. Egerton, *Life of Th. Egerton*, p. 101; in Lingard, p. 453, *n*.

² Morris, pp. 284, 287.

³ *The Scottish Queen's first answer*, R.O., *Mary Queen of Scots*, xx. 12; Boyd, ix. 97.

Burghley told Hatton he thinks that both

"Nau and Curll will yield somewhat to confirm their Mistress's crimes. But if they were persuaded that themselves might scape, and the blow fall upon their Mistress betwixt her head and shoulders, surely we should have the whole from them," and then he went on to ask in words already quoted, for more of their drafts, which "shall serve us the better, and spare our threatenings to them." '[1]

Walsingham desired the Queen's mercy for Curll, in hopes of his bearing witness against Nau. As the minute of her answer is not 'extant,' it seemed necessary to work in this way; and he (Walsingham) had in fact already promised his aid to Curll. Phelippes wanted the execution of both the secretaries, and showed in a letter of the same day, 4 September, how it could be accomplished. This blood-thirst rose partly from the greater cruelty of an underling, whose lust for Mary's death we have already heard, and still more from his desire to put out of the way those who might perhaps charge him later on.[2]

Still on this occasion both Phelippes and Hatton appear to have used their influence with Elizabeth to obtain the grace proposed; but to the credit of the secretaries be it added, that as they would not bend to fear, so neither did they yield to any offers of favour. They were deceived, however, about the 5th or 6th, into believing that some letters of overwhelming force had been discovered. This caused a great and immediate change in both: they thought that all chance of further defence was gone.

Nau in a later apology to James I. wrote, ' C'est affaire ayant esté approfondy et avoué en leur proces (*i.e.* that of the conspirators) tant par lettres, chiffres, mémoires,

---

[1] *Bardon Papers*, p. 43.
[2] Boyd, viii. 673, 678; P. F. Tytler, iv. 335, 336. It is interesting to see the same blood-lust in Gilbert Gifford: '*Guai a noi*,' he cries, ' if they be ever in libertie,' etc., *Domestic Elizabeth*, cc. *n*. 65; cci. *n*. 42.

instructions, et aultres papiers, *qui furent pris en leur logis, ou il se trouva aulcuns de sa Majesté*, que par leur propres adveus, recognaissances et confessions.'[1] Probably, however, no letters at all were found at Babington's lodgings; certainly none such as Nau here describes, *i.e.* some of Queen Mary's own letters. Indeed, as she only wrote twice, this amounts to saying that the original ciphers to Babington had been seized and were in the hands of the prosecution. This very gross imposition reappears also in Curll's *apologia* when discharged from prison.

'They did show me the Queen's Majesty's letters to my Lord Paget, Mr. Charles Paget, Sir Francis Englefield, and the Spanish ambassador—all penned with my own hand,[2] which I could not deny . . . [and they treated] the same matter whereof she answered to Babington.

'Moreover, they showed me the two very letters written by me in cipher and received by Babington, and the true decipherments of both word by word, with the alphabet between her Majesty and him.[3] (MS. burnt for about 2 lines) . . . Also . . . the answer . . . acknowledged by Mr. Nau . . . not to trust Poley[4] was found written in my own hand. . . .

'Upon which so manifest and unrecusable evidence, I could not deny . . . but it behoved me to confess, as I did, that I had deciphered Babington his principal communication to her Majesty, and that I received from Mr. Nau by her commandment her answer thereunto, after she had read and perused the same in my presence, which answer I translated into English and after the perusing thereof by her Majesty, put it in a cipher as it was sent to Babington.[5]

To all who have studied the collection of papers which have come down to us from Phelippes these words of

---

[1] *Caligula*, B. v. 233.
[2] Of these four drafts *in Curll's hand* none seems to survive.
[3] This cipher alphabet is still extant, see *above*, p. clxxxv. *n.*
[4] This now only exists in Phelippes's hand.
[5] B.M., *Caligula*, D. i. f. 90b, written and dated 6 August 1587. The burnt lines can be supplied from Harleian MS., 4647, and the reconstructed passage will be found in Lingard, vi. 703. Cf. F. v. Raumer, p. 327.

Curll will seem quite incredible. 'They did show me the two very letters written by me in cipher, and received by Babington, with the true decipherments of both, word by word.' What can be clearer than that Curll thought that the two original cipher-letters to Babington, which he, Curll, had Englished, and put into cipher-characters, were in the hands of the prosecution, together with the decipherments? And yet it was only by gross deception that both Curll, and also Nau, can have been separately brought to that opinion. For Babington was told to burn them, and no doubt he did so. Nor was it the secretaries only who were deceived. Holinshed says, 'It were needless to express more particularly the contents of his and her letters, the originals themselves being extant and surprised.'[1]

How the deception was effected we cannot say. Perhaps the artful edition with Babington's signatures and those of the Council played part in it; perhaps also Phelippes's copy of the ciphers, for his hand was not unlike that of Curll, and he was fully primed with the malice necessary to play the trick, for which his letter of 4 September[2] may have prepared the way. Anyhow, both secretaries had now fallen, and were henceforward pliable at Walsingham's will. They, too, attested the Babington correspondence, though slowly and against the grain.

'Then must I, and do confess to have deciphered the like of the whole above written,' wrote Curll on the 5th of September, with similar forms for the other letters. Nau on the 6th wrote, 'Je pense de vray que c'est la lettre escripte par sa Majesté à Babington, comme il me souvient.' The statement made at the trial, that both confessed voluntarily, when they saw the papers, is a gross falsehood. They were, and with reason, in fear for their lives; and they spoke only under constraint and after long resistance;

---

[1] Holinshed, *Chronicles*, ed. 1808, iv. p. 925.   [2] *Above*, p. clxxxviii.

and above all, they had been grievously deceived as to the papers before them (*below*, p. 148).

These statements by Mary's secretaries decided the case against her. They were afterwards repeated, and amplified, on the 21st or 23rd of September. But these elaborations in effect weakened the force of the previous statements, for the secretaries were now required to enumerate 'the principal points' of the letters, in the exact words which Mary had used two months before. It was unlikely that either, impossible that each, should have remembered the same phrases verbatim at so long an interval. They must therefore, in effect, have been reading copies placed before them, written by Phelippes. Those further statements, therefore, did not contain any really new evidence.

When the evidence of the secretaries was read in court, Mary rejected it with energy and some contempt. Nevertheless it made a deep impression, and Walsingham was probably right, from his point of view, when he wrote next day to Leicester that, 'the testimony of her two secretaries had been sufficient proof of the matter . . . so as in the opinion of her best friends that were appointed commissioners, she is guilty.'[1] And, again, when the Queen was told she must die, she is reported to have said, 'Where is Nau? Must I die for him?' showing that she felt fully the weight of his evidence. In her last dispositions, however, she wished both him and Curll to have a chance of justifying themselves.[2]

However deceitfully obtained, their evidence did in effect bring home to Mary her correspondence with Babington. But the responsibility for their action lay with those who deceived and coerced them.

---

[1] *Caligula*, C. ix. f. 502.
[2] Labanoff, vi. 487. Chantelauze, *M. Stuart*, 1876, p. 394; Maxwell-Scott, *Fotheringay*, p. 193; Jebb, ii. 663.

INTRODUCTION

Again, though the evidence of Nau and Curll was then made to seem so conclusive, we must also remember that the prosecution could have easily done without it, though they would have had to conduct the case differently. It might not then have been so easy to satisfy the public. Inquiry might not have been quite so effectively cut off. Though a just verdict was never possible, history might not have been so successfully silenced, or for so long a time as it actually has been.

3. *Queen Mary's Trial.*

Queen Mary's trial, which began on the 14th of October, was deeply influenced by the monstrous Band of Association, according to which no evidence was necessary against the accused. Proof that Babington had plotted against Elizabeth's life for Mary's advancement, made the captive liable to death, whether she had consented or not. Nay more, her judges, perhaps without exception, had already sworn to pursue her to the death, if such proof were offered; and Elizabeth repeatedly insisted on this in the Davison episode. What chance was there of men, thus pledged, acting with impartiality? But by the Act of 27 Elizabeth (*above*, p. xxv.) a formal trial was required.

As usual in such trials no witnesses were called, but extracts from the written confessions were read, and these are still in our possession.[1] We see the utmost that the prosecution could prove, and Mary was asked to recognise the handwriting of Nau and Curll. This she did not deny, and so the case was proved to the satisfaction of the crown lawyers. Elizabeth, however, before the verdict was passed, recalled the judicial commission to London. Eventually on the 29th of October, the commission passed the sentence

---

[1] B M., *Caligula*, C ix. 340-405. See *below*, p 136.

of death unanimously, though Lord Zouche had found that, while Mary was 'privy' to the plot, she had not 'compassed and practised' the Queen's death.[1]

One point in her defence, the significance of which may escape the casual reader, is her insistence on her being a queen. A queen is not bound to take cognisance of the plots against a neighbouring sovereign. If Mary had had her rights in this matter, she would have gone free. So far therefore, as Elizabeth's ministers could do so, she was deprived of royal honours from first to last. That was their object in the indictment, in the rude tearing down of her dais, in the insufferable cant of Sir Amias, in all the indignities heaped upon her. Yet it was impossible not to allow her a certain pre-eminence, and more impossible still for her rights not to be emphasised by the attempts made to obscure them. Scotland was awakened, and Elizabeth feared to act. That was already much, and it was the result of Mary's own courage.

If it seems to us astonishing that Mary's pleas should have been so entirely ignored, we must also remember that Mary was not anxious to have every detail known. To have pleaded in so highly prejudiced a court that she had left the issue of the assassination to providence (as she wrote to Mendoza) would have prejudiced her greatly, would have been quite fatal. She therefore asserted her innocence and her royal dignity, and did not stand upon explanations which would neither have been comprehended nor admitted, except perhaps by Lord Zouche.

Besides, that was all she could do. Allowed no papers, no witnesses, no advocate, she could do nothing but protest. And barbarous as this treatment was, it may have helped

---

[1] *Hardwicke State Papers*, i. 224, but I cannot find the passage in MS. *Caligula*, C. ix. f. (400)=497. Lord Zouche also said something during the trial which pleased Mary. Morris, p. 300.

INTRODUCTION

her in the end. Had she been in a position to fight the evidence, the overwhelming forensic talent against her must have gained an apparent victory. But her cries of innocence, her invocation of the divinity that hedges round the crown, were re-echoed from Land's End to John o' Groat's, and will for all time awaken the sympathy of loyal hearts.

4. *Mary's Protests of Innocence.*

A word must also be said here in explanation of Mary's protestations of innocence. They fall into two classes: (1) Those found in the reports of her trial; (2) those written in letters by herself. As to the former we must admit many possibilities of misstatement. She was inevitably in a state of great excitement; and allowance should be made for her denying any charge till it was proved, especially as she was tried by bitter enemies, who had no valid jurisdiction over her. In the enemy reporters too there was violent prejudice, misapprehension of her line of defence, and subsequent alterations of the record.

Nevertheless, the records, if we do not stand too close to the letter, show Mary's mind fairly well. In her first answer to the commissioners, 'She protested that she had not procured or encouraged any hurt against her Majesty.'[1] In her second answer, she said that her first answer was 'according to her meaning, and such as she was to maintain.' In her third answer, she said, 'If the commissioners will take her word, she will affirm and say before them that she never meant evil to the Queen, nor to the State of England.' On the other hand, she said openly that she had sought to gain her liberty by the intervention of foreign arms.

In her letters we find several passages relating to her

---

[1] Labanoff, vii 38

plea. They too fall into classes. To the Duke of Guise, and to the Archbishop of Glasgow, she wrote accounts of her trial, which they were to circulate in France. In these she describes her pleas, but she does not go on to explain whether they represent her mind truly and fully, or only her formal pleadings. In any case they are so brief that we learn little from them. In the one she says:

'They charged me with practising against the life of their Queen, or to have consented thereunto. But I said, as is true, that I know nothing about it (que je ne scais ce que c'est). They said that they had taken certain letters to one Babington and one Charles Paget, and his brother, which proved the conspiracy, and that Nau and Curll had avowed it. I said that they could not, unless they made them say more than they knew, by force of torments. "Voilà tout ce que l'on m'en a dit."'[1]

To the Archbishop of Glasgow she wrote, dwelling on the religious side of her defence, but interjects:

'As to having plotted, counselled, or commanded her death, I had never done so. For my private advantage I would not suffer one fillip to be given her.'

Writing to Mendoza on the 23rd November, she follows a different line of thought, and her statement is instructive:

'My very dear friend . . . Praise God for me that, by His grace I had the courage to receive this very unjust sentence of the heretics with contentment, for the honour (which I esteem it to be) to shed my blood at the demand of the enemies of His Church. They honour me so much as to say, that theirs cannot exist, if I live. The other point they affirm to be, that their Queen cannot reign in security, and for the same reason. On both these conditions I, without contradicting them, accepted the honour they were so anxious to confer upon me, as very zealous in the Catholic religion, for which I had publicly offered my life.

'As to the other matter—[*i.e.* that of Babington]—although

---

[1] Labanoff, vi. 439.

I had made no attempt nor taken any action to remove her that was in place, still as they reproached me with what is my right and is so considered by all Catholics, as they say, I did not wish to contradict them, leaving it to them to judge.

'But they, angry at this, told me I was talking in vain: that I should not die for religion, but for having wanted to have their Queen murdered. This I denied to them, as being very false. Moreover, I had never attempted anything of the kind; indeed, I had left it to God and the churches to settle for this island, and what depends upon it, in that which regards religion. 'This bearer [? Gorion] has promised me to tell you, how rigorously I have been treated by the people here, and how ill served by others, whom I could wish had not shown in so just a cause their fear of death or other inordinate passions. Whereas from me they only obtained the avowal that I was a free Queen, catholic, obedient to the Church, and that for my deliverance, I was obliged—after having tried for it by good means without being able to obtain it—to procure it by the means offered me, without consenting [*i.e.* approving them].'[1]

There is a distinction in her mind between 'intending to assassinate,' and 'leaving to God and the Churches [an odd phrase, perhaps misread in cipher, for " The Catholics under God's Providence "] to take such measures as they can,' as to which she bears herself a neutral. This distinction seems to convey her mind as clearly as she was likely to set it down on paper.

Nau, her secretary, puts the matter quite plainly (Labanoff, vii. 208). After describing the many reasons she had for desiring to escape—

'Voyant par là [*i.e.* by Babington's offer] son eschapper luy estre offert et proposé, elle s'est laissée aller à l'accepter, et, en conséquence d'icellui, donner advis pour le support estranger, sans se meller aucunement du troisième poinct, ne s'estimant ès termes ou elle se voyoit estre obligée de la réveller.'

---

[1] Labanoff, vi. 458, 459, dated 23 November. It did not reach Mendoza until 15 October 1587, ten months later; after Mary's servants were allowed to depart. See the *Spanish Calendar*, 1587, pp. 152-5.

On the scaffold Mary is reported to have protested—

'As for the death of the Queen your sovereign, I call God to witness that I never imagined it, never sought it, nor ever consented to it.'

None of these protests are inconsistent with Mary's extant letter to Babington, in which Elizabeth's death is nowhere suggested, counselled, or commanded. Some disclaimers, like that to Archbishop Beaton, 'Je ne souffrirois que, pour mon particulier, une chiquenaud luy fust donnée,' 'I would not suffer her to receive a fillip for my particular interests,'[1] are overstated. This may well have represented her normal attitude towards the Queen, but on the day when the hope of escape was dangled before her, other feelings passed through her mind. Still on the whole, considering her very trying circumstances and the secrets she still had to keep, the exaggeration is very slight. Taken together, her declarations of innocence do not overshoot the mark. She did not plead falsely.

5. *The Execution.*

Finally on the 8th of February came the execution, the glorious day of Mary's everchanging fortunes. Never did she show greater courage, greater love, greater humanity. On this occasion her foils were Henry Grey, Earl of Kent, and Fletcher, Dean of Peterborough; fanatics indeed, both rude and inhuman, but just the men to stimulate her to her highest flights. They worried themselves little with the arguments about her complicity, but exulted openly in the hope of washing their hands in her blood. 'Your life would be the death of our religion,' said the Earl on the evening of his arrival, 'your death will be its life.'

These words gave Mary a keen satisfaction, and she

---

[1] Labanoff, vi. 468.

returned to them that evening frequently and with smiles. 'Oh, how happy Lord Kent's words have made me! Here at last is the truth. They told me I was to die because I had plotted against the Queen, and here is Lord Kent sent to convert me, and he says I am to die on account of my religion' (Chantelauze, p. 393).

Yet this woman was no milk-and-water saint. That evening she had spoken bitterly of her son as having betrayed her. 'You should die at peace with all men,' cried the carping puritans. 'I forgive every one, and accuse no one,' was Mary's ready answer; 'yet I may follow David's example and pray God to confound and punish His enemies, and those of His divinity and religion; and to pardon my own enemies.' That same night she sent a long message to King Philip bidding him remember, if the Armada were successful, that Walsingham, Burghley, and their party had been his worst enemies as well as hers.[1]

The last night was passed in arranging little presents for her servants, in writing her last letters, and in prayer, for she had been cruelly refused the services of her chaplain, de Préau. When Shrewsbury and Kent came to lead her out next morning, it was before the little altar that they found her. At first they wished to separate her at once from all her servants; but at her prayers and tears, she was allowed the service of four men-servants and two maids for her last unrobing.

After the sentence had been read by Beale, Fletcher came forward, and despite Mary's objections, began a long denunciation of popery, during which the Queen read her book of Hours. When quiet had been restored, she prayed for some time in English for the peace of Christendom, for the conversion of England, for her son, for Elizabeth, for

---

[1] Chantelauze, *Journal de Bourgoing*, 1876, p. 575; *Spanish Calendar*, 1587, p. 155.

all her enemies. Then came the disrobing, Mary bravely controlling her tearful ladies, while the brutal hangman Bull of Tyburn, stepping in, wrested from them the cross from Mary's neck, which he claimed and kept as his perquisite. Amid breathless silence Mary's gentle prayer, ' *In manus tuas, Domine, commendo spiritum meum*,' was heard throughout the hall; Shrewsbury by a sign gave the signal to Bull, and then turned away. Two blows and the neck was severed; a third and the head rolled upon the scaffold. Picking it up, Bull cried, ' God save Queen Elizabeth '; while Kent standing over the corpse with his white wand, and supported by the Dean, called out, ' So perish all her enemies. Amen.'

SECTION X

Exeunt Omnes.

The interest attaching to Queen Mary's wonderful personality is so great, that when she is taken away, all else seems to fade into insignificance. But before we close our account of the plot, some final words must be said about a number of secondary subjects and less important persons, who have passed before us.

1. In the first place we must agree that the death of Mary ended in success for that revolutionary protestantism, which had perfidiously achieved it. The failure of the Armada in the year following, with the assassination of the Guises and the advent of the Huguenot Henri iv. to the throne of France, were all disappointments or disasters to the cause of the ancient religion. Without question the permanency of the new religion gained much from the removal of the catholic heiress. When Doctor Allen was made a cardinal, Pope Sixtus mentioned in consistory, as

the primary reason for his act, the desire to make up, as far as he could, for the loss and discouragement caused by Queen Mary's death. As far back as 1582 Mendoza had told King Philip that Mary's courage was, as it were, the heart of political aspiration among catholics.[1]

The actual loss to catholicism, however, fell chiefly upon those who had already yielded much to the persecution. The total number in the seminaries did not notably change, but rather tended to increase; so too did the number of priests in England and the flocks to which they ministered. For the fervent Mary's death was something near to martyrdom, and *sanguis martyrum, semen ecclesiæ*.

But hope of political success began to fail. Both England and Scotland were now firmly held by the reformers. Heretofore there had been many a chance that in one or other country a split might be effected, which would end in the majority regaining their religious freedom. It was not that Mary's friends were very efficient, or her propaganda very powerful, it was her rights as Queen and heiress which appealed continually to the great conservative majority, who were also at heart inclined to the ancient religion. But now Mary's natural rights were devolving on her protestant son.

Had it not been for Elizabeth's extraordinary tyranny in not allowing her successor to be named, the issues raised by Mary's death would have been settled sooner than they eventually were. But so long as the English Queen prevented the recognition of James, she was virtually fostering the claims put forward by those extremists who advocated the claims of the remoter descendants, whether catholic or protestant, of the House of Lancaster.

2. Next after Queen Mary, our curiosity will probably turn to the rascals whom Walsingham employed in his

---

[1] *Spanish Calendar*, 1582, 9 February and 1 April, pp. 291, 323

work of darkness : and first to Gilbert Gifford. There is, however, but little to add to the record of his correspondence, *below*, pp. 118 to 130. His course tended steadily downwards, and his new start was to get himself sacrilegiously ordained a priest, in order to carry on his abominable trade with greater success. Not only Walsingham and Phelippes, but Elizabeth too took interest in the fortunes of this clever scoundrel, who was awarded the then handsome pension of £100 a year for sending 'intelligence' which might excite the interest of her Majesty.

But this gleam of fortune did not last long. Not only did he get into serious trouble with the English ambassador in Paris, but he was arrested in a brothel in December 1587. Being a priest, he was confined to the Archbishop's prison, from which he never came out alive.

Efforts indeed were made by Phelippes to help him, and in some details these efforts were successful. An endeavour to prosecute him was made by the Nuncio in Paris, in the absence of any English catholic bishop with jurisdiction over him. But no evidence against him was obtainable. No one knew how Queen Mary had been entrapped ; there were no papers of importance. Richard Verstegan, the author, is said to have got up the case against him, and to have worked this up into a little book. William Pierce and George Birkhead (who became men of some note among the English clergy in later years, and were then taking their degree of Doctors at the Sorbonne) helped to prepare the case against the accused. But neither Morgan nor Paget, neither Nau nor Curll, would, or perhaps could, give effective evidence. The result was that about March 1588 the case was abandoned. When the papers of the Paris Nuntiature are in better order, more information will perhaps be forthcoming. At present the evidence about it is very scant indeed. Verstegan's book is said to have been bought up by money provided by Lord Paget, and destroyed.

Gifford would now almost certainly have worked himself free but for that book against the Jesuits, of which we have heard before. Phelippes is said to have sent it over to Lily, one of Gilbert's enemies in the house of the English ambassador, Stafford, who had reasons of his own for taking sides very strongly against the imprisoned spy. Grately too was imprisoned at Padua before August, also on account of this luckless book.[1] We shall later on find the book brought up again against Morgan.

Gifford and Grately lingered on for two years in their respective cells, Gilbert dying about the beginning of November 1590. His secrets were buried with him, until 'the opening of the Archives' in the last century, when his letters and those of Phelippes came to light. It is a sad story certainly which they tell, for the mischief-maker had once been a clever and attractive fellow. Fortune gave him the choice between doing great good and great evil; he chose the latter, and by his treachery towards the hapless Queen, ruined himself in destroying her.

3. Next after Gifford as an evil genius, most people will reckon Thomas Phelippes. It is clear from all the secret correspondence, and even from the preparation for the trial, that he had, in his sphere, an almost free hand, and a heart even more viciously set on bloodshed than his master. Some have praised his skill as a decipherer in terms as high as though his talent had been phenomenal. But in

---

[1] It appears that the book was in the form of two letters, one from a Jesuit in Transylvania to a Dominican in Rome, in which he exaggerates and belauds the doings of his order in England. The other letter is the answer of the Dominican. In this the Jesuit's claims are, of course, overthrown and condemned with great emphasis, and living persons, especially Father Persons, are freely introduced and reproved. No existing copy has yet been recognised. C. Grene, *MS. Notes for Bartoli*, E. f. 30.

this particular case he had really no scope for extraordinary powers, because from the very first a new set of cipher keys was introduced, of which he at once obtained copies. The actual deciphering was therefore always quite easy.

As to his good faith, it is true that we cannot rely upon it where it stands alone, especially when he was speaking or writing against Mary. The history of the postscript and of the drafts for Mary's letter prove this beyond a doubt. But other corroborative considerations may sometimes come into play, and give his word a new value. I think his loyalty to Walsingham does supply one such corroboration. There may, after all, be honour among thieves. I have tested his deciphers for Walsingham repeatedly, and I have always found them truthful. In unimportant letters he sometimes abbreviates; sometimes he makes the sense clearer, but in ways which Walsingham would presumably have approved. Examples will be found in the later correspondence with Gilbert Gifford.

During the small residue of Walsingham's life (he died April 1590) Phelippes continued to prosper; and in June 1590, I find a letter addressed to him (but perhaps in error) as a Secretary of the Council.[1] After this his creditors began to press him more urgently; most of the year 1596 was passed in prison. He was then occupied in sending out discouraging news to Charles Paget and other exiles, and for this purpose he made much use of Thomas Barnes. He also traded for Spanish largess, by supplying news. In 1607 he was again under arrest; in 1622 he petitioned for some minor post in the Church of England (!), as a relief from his long struggle with debt. It is needless to inquire into the details of his later years. Enough to say,

---

[1] He really held the very lucrative post of Collector of Customs for the harbour of London. *Domestic Calendar*, 1590, p. 675.

though a clever fellow and faithful to Walsingham, he was a spendthrift, without steadfastness or credit.

4. Much the same may be said of Poley. After a year's imprisonment *pro forma*, during which he was believed to have poisoned Richard Creagh, the saintly Archbishop of Armagh, he was freed and employed in the diplomatic service, as a special messenger to Denmark in 1588. But in 1589 he was in prison again, charged with 'lewd words against Walsingham,' and then with seducing his gaoler's wife. In 1593 he was employed as a spy in Flanders and again in 1595. Men like this are the reverse of a credit to their country, and the same may be said of Mawde, Barnes, and others of Walsingham's crew. Of the misfortunes of Secretary Davison I have nothing special to say here. They did not exactly befall him in consequence of Babington, but because of his royal mistress, whose ideas of honour were capricious. Though as a rule she accepted the opinions of the ministers she had chosen, she sometimes showed strong resentment at being managed by them.

Of the conspirators little remains to be said. Their personal property was confiscated by the crown,[1] and granted to the Queen's favourites, especially to Sir Walter Raleigh,[2] whose name had been mentioned by Babington quite casually, as the patron of Langhorn or Flyer, obscure and probably harmless persons, of whom Ballard had formed some baseless hopes. It looks as though Elizabeth wished to recompense the imagined injury done by having been mentioned by a man condemned for treason.

Walsingham's underhand encouragement of the plot was sufficiently known to make catholic apologists ascribe the

---

[1] R.O., *Miscellanea of the Exchequer*, 15/3, *nn*. 7, 8.
[2] For Babington's property and its redistribution, see *The Reliquary*, April 1862, pp. 177-99, by W. Durrant Cooper, *above*, p. civ.

guilt of it primarily to him, and to represent Mary and also 'the twelve gentlemen' as victims to religious odium. But their names were not enrolled in the long catalogues of martyrs, so frequent in the late sixteenth and early seventeenth centuries. This is the more noteworthy when we remember that, in some preface or parenthesis, hardly any of these lists fail to mention the case of the Queen of Scots as a vivid illustration in its way of hatred towards the catholic faith on the part of Elizabeth's government.[1]

5. Turning now to Mary's friends and servants, a few more words still seem needful about Thomas Morgan. That his indiscretions were a primary cause of the Queen's death appears but too clearly from what we have already seen; but to what extent Mary was aware of it, is uncertain. During her trial she defended him briefly but warmly, when he was charged by Lord Burghley with having tempted Parry to plot. She declared that she had 'terrified the man from any further such attempt.' Alas, a complete illusion! She should certainly have discharged him for his low standards in the matter of political assassination. The fact seems to be that Mary, brought up amid the turmoils of civil war and revolution, did not sufficiently oppose fighting and quarrelling among her followers. She highly esteemed Morgan for his impetuous activity in her service, and his zeal to procure her news. From early

---

[1] An analysis of the martyr-lists for this year 1587 will be found in *Catholic Record Society*, v. p. 10. The analysis shows the frequency with which her name recurs, but of course not the modifications under which it is found in each case. For these Challoner's *Missionary Priests* (vol. i. under No. 41) may be consulted as a model.

The 'twelve gentlemen' are never mentioned in the martyr-catalogues. But Brother Henry Foley, S.J., by inadvertence, has placed Ballard in his miscellaneous list of sufferers for religion. He was, however, so far from recognising his man, that he describes him conjecturally as having died in prison! Further on he mentions Ballard's *alias* of 'Thomson' as though this were the real name of yet another, hitherto unknown, sufferer. *Records, S.J.*, iii. 801, 808.

years she passionately loved the receipt and discussion of news. Randolph, then English agent at Edinburgh, frequently mentions it in his dispatches. This amiable weakness now proved her undoing. Poulet would glut his cruelty, sometimes by 'keeping her fasting from all news'—sometimes by reporting to her the calamities of her friends. This to his diseased imagination was 'like throwing salt in her eyes.'

Morgan played on the same weak point, but in the opposite way; he staked her life and fortunes on the safe arrival of her letters. Neither man nor mistress realised the ruin which might follow. We cannot at this distance of time profess to state exactly where his chief indiscretions lay; but if Morgan had taken the obvious precaution of inquiring from the heads of Gilbert Gifford's seminary, whether he were a safe man in whose hands to place the Queen's life, he would surely have received an answer that would have effectively prevented that young man's employment.

But whatever the extent of Morgan's responsibility, Mary's warm appeals for him to Mendoza and her other friends proved ultimately to be his fortune. Mendoza procured for him a small pension, and the Pope, at the suggestion of another Welshman, Owen Lewis, Bishop of Cassano, pressed for his release, which was now granted, though Elizabeth was deeply offended.

Morgan and Charles Paget would take no effective part in the prosecution of Gilbert Gifford, which clearly showed their fear of being countered by him. In 1588 Mendoza sent them to Flanders in the interests of the Armada. They went, and entered again into correspondence with Phelippes, but whether for the profit of their new paymasters or not seems doubtful. Morgan was soon in difficulties again; possibly they arose out of that luckless book against the Jesuits, which had in part been laid to his charge by

Gilbert Gifford. Morgan's examination, taken 12 February 1590, will be found in the *Spanish Calendar*. The examiners were hostile in tone to him; and their report was sent to King Philip before action was taken upon it. A counter-protest in Morgan's favour was issued by the Bishop of Cassano on the 24th following.[1] The evidence on both sides was very inconclusive. Eventually, after two years, he was freed, but had to leave Flanders.

From Brussels he wandered to Turin, where he obtained, again through Owen Lewis, a Papal letter of commendation to the King of Spain. Going on to Spain, he was at Madrid when Cardinal Allen died in October 1594, on which occasion he began to urge the advancement of Owen Lewis to the cardinalate with so much vigour that attention was attracted to him, and to the fact of his banishment from Flanders. This led to his expulsion from Madrid, after which he returned to Paris.

Upon the accession of King James in 1603, Morgan thought that his hour of fortune had arrived. He began to write to him, just as he had addressed Mary, in long, inflated, egotistical letters. The 'French Correspondence' in the Record Office contains seven such missives between 14 August 1603 and 4 July 1605. But between those dates there had been renewed troubles. He had gone back to England, where he was promptly imprisoned, then deported. Then he became involved in a French court intrigue, connected with the custody of the natural children of Henri iv., which led to a new imprisonment in the Bastille, from June 1604 to April 1605. The last of his letters to James which I have seen is dated 4 June 1608, at which time he had again returned to England and was again in prison. How this adventure ended is not known. He is believed to have died not long after.

---

[1] Dodd, *Church History of England*, 1737, ii. 267.

A troubled life certainly; and the contests are all with men of his own side, and such as others avoided. The brighter side of his character consisted in his energetic devotion to his mistress. He thoroughly understood how to please her, and he was untiring in his efforts to serve. So far as I can see, he was both faithful and steadfast: but he was far indeed from being the man to whom authority and a high place could safely be given, and his political morality was low.

Mary was ever as strangely bad a judge of men (considering her great qualities) as Elizabeth was a good one. This weakness is strikingly manifest in the story now told. Mary has been entirely mistaken, not only in Gilbert Gifford, Barnes, and his gang of rogues, but also in Babington and Nau, in Morgan and Mendoza. If she had but kept Morgan in his own humble position, how different might not the end have been![1]

6. Charles Paget was the associate of Morgan in all that led to Mary's downfall; and he was the less excusable in that he was free, could go about and make inquiries. On the other hand, he was far more deep and artful than his Welsh leader, and cunningly succeeded in extricating himself from the consequences of his misdeeds. A gentleman of means, there are ominous rumours that his voluntary exile was due less to religion than to being mixed up in a divorce suit.[2] Like Morgan, he let Gilbert Gifford escape, and then went with a Spanish pension to Flanders to join the Armada. Keeping clear of Morgan's violent quarrels, he perceived, before long, that the future lay with King James, after which he gave every kind of underhand

---

[1] For Morgan's later life, besides many references in the *Domestic Calendars*, and those for Spain and Hatfield, and the Catalogues of the British Museum, see especially *Titus*, B. vii. 414, and *Additional MSS.* 30,609, ff. 96b to 112.

[2] *Catholic Record Society*, ii. 183.

assistance to the Scottish succession. When this made his position as a Spanish pensioner untenable, he slipped over to France, and in 1598 appealed to Elizabeth for mercy. As a sign of the thoroughness of his change of mind he volunteered to betray catholics, and sent in a list of charges. The first of these was that the Jesuits had encouraged Savage in his conspiracy, that is to say in the very conspiracy in which he had himself been a ringleader.[1] But he was ironically told that the memory of his treasons was all too fresh for him to expect pardon. Phelippes, moreover, out of spite, sent his list of charges to Flanders, with disagreeable consequences for Paget.[2]

But when King James succeeded, Paget's assiduous courting of that monarch obtained its reward. He was allowed home, was pardoned his crimes, and received several handsome grants from the crown. He was now able to take revenge on Phelippes;[3] and, for all we know, lived happily the rest of his days. A dishonourable, disagreeable character; neither in good nor in evil fortune was he the man to be Queen Mary's counsellor.

7. Of Gilbert Curll and Jacques Nau there is little more to say. Mary called them disloyal, because she did not see through the garbled accounts put out by the government, and because she was never told of the quasi-impossibility of their denying their own handwriting. In reality they

---

[1] Paget's charges may be conveniently found in the *Domestic Calendar* for 1598, p. 68, with answers by Verstegan, p. 234, and by Persons (*Stonyhurst MSS., Anglia*, ii. 46; also R.O., *Roman Transcripts*, Bundle 86).

[2] This correspondence, which is bulky, may be found in the *Domestic Calendars* for 1598, etc., the *Additional Calendar*, especially p. 215, where Barnes calls him 'an inconstant fellow, full of practices, true to no side.' In the corresponding *Spanish Calendar* he is found tendering his services to Spain, p. 671. The Spaniards offer to take his information, but they agree that they won't pay, unless his news turns out to be true.

[3] Phelippes, from the Tower, about April 1606, writes that 'Paget's malice causes his troubles.' *Domestic Calendar*, p. 314.

had good excuses; but they were not heroes. They even appeared in the Star Chamber, swore to their confessions, and blamed Mary in public. That was not loyal. But they were then broken men, overwhelmed with grief and fear. After another year of close imprisonment, they were returned to France, and it was said that Nau would examine Gilbert Gifford, but he never did so. In his final defence [1] sent to King James, he can only say that he 'thought' that Gifford or Poley had been the traitors who brought about the catastrophe. This shows how little he *knew*, and how well Phelippes's secrets were kept. It is a disgrace to King James that he should have left those doubts unsolved. For the rest Nau's apology, though a good one, would please us better if there had been fewer protests.

8. Mendoza did not leave the Paris embassy with a heightened reputation. Philip had sent him there as an answer to the insolence of Elizabeth's government in expelling him from England. But the ambassador's hot temper did not cool with time, and made him many an adversary amongst his own followers, as well as among his political opponents. He grew nearly blind, had to trust entirely to subordinates; and we have seen the facility with which Gilbert befooled him. He took the side of Morgan and Paget against the other English catholic exiles, which did not tend to peace. On the other hand, he bore himself with distinguished courage during the memorable siege of Paris in 1590. Finally he returned old and out of favour; rather a sad ending, considering the courage with which he had so long defended an untenable position. But de Quadra and de Silva, who had been ambassadors before him, were far more successful in diplomacy than he.

---

[1] B.M., *Caligula*, B. v. 233-7, unprinted.

9. One frequently reads in our popular handbooks of history that Elizabeth's life was the object of perpetual plots on the part of catholics. Does the history we have just finished support the contention that plots were widespread? Doubtless the existence of men like Morgan and Ballard does make to some extent in favour of the popular theory; and again when there was so much cruel persecution, one cannot wonder at the rise of some such characters as theirs. Nor can we be surprised if some exiles, in desperation, thought of desperate remedies. Yet what is clearer than that on English soil this plot could not have progressed an inch without Walsingham's active assistance? Walsingham's victims only began to plot some months after he had furnished them with the opportunity, and with the tempters to lure them on. He need never have given them those incentives; he need never have let them begin. Had there been any real danger he could and would have arrested them immediately. That Elizabeth was ever in the least peril, either from this or any other conspiracy, still stands without any historical proof.

This book has been some years upon the stocks. Begun in 1907, I could not complete it until Mr. Boyd's *Calendars* had covered the period under review. After the war it was difficult at first to find any means of bringing the book before the public. I have once more to thank my colleague, Father P. Ryan, whose accuracy and care in collation, and in the re-deciphering of the secret correspondence has been invaluable. I have also once again to thank Mr. Mills for admirable craftmanship in compiling the Index, and Mr. J. E. Neale for his care in revising proofs.

J. H. POLLEN, S.J.

31 FARM STREET, LONDON, W.
16 *March* 1922.

SECTION I

THE SECRET CORRESPONDENCE OF THOMAS BARNES, GILBERT CURLL, QUEEN MARY AND ANTHONY BABINGTON.

QUEEN MARY'S SECRET POST.—The institution of this post has already been explained, *Introduction*, § iii The first letter was passed in by Gilbert Gifford on the 16th of January, and by degrees more and more followed, until in March Mary began to receive the packets which had arrived for her at the French embassy during the past few years, but which could not be sent on before. It naturally took a longish time to decipher, read, and digest these letters, and so her letters out became few. For this and other reasons Gifford got leave for a holiday abroad Writing to Curll, 24 April/4 May (*below*, p 99), to say that a second substitute would take his place, Thomas Barnes came ushered in by introductory letters, composed in the deceitful style of Phelippes and Gifford These little fictions so evidently pleased Mary that the deceivers maintained until the end the soothing allurements which they had attached to the name of Barnes, which name was improved to the more familiar and endearing form of Barnaby In reality, however, Thomas Barnes was used as a letter carrier twice only

THE CORRESPONDENTS.—(i) On Mary's side the penman is always Gilbert Curll, her secretary for English, an accurate, faithful, well-mannered clerk who wrote an excellent hand, but does not display any other great gift Though accurate, he was not infallible, and he was especially troubled by the introduction of the 'New Style' in October 1582 (see *Introduction*, p. lxiv) England had not yet adopted it, and was therefore ten days behind France, Spain, and Rome, which had done so. As it was with these countries that Mary's diplomatic correspondence was chiefly conducted, she employed it when writing to them; though at Chartley itself the old style remained in use. Bourgoing's Journal, for instance, follows this style Hence we should have expected that when writing to Barnes, Curll would have used the old style; and we can see from his slips that he was much inclined to do so. Indeed, it may be that his first letter (No. 2) really was in the old style.

But Phelippes—perhaps craftily (wishing to improve his disguise by adopting a Catholic style), perhaps because he already knew (though intercepted letters) that Mary sometimes used new style—took this date also for new style, and told Curll that he would follow that style (p. 11). Curll accordingly did the same, and we find this style used in all letters addressed to Barnes. But when Mary wrote to the unrecognised messenger, No. 5*a*, or to Babington, No. 7, she again used old style.

(ii.) The outside correspondent in all cases was presumably Phelippes. This appears by the handwriting itself in the later letters, and in his hand we also have the first words of No. 4. Letters 1 and 3 are not in his hand, but considering what an important part they took in his scheme of deception, and remembering that he was not the man to leave important matters without personal supervision, the conclusion as to their authorship, or at least as to their dependence on him, is fairly certain, and is confirmed by the unity of style, of craft, of character, with his other letters. If they were penned by his confidant Gilbert, they would have been either written in his office or communicated to him later (*below*, p. 101, *n.*). The signature, however, of all these outside letters is that of Barnes, who here goes under the byname of Barnaby, represented by the cipher sign *ff*. A few words about him will not be superfluous in order to take the measure of his slippery character.

Thomas Barnes appears to have begun as a Catholic. He speaks of himself as 'having endured somewhat for conscience' (*Confession*, §§ 1, 6), while to Mary he wrote of his 'long imprisonment' (No. 3). He was also familiar with the martyr-priest Stephen Rowsham (*Confession*, § 6). It seems therefore that his mission may have begun in good faith, under the spell thrown over him by 'his cousin Gilbert,' who had tested his pliability by sponging on him for lodgings (*Confession*, § 1), and had found him responsive to offers of money (*below*, p. 3). Gilbert having promised him some work, 'agreeable indeed to the service of God,' but 'greatly to his commodity,' began by making him copy out certain cipher-keys, then prevailed on him to become Mary's postman (whilst he, Gilbert, was away), to fetch letters to and from the French ambassador. But ' what their contents were, or whose, I was not [made] acquainted' (*Confession*, § 2). Gilbert did not at first tell Phelippes the name of Barnes. He mentioned that later, on the 7th of July (*below*, p. 104). To Sir Amias and also to Phelippes the man was first known as 'the second messenger' (Morris, *Letters of Sir Amias Poulet*, 1874, pp. 210, 213), or 'your friend's [*i.e.* Gilbert's] substitute in London' (Morris, p. 212).

I take Barnes to have been a weak, impecunious, venal fellow, whom Gilbert had recognised as a tool who would be useful to any daring villain; for he would sign or deliver as his own, without knowing its contents, any letter put before him; as the papers below most clearly show.

When the tragedy was over, Gilbert wrote from France to Phelippes (end of 1586), 'If you have Barnes, keep him close; if you have him not, I would you had him in your hands' (*below*, p. 123; Boyd, ix. 220). But it was March 1588 before Phelippes 'had him in his hands,' and ex-

§ I. THE SECRET CORRESPONDENCE

tracted the following inedited *Confession*, which is our chief authority for Barnes's life :—

THE CONFESSION OF BARNES

[17 *March* 1588.]

R.O. *Dom. Eliz.*, vol. 199, n. 86. Barnes's autograph, undated. On the same day he wrote a letter offering himself as a spy, and sending on this paper. This letter is printed in Morris, p. 379, from *M.Q.S.* xxi. n. 26, and is dated 17 March 1587/8.

1.] To the first I answer that about the myddell of Easter tearme next shalbe two yeares, my Cosen Gylbert (having had a moneth or two before recourse to my chamber, as lodginge most commonlye or at the lest wyse at his pleasure wth me) brake wth me, as he tearmed hit, in a peece of service, w^{ch} (in respect of the conscience I professed & had indured somewhat therfore) should be agreable to the service of God & redounde likewise most greatlie to my commoditie. Upon w^{ch} & the like persuasions I did undertake to convaye such letters unto the Q. of Scottes as should be sent from him or Morgan, and I made several alphabets for divers persons, as one for the Queene, an other for Morgan, the thyrde for my Cosen, the fourthe for my selfe, and the last for Savage to directe unto me those letters, by [*sic*] wch might by chance come unto his handes from beyonde, at my remaynder or abode in the cuntreye.

2.] As touchinge the seconde [question];—my Cosen Gyfforde delivered me a packett of letters, sealed up wth divers seales, wch he him selfe had receaved, as he told me, to convaye; but havinge other occasions of busynes, presentlie to passe the seas, and havinge thouroughlie perswaded me to take upon me those matters in his absence, willed me, accordinge unto his instructions, to deliver them to the Queene of Scottes Brewar, wch dwelt at Burton upon Trent, in a howse wch was sometimes the Lord Pagetts. W^{ch} I effected accordinglie; although not so soone, in respect of my sicknes at that present, as I promised; but what the contentes were or whose, I was not acquainted wth but thus farre, that my Cosen tolde me they came from Morgan.

3.] To the thirde, I protest upon my faythe and salvation, that I was not particularlie acquainted wth any enterprise against her Maiestie, as sithens is more then manifest, was then in hande; yet notwithstandinge did gather by some generall speeches cast out by Savage and my cosen at our sundrie meetinges that ther was some extraordinarie matter to be putt in execution; but when or what,

I was altogether ignorante. Of George Gyfforde I never harde any mention, nether was I acquainted wth any of them that suffered, but Savage and Charnocke.

4.] Touchinge the fourthe, I confesse I wrote to the Queene, and hit was at that time as I convayed the packett aforesayd. The effect I neede not to declare; because you have hit extante: but answer I receaved none againe; though I had ben divers times in hande wth the Brewar, for one.[1]

5.] Concerninge the fifte, I do most certainlie assure you that my Cosen Gilbertt did not acquainte me wth the name of any other but him selfe (whose turne he persuaded me to supplie) that should deale in that intelligence wth the Queene. For, yf he had, I should not so willinglye have taken the matter in hande; as more certainelye subiect to perill & danger.

6.] To the sixte, I answer that I never acqainted any man or woman wth the particulars of my dealinges for the Queene; but only this, as I was in iorneye towardes Burton wth the aforesayd packett, I mett one Rowsam a preste[2] at Stretforde upon Haven on foote, whom I requested to pray for me, because I had divers thinges about me wth the w^{ch}, yf I should be apprehended, would turne me to as great trouble as I had sustained afore, yf not more.

7.] As touchinge the seventh, I confesse I receaved one letter from Morgan, wherin he gave me to understande that he had recommended me and my service unto the Queene.

8.] To the last I answer that I never harde but two wayes howe the conspiracie was revealed: the first should be by Savage's boye, wch was the generall voyce allmost of all men at that time that I harde talke of hit; the seconde was that hit should be descried

---

[1] This, however, was not Mary's fault. Gilbert carried Mary's letter to him (and presumably also his tip) to London early in July, and it will be found below, No. 6 (see Morris, pp. 217-20).

When Barnes says that he interviewed the brewer 'divers times,' this does not signify that he made more than two journeys as a letter carrier to London, but that he went to see 'the honest man' at home, or in his neighbourhood, in May or June when no letters were coming out, and asked vainly for a letter.

[2] This was the martyr Stephen Rowsham, for whose biography see Burton and Pollen, *Lives of English Martyrs*, i. 279-87. As he was already dead Barnes does not mind calling him a priest. He had returned from exile in the February 1586, but nothing is known of his labours in Shakespeare's Country.' He was arrested in Gloucestershire in the house of Widow Strange, and executed for his priesthood about March 1587.

by my Cosen Gylberte, and that I never harde but once, and that was at Candelmas tearme last was twelue moneth, by one Yardeleye,¹ prisoner in the Clynke at that time.

By me THOMAS BARNES.

From thenceforward Barnes surrendered entirely to Phelippes, and spent his days in worming himself into the confidences of Catholics like Charles Paget, writing him letters according to headings provided by Phelippes; while Paget supplied him with such secrets as he could extract from his patrons the Spaniards, on whose alms he was living. Our *Calendars of State Papers* provide superabundant evidence of these treacheries till the end of Elizabeth's reign.

To return to the correspondence before us. Barnes acted as Gilbert's substitute during the two journeys made to France by the latter, from about 24 April to 25 May, and from 6 to 26 June. Poulet then became suspicious of substitutes (see *Introduction*, § vii. No. 4), and they were discharged: Morris, p. 212 (29 June) and p. 217 (7 July). Barnes does not reappear. Curll, indeed, continues to write to him until the end, but it is Phelippes who answers him under the name of Barnes.

No. 1

THOMAS BARNES TO GILBERT CURLL

[*London, 28 April* 1586.]

Hatfield MSS., Cecil papers 164/55; *Calendar*, iii p. 180; called 28 April in No. 5 *below*. Original decipher by Curll on a half-sheet of pot-paper. From No 5 *below* we learn that it arrived a week before No 2, i e. on 13 May. This is probably 'new' style, therefore=3/13 May. But there is also the possibility of the style being 'old'; and then the date of arrival would be 13/23, which would suit the circumstances better. As ciphers do not have punctuation, capitals, or paragraphs, wherever such things occur, here and hereafter, they are later or editorial additions.

Sʀ,—Having taken uppon me the charge of the packets at London, there was some cause of my stay [? afore] the delyvery and wilbe for a tyme, wherupon I have sent them downe to my brother,² who, I am sure, will tak

---

¹ For Roger Yardley, *alias* Bruerton, see *Cath Rec Soc* ii and xxi. *passim*

² This 'brother' is a mystification not yet fully cleared up. He seems to be later on called 'Emilio' in the endorsements to No 9 and to No 16. Phelippes later on wanted an explanation of the name from Gilbert, who would not give one, thus perhaps showing that he had already told inconsistent stories about it. Eventually they agreed that it should be

order for the sauf conveyance according to the plott layed by ♃ [*cipher sign for Gilbert Gifford*].

I will not trouble yow wth many wordes, especially in this unacquainted and cumbersome maner of wryting towching my devotion towardes her maiestie, which I intend to shew by deedes and not by circumstance of speache. I pray God only my habilite may answer myne owne desire and her maiesties expectation, and I shall think my self happy to have bene any instrument of her contentation.

I am humbly to crave at her maiesties handes and yours that the intelligence wrought by us be not made common to any other of her servantes [1] then suche as have ther address from the Ambas[sador] of fr[ance] at london, at whose handes whatsoever we receave shall surely cum to her handes; as, on the other syde, whatsoever yow delyver unto the honest man, your domesticall frende, will cum sauf [to this] cuntry, I can assure yow, as the matter is ordered. It wer to small purpose to have [the nameys] so curiously concealed, as our cousen ♃ [Gilbert

---

said to represent one of the conspirators who had been executed. But in this correspondence he seems to be Barnes's fictitious brother. In this letter the brother is supposed to be at Burton or Lichfield, but the mystification is not kept up consistently.

The object of the mystification is clearly to create trust in the Scottish Queen. If she had known what an insignificant fellow Barnes was, she would probably not have used him. But she was inclined to confide in the alleged pair of catholic brothers, so intimately united together, and 'cousins' both of the Giffords, the Throckmortons, and Foljambes, knightly families, whose names are casually mentioned later, and who had really suffered in her cause. 'Honest brethren,' she calls them, 'kinsmen of [Gilbert] to serve [his] turn in his absence' (Labanoff, vi. 355).

When dealing with the protestant brewer, Barnes boasted in the same way, only now his relatives are noted puritans, Sir Walter Aston and Mr. Richard Bagot. Poulet's curt but pungent comment is, 'untruly, I doubt not' (Morris, pp. 213, 214). It may also be remarked that Gilbert when writing to Phelippes about Barnes, never calls him 'cousin.'

[1] To keep Mary's correspondence confined to the one channel, which the government was carefully watching, is the object of these two paragraphs: and we must needs regard this as another indication of the cloven hoof. We find Poulet also constantly anxious for the same thing. We cannot doubt which side inspired these lines. Another indication of the same thing may be said of the use of the words 'honest man,' etc.

§ I. THE SECRET CORRESPONDENCE

Gifford] assureth us, from her maiestie her self, If the instrument is a worke to be made common to any other.

If besydes the danger we have sene others fall into before us, namely o^r cousen fr: T. and God: fol: [*i.e.* Francis Throckmorton and Godfrey Foljambe], If yow knew what hazard for myne owne parte I have sene her maiesties secret instrumentes do live in, by reason of the division of her servantes on the other syde the sea, yow wold not marvell that other men be fearefull, and wee warye, how they deale in that wch cummeth from them. For, in trewthe, as they be devyded in affection one from another, so are they in opinion of her maiesties servantes. And if any one of us wch be knowen to be her maiesties, seme to depend or honor them of the one syde, he must looke for all persecution from the other. And any man of qualitie to live in amitie wth both is unpossible.

We are therefor resolved to manage this intelligence as is agreed, not doubting but, if yow be warye enough of the watchefull knight Paulet wthin doores, all shall go currant w^{t}hout rubb abrode. And, rather then fayle, If her maiestie have not othervise meane, I will not stick to mak a way of intelligence for Scotland,[1] being advertised of some course from π [? Morgan], w^{ch} ♃ [Gilbert Gifford] attendeth by his promes.

Thus, attending her maiesties commandementes and directions, I tak my leve for this tyme.   London [28 April].

Endorsed, probably by Curll.   *ff* [cipher mark for Barnes] in May 1586.

At end, in more faded ink.   From Barnaby—disciphered by me Gilbert Curll.   vth october 1586.

Still later hand by a librarian.   A letter decypherd by Gilbert Curle. The Name Gilbert Curle seems to be in ye same Hand as transcribed the Letters from Morgan, Charles Paget, etc.

---

[1] In March (Morris, p. 156) Phelippes had wanted to palm off one of his creatures on the French ambassador, as messenger to Scotland. Here he is trying again.

No. 2

GILBERT CURLL TO THOMAS BARNES.

[*Chartley,* ' 20 *May* ' 1586.]

R.O. *Mary Queen of Scots*, xvii. n. 73; Boyd, n. 413. Curll's original cipher, to which Phelippes has appended his decipher, and then begun his draft answer, but he comes to the end of his line after writing the first eleven words of what is now No. 4. The rest is torn off.

The cipher is written lengthwise on a quarter of a folio sheet; but the flysheet, which presumably bore the address *ff*, has been torn off, so that the page now measures 8 × 3½ inches only.

What follows is Curll's cipher redeciphered. Phelippes's decipher is quite accurate, but he substitutes his own English spelling for Curll's Scotch spelling.

SIR,—H^r M. lykeeth very vvell of the ordor of this convoy, & acordinn to your desyre, vvill haue your securitie regarded carefully. Let me know if I shall send an alphabet to your brother in caise this be not commoun betvven you.

The packet here inclosed [1] is for the French Ambassador.

Excuse, I pray you, for this tyme my breuity, proceding only of the bearer's soonear departure then he was appointed. God preserve you. Of may this tvventeth. Curll at Chartley.

No. 3

THOMAS BARNES TO QUEEN MARY

[*s.l.* ' 10 ' *June,* ? *N.S.*, 1586.]

R.O. *Mary Queen of Scots*, xviii. 6; Boyd, n. 466; Morris, p. 375. Decipher by Curll on a half-sheet of paper, with later attestations by different hands. It is answered in No. 5, whence we learn that it was not signed. Gilbert Gifford went abroad again after 7 June. Barnes, therefore, now reappears as a messenger.

[Headed by a sign, probably *ff*, roughly written.]

MADAME,—the dewtifull good mynd I have alvise inwardly to your Heignes borne, hath bene such as I haue not only quyetly lamented yor vndeserued estate, but have

---

[1] There were originally nine enclosures in this packet to Morgan (see Labanoff, vi. 329), to Englefield, Paget, Bishop Leslie, Dr. Allen, Mendoza, Liggons, Archbishop Beaton, Foljambe, Du Ruisseau. All are preserved except the two last. This was Mary's Post 1.

lykevise sought by all meanes to me possible, wch asmuch as in me lay, I might any way yeald yow confort in this your distressed caise, or imploy my self, and that litle I had, to do you service. All wch intentions of myne, partly throwghe my long imprisonment, and partly for dyvers other causes as [? also] hitherto could take no effect; vntill of late having conferred wth a certaine kinsman of myne about such affayres, he imparted to me this kynd of service, wch he could not so ernestly recommend to me, as I did willingly and affectuously accept of the same. And surely in this he hath satisfyed me this far that I think not my self so much bound unto him in respect of o^r consanguinitie as I do acknowledge my self redevable [1] and beholden to him for this his trust and courtoisy. And therfor not only this way but howsoever it shall please yor H[ighness] to imploy me, yow shall fynd me redy, according to my habilite to performe as yow shall vpon occasiones think convenient to command.

I have here sent yow a packet from france,[2] wch yow had receaved ere this, if I had not in this strange cuntrey lighted in the handes of theaffes, who having spoyled me of my horse & money, have enforced me to go on foot the best part of my way.[3]

I expect yor answer for the recept assoone as may be, for that I wold presently repayre agayne to London to furnish my self of necessaryes. I pray yow send me a

---

[1] Redevable—indebted. See Murray's *English Dictionary*, which notes that the word is obsolete.

[2] This packet, says Barnes (*Confession*, § 2), was from Morgan, and the decipher of his letter of '24 April' is preserved at Hatfield (*Calendar*, iii. 139, printed in full, Murdin, pp. 510-512). Mary gives a full account of its reception in her letter to Morgan, 22 June-'2 July' (Labanoff, vi. 354), together with the present note.

[3] The real object of this paragraph is, no doubt, to solicit a gratuity, and hence the moving terms his '*long* imprisonment,' and the story of his being robbed by highwaymen, about which there is not a word in his *Confession*. It is probably a mere pretence. Still Barnes did go down to Burton, though he could not get an answer, in spite of many petitions to the brewer; perhaps because he forgot to sign his letter. The answer, probably with a donation, came by Gilbert 11/21 July (Morris, 220), and also a cipher alphabet.

new *Alphabet*, for that wch I wryte by was worne owt because I had it of my cousen. Thus, my humble dewtie to yor Heighnes not forgotten, I commit yow to God, whom I beseche long to preserve yor maiestie in lyffe, and shortly to delyver yow out of the handes of yor ennemyes. Dated this x^th of June.[1] [No Signature.]

Written later. Deciphered by me, Gilbert Curll—v^th October 1586.

Written still later. This is the copie of the true & onlie letter I sent to the Queene of Scottes.

By me   THOMAS BARNES.

Endorsed in Phelippes's hand. ff, [*Barnes*] xvj^th and x^th of June 1586.

In a modern pencil. See the answer to this letter by the Scottish Queen, posted 19 June.

Signed,   P. F. T[YTLER].

No. 4

THOMAS BARNES, 'BARNABY' [*really* PHELIPPES] TO CURLL

'*Lichfield*' [*really London*] 6/16 *June* 1586.

R.O. *Mary Queen of Scots*, xviii. 6; Boyd, n. 473. The beginning of the draft, in Phelippes's hand, has been described under No. 2. This is written on the recto side of the last, on a half-sheet of pot-paper. It is Curll's decipher in his autograph, followed by his attestation in October.

As Phelippes was in London, we see that the place-name of Lichfield is fictitious; and so, perhaps, are most of the details. They are all clearly intended to play upon Mary's generosity. The idea of the foot-boy running the 150 miles to London proved a good bait. He is alluded to, we shall see, in almost all the future letters from Chartley; and Mary 'gave credit' to the idea of his being rewarded by the French ambassador in hers of the 13th of

---

[1] As this letter is not signed; as it also begins without any reference to his previous letter of 28 April, or to its answer, which he ought also by this to have acknowledged; as it also contains no reference to his alleged brother at Lichfield (to whom, one would think, he would have gone, instead of returning at once to London)—for these, or similar reasons, we shall henceforward find Mary and Curll treating this 'messenger' as a new person. So that Barnes is now *triplicated* into himself, his brother Emilio, and his messenger; and the messenger is answered in No. 5A.

July: 'Continuez, je vous prie, toujours à gratifier ce laquay de ce que trouvez bon, toutes et quantes foys qu'il portera aulcunes lettres de ma part, et l'employez sur mes parties.'—Labanoff, vi. 374.

From Barnaby vnto me.

S^R,—In the way from London I mett yours of the [1] xxth May, according to the reformed Calendar, (wch I will hereafter follow), wch the bearar therof delyvered, and is returned wth this only lre. I was bold to pray the Ambassador to bestowe an Angel vpon him, wch wold be a gret encouragement to him, being a foot boy to run it, being also of the maner of o^r nation, and a trifle in the wholl yere to her Maiestie. Whrefor it may please yow to geve credit to this motion, by your next to the sayd Ambassador, wch was done in treuth for her Maiesties better service. My brother desyreth to be troubled as litle as he may wth wrytinge,[2] but is content to beare any charges, as I am any paynes, for her Maiesties good: howbeit the *Alphabet*, in respect of any occasion that may happen in my absence, is common betwen us, yet I shall not be long at any tyme so far of but your directions may be sent to my self, the xxiijth of this present I will repayre for answer. God have you in his kepeing.

Lechfeld, xvjth of June 1586.

Decyphered by me, Gilbert Curll, vth October 1586.

No. 5

GILBERT CURLL TO BARNABY

[*Chartley*, 19/29 *June* 1586.]

R.O. *Mary Queen of Scots*, xviii. 10. Curll's draft, much corrected, with later attestation. An answer to Nos. 1, 4.

S^R,—At a seuennight before my former,[3] yo^{rs} dated the xxviijth of Aprile wth your Cousens [4] and the wholl men-

---

[1] Phelippes's draft, commenced on letter 2, had stopped with this word.

[2] This is in answer to Curll's question in No. 2, whether he shall send 'the brother' an alphabet.

[3] 'My former' was No. 2 above, of 10/20 May.

[4] 'Cousin' Gilbert's letter was 24 April (Boyd, n. 359), *below*, p. 99.

tioned therin came sauf to her maiesties handes : So did on the xxth of this instant your other dated the xvjth of the same, conforme to the reformed calender : wherof before now I could not advertise yow.

Her maiestie thinketh her self not a litle beholden to yor sayd Cousen for the fynding owt of yow & your brother to pleasure her maiestie in this intercourse; nor lesse obliged unto your selfes for your so willing acceptance of the payne & travell, that therby yow shall have; wch her maiestie hath commanded me to signify unto yow in hir name, and with all to assure yow of her goodwill & thankfull mynd, to recognosce the same in effect towardes yow & all your^s, whensoever occasion & meanes may offer therunto.

By any erro^r or wante of circumspection, either in her maiesties self or any here about her persone, yow may be assured, ther hath no inconvenient hapned unto any man whom her maiestie hath had intelligence wthall, or imployed as yow are, having alvise kept that order and rewle on her syde for the surest, that never one almost shold know of an other dealing for her maiestie. But that wch hath overthrowen many (to her maiestie's extreme gret greffe) hath bene ther owen too gret curiositie to know more then was requisit for ther securitie, and jalousye one of an other after ther too liberall revealing amongst them selves of ther goodwills in the cause. Towardes whom and ther posteritie her maiestie notwithstanding estemeth her and hers bond to acknowledge her obligation therin effectually, and wilbe no lesse carefull, in the meane tyme, of your preservations every way then of her owne; wch her maiestie maketh not so much accompt of for any particular contentment she wisheth to her self, as she doeth for the mayntenance of Godes cause & the commen good of this ysle : to wch end her maiestie hath dedicated both her lyffe and labors.

On Monday last [1] this bearer browght hither a lettre written to her maiestie in ♃ [Gilbert Gifford] his Alphabet,

---

[1] 'Monday last' was 13/23 June. The letter was No. 3 above.

w^thowt any name or signe who he may be that wrote it, except only that 'a certaine kinsman of his imparted this way to him.' The inclosed is for him, desyring to know his name, w^thowt the wch her maiestie can ground no sure intelligence wth him.

For this day fourtnight, wch wilbe the xiij^th of July, her maiestie will have a packet finished, to be sent unto the french Ambassador: wherfor desyreth yow for that tyme to hold your boy in reddynes; and towching his encouragement her maiestie shall lett the Ambassador know her intention, to your contentment. What correspondence I may give yow, for my owne part, in this trade, yow shalbe sure to have, as also the pleasure and service my poware can othervise do yow, whom I pray God to preserve. Chartley this xxix^th of June.

I have thowght good to change the chifred wordes added to this Alphabet in other simple Caracters, as are herein noted; wch I pray yow vse in tyme cumming, as I will, to thend o^r ordinary wryting—in caise of interception or losse of our lettres—be not discovered (as might by the other) & so by consequence o^rselfes.

Later attestation, From me to Barnabie, at the Queenes Maiestie my mistress' commandment.

GILBERT CURLL, v^th October 1586.

No. 5A

QUEEN MARY TO BARNABY

[*Chartley, 19/29 June 1586.*]

R O *Mary Queen of Scots*, xviii. n. 10; Curll's draft, on the verso side of No 5 It answers No. 3, which is not signed, but dated 10 June

Whosoever yow be, that hath written a lettre unto me in the Alphabet hereof dated the xth of this instant, (wherunto before now I could not answer), I must thank yow right hartely for the affection declared therin, wch yow beare unto me, and the offer yow make to lett me effectually know the same. But I wold more boldly accept therof and imploy yow, if I did know your particular intention: wherin and by what way yow wold pleasure me, and what is yor name, omitted in yor sayd lettre, wch by yor next I pray yow to vtter. In the meane while I do herewith send yow a new Alphabet, conforme to your desire, & pray God to preserve yow. This xix^th of June according to the new computation.[1]

Endorsed (1) To *ff* the xix^th of June 1586.

(2) *Mr. Lemon's note*, A mistake; June 19 *stylo veteri*.

No. 6

GILBERT CURLL TO BARNABY

[*Chartley, 25 June/5 July* 1586.]

R.O. *Mary Queen of Scots*, xviii. n. 16A redeciphered; printed in Morris, p. 378. In this interesting dispatch we have the little quarter sheet in Curll's beautifully regular hand. Phelippes's decipher, very hard to read, is written below the ten lines of cipher. Phelippes has also turned the note, and copied on the back the cipher-letter to Babington, the original of which he was to seal up again and forward. The deciphering may have been done later, and in any case the ciphers would be needed for reference or as evidence.

On Sonday last I vvrote vnto yow by this bearer, having had nothing from yow since your letter dated the sixteenth of this instant. I hope to have hir M. embassador dispatche, mentioned in my foresayd, redy for to-morrow seuennight conforme to the appointment.[2]

In the meane season her Maiestie prayeth yow to send your footboy, so closely as yow can, with these two litle bils inclosed: the one, so)— marked to Master Anthony Babington, dvvelling most in Derbyshyre at a house of his

---

[1] See Mr. Lemon's endorsement.

[2] Sunday before 'Saturday,' 25 June/5 July, was 19/29 June. The bearer of the letter of that date to Barnaby was 'the honest man.' 'This instant' is a slip, for the date of this letter is given in *New Style*, according to which the month was July, not June, while the letter to Babington was Old Style. Hence we see again that Curll, as we might say, thought in Old Style, not in the New. The 'appointment' for Mary's 'embassador dispatche' was in the last letter Sunday, 3/13 July, and this he calls '*to-morrow* sevennight,' so that Curll has in mind that the day he was writing on was Saturday 25 June/5 July; not 4 July, as he writes by slip at the end.

§ I. THE SECRET CORRESPONDENCE

ovvn,[1] within tvvo myles of Winkfeild, as I doubt not but yow knovv, for y^t in this shyre he hath both frends and kinsmen. And the other bill without any mark or superscription to one Richard Hourt,[2] mercer, dvvelling most in Nuttingame. Unto nether of the tvvo foresaid personages your said Boy nedeth not to declare vvhose he is: vnless he be alredy knowen by them vvith vvhom he shall haue to doo, but only aske ansuer, and vvhat is giuen him, to bring it to your handes, which her M. assureth herself, you vvill with conuenient diligence mak come vnto her. As Her M. desyreth y^t you wold on euery occasyon you haue to write, participate vnto her such occurrentes as come unto your knovvledge either foreyn, or within the realme, and in particular what you vnderstand of the Erle of Shrevvsbury his going to court.[3] God preserue you.

At Chartley, of July the fourth on Setterday. CURLL.

Addressed, ff. Calendarer's note in pencil, The day of the month is the 5th and according to the New Style.

No. 7

QUEEN MARY TO ANTHONY BABINGTON

[*Chartley*, 25 *June*/5 *July* 1586.]

R. O. *Mary Queen of Scots,* xviii. 16A verso: described in the preceding letter. It is here redeciphered and is equivalently a new text, which, however, offers no variants from those hitherto published, except that Curll's Scotticisms take the place of Phelippes's Englishisms. For the MS. copies and the editions, see under No. 15.

MY VERY GOOD FREND, Albeit it be long since you hard from me, no more then I haue done from you, agenst my

---

[1] Babington's house was Dethwick, two miles S.E. of Matlock. Mary, it will be noted, believes that her humble correspondent really belongs to the county families, and knows every one. This was because Gilbert had told her (24 April) that 'my kinsman has good friends in the courte,' and 'will be able to inform you of the state of this council, as you shall direct him.' Hence also the inquiry about Lord Shrewsbury, answered in No. 9.

[2] This Richard Hourt, or Hert, was a creditor from whom Mary had borrowed money. See Mary to Morgan, '2 July'; Labanoff, viii. 354; Boyd, n. 497. But Labanoff reads 'Charles Paget' in place of Hert, I suppose by an erroneous identification.

[3] See also Babington's Examination, *below,* p. 89.

vvill, yit vvodd I not you shold think, I haue in the meanevvhyle, nor will euer be vnmyndful of the effectuall affection yow haue shewen heretofore towards all y^t concerneth me. I haue vnderst[ood] y^t vppon the ceassing of ovvre intelligence there vvere addressed vnto you both from France and Scotland some packets for me. I pray you, if any haue come to your handes, and be yet in place, to delyuer them vnto the bearer hereof, who will mak them to be sauf conuoyed to me, and I vvill pray God [for your] preseruation.

Of June the tvventy fyfth, at Chartley.
  Your assured good frend,   Marie R.

Address in the left corner, Babington.

No. 8

GILBERT CURLL TO BARNABY

[*Chartley, 2/12 July* 1586.]

R.O. *Mary Queen of Scots*, xviii. n. 30 redeciphered. A slip of paper containing four lines of cipher characters by Curll, and also the decipher by Phelippes (printed in Morris, p. 378).

The last of yours vv^ch came to my hands vvas dated the sixtenth of Iune. Since the vvhich I have vvritn to you tvvyse, the one on Sonday vvas a seuennight, & the other the fourth of this instant, but haue had no vvord from yow of the recept of ether of the tvvo.[1]

Herevvith is the packet mentioned in both, which her Mai. prayeth yow to send by your boy, or othervvise surely, to the Fr. Amb.[2]

So expecting yow vvill by the next commoditie communicate to her M. such newes as yow heare, I pray God to preserue yow.

This Setterday at Chartley tvvelfth of Iuly. Curll.

Addressed, ff.[3]

---

[1] These two letters are numbers 5, 6, *above*.
[2] This was Mary's Second Post out.
[3] This sign means Barnes, but he probably never received the letter. Gilbert Gifford, whom Sir Amias expected on the 29th of June (Morris,

No. 9

BARNABY TO GILBERT CURLL

[?Chartley, 10/20 July 1586.]

R.O. *Mary Queen of Scots*, xviii. n 63; Boyd, n. 606; Morris, p. 379. Phelippes's draft, much corrected, and occasionally wanting in connecting words, which deficiencies are here shown by dashes. The letter must have been written by Phelippes on his arrival at Chartley, and it covered Babington's first letter to Mary.

SIR,—I have received your last of the 12th of July [No. 8] by my cousin Gilbert, as also your other two therein mentioned which in my absence came to my brother's hands, who took order for the satisfaction of her Majestie touching the contents, but forbears to write, as a thing which he always desired he might not be charged with.

The present packet [*i.e.* Post ii.] committed to my cousin Gilbert, to be by himself delivered; who hath likewise signified (as he tells me) [? so much that may content the ?] second messenger, as I hold it nedeless to trouble you with anything myself touching that point.

Ye delivery of the letters in cipher [to Babington, No. 7] enclosed in yours of the 4th [No. 6],—my brother at London—despatched it accordingly thither. In turne he received the packet sent herewith, which, Babington said, required great haste; and therefore the boy returned without staying for any despatch from the French Ambassador, who attendeth letters, he saith, daily out of France. I will take order for the delivery of Hurt's letter myself.

---

p. 212), arrived in time to receive this letter, as well as Mary's letter to Barnes (No. 5A *above*), and probably also Barnes's reward (Morris, pp. 217, 220). Sir Amias wanted Barnes discharged (Morris, p. 212), and Gilbert promised 'to cut him clear off from this course' (Morris, p. 217).

Gilbert also took the 'Second Post,' and it was sent up to London by Sir Amias's courier.

Mary refers to Gilbert's letter to her in her letter to Morgan, 17/27 July, (Labanoff, p. 421; Boyd, n. 624), and in writing to Chateauneuf (*ibid.*, Labanoff, p. 428) she says he had promised to be back before the end of the month.

I find the Earl of Shrewsbury¹ he was greatly grieved with a stay that the Quene of England made of a book, printed by him about one Babsthorpe, a gentleman, upon the statute of *scandalum magnatum*, for lewd speeches uttered by the said Babsthorpe against the Earl. Howbeit the Earl, since his going up hath prevailed so far with his reasons of discontentment that the Q. of England is content the Law shall have course.

For other matters I refer to the next: this both sudden and speedy because of Mr. Babington's request. I received your alteration of the alphabet & concurred in the reason. I wish, for greate expedition also in writing, that you would assign special characters for a number of the most common words. So God preserve you.

The 20th of July.

Endorsed, Emilio, cifer 1. *Numbered*, 52 [? 32].

No. 10

ANTHONY BABINGTON TO QUEEN MARY

[*n.d.* ? London, ?6/16 July 1586.]

R.O. *Mary Queen of Scots*, xix. n. 12, official copy. This letter is always found in conjunction with Queen Mary's answer, and its authenticity must depend upon that. This question will be discussed fully below; the MS. and printed copies with which the collations are made are also explained below.

i. Moſt mightie, moſt excellent, my dread ª ſoveraigne Ladie and Queen,² vnto whome only I owe all fidelitie and obedience. It maie pleaſe yoʳ gratious Maᵗⁱᵉ to admitt thexcuſe of my long ſilence and diſcontenewance from the dutifull offices incepted. Vpon the remove of yoʳ royall pſon from the auntient place of yoʳ aboade to the cuſtodie of a wicked puritan and meer Leiceſtrian,ᵇ a mortall enemie

---

a. dread,—Bresslau, dear.
b. mere Leicestrian,—K. *omits*.

---

¹ This answers the question put in No. 6.
² For the exaggerated tone throughout, see Babington's *Confessions*, viii. p. 91.

both by faith and faction to yor Matie and the State Catholick : I heald the houpe of o^r Contries weale depending next vnder god vpon the lief and health of yor Matie to bee defperate, and therevpon refolved to depart the land, determining to fpend the remainder of my lief in fuch folitarie fort as the wretched and miferable ftate of my Contrie did require : daily expecting according to the iuft iudgement of god the deferved confufion thereof, which our Lord for his mercies fake prevent.

ii. The wch my purpofe being in execution, and ftanding vppon my departure, there was addreffed to mee from the partes beyond the feas [1] one Ballard a man of vertue and learning, and of finguler zeale to the Catholick caufe, and yor Ma^{ts} fervice. This man enformed mee of great preparation by the Chriftian princes (yor Ma^{ts} allies) for the deliverance of o^r Contrie from thextreame and miferable ftate wherein it hath to long remained :

iii. wch when I vnderftood my fpetiall defire was to advife, by what meanes with the hazard of my lief and frendes in generall I might doe your facred Matie one good daies fervice. Wherevpon moft deare [a] foueraigne according to ye great care wch thofe princes haue of the prefervation and fafe deliverie of yor Ma^{ts} facred pfon, I advifed of meanes and confidered of ye circumftances according to the weight of the affaire : and after long confideration and conference had with fo manie the wifeft and moft truftie, as wth fafetie I might commend the secrecy [b] thereof vnto,[2] I do [c] find (by the affiftance of o^r Lord

---

a. dear,—K. dread.

b. secrecy,—*so* B. R.O. *reads* safety—a duplication from the previous line.

c. do,—*so* Cal. and K.

[1] We may fairly assume that Morgan directed Ballard to Babington; but we should remember that Gilbert Gifford was also capable of having done this. For this mission, and for the bogus league of princes, etc., see *Introduction*. Babington evidently believed in the league. Mary, to judge by her answer, and much more by her letters to Mendoza, and the rest, did not, though she did not contradict Babington.

[2] These words are explained in Babington's *Confessions*, viii. § 1.

Jefus) affurance of good effect and defired fruict of o^r travailes.

iv. Thefe thinges are firft to bee advifed [1] in this great and honorable action vpon the iffue of wch depend not only the lief of yor moft excellent Matie (wch god long preferve to our ineftimable comfort and to the falvation of Englifh foules) and the lief of all vs actors herein, but alfo the hono^r and weale [a] of o^r Contrie, farr then our lives more deare vnto vs, and the last hoape ever to recover the faith of o^r forefathers, and to redeem o^r felves from the fervitude and bondage wch herefie hath impofed vpon vs with the loffe of thoufands of foules : [a] ffirft affuring of invafion : [b] fufficient ftrength in the invado^r : [c] Portes to arrive at appointed,[b] [d] with a ftrong partie at everie place to ioyne with them and warrant their landing. [e] The deliverance of yor Matie. [f] The difpatch of the vfurping Competitor. ffor the effectuating of all wch yt it maie pleafe yor Ex^{tie} to relie vpon my fervice.

v. I vowe [2] and proteft before the face of almightie god (who miraculoufly hath long preferved your facred pfon no doubt to fome vniverfall good end) that what I haue faid fhalbee pformed, or all our lives happely loft in thexecution thereof : which vowe all the chiefe actors herein haue taken folemnly and are vppon affurance by yor Ma^{ts} lres vnto mee to receave the bleffed facrament therevpon, either to prevaile in ye churches behalf and yor Ma^{ts}, or fortunately to die for that honorable caufe.

vi. Nowe for as much as the delaie is extreame dangerous : It maie pleafe yor moft excellent Matie by yor wifdome to direct vs [3] and by yor princely authoritie to

---

a. honour and weal,—Cal. weal, K. wealth.
b. invaders ... *to* ... appointed,—K. *reads*—invaders ports to arrive well appointed. *French version has the same.*

---

[1] Mary's answer to this is in her §§ 3, 4. In effect she says, '*You must look to them and consult Mendoza.*'
[2] On this 'vow' and on 'sworn servant' at the end, see *Confessions*, viii. §§ 6, 9.
[3] This is answered in Mary's § 12.

enable ᵃ ſuch as maie advaunce the affaire¹: foreſeing that where is not anie of the nobilitie at libertie aſſured to yoʳ Maᵗⁱᵉ in this deſperate ſervice (except vnknowen to vs) and ſeing it is verie neceſſarie that some there bee to become heades to lead the multitude, ever diſpoſed by nature in this land to follow nobilitie conſidering withall it doth not only make the comons and gentrie to followe without contradiction or contention (which is ever found in equalitie) but alſo doth add great corage to the leaders. ffor wᶜʰ neceſſarie regard I [would] recommend² ſome vnto yoʳ Maᵗⁱᵉ as fitteſt in my knowledge for to bee your Lieutenants in the Weſt partes, in the north partes, Southwales, North Wales and the Counties of Lancaſter Derbie and Stafford: all which Contries by parties alreadie made and fidelities taken in your Maᵗˢ name I hould as moſt aſſured, and of moſt vndoubted fidelitie.

vii. My ſelf with tenne gentlemen and a hundred oʳ followers will vndertake the deliverie of your royall perſon from the handes of yoʳ enemies.

viii. †ffor the diſpatch of the vſurper, from the obedience of whome wee are by thexcommunication of her made free,³

---

a. enhable,—*so* Cal. *State Trials*, 1729, p. 142, *reads*—enable us and. All MSS. *omit* 'us and'; Cal. *however has* 'us,' *but it has been cancelled.*

---

¹ The weight of MS. authority (see the variant readings) is against the introduction by Babington of the request that Mary should 'enhable us,' *i.e.* that he should be appointed leader, tempting though it may be, to imagine that he would have made such a suggestion.

² Babington was re-examined on this passage, viii. § 4. He then 'denied that he did recommend any gentleman by name to the Scottish Quene, to be Lieutenant; but the effect of his letter in that point was that he would afterwards recommend some unto her.' 'Would' must therefore be supplied.

³ Pius v. gave no warranty whatever for assassination; *Introduction*, p. xxi. (see *Bullarium* under date 25 February 1570; or Sander, *De Schismate Anglicano*, ed. D. Lewis, p. 301; or *Venetian Calendar*, 1570, p. 449; or *Rome Calendar*, p. 328; or Pollen, *English Catholics in the Reign of Elizabeth*, 142-59). Babington, moreover, was uncertain whether the bull was still of force (*Confessions*, ii. 2). He was also speaking untruly when he stated that six gentlemen were ready 'to undertake the tragical execution.' He himself insisted on this later (*Confessions*, ii. § 22, and iii. § 7). Ballard declared that 'for all Babington's brag he could not see that he could assure himself of more than two' (Boyd, p. 683). For the †† see p. 31.

there bee fix noble gentlemen all my private frends, who for the zeale they beare to the Catholick caufe and your Ma^te fervice will vndertake that tragicall execution†.

ix. It refteth that according to their infinite good defertes and yor Ma^ts bountie their heroicall attempt maie bee honorably rewarded in them yf they efcape with lief, or in their pofteritie, and that fo much I maie bee able by your Ma^ts authoritie to affure them.

x. Nowe yt remaineth only that by yor Ma^ts wifdome it maie bee reduced into methode; that yor happie deliverance bee firft, for that therevpon dependeth our only good, and that all the other circumftances fo concurre ^a that the vntimely beginning ^b of one end doe not overthrowe the reft. All which your Ma^ts wonderfull experience and wifedome will difpofe of in fo good maner, as I doubt not through gods good affiftance all fhall come to defired effect; ffor the obteining of which everie one of vs fhall thinck his lief moft happely fpent.

xi. vpon the xij^th of this moneth I wilbie at Lichfield [1] expecting yor Ma^ts anfweare and letters in readines to execute what by them fhalbee comaunded.

Yo^r Ma^ts moft fathfull fubiect & fworne fervant,

ANTHONY BABINGTON.

To Mr Nau, Secretarie to her Matie.

Mr Nau I would gladly vnderstand what opinion you hould of one Robert Pooley, whome I find to haue intelligence with her Ma^tis occasions.[2] I am private with the man and by meane thereof knowe somewhat but suspect more. I praie you deliver yor opinion of him.

---

a. concur,—B. occur.
b. beginning,—K. fall.

---

[1] The answer was delivered to him at London on the 29th of July.
[2] Occasions (see *Oxford English Dictionary*, meaning No. 7)=Necessary business, affairs. This example is earlier than any of those there cited.

§ I. THE SECRET CORRESPONDENCE

Attestations in the same hand. (1) *To the letter for Mary.* This is the true copic of y^e l̃re wch I wrott to y^e Queene of Scottes.
ANTHONIE BABINGTON.

(2) *To the letter for Nau.* This is the true copie of the letter wch I wrote to Nau.
ANTHONIE BABINGTON.

No. 11

GILBERT CURLL TO BARNABY

[*Chartley*, 12/22 *July* 1586.]

R.O. *Mary Queen of Scots*, xviii. n. 42, redeciphered; Boyd, n. 585; Morris, p. 379. Six and a half lines of Curll's cipher, with Phelippes's decipher below. Curll is now triplicating Barnes; *viz.* Barnaby in the address, 'your brother,' and 'the second messenger.' He believes them all to be distinct and different persons. This letter of acknowledgment covered the one from Nau, which follows.

SIR,—Yisternight your letter, dated the tvventeth [1] of this instant with the inclosed, her M. received right thankfully of yow, vvith dilligence yow shevv to pleasure her in all she desyreth.

I trust yow have caused deliver her M.'s answer to the second messinger, although to say trevvly, her M. agreeth with cusin Gilbert his advice not much to imploy the man. Neither hath her M. ben vvilling at any time unnedefully to exerce this course for her part vvith any mo then your self, your brother and cusin Gilbert.

If Master Babington come dovvne in the cuntrey for vvhom this ·x· caracter shall servve in the tyme cuming, her M. prayeth yow to cause conuoy to him this inclosed: other vise to stay it untill yow hear from her M. agayne.

With my next I shall doo my best to satisfy yow toucheing the other caracters. God have you in protection.

Of iuly the xxij. Curll, Chartley.

Addressed, ff=Barnaby.

Numbered, 48.

---

[1] Phelippes in error wrote 12.

No. 12

CLAUDE NAU TO ANTHONY BABINGTON

[*Chartley*, ' 13 '/23 *July* 1586.]

R.O. *Mary Queen of Scots*, xviii. n. 43. Copy by Phelippes; Boyd, n. 586. Babington's covering letter to Nau appears to be lost, but Babington's recollections of it are given *below*, p. 90, where he also gives a remarkably accurate recollection of the letter which follows. This is Phelippes's decipher. The original was penned by Curll, as he afterwards confessed, because he was English secretary.

S^r,—Yesternight her Ma^{ty} receaved your letters and therin closed, wch before this bearer's [1] retorne cannot be decifred. He is within these two or three dayes to repayr hither agayne; agaynst which tyme her majestyes answer shalbe in redynesse.[2]

In the meane while I wold not omitt to shew you, that there is great assurance given of Mr. Poley his faythful seruing of her majesty, and by his owne letters hath vowed and promised the same. As yet her majestyes experience of him is not so great as I dare embolden yow to trust him moch: he never hauing written to her Majesty but once, wherunto she hath not yett answered,[3] for not knowing of his abode, neyther assuredly to whose handes he first committed his sayd letters. Let me know playnly what you understand of him. And so I will pray God to preserve yow. This 13 of Julye.[4] At Chartley. NAU.

Endorsed by Phelippes, 13 July 1586, Nau to Bab. *Numbered*, 53.

---

[1] 'This bearer,' *i.e.* the 'honest man.'
[2] In fact the answer took a fortnight to prepare.
[3] So Mary seems to have kept the letter, but it is now lost.
[4] Old Style, because addressed to an Englishman following that style.

No. 13

GILBERT CURLL TO BARNABY

[*Chartley*, 17/'27' *July* 1586.]

R.O. *Mary Queen of Scots*, xviii. 57; cipher redeciphered; Boyd, 599; Morris, 379. Curll's writing (seven lines) followed by Phelippes's decipher.

SIR,—This afternoone hauing receaued your letter of the tvventy fyue of this instant,[1] and letten her M. see the same vvholly descyphered, which hath not a litle augmented the good opinion she had conceaued before of your affection towards God's cause and hers, she hath commanded me hereby to give yow her right harty thankes herfore, & to pray yow in her name, untill farther occasion shall offer to imploy yow otherwise, that you vvil continevv in occurrentes [2] as yow promes & novv haue done.

& to mak this inclosed [3] be surely [deliver]ed in the hands of Anthony Babington, if he be come dovvn [to] yow in the country. Otherwise, that it be kept still in yours or your brothers keeping, untill Babington his arrivall; or for an tenn dayes, within which tyme her M. intendeth to haue a [packet] redy to be sent to the Fr. Am. by your boy,[4] who by the same meane may also carry the other to Babington at London, if he come not douune soonar.

Giuen herewith is the addition to this alphabet, and so I pray God to preserue you. Of iuly the tvventy-seuenth.

CURLL.

Addressed, ff; Numbered, 50.

---

[1] This letter seems to be lost. It was probably written to reassure.

[2] Mary's pleasure in hearing news is attested now in every letter since No. 6. Gilbert, in sending Barnes to her (letter of 24 April, *below*, p. 101), promised her that he had the news of the court; and Phelippes, while weaving his fatal toils around her, is lulling her into a feeling of security by his stories.

[3] This was the fatal letter to Babington.

[4] The promised packet would contain her 'third post.'

No. 14.

QUEEN MARY TO ANTHONY BABINGTON

[*Chartley,* 17/27 *July* 1586.]

R.O. *Mary Queen of Scots,* xviii. n. 53. Judging by the cipher signs which remain in this transcript, one infers that this copy is an extremely early one. We cannot point to any copy as definitely earlier.

Mary's letter to Babington, of 17 July 1586, is confessedly the chief document of this entire episode. Phelippes endorsed it at once with the gallows' mark. Babington knew it practically by heart. Mary entirely denied its blood guiltiness, 'I am to be tried by my own words. By them you will not find me guilty.'

Both sides therefore regard the letter as all-important; and whatever our answer to Mary's challenge, there is no question that it demands a very careful study. Its difficulties are many, subtle, and long-standing. 'The English Councillors . . . say that this letter is the most artful and cleverly worded they have ever seen.' That was Mendoza's report, 8 November 1586 (*Spanish Calendar,* p. 645).

§ 1. THE AUTHENTIC TEXT.

There are two families of texts. The authentic text and the *textus receptus,* as we may call it.

The authentic text was that of the letter which Mary sent off. Looking at the *Introduction,* p. cxlvi, we find its history, which may be reduced to the following chronological heads. Written between the 10th and 17th of July, it had at first been thought out by Mary herself, perhaps with a note or two in MS. Then it was written in French by Nau; and finally translated into English by Curll, Mary having revised *and approved* the letter at each stage. Afterwards Curll put it into cipher and sent it off.

This authentic text was, as we see, in English. Labanoff, who printed it in French, and the officials of the Record Office, who bound up their French copies before the English, were mistaken. Even if the existing French had been Nau's draft (which is in reality not preserved), it would not have been the authentic text. In point of fact the existing French versions are enemy translations of the *textus receptus,* made either for the examination of Nau, or else after the trial for transmission to France.

§ I. THE SECRET CORRESPONDENCE

The authentic letter, after being posted by Curll on the 18th of July, was brought back by 'the honest man' that same night, and given to Phelippes, who immediately deciphered it. This decipher is the original of the *textus receptus*.

On the 19th the decipher was sent up to Walsingham; Phelippes, bringing up the authentic letter, arrived in London on Friday the 29th. And after dusk that same summer evening, the letter was handed on to Babington, but now furnished with a postscript, asking the names of the 'six gentlemen.'

Next day the letter was deciphered by Babington, aided by Tichborne. There is no trace of any copy having been made or kept; and Babington (*Confessions*, ii. § 22) denied having done so. Poley indeed commenced a copy; but being detected by Babington he tore up his copy before Babington's eyes (Boyd, p. 601). Mary had ordered the immediate destruction of the letter, and there is no question that Babington would have obeyed. His accounts of it in his confessions written by memory, are so accurate that we feel sure that he had deliberately committed the letter to memory; and he would not have done that except in some necessity of making away with the paper itself. He knew that he was in danger; and he had plenty of time to destroy it. He cites the postscript, so does Dunne. The obvious conclusion is that Babington made away with the cipher and the decipher as soon as he and a sufficient number of witnesses had seen it. This would have been about the 1st to the 4th of August. The only records now remaining of it *as a text* are the excellent recollections of Babington in his examinations below, with others in gradually diminishing value, from Ballard, from Dunne, from Tichborne, and also from Robert Poley, all of which are independent of each other.

Of the many extant copies of Mary's letter any derived from the authentic text should give the postscript. But no known copy contains it.

§ 2. THE DRAFTS FOR THE AUTHENTIC LETTER.

We know that there were several drafts for the authentic letter; possibly, though not probably, one by Mary, one by Nau, and one by Curll.

1. On the 3rd of September Nau acknowledged that Mary's minute had been seized with the other papers. 'It pleased her to deliver to me a minute of a letter written by her hand to be corrected and fairly written, as appears to your honours [*i.e.* to the

Privy Council] to have been done, having both of them in your hands.' (Boyd, p. 665.)

But Nau is not a good witness here. He was already confused, frightened, unable to defend himself. He had been made to believe that more papers were captured than was the case. It is clear from his words that he was relying here on this false information.

Besides this, Nau is here going beyond his province. The keeping of Mary's papers was not his business, but that of Curll.

In subsequent confessions, moreover, after the 3rd of September, he gives a slightly different account, which seems to exclude a draft in Mary's hand. He says that he 'had taken down the points of the letter to Babington *out of the Scottish Queen's own mouth.*' And again, 'These points were . . . first delivered by the same Queen unto this examinate by her own speech,' p. 145, *below*.

Walsingham, on reading Nau's first confession, at once, 3 September, wrote earnestly to Phelippes about it, 'I would to God these minutes were found!' (Morris, p. 284). Next day, 4 September, he has been convinced that 'the minute of her hand is not extant' (Morris, p. 284; Boyd, n. 753). With these words the prosecution seems to give up all attempt to learn more about the draft by Mary. Nau's statement may have been an exaggeration due to over-wrought nerves, after he had been misled by Lord Burghley's calculated flourishes.

2. Of Nau's own draft also nothing more was said. It certainly existed, and appears to have been preserved. But nothing more is heard of it now.

3. *Curll's English draft,* from which the authentic letter to Babington was put into cipher.—This draft had been preserved by Queen Mary. Curll, a much more staid witness than Nau, declared this quite plainly on the 21st of September. 'That which was Englished by this examinate, this examinate did put into a trunke which was in the Scottish Queen's cabinet (*i.e.* her writing-room) under lock and key' (*below,* p. 147). We should mark this attentively, for some official abbreviator of the evidence has deliberately falsified this record in a later paper, which purports to summarise this examination of 21st September. Compare *Hardwicke Papers,* i. 249, 250, with p. 147, n.

The conclusion seems to be that while there may have been notes by Mary which might be called a draft, and while there certainly were drafts both by Nau and by Curll, none of these were produced, though much desired. The draft by Curll was certainly kept, and therefore certainly seized, and an attempt was made to falsify the record of its preservation. How can this be explained? I suggest that Phelippes, on seizing the papers, destroyed the drafts which would have betrayed his postscript. When Walsingham regretted their non-appearance, Phelippes told him the reason; and he acquiesced, 'the minute of her answer is not extant.' In the same spirit, when a summary of the trial was prepared for some form of publication (ultimately in the *Hardwicke State Papers*), it was so doctored that the evidence of preservation should disappear without exciting comment; the record was *spurlos versenkt*.

§ 3. THE TEXTUS RECEPTUS AND ITS HISTORY.

The text in general circulation, which is also printed below, may be called the *textus receptus*. Copies are numerous, in manuscript, in print, and in translations. As generally happens with such oft-copied pieces, copyist errors are frequent, but in essentials the text is the same everywhere.

Phelippes deciphered and copied the authentic letter that passed through his hands on the 19th of July; and hereby ensued a new text. But what can be more clear than that Phelippes's copy lacks all 'authenticity.' We know that he forged a postscript to the letter itself before he sent it on. How, with that in mind, can we trust his *authority*? Elizabeth's government was afraid to produce his story in court. Why? Because they knew that the whole world would have cried out, and would have accounted him the worst criminal in the proceedings. If then Elizabeth's government feared to commit themselves publicly to Phelippes's authority, with how much better reason should not we abstain? The text lacks all external authenticity: and if we eventually see our way to trust it, this can only be for reasons extrinsic to Phelippes's reliability. In any case, however, as it was everywhere received, we may very well call it the *textus receptus*.

At first while the conspirators were being examined, we hear but little of Mary's letter. Babington, however, confessed at once (? 18 August) all that he could remember about the letter and the postscript. On the 20th of August (*Confessions*, iv.) he was shown further clauses copied often literally from Phelippes's copy, and he was fraudulently told that they had been confessed by the other conspirators. These points (which did not comprise the postscript) Babington at once confessed, and re-wrote them in improved order and the commissioners countersign his welcome concession.

Next he is asked to attest Phelippes's copy entire, and he does so. Nau, seeing this, follows suit. Finally Curll does the same. Thus was the *textus receptus* at last established (pp. 79, 139).

Babington had been carried away by his desire to oblige the government, and he had apparently not noticed the absence of the postscript, which he had rightly mentioned in his first confession. By this careless weakness, he had done Mary's cause a great, if unintentional, injury. For if he had insisted on the introduction of the postscript, Curll or Nau would have detected the fraud when they were asked to sign a day or two later. This gullibility is characteristic of Babington.

The attestations of Nau and Curll (*below*, pp. 142-147) are expressed so very guardedly, as almost to suggest the presence of errors. To prevent any doubt settling upon the parts which the government considered vital to their case, they extracted *Certain Principall Points*, six in number: Curll and Nau had to subscribe these on the 23rd of September. The parts quoted are marked in the notes to the text below.

The letter was read to Mary at the trial (15 October). She asked for a copy: denied that she had written any such letter, and again protested in general 'that she was not to be charged, but by her word or by her writing, and she was sure they had neither the one nor the other to lay against her.' In Mary's own mind that meant, no doubt, I am not to be tried by Babington's letter, but by my own, taken *strictly* by itself alone. By that *alone* I cannot be proved guilty. But nobody saw her point, and the court would only have jeered if they had seen it. In the 'Association' they had sworn to murder her, if it were but proved that such a one as Babington had conspired in her favour.

After the trial a French version of the letters was sent to France, carried by Sir Edward Wotton, whose instructions are dated 29 September. It was hoped that the § xiii. against trusting the French King, might cause Henri III. to refrain from interfering on behalf of Mary his sister-in-law. It is probable that these letters had been translated previously, in order to lay before Nau: and there was another translation later, of which immediately.

After Mary's execution the letters were printed in English, in an anonymous book, *A defence of the honourable sentence and execution of the Queen of Scots*, printed by John Windet, and conjecturally ascribed to Maurice Kyffin. This tract is extremely rare. It has some peculiar omissions, evidently those of the court censor, as will be seen below. These peculiarities are not found in subsequent editions, those, for instance, in the *State Trials*, of which the first edition was before 1729. The inference therefore is, that for them recourse was had to manuscript sources, which are, of course, abundant. There was, however, a French translation of this tract in 1588, which follows the peculiarities of the English edition, though, as we have seen, the letters had in fact been translated into French officially and fully at an earlier date.

§ 4. Suspicions of the *Textus Receptus*.

Camden tells us that Phelippes added to the text the postscript, *si non et quaedam alia*, 'if not some other things also.' Partly from this, partly from other reasons, some critics favourable to Mary, as Labanoff and Lingard, have pointed out that if a few clauses in Mary's letter, and they the most liable to hostile attack, are omitted (they are marked below by daggers), the whole letter reads more naturally, and corresponds better with the circumstances of the case. They point, for instance, to § ix., where Elizabeth is represented as consigning Mary to a life-long dungeon, and they contrast this with § vii., where it is arranged that the assassination must be the first step of all. Here, say they, are two conflicting ideas. If, however, the passage in § vii. is omitted as having been inserted or altered by Phelippes, the sense of the whole is improved. With a change or two like this, Mary's letter is disconnected from Babington's plot, and refers only to escape and final deliverance with foreign aid. This conclusion is strengthened by further excisions in Babington's letter. It is pointed out that Morgan had previously cautioned Ballard and Gilbert Gifford against telling Mary of the plot. After that, say they, we may be sure that Babington would not have written to her about it; and so the assassination passages in Babington (§ viii.) are similarly confined with daggers. When this is done, both letters may be read together, and still nothing will transpire about the murder-plot.

As to the above arguments, we must say, in the first place, that they proceed on an altogether wrong principle. The true canon for a case like this is the following, *Lectio difficilior, ergo verisimilior*. But without enlarging on this abstract principle, we should say that the aforesaid inference might have seemed to us plausible in earlier times, when documents regarding this case were extremely rare. But now that we have so many independent witnesses, they are quite inadequate for the occasion. Some of the inferences are directly invalidated by further research; *e.g.* the letter from Morgan against communicating with Mary did not reach Ballard till the 21st of July, whereas Babington's letter was written on the 6th of July.

The striking catena of witnesses to Mary's authentic letter, Babington, Ballard, Dunne, Tichborne, Poley, is passed unnoticed. But they all understood her to have actually approved of the plot, to say nothing of Nau and Curll, though their evidence is certainly very strong and was held at the time as decisive. When Dr. Lingard wrote his extremely clever note S., he had no chance of weighing any part of that catena; he had not studied the collections of the British Museum or the Record Office, and relied upon the extracts given in Tytler and supplied to him by friends; he only speaks conjecturally.

§ 5. Reasons for accepting the *Textus Receptus*.

Though this text comes to us through a forger, and is for that reason to be received with the greatest suspicion, yet that is not the same thing as saying that it can never be admitted. If sufficient and independent evidence for it can be obtained, it must certainly be accepted. It appears to me that our evidence is sufficient. We have seen a catena of witnesses for the *textus authenticus* which is strong and ample — Babington, Ballard, Dunne, Tichborne, and Poley. They are independent, they speak to all the important passages; and as to these, they are at one. Nau and Curll concur. At the time their evidence was the chief authority, and it must still be considered most important. This purely extrinsic evidence seems to me abundant. I accept the *textus receptus* throughout, apart from errors of transcription. I believe that the postscript was the only forgery which Phelippes was allowed.

Moreover, it seems to me that the letter agrees in a marked way with Queen Mary's defence. It is incredible that Walsingham and Phelippes should have forged or manipulated a letter so that it would suit the plea which Mary was going to put forward in her defence; and far more incredible still, if the text was really influenced by manipulation, that Mary should have known, before seeing the document objected to her, that her peculiar line of defence would be applicable to it.

Mary's well-known protest was that she was not to be tried except by her own words, and that in her own words, there would be no consent or incitement to assassination. With these letters before us, her meaning becomes much more pertinent than at first appears. When she said she was only to be tried by her own words, she meant that she was not to be tried by Babington's letter. The blanks in her letter were not to be filled up by statements of his, and his intentions must not be read into her mind. And, in fact, we find that if she is tried by her own letter alone, even in the received text, she must be pronounced free of having encouraged assassination. Her defence will stand.

§ 6 WHILE PRAISING BABINGTON'S ENTERPRISE IN GENERAL, MARY REFUSES CONSENT TO THE MURDER CLAUSES.

Mary's letter from first to last is one of praise and agreement. Nevertheless, if we look to the points for which Babington explicitly solicited her consent and approval, we find that these are refused. This was not a side issue. Babington declared (and Ballard was of exactly the same mind) that the Queen's consent was an absolute necessity; and he therefore asks for consent in a clear and tangible form.

1. He begged her first 'to reward the six gentlemen who undertake the tragical execution' (§§ viii. ix.)

Mary in reply does promise rewards, but not to the six nor for the special work of the six. She undertakes 'to recompense by effects your deserts for my delivery' (§§ ix. xv.)

2. Babington again (§ ix.) asked for 'your Majesty's authority to assure' the six of 'honourable reward.' Mary answers this (§ ix.), 'To yourself in particular I refer, to assure the gentlemen above mentioned [she has last mentioned "our principal friends"] of all that shall be requisite on my part for the entire execution of their good-wills' And again at the end, 'I do and will think myself obliged, as long as I live towards you, for the offers you make to hazard yourselves, as you do, for my delivery.'

Looking for the moment not to the morality of the offers but only to the strict meaning of Mary's words, we see that they contain at this critical point a distinct withdrawal. Asked to reward the six, she promises rewards—(1) for her 'delivery,' which was not the work of the six; (2) To 'the gentlemen above mentioned,' *i.e* to all active friends; (3) Babington may not give her royal assurance of recompense, but only his own, (4) Moreover, he may not attach rewards to definite acts. her rewards will be ' as shall be requisite.' It is obvious that there is a withdrawal here, at the critical point. It does not require any superlative cautiousness to see that.

But of course the conspirators, at that moment anxiously catching at every straw, were the last people in the world to interpret Mary's letter strictly, clause by clause. The general tone was that of consent, and they applied this to all their plans. Babington indeed said, 'I think Tichborne made some question of the Scottish Queen's letters (*Confessions*, iii. 1), but I remember not in what manner.'[1] We may say then that Mary's reserves made no impression on the conspirators.

Returning now to Mary's plea, that her words would not substantiate the charge against her, we can now see how full of significance that plea is, and how minutely the *textus receptus* agrees with what she contends her answer really was. Where we are dealing with negative evidence, we must be specially cautious in our conclusions, but at all events we may say that the text stands the test imposed by the Queen's words.

§ 7. An Obscure Passage.

In the last section we saw that to the crucial point, where Babington explicitly asked for rewards to the six gentlemen, Mary gave no consent. We still have to consider another allusion to the murder plot. In § iii. (6) she said, 'Examine deeply by what means the six gentlemen do deliberate to proceed,' and further on, § vii., she says, 'Then shall it be time to set the six gentlemen to work.' *Without Babington's letter we should not know what the work of the six gentlemen was:* from § viii. of his letter we know it was assassination.

Moreover, her orders about 'the time' are different from Babington's. Babington had put her escape first of all. Mary puts 'the work of the six' first. With this before us we cannot absolutely say that she shows no *knowledge* whatever of the murder plot. But the important question is, Does she also approve *by these words*?

It would seem not, if the refusal conveyed elsewhere is sufficiently intelligible. She is not prescribing here any line of action.

---

[1] Tichborne's confession is lost. All that remains is a note or summary by a hostile hand, comprised in a single sentence (Boyd, ix. p. 185). This makes no question at all of Mary's consent even in the passage noted above, where the *textus receptus* represents her as making limitations.

§ I. THE SECRET CORRESPONDENCE

In case Babington had resolved on any other plan, *e.g.* one of capture and carrying off, as several of the conspirators proposed, these words of Mary would not at all stand in the way; while the refusal of her consent, alluded to above, would have strengthened such a proposal.

No doubt the point is an obscure one: we must not wonder if some people are unable to take the view here proposed. There can be no doubt that the puritans of that day considered this, and indeed every passage in Mary's letter, as a capital offence.

Mary's defence turned upon her being an independent queen, unrightfully kept in duresse. From her point of view even an act of war was licit, in order to obtain liberty. If she had written in perfectly plain language on this obscure passage, I fancy she might have said, 'It is not for me to approve or condemn the assassination. But if it is done at all, it should be done first'

From Babington's own point of view the plot was utterly illicit, supposing that it was only made on his private authority. Hence his anxiety to obtain a declaration from 'authority' through Gilbert Gifford (*Confessions,* i § 9) 'that this action was directly lawful in every part.' In this letter also he is asking Mary to assume the necessary authority, and to persuade her he exaggerates constantly, as he owns in *Confessions,* viii. § 1. With the same ill-balanced, uncertain spirit, he prepared, not long after writing this, to give up Ballard, whom he here so much praises. Finally, when captured he laid all the blame on his companion, and surrendered all claim to defend the goodness of his cause.

Mary's conduct was very different. She never wavered in the defence of her cause, which was certainly very much stronger than that of the rest.

Both Mary and Babington's letters abound in character strokes. Babington is youthful and enthusiastic, clever but shallow, and remarkably credulous His style is dignified and impressive. Mary is far more masculine and mature than the English gentleman. Though enthusiastic and rash, she is less so than he. The *exalté* tone which pervades Babington's letter is absent. She is far-seeing and sensible, and her courage never falters.

§ 8 Contemporaneous Copies

There are many contemporaneous transcripts of this set of letters, and they are all so nearly equal in value, that it is not easy to assign a preference for one rather than another.

1. The best seem to be in the Record Office, *Mary Queen of Scots*, xix. n. 12, ff. 75-79, and xviii. n. 53, ff. 114-122. All are in the same hand, but they have belonged to two sets. They are in wrong order because Babington's undated letter is bound after that which is dated (*i.e.* No. 10 *above* is under No. 15 *below*).

This group presumably descends more directly from the originals than any other for these reasons. It retains the original cipher signature for Queen Mary,)—(. It has the Jupiter mark ♃ (more than once), which was used in Walsingham's office, more or less in the sense we now use N.B. This, joined with the fact of its being in the Record Office, makes it probable that the copy was written by one of his clerks. It also contains two or three small contemporary corrections, and everywhere shows great care. This is the text selected for printing.

The date of the copy must be later than the attestations of Nau and Curll, which are entered in the same clerk's hand. Therefore it is not earlier than September. But we do not definitely know any copy which is earlier still. I call it R.O.

Another text of good authority is that in the official record of the evidence during Mary's trial, now B.M. *Caligula*, C. ix. ff. 463 to 466, and ff. 467 to 474. This is a fair copy: the official 'Writers' at the trial were 'Edward Barker, principal Register to the Queen's Majesty, and Thomas Wheeler, public Notary, Register of the audience at Canterbury.' This text is also very careful and accurate, but owing to the frequent contractions then used by law-clerks, it gives less aid in settling variant readings. The date will be shortly after October. I call this text Cal.

Besides these I have used H. Bresslau's text in the *Historische Zeitschrift* (von Sybel, at Munich 1883), bd. 52, pp. 270-318, made by collating the four copies at R.O., which are all good. Sepp reprints this in *Briefwechsel mit Babington*, 1886. Referred to as Bres.

Important in its way is the *first printed edition* of the letters, from *A defence of the honourable sentence and execution of the Queen of Scots*, at London, printed by John Windet; in B. Museum, G. 1737, ascribed by conjecture to M. Kyffin, 1587. The letters occur at the end on a new signature, D. to E. 3. The tract is very rare (see J. Scott, *Bibliography of Mary Queen of Scots*, nn. 145, 163). There is also a French translation of this, *Apologie ou Défense de l'honorable sentence*, &c., 1588, which follows the readings of the English. Two of these are peculiar. Babington called

§ I. THE SECRET CORRESPONDENCE

Poulet 'a mere Leicestrian,' and Mary advised Babington to look for a leader among the Howards. Both these phrases are omitted, evidently in order to avoid offending a man or a family which was powerful at Court. This text will be referred to as K (Kyffin).

The MSS which I have collated in the Yelverton Library (*Yelverton MSS* xxxi 206) follow the K. text. The French version (*ibid.* 243) is closely connected with the French copy at R.O., printed by Labanoff, vi 385, and gives the signatures of the Commissioners at the end. Referred to as Y.

The Bardon MS., printed by the Camden Society in 1909, and edited by Dr. Conyers Read, shows a text very closely related to the Record Office copy. Referred to as Bar.

Modern paragraphs (numbered), as also punctuation, are used. They are far more easy to refer to, and no ancient copy sets a standard which is authoritative in such things. The original cipher would have been all one paragraph, without even a distinction between the words.

It must be remembered that the ancient copyists of these letters did not aim at literary (much less at literal) accuracy, only at legal fidelity to the text before them: and they were quite eclectic about such variants as 'hath' and 'has,' 'my,' 'mine,' 'my own,' the singulars and plurals of collective nouns, *e.g.* force or forces. It would be labour wasted in collating to enumerate exhaustively all such variants. We cannot get back beyond the accuracy of our earliest texts. I have not attempted to give here more variants than may be sufficient to identify the families of texts noted in this section.

§ 9 Linguistic Peculiarities.

As this letter was originally written in French and translated by a Scotsman, several Scotticisms and foreign constructions may be traced.

Scotticisms. § vi. 'unnaming' *for* not naming; § ix. 'unbeing assured' *for* not being assured; § ix 'unhap' *for* mishap; § x. 'take hold' *for* succeed.

Unusual turns probably due to translation. § iii. 4°, 'which would be compassed conform to the proportion to yours' *for* which should be in proportion to yours; § xii. 'To seek upon the young earl' *for* to make inquiry about the young earl.

i. Truſtie and welbeloved/According to yᵉ zeale and entier affection wᶜʰ I haue knowen in you towardes the comõn cauſe of relligion and mine, having alwaies made accompt of you as of a principall and right worthie member to bee emploied both in the one and the other: It hath been no leſſe conſolation vnto mee to vnderſtand yoʳ eſtate as I haue done by yoʳ laſt, and to haue found meanes to renewe my intelligence wᵗʰ you, then I fealt grief all this while paſt to bee without the ſame. I pray you therfore from henceforth to write vnto mee ſo often as you can of all occurrences which you maie iudge in anie wiſe important to the good of my affaires: wherevnto I ſhall not faile to correſpond with all the care and diligence that ſhall bee in my poſſibilitie.

ii. ffor divers great and important conſiderations, which were here to long to bee deduced,ᵃ I cannot but greatly praiſe and comẽend your comõn deſyre to p̃vent in time the deſſeignements of our enemies for the extirpation of our relligion out of this Realme with the ruine of vs all. ffor I haue long agoe ſhewen vnto the foraine Catholick princes, and experience doth approve it, the longer that they and wee delay to put hand on the matter on this ſyde, the greater leaſure haue our ſaid enemies to prevaile and win advantage over the ſaid princes, as they haue done againſt the king of Spaine, and in the meane time the Catholickes here remaining expoſed to all ſortes of p̃ſecution and crueltie doe daily diminiſh in nomber forces meanes and power. So as yf remedie bee not therevnto haſtely p̃vided, I feare not a little but they ſhall become altogether vnable for ever to ariſe againe and to receave anie aid at all, whenſoever it were offred them. ffor mine owne ᵇ part I pray you to aſſure our principall frendes that, albeit I had not in this cauſe anie particuler intereſt (that wᶜʰ I maie pretend vnto being of no conſideration vnto mee ᶜ in reſpect of the publicque good of this ſtate)

---

a. deduced, *so* R.O., K., etc.,—Cal. and Bres., etc., deducted.
b. mine owne, *so* R.O., Bres.,—Cal. my.
c. unto me, *so* R.O., Cal., and K.,—but French version *omits*. B. *repeats* particular *before* consideration.

§ I. THE SECRET CORRESPONDENCE

I fhalbe alwaies readie and moſt willing to emploie therein my life and all that I haue or maie ever looke for in this world.

iii. Nowe[1] for to ground fubſtantially this enterprife and to bring it to good fucceſſe you muſt firſt examine deeply.

1°. what forces afwell on foote as on horfe you maie raife amongeſt you all and what Captaines you fhall apoint for them in everie fhire, in cafe a chief general cannot bee had.

2°. of what townes portes and havens you maie aſſure yorfelves, afwell in the Nort west as South to receave fuccors from the lowe Contries Spaine and ffraunce.

3°. what place you eſteem fitteſt and of greateſt advantage to aſſemble the principall companie of your forces at; and the fame being aſſembled, whether or wch waie you haue to march.

4°. what foraine forces afwell on horfe as foote you require (which would bee compaſſed conforme to ye proportion of yours) for howe long paied, and munition and portes the fitteſt for their landing in this Realm from the three forefaid foraine princes.[a]

5°. what pvifion of money and armo^r (in cafe you want) you would afke.

6°. By what meanes doe the †fix†[2] gentlemen deliberate to proceed.

7°. and the maner alfo of my getting forth of this hold.

iv. Vpon which pointes having taken amongeſt you, who are the principall authors, and alfo as fewe in nomber as you can, the beſt refolution, my advice is that you impart the fame with all diligence to *Barnardino de Mendoza* ambaſſado^r lieger[3] for the king of Spaine in ffrance, who

---

a. princes, *so* R.O.,—C. and K. *read* countries.

[1] The first of the *Points out of the Scottish Queen's letter*, subscribed by Curll, 23 September. Printed in Kyffin, sig. F.2. This point covers § iii. As the title indicates, a few unnecessary words and phrases are omitted.

[2] For the daggers see introductory paragraphs, § 4.

[3] Lieger means a 'resident' ambassador: allied to our word 'ledger.'

besides thexperience hee hath of the estate of this syde, I maie assure you will emploie him therein most willingly. I shall not faile to write vnto him of the matter wth all the earnest recomendations that I can ; as I shall also to anie els that shalbee needfull. But you must make choise for managing of this affaire with the said *Mendoza* and others out of the Realme of some faithfull and verie secreate personage vnto whome only you must comitt yo^rselves, to thend thinges bee ^a the more secreate which for yor owne securitie I recommend vnto you above the rest.

v. If ^1 your messinger bring you back againe sure pmise and sufficient assurance of the succo^r you demaund, then thereafter (but no sooner, for that it weare in vaine) take diligent order that all those of yor ptie on this side make so secreately as they can, provision of armo^r, fitt horse & readie money, wherewith to hold them selves in readines to march so soone as yt shalbee signified vnto them by their chief and principalls in everie shire.

vi. And for better coloring of the matter (reserving ^b to the principall the knowledge of the ground of the enterprise) yt shalbee inoughe for the beginning to geve out to the rest, that the said provisions are made only for fortefying yo^rselves in case of need against the puritans of this Realme: the principall whereof having the chief forces of the same in the lowe Contries, haue (as you maie lett the brute goe) desseigned to ruine and overthrowe, at their returne home, the whole Catholicques, and to vsurpe the Crowne, not only against mee and all other lawfull pretendors therevnto, but against ther owne Queen that nowe is, yf shee will not altogether comitt her self to their only government. The same pretextes maie serve to found and establish amongest you all an association and confederation generall, as done only for your owne iust preservations and defence, aswell in relligion as lives, landes, and goodes against the oppression and attemptes of the said puritans, w^thout touching directly

---

a. be, Cal. *inserts* kept,—*all others omit*.
b. reserving, *so* Cal., R.O., B.,—K. referring.

[1] The second of the *Points out of the Scottish Queen's letter* begins here, and goes on to 'Puritans of this realm' in § vi.

by writing anie thing againſt that Queen, but rather ſhewing yo^{r}ſelves willing to mainteine her and her lawfull heires after hir, vnnaming mee.

vii. The affaires [1] being thus p̄pared and forces in readines both without and w^{t}hin the Realme, then ſhall yt bee time to ſett the †ſix† [2] gentlemen to woork, taking order, vpon the accompliſhing of their deſſeying, I maie be ſodainly transported out of this place, and that all yor forces in the ſame time bee on the field to meete mee in tarying for ye arrivall of the foraine aid, wch then must bee hastened with all diligence.

viii. Now, for that there can bee no certeine daie apointed of the accompliſhing of the ſaid gentlemen's deſſeignement, to thend that others maie bee in readines to take mee from hence, I would that y^e ſaid gentlemen had alwaies about them, †or at the leaſt at Court†,[2] a fower ſtout men furniſhed with good and ſpeedie horſes, for, ſo ſoone as the ſaid deſſeing ſhall bee executed to come with all diligence to advertiſe thereof thoſe that ſhalbee apointed for my tranſporting, to thend that immediatly thereafter they maie bee at the place of my aboade, before that mie keeper can haue adviſe of thexecution of the ſaid deſſeing, or at the leaſt before he can forteſie him ſelf within the howſe, or carie mee out of the ſame. It were neceſſarie to diſpatch two or three of the ſaid advertiſers by divers waies, to thend that, yf the one bee ſtaied, the other maie come thorough ; and at the ſame inſtant were yt alſo needfull to aſſaie to cutt of the poſtes ordinarie waies.

ix. This is the platt [3] wch I find beſt for this enterpriſe, and the order wherby you ſhould conduct the ſame for our comon ſecurities. ffor ſturring on this ſide before you bee well aſſured of ſufficient foraine forces, yt were but for nothing [but] [a] to putt yo^{r}ſelves in danger of following the miſerable fortune of ſuch as haue heretofore travailed

---

a. for nothing but, *so* Cal.,—*others* but for nothing.

[1] The third of the *Points* goes on to § viii., ' out of the same.'
[2] For the daggers see the introductory paragraphs, § 4.
[3] The fourth of the *Points* : two lines only to ' securities.'

in like occasions. And to take mee forth of this place, vnbeing before well assured to sett mee in the middest of a good armie, or in some verie good strength, where I may safely staie on th'assembly of your forces and arrivall of the said foraine succors, it were sufficient cause geven to that Queen in catching mee againe, to enclose mee for ever in some hole, forth of the wch I should never escape, yf shee did vse mee no worse, and to pursue with all extremetie those that had assisted mee, wch would grieve mee more then all the vnhap [w^{ch}] might fall vpon mie self. And therfore must I needes yet once againe admonish you so earnestly as I can to looke and take heed most carefully & vigilantly to compasse and assure so well all that shall be necessarie for effectuating of the said enterprise, as with the grace of god you maie bring the same to happie end : remitting to the iudgment of our principall frends on this side wth whome you haue to deale herein, to ordaine [and] conclude vpon this present (which shall serve you only for an overture and proposition) as you shall amongest you find best : and to yor self in particuler I refer to assure the gentlemen above mentioned of all that shalbee requisite of my part for the entier execution of their good willes.

x. I leave also to your common resolutions to advise ^a (in case their desseignement doe not take hold as maie happen) whether you will or not pursue mie transport and thexecution of the rest of thenterprice. But yf the mishap should fall out that you might not come by mee being sett in the tower of London or in anie other strength wth greater gard : yet notwithstanding leave not, for god's sake, to proceed in the rest of thenterprice : for I shall at anie time die most contented, vnderstanding of yor deliverie forth of the servitude wherein you are holden as slaves.

xi. I shall ¹ assaie that, at the same time that the work shalbe in hand in these partes to make the Catholicques of Scotland arise and to put my sonne in ther handes, to

---

a. to advise,—Cal. *and* K. *omit.*

¹ The fifth of the *Points* : to end of § xi.

§ I. THE SECRET CORRESPONDENCE

theffect that from thence our enemies here maie not prevaile of anie fucco^r. I would alfo that fome fturring in Ireland weare labored for, and to be begonne fomewhile before that anie thing weare done here, to thend the alarme might bee geven therby on the flatt contrarie fide that the ftroke fhould come from.

xii. Your reafons to haue fome generall head or chief, mee thincketh, are verie pertinent, and therfore were it good to found obfcurely for the purpofe the Earle ^a of Arundell or fome of his brethren, and likewife to feeke vpon the yong Earle of Northumberland, yf he bee at libertie. ffrom over fea the Erle of Weftmerland maie bee had, whofe howfe and name maie ^b much, you knowe in the north p̄tes: as alfo the L. Pagett, of good abilitie in fome fhires hereabout; both the one and the other may be brought home fecretely: amongeft wch fome mo of the principall banifhed maie returne yf the enterprife bee once refolute. The faid L. Pagett is nowe in Spaine, and maie treate there all wch by his brother Charles or directly by him felf ^c you will committ vnto him touching this affaire.

xiii. Beware that none of your meffingers, whome you fend forth of the Realm, carie over anie letters vppon them felves, but make ther difpatches bee conveied either after or before them by fome other. Take heed of fpies and falfe brethren that are amongeft you, fpetially of fome prieftes [1] alreadie practifed ^d by our enemies for your difcoverie, and in anie wife keepe never anie paper about you that in anie fort maie doe harme: for from like errors haue come the only ^e condemnation of all fuch as haue fuffred heretofore, againft whome could there otherwife

---

a. K. *omits from* The Earl . . . *to* . . . at liberty.
b. B. *inserts* do.
c. or directly by himself, Cal. and K. *omit*.
d. practised by our enemies,—K. by our enemies wrought.
e. have . . . only,—Cal. have only come the.

---

[1] It would be interesting to know whom Mary had in mind at this place. Several priests indeed had fallen through fear, as others had done, but none of these had been systematically 'practised for betrayal.' She was probably thinking of ex-seminarists, but not priests, like Nichols, or Munday, or Caddy, who troubled the Catholics much about the time

haue been nothing proved. Difcover as little as you can yor names & intentions to the ffrench Amb^r nowe Lieger at London: for althoughe hee bee, as I vnderftand, a verie honeft gentleman, of good confcience and relligion, yet feare I y^t his M^r enterteineth with that Queen a courfe farr contrarie to our deffeignementes: which maie move him to croffe vs, yf it fhould happen hee had anie particuler knowledge thereof.[1]

xiv. All this while paft I haue fewed to change and remove from this howfe, and for anfweare the Caftle of Dudley only hath been named to ferve the turne: fo as by apparance within the end of this fomer I maie goe thither. Wherfore advife, fo foone as I fhalbee there, what provifion maie bee had about that part for my efcape from thence. If [2] I ftaie here, there is for that purpofe but one of thefe three meanes following to be looked.[a]

The firft that at one certeine daie apointed in my walking abroad on horfback on the moores betwixt this and Stafford, where ordinarely you knowe verie fewe people doe paffe, a fiftie or threefcore men well horfed and armed come to take mee there, as they maie eafely, my keeper having with him ordenarely but eighteen or twentie horfemen only with dagges.

The fecond meane is to come at midnight or foone after to fett fyre in the barnes and ftables, which you knowe are nere to the howfe, and whileft that my Gardian his fervants fhall runne forth to the fire, your companie (having everie one a marke whereby they may knowe one

---

[a.] looked, *State Trials adds* for. For *look* in the sense of *look for* see Murray's *Oxford Dictionary* under *Look*, I. 6. d.

---

of Campion's death. Nevertheless, the advice was excellent. Gilbert Gifford, the deacon, was the evil genius of the plot; and the priest Ballard, though no traitor to his own side, was the unbalanced enthusiast, who carried the conspirators into their fatal errors. Unfortunately it was Mary's own servant Morgan who set both to work on lines which led up to the great calamity.

[1] This passage was, of course, used in subsequent diplomacy in order to make Henri III. withdraw from Mary's defence.

[2] The sixth *Point* begins here, and goes on, two and a half paragraphs, to 'suddenly away.'

another vnder night) might furprife the howfe, where I hoape with the fewe fervantes I haue about mee, I weare able to giue correfpondence.

And the third, fome that bring Cartes hither ordinarily comming early in the morning, their Carts might bee fo prepared and with fuch Cartleaders that being iuft in the middeft of the great gate ye Carts might fall downe or overwhelme,[a] and that therevppon you might come fodainly with your followers to make your felf M^r of the howfe, and carie mee awaie: fo you might doe eafely, before that ever anie nomber of fouldiers (who lodge in fondrie places forth of this place, fome a half and fome a whole mile off) might come to the relief.

xv. Whatfoever yffue the matter taketh, I doe and will thinck my felf obliged, as long as I live, towardes you for the offers you make to hazard your felf as you doe for mie deliverie, and by anie meanes that ever I maie haue I fhall doe my endevo^r to recognife by effectes yor defertes herein. I haue comaunded a more ample [b] alphabett to bee made for you, wch herewith you will receave.

God almightie haue you in protection.

    Your moft affured frend for ever)—(.
ffaile not to burne this prefent quickly.

[*The forged Postscript. Mary Queen of Scots*, xviii n 55. Cipher in Phelippes's hand Redeciphered and collated with the decipher of the late Mr. Lemon See P. F. Tytler, *History of Scotland*, 1864, iv 127]

P.S.—I wold be glad to know the names and qualities of the sixe gentlemen, which are to accomplish the designment, for it may be, I shall be able upon knowledge of the parties to give you some further advice necessary to be followed therein; and even so do I wish to be made acquainted with the names of all such principal persons [&c.] as also from time to time particularly how you proceed, and as soon as you may, for the same pur-

---

a overwhelm, *so* Boyd, Bar., Y.,—Bres. *reads* overthrow. But overwhelm is also used intransitively. *See* Murray, *Oxford Dictionary*, Overwhelm, I d.

b ample, *so* Cal. and K,—Bres. ample. Both Cal and K *end with the word* receive.

pose, who be already, and how far every one [is] privy hereunto.[1]

End. by Phelippes.—Postscript of the Scottish Quenes lettre to Babington.

No. 15

ANTHONY BABINGTON TO QUEEN MARY

[*London, 3/13 August* 1586.]

R.O. *Mary Queen of Scots*, xix. n. 10. Official copy, marked iv, and contains the authentication. 'This is the true copie of the last lettre which I wrote vnto the Queen of Scotes, Anthonie Babington.'

Your letters I receaved not vntil the xxix[th] of July. The cause was my absence from Lichfield contrarie to promise. Howe dangerous the cause thereof was by my next letters shalbee imparted.[2] In the meane time your Maiestie maie vnderstand that one Mawde (that came out of ffrance with Ballard, who came from Mendoza concerning this affaire) is discovered to be for this State. Ballard acquainted him with the cause of his comming, and hath emploied him of late into Scotland with letters. By whose trecherie vnto [what][3] extreame danger my self haue been, and the whole plott is like to bee brought, and by what meanes we haue in parte prevented, and purpose by gods assistance to redresse the rest, your Maiestie shalbee by my next[4] enformed.

Till when, my soveraigne, for his sake that preserveth your Maiestie for our common good, dismaie not, neither doubt of happie issue. It is goddes cause, the churches and your Maiesties, an enterprise honorable before god and man, vndertaken vpon zeale and devotion, free from

---

[1] The composition of this postscript should be compared with the beginning of Mary's letter, where she makes much the same request. Her style, it will be seen, is queenly and sincere: here there are constant repetitions and a want of all inspiration. When once the cloven hoof is recognised here, its trail will be recognised throughout the postscript.

[2] Bardon adds 'at large.'

[3] Here the text reads 'my,' so also xix. 11, and xix. 12, and the Bardon text. But the sense requires 'what,' and it is probable that we should read 'this treachery,' for 'whose treachery.' [4] Bardon here adds 'letter.'

§ I. THE SECRET CORRESPONDENCE

all ambition and temporall regard, and therfore no doubt will succeed happely. We have vowed and wee will performe or die. What is holden of your [Maiestie]¹ propositions together with our finall determinations, my next shall discover.

In the meane time resting infinitely bound to your highnes for the great confidence it hath pleased you to repose in mee, which to deserve by all faithful service I vowe before the face of our Lord Jesus, whom I beseech to graunt your Maiestie a long and prosperous raigne, and vs happie successe in these our vertuous enterprises. London this third of August 1586.

No. 16

GILBERT CURLL TO BARNABY

[*Chartley, Friday,* 29 *July*/8 *August* 1586.]

R.O. *Mary Queen of Scots*, xviii. n. 86. Curll's cipher, 15 lines, redeciphered. Phelippes's decipher is No. 87, and it is endorsed by him 'Curle to Emilio.'² This note covered the dispatch of Post iii, which shows the influence of Babington's plans.

Sir,—Her Maiestie geueth yow continual thankes for yowr care and trauel taken to lett her vnderstand of such occurrences as yow doo, wherof frequently her Maiestie cannot be aduertised by others, as by the rare cuming of secret letters vnto her handes which passe throg yowrs, yow may well iudge.

Yowr desyre to have warning beforehand shall be satisfyed so wel as may be, which hithertil hath not much bene forgotten and specially for the sending of this inclosed

---

¹ Maiestie; wanting in all the R.O. texts, but Bardon reads 'mo.'

² The name Emilio does not occur on the cipher No. 86, but on the back of Phelippes's decipher No. 87. It has also occurred on the back of No. 9. But it makes little difference who was meant by this name. Whatever the original object of the name was, the personage was certainly fictitious; a man of straw, at this stage. The recipient was Phelippes. A fortnight earlier Phelippes had used the name Emilio Russo for quite a different impersonation (see Morris, pp. 225, 226).

packet[1] wherof I wrote to yow ten dayes before the day appointed for the dispatching therof and shold haue bene sent to yow on Monday last were [it] not that those which came with yowrs the same day cawsed it thus so long to be delayed.[2] Her Maiestie prayeth yow now to send it away by yowr boy to the French Ambassador so soone as yow may goodly.

And if yow think that yow can find Babington at London, by the same meanes to mak her Maiesties two letters,[3] which yow have alredy, be surely delyvered to him.

Doubting by yowr foresayd (wch to tell yow fryely I founde difficil in discipring and therfor some pointes lesse intelligible then I wished) that myself haue erred in dowbling[4] of the addition which I sent yow, throw some haste I had then at dispatcheing therof. I pray yow to forbeare the using of the sayd addition untill that agaynst my next I may put the wholl at more leasure in better ordor as I hope to doo both for yowr gretar ease and myne.

If I have not mistaken yowr meaning towcheing the mark that is for yow it is yowr desyre that in yowr absence her Maiesties letters or mine requyring spedy disciphering that on the back therof for yowr brother his better direction, as yow name it, yowr sayd marke may be written twyse or thryse, which (untill yow let me know the contrary) shal be so.

God almighty preserue yow. Fryday the seuenth of August.[5]—CURLL.

Addressed, ff. See also p. 47, n. 2.

---

[1] Post iii, with letters to Mendoza and others on the general situation caused by Babington's plans.

[2] The sense is, 'I wrote (No. 13 *above*) giving you ten days' notice for this post, *i.e.* appointing Wednesday last. It would have been ready last Monday, but for Babington's letter.'

[3] Two letters to Babington, *i.e.* Nau's about Poley, No. 12, and Mary's answer, No. 14.

[4] Phelippes erroneously deciphered ' doubling ' as ' setting down.'

[5] There is in the date another mistake in the style. Friday was 29 July Old Style, and 8, not 7, August New Style. Friday is likely to be right, for Poulet sent it up to London on Saturday 30 July Old Style (Morris, p. 247).

SECTION II

CONFESSIONS AND EXAMINATIONS OF ANTHONY BABINGTON

No. 17

BABINGTON'S FIRST CONFESSION

[*Ely House*, 18 *to* 20 *August* 1586.]

Very little has hitherto been known of this important paper, by far the clearest and fullest contemporary source for the history of the plot, which is yet accessible. In the *Hardwicke State Papers*, i. 225, an abstract was printed of its first page, and of § 11. This abstract was derived from the official record of the trial already cited, now B.M., *Caligula*, C. ix. ff. 456-459. This Caligula text, though so short, gives readings which are everywhere superior to those of the Yelverton text now published; it also gives the authentication at the end (p. 66, *below*).

The complete text, now published, is taken from MS. Yelverton, vol. xxxi., ff. 218 to 223. (See *Catalogi librorum MSS. Angliæ*, &c., Oxford, 1697, No. 5270.) Its date is about 1600; the hand is the ordinary clerk's hand of that time, and the copyist errors are numerous. When very, very small these have been silently corrected; sections and paragraphs are inserted. The collector of the papers was Robert Beale, once clerk of the Privy Council. His signature appears on some of the documents in this volume. The late Lord Calthorpe (a descendant of Beale) permitted me to photograph these papers, and for his great kindness I shall ever be grateful.

[§ 1, f. 218. *First acquaintance with Mary's party,* 1580-86.]

Passing into Fraunce without licence the yeare 1580, I remayned there six months, for the most part at Paris, the rest of the time at Roan. I conversed most with Mr. Thomas Worseley, Chideoke Tichborne and Mark Ive. During the same time Thomas Morgan, being in Paris, came as of courtesie to visit me, offered to me all friendship, and in the end conducted me to the house of the Bishop of Glasgow, Ambassador Ledger in France for the Queene of Scotts. They both recommended their mistress to me as a most wise, virtuous and catholique Princess; declaring withall the certayne expectation of her future greatness in that land, by reason of her undoubted title to this croun as the next in succession[1]: whereof I myself made no question. By these insinuations [I was] induced to respect her.

Then by their letters after my departure out of Fraunce (as it appeared) they commended me unto her. Where[upon] she writes unto me a letter of gratulation. It came to my hands by the means of Mris Bray dwelling in Sheffield. Not long after my journey to London, de Courcelles, Mauvissiere his secretary, came unto my lodgings, and delivered me letters from Morgan, by which I was solicited vehemently to procure the delivery of a packet therein closed, afferming the service to be very meritorious, full of honour and profit, and a matter of small moment if discovered.

By which means moved I sent the packet to the Queene by means of Anthony Rolston, whose means only, together with Mris Braye, I used for the convey of all such packets as I sent unto the Queene, which to my remembrance were five at several times during the space of two yeres. Being weary of which service (as it was of great danger and more hurtful to this state then before I conceaved) I was desirous to cease from further proceeding in that course. [This] I did three moneths before her remove from the Earl,[2] and ever since, till Julie[3] last paste, as

---

[1] Babington would not have written thus if (as our popular historians assert) he had previously been her page, and was enamoured of her. *Introduction*, p. cv.

[2] Mary was removed from the Earl of Shrewsbury's custody to that of Sir Ralph Sadleir, 25 August 1583.

[3] 'July.' This is the reading of MS. Caligula, for 'June' of Yelverton. Mary's letter, written on 25 June, was answered on the 6th of July, and therefore probably received on the 4th or 5th. The letters from Morgan, then forwarded, cannot now be identified. In *Hardwicke State Papers*, i. 227, the sense is inverted. Mary is represented as wishing to send packets to Babington which she has received from Morgan. (See also *below*, §§ 9, 11.)

The passage printed in *Hardwicke State Papers* stops five lines further on.

§ II. CONFESSIONS OF BABINGTON

I remember, when I received by a boy unknown to me, letters in sifer, signifying her discontentment for the breache of intelligence, [and] requiring me to send by that bearer, as I did, certain letters which I had received from Thomas Morgan in Aprill (as I remember) last past directed unto her. Which letters I was earnestly entreated to convey unto her, but did not seke the means: only I kept them in safety, having immediately before the same sent back unto Morgan another packet directed likewise unto her, utterly refusing to deal any further in those affairs.

[I] purpos[ed] to travell into France, Sir Edward Fitton[1] being meanes for licence for me and Mr. Salisbury, there and in Italy to have spent my time, until it might please God to have dedicated my[self] to his service and study, and not once to have intermeddled in matter of state or practise against the state present. Which course of travell we found very convenient, our states and the danger of the time considered, with the capital laws against the entertainment or accompanying of Catholique prestes,[2] without whome we desier not to live, holding them more necessary for our souls [than] food for our bodyes.

Which pretended iourney not taking effect, through our misfortune, Sir Eduarde not prevailinge in the suite for our license, such was our hard destinye by God's iust iudgment for our sinnes, that remaining heare at London togeather, it was our mishap to be drawen into these cursed courses, by the persuasion of such as abused our zeal in religion,[3] and the youthful ability of our bodies and mindes, ambitious of honour and fame. Woe be to them there-

---

[1] Sir Edward Fitton the younger, see *D N B*, also *Gillow*, under Peter Fytton vere Biddulph. The trial says that he went to Ireland, and Father Persons (see next note) mentions him as an active Catholic who eventually died there.

[2] This confirms Weston, as quoted in the text (ch. v.), and Persons, *Life of Campion* (privately printed, Roehampton, 1877), p. 29, that Babington had been one of those who 'accompanied priests' at the time of the Jesuit Mission. But it does not support Mr Simpson's surmise that a secret society was formed to do this. (See *The Month*, June 1905.)

[3] See *below*, Interrogation 1.

fore, that have overturned so many happy estates, and defiled such and so many familyes heretofore of unspotted fidelitye with so infamous and hatefull an accion, in depriving us of life and desire of lyfe, and the commonwealth of the service of men most resolved in whatsoever they apprehend.

[§ 2, f. 218. *Ballard comes to Babington.*]

About Maye last as I remember, ther came unto me at London, at my lodginge in Hernes rentes,[1] one Ballard, a man whom I had knowen before his departure last into Fraunce. He toulde me he was retorned from Fraunce uppon this occasion. Being with Mendoza at Paris, he was informed[2] that in regarde of the iniuries don by our state unto the greatest christian princes, by the nourishinge of sedition and divisions in their provinces, by withholding violently the lawful possessions of some, by invasion of the Indies and by piracy, robbing the treasure and the wealthe of others, and sondry intollerable wronges for so great and mighty princes to indure, it was resolved by the Catholique league[3] to seeke redresse and satisfaction, which they had vowed to performe this sommer without farther delay, havinge in readiness suche forces and all warlike preparations as the like was never seene in these partes of Christendome.

The Pope was chiefe disposer, the most Christian kinge

---

[1] According to the indictment (*Fourth Report of Dep. Keeper*, Ap. ii. p. 276) the visit took place at the very end of May. I cannot identify Herne's Rents. *The Alphabetical index of the Streets, Squares, Lanes, Alley's, &c.* in *Roques' Survey of London*, 1747, does not give the name, though a long list of 'Rents' shows that the term was then still in vogue in London. Boyd (p. 615) mentions 'Heron's Rents.' Holinshed, iv. 260, speaks of 'Hern's Rents, Holborn.' This place was the scene of most of the meetings now to come, and its identification would be interesting. It was presumably near St. Giles's Church, facing which the conspirators were executed; the spot being chosen as representing the scene of the crime. Cf. also p. 71, 'My lodging at Mr. Cooks.'

[2] Mendoza's real message was very different. *Introduction*, p. xciv.

[3] All that follows about an international Catholic League is popular fiction (see *Introduction*, p. xvii.).

§ II. CONFESSIONS OF BABINGTON

and the kinge Catholique with all other princes of the league concurred as instruments for the righting of these wronges, and reformation of religion. The conductors of this enterprise for the French nation, the D. of Guise, or his brother the D. de Maine [1]; for the Italian and Hispanishe forces, the P. of Parma; the whole number about 60,000.[2]

And hereupon he cam ouer to informe thus muche, and to sounde the Catholiques of this land, for assisting in this enterprise [and] for the preservation of their possessions, uppon which the stranger would enter by right of conquest, without sparing any, in case they did not declare them selves [3] with [the] performers.

I tould him I held the princes so busied with home affaires, as I thoughte they coulde not intende the invasion of this countrie, untill their owne were setled: wherof ther was little expectation as yet. And if they would invade, I could not conceive from whence they should have so many men or means to transport them.[4] Further, that I held their assistance on this side small, notwithstandinge the excommunication (which either was or should be revived),[5] so longe as her Maiestie dothe live, the state beinge so well setled.

He answered that difficultie would be taken away by meanes already layde, and that her lyfe coulde be no

---

[1] In MS. Demaine.

[2] It sounds suspicious that Savage thought the army of 60,000 men was to be raised in England (Boyd, 611)

[3] In MS. sent *for* selves

[4] Although Babington here represents himself as having talked very good sense, yet he spoke at the time as though he quite believed in the Papal League (see his letter to Mary, § 2). Mary, however, did not answer this

[5] See Interrogation 2 The statement is made doubtfully, because there was an erroneous report made in 1579, that the excommunication was renewed What, then, happened was, that the bull was reprinted unofficially by some Catholic opponents to the Alençon match. In 1583 the bull was actually renewed in secret, but not reprinted, for an *empresa* of that year This has only recently come to light (see *The Month*, April 1902).

hindrance therein. He told me the instrument was Savadge,[1] who had vowed the performance thereof, and some other, whose names he tould not, neither was I inquisitive, as I gesse Gifforde, and one in courte neare sir Walter Raweleye.[2]

[§ 3, f. 219. *Discussions with Salisbury, Tichborne, and Barnewell, June* 1586.]

We departed for that tyme. Soone after Mr. Salisbury, Mr. Tuchburne, and Mr. Barnewell, inquiring what I thought herein, I tould them that we seemed to stande in a dilemma. On the one side leaste by a massacre (as enoghe hath been doubted) the magistrates here would take awaye our lives, or by the lawes allready made, by meanes whereof there is no Catholique, whose life is not in theire handes. And on the other side lest the straunger shoulde invade and sacke our Countrye, and bringe it into servitude to forenners.

Twixte which daungers hanginge, we discoursed much of bothe. In the reformation we found conclusion of our estates, dishonour and desolation of our countrye: in the delaye thereof extreame hazard. The evill opinion, which the State had of Catholiques being manifested by sondrye bookes imprinted, that all Catholiques are traytores, and that it was not possible for a Papist to be a good subiecte, which opinion holden, must needes assure us of the desire of our extirpation, if there were meanes. Which, that there wanteth not, is apparent; it remayninge in their powre by the late statutes[3] to prove any Catholique, how precise of conversation so ever, a traytor.

---

[1] Savage was really only an inferior agent in George Gifford's plot. But George was in the Queen's favour, so his name was carefully removed from the records of the trial. Babington here and below alludes to him (*below*, § 8, and *Confessions*, iii. § 5), but the Christian name is omitted, and people would think that William or Gilbert Gifford was intended.

[2] 'The person near to Sir Walter Raleigh.' Here again a clue connected with a court favourite, which was never followed up. On the contrary, Raleigh received part of Babington's estates, because forsooth Babington had taken his name in vain. The words are repeated *below* (§ 8).

[3] By 'late statutes,' Babington, no doubt, referred to the bloody law

§ II. CONFESSIONS OF BABINGTON

This considered, how lamentable our estates seemed, may welbe discerned. And let any man iudge what spurres these desperat perills be to pricke forwarde men of suche bodyes and mindes to perpetrate any thinge, to adventure their delivery from suche extream termes, or at least their countryc and fellowes in faith, by their deathes holden honorable. And likewise in what daunger the state dothe staund, in which remaine infinite number of men in the same termes, and by consequence of the same mindes; whome either utterly to root out, or by some more easy toleration to holde better content, seemed to be expedient for the security of the state. That any toleration would ever be admitted was dispaired of. Extirpation therefore[1] was to be loked for, upon the first assurance of any such occasion, as might seem sufficient to excuse the fact somewhat abroad and hold satisfied the multitude at home.

Thus we discoursed. In fine for conclusion I told Mr. Salisbury that for the avoiding of both those extremities, I held the best course to depart the realm, with licence, if it were possible, if not without, rather then to stay; aswell in regarde of the daunger by this present state threatened, if it so remaine, as allso in regarde of the miserye and wretched estat, which this realme was like to be brought unto in every man's expectation, when her maiestie should be taken away, by the sundry competitors of great habilitie, both within and without the realme; and that, as there was small conceit of any securitie, the state standing as it dothe, and the opinion of us as it is. So likewise remaineth there smale hope of any happiness after her Maiesties decease, the Queene of Scotts her

---

of 27 Elizabeth c. ii, *Introduction*, p xxv, just passed, 'Against Jesuits, etc,' under which so many martyrs suffered. Indeed, no Catholic could escape it, 'how precise of conversation so ever,' when magistrates were bent on a conviction The 'sundry books' cannot so easily be identified He may have meant the many printed attacks upon the martyrs, on Throckmorton, Parry, etc, which were singularly brutal; and so, too, were many of the sermons and political addresses during the fanatical election of 1584.

[1] The MS reads 'despaired The extirpation thereof'

person remaining in great daunger at that day, whensoever it should fall, and not like to live longe though she should come unto the crowne by reason of her age and healthe, her son a prince of whome we had smale expectation of any good in religion; no other Catholique claiming except a stranger, whome to admit I could never thinke the catholique partye woulde [agree].[1] Which sorrowful considerations moved a conclusion to depart the realme, in which intention we left each other for that time, hasteninge Mr. Poolye the pursuite of our licence, which he had undertaken and had brought me to Mr. Secretarye once before, unto whome I made proffer of service in generall tearmes, and with many honourable speeches was dismissed.[2]

[§ 4, f. 220. *Babington becomes leader*, 5-9 July.]

After returning unto London I met with Ballard[3] nere my lodginge, and asked him how he had found the Catholiques whom he had sonded, affected.[4] He answered, those that should be most forward were most slowe, and the older the colder, and wished me to undertake to sound the whole realme: I told him there were sundry other more fit, of greater age, authoritie, conscience, and experience; and that it would be helde extreame of presumption for me or any younge man to undertake the managinge of so great an accion. He said they would not; and by sondrye agravations of the daungers before mentioned wherein we

---

[1] Babington had been grossly deceived by Ballard (or Gifford), if he really thought that any stranger had claimed the English Succession. Speculation, indeed, on a Spanish successor had commenced, and as to this Babington spoke at greater length in *Confessions*, v.

[2] Babington's first interview with Walsingham was late in June, at Greenwich, the second was at Barnelms in the first days of July (see Poley's *Confession*, M.Q.S., xix. 26, Boyd, p. 595).

[3] The earliest definite date which we have for Ballard's return from the North to London is Saturday, 9 July (Morris, 221), when he asked for letters at the French embassy. But he may have been back a few days sooner.

[4] See Interrogation 4.

live, by commending the acte to be of great honor, of singular merite, easy to effectuate (the meanes considered), and the not undertaking thereof both hurtfull and dishonorable: that, if I would undertake it, I should have at the handes of the same league whatsoever was necessary. I entertained the discourse of it, upon condition he would surceas from further proceeding other then I should direct him. Further, I advised that Savadge should surcease from proceeuting his intention, which he said was to kill her Maiestie, but whether by swords or pistolls I know not neyther the manner, as a thing reiected upon the first knowledge thereof.

[§ 5, f. 220. *The Surprise of the Queen's person.*]

During this time there was a proposition by Mr. Edward Abbington to surprise the person of the Queene [1] and to have carried her to some strength, ther to have advised her to graunt toleration in religion, if not reformation; and that so doing we should have taken care of the preservation of her health and life, removing from her such as should be thought meet, and placing other Catholiques in their room.

I conferred concerning the action [2] of the Queene's person with the three aforesaid gents (whome my love and interest drue into this practise as parties) though before they had had understanding thereof [3] (yet without doubt I presume they had never dealt therein but in regarde of me); and with Mr. Tilney and Mr. Abbington; which five, Mr. Salisbury excepted, were disposed to undertake the exploite for the Queene's person, if it were holden lawfull, whereof Mr. Barnwell doubted and some others; but for the invasion and surprising of her person they made no doubt.

---

[1] See *below*, Interrogation 5
[2] By 'action' or 'exploit' of the Queen's person Babington here clearly means assassination by 'surprise' her capture only
[3] See Interrogation 3

[§ 6, f. 220. *Dealings with individuals.*]

Not any durste communicate this action vnto Sr John Arundell, Sr Thomas Tresham, Sr W. Catesbie or Mr John Talbot of Grafton, for that it was harde say, they should saye, 'It behouethe vs to suffer with Christian patience whatsoeuer affliction authoritie might impose vppon vs.' And if any should come to sounde them, they would be the first accusers of them.

John Savadge was contented to surcease from further attemptinge what he had vndertaken, vppon condition that he might be imployed in the same action, which was promised him by me; otherwise he would not, in regard of his vowe,[1] which he had solemply taken.

With Tuichburn I never spoke touching any parte of the practise neather did I knowe whither he was privie thervnto or no, notwithstanding we recommended him one, in regard he was a verye stoute man, resolute and zealous in religion, whome in our intention Balard and I reconed one of the six with Mr Abbington, Tilney, Tichborne, Barnwell and Savadge. I dealt with Charnocke, and so had Ballard, Don, and Savadge, but never had his expresse resolution therin.

[§ 7, f. 220. *Dealings with Poley.*]

I conferred with Robin Pooly concerninge this action, who I presume hath discovered that parte longe since.[2] I proposed vnto him three Courses, in any of which he vowed to followe me before he knew what they were. I told him I disliked of the course holden with Mr Secretary bothe by him and me, indifferent betwixt the two states, and not very sincere vnto ether.

Mythought it was better to aduise eyether to dedicate ourselves to the preservation of this from all practises daungerous to the Queene person or the state, which I presumed, by reason of my credit with the Catholiques

---

[1] For Savage's vow, see *above, Introduction,* p. xlv.

[2] Interrogation 6, p. 69 *below*, clears up some of the obscurities here.

here and elswhere, did lye expressly in my power, or otherwise to the subversion of the present, or lastlye to leave the service of bothe and dedicate ourselves to a contemplative life, leaveinge the practize of all matters of estate.

He with an indifferent conscience swore vppon his salvation to follow me and my fortunes in any of those directe contrary cources that I should vndertake, asked me which I liked beste.

I tould him the contemplative life, so should we beare no blame of any or ether partye, and spend our tyme there in securitie, with profit in study, whilest this state stoode, and after, if it please god to sende a good world, we mighte take the ffruit of other mens labors, exempted from the daunger accompanyeinge the chaunge.

He helde the Course to departe the realme beste for any particuler, but added withall that he had euer founde me to reckon little of my particuler in question of any common good, and that no doubt one of the other two Courses were better, if it could be advised, which I proposed vnto him, then preservation of the present estate with the hazarde of the other, which he allowed not. It rested then of necessatie to imbrace the last, which he did willingly in apparaunce.

[§ 8, f. 221. *Lingering.*]

And thervppon I persevered therin, who otherwise (if so he had aduised), had departed the Realme with these other gentlemen my adherentes. But beinge by extreame fortune denyed meanes to travell, and perswaded by this man and Ballarde that this course was beste, I still enterteyned the practyze, but with suche extreame delayes as might well bewraye the repugnance which was in my nature, and the dislike which in conscience I had of this facte; by meanes wherof no doubte her Maiestie's lyfe was preserved.

Ballard oftentymes reproved my slownes, and tolde Henry Donne that he doubted I would discouer it vnto the Queene her selfe, vnto whome he harde I should be brought: the which no doubt I had don, if [I] might haue bene in assured hope of pardone for the rest, whome I loved so muche that I could not indure to discouer it to there overthrowe.

This lingeringe, as no man of resolved malice could haue don in a case so extreame daungerous, we debated *obiter* (to entertayne the tyme and their expectations) of many fowle practices, as What if the shippes were burned? which I liked not, beinge the strengthe of the realme.

Ballard said the gunnes might be poysoned they could never be discharged. Pooly saide it was convenient for to take awaye my L. of Leycester by poyson or violence. I thought there were men, and he meanes, to doe it.

He named likewise my L. Threasurer and Mr Secretarye, who mighte easely be taken away.

These three thinges beinge onlie spoken of, rested so; and was not resolued by whome nor when, neyther in what exprese manner, nor assuredly to be put in execution at all.[1]

They still cryed out of my delaye [2] as a thinge tendinge to the discouerye therof. I excused it with the expectation of Gilbert Gifford's retorne,[3] uppon which I did affirme somewhat to be don.

[§ 9, f. 221. *Gilbert Gifford revives the plot,*
June 26 to July 11.]

Gilbert Gifford before this was come over to Savadge, muche discontented that he left of to execute what he had vowed, and that he could not be discharged in conscience, vppon the pretences which I made, of his discontinvance from prosecutinge the same; all which he harde as meare delayes.

---

[1] See Interrogation 7.   [2] See Interrogation 8.
[3] Gilbert made two journeys abroad, and two returns. The plot was only started *after the first return*, in early June. So the only return which could have been *expected*, was the second, at the end of June. As to this he said in his confession, 'Revera autem ex parte mea totum hoc ideo erat factum ut negotium illud de interficienda Regina Angliae conficeretur, quod tunc agebatur.' This is said in regard of 'ultimi mei reditus in Angliam.'—*Hatfield Calendar*, iii. 348, 14 August 1588.

§ II. CONFESSIONS OF BABINGTON

I tolde [him] that I would he should assure vs from be-yonde the Seaes by authoritie,¹ that this action was directly lawfull in every parte; that there might be assur-ance geven of the readines of all suche provision as was required²; that some authoritie were granted³ for the int⁴ [? advancing] of men to dignities and some offices, and to haue rewards granted for suche as should vndertake any daungerous attempt. Vntill all which were don, I aduised him to with holde suche as were imployed against the Queene person, which then was Savadge, Gifforde, and one as I remember said to be nere Sr Walter Rawley.⁵ If he did not, I protested and swore I would discover it vnto the Queene, which he much disalowed, as Savadge tolde me. He went ouer⁶ dislykinge muche my courses, he said he was to passe by meanes of the frenche Ambasador as a frenchman.

Haveinge meanes to send to the Queene of Scotts by the boye that came for her packet, I writt vnto her touchinge everye particuler of this plott, vnto which she answered xx or xxx dayes after accordinge as in my former confessions is declared, which if theire honors Comande, I shall repeate.⁷

---

¹ 'Authority' for the lawfulness of the action was probably to be asked from Dr. Allen, or some ecclesiastic in high position, as the Nuncio in Paris, but we know no details. We do not know that Gilbert ever attempted to execute this commission, except perhaps sardonically, when he provoked Mendoza to write. As to which see *Introduction*, p. clxxiv.

² 'Assurance of readiness'. Mary was very insistent that this should be asked from Mendoza (Letter III). But Babington cannot have known this when giving Gilbert Gifford this commission before 21 July, as Mary's letter only arrived on the 29th of July (see Letter IV). But the precaution was an obvious one.

³ See Interrogation 9, and Babington's answer to it, *below*, p. 70.

⁴ Blank in MS. See p. 21, *nn* 1, 2.

⁵ The same words have occurred before, *above* p. 54.

⁶ He went over 21/31 July (Chateauneuf's *Memoire*, Labanoff, vi p. 292).

⁷ Babington's letter was about the 6th of July. He returns to his correspondence with Mary in § 11.

The 'former confessions' here mentioned are no longer forthcoming. This present confession probably covers the same ground.

[§ 10, ff. 221, 222. *Details. Probably Answers to further questions.*]

Edwarde Windsor was made privy vnto this action by Ballarde, and after I confered with him at the request of Ballarde touchinge the deliverye of the Queene of Scotts, or the takinge of Killingworthe Castell.¹ He offered to doe his parte in eyther of them. The meanes to take the Castle I never knewe; the rest I communicated vnto him, wherof he allowed.²

The meanes of the attempt of her Maiesties person nor the manner was never resolued, but rather left to the discretion of the parties. It was spoken of in her Coche, ridinge on horsbacke or walkinge into the perke or other like place, or it was holden that any of these havinge accesse into the Chamber, with sure expence of his life, might without fayle performe it there.

Mʳ Barnewell I resolued to haue sente vnto London, to the house of an Onckle of myne Richard Babbington in Tuttle streate, or to the house of one Winde in Sᵗ Johns Streate to knowe [if ignorant of these broyles] †³ which I presumed had not bene so greate, they would have received me, where I would haue remayned close, vntill the storme had bene past. During which tyme we would haue endevored passadge by meanes of father Edmonde the Jesuite or some other, and to haue sought by some meanes for a passadge downe the Temes, or to haue gon into an Ilande in the west⁴ vppon Mʳ Tuchborne his direction geven therin. We thought to haue wone to Wales or towardes Lirpole; so to Irelande or Scotlande; but to the houses of any Catholique any frinde I never ment; except to Mʳ Salisbury, if his Countrye had risen, as I presumed.

Mʳ Edwarde Abbington proposed the L. Strange his title, in case the Queene of Scots should dye. His opinion was that eyther he was disposed of him selfe, or at leaste

---

¹ Killingworth. This variant for Kenilworth, as the *State Papers* show, was then fairly common.
² See Interrogation 10.   ³ Some words seem to be missing.
⁴ The 'Island in the west' may have been Lundy (see Interrogation 11).

§ II. CONFESSIONS OF BABINGTON

a Septer woulde make him become a Catholique, and we thought that mans title would be beste admitted which they singulerly favour, next to that of Scotlande, and I thincke preferre it before the yonge prince, in case he persist in religion. Other talke concerninge that I remember not.

I talked with Mr Charnocke[1] and he referred him selfe to be disposed by me, this action by me. [*Sic.*]

I talked with Sr Thomas Gerrerde[2] of the takinge of the Queene of Scottes, wherin he should haue bene an actor.

That euer I comitted [? conversed] with any other touchinge this plott I doe not at this tyme remember. If there Honors do conceaue any thinge to be inquired herevppon I shall answere therevnto accordinge to my knowlidge.

Mr Barnwell and I were resolued to stand to the denyall of euerye parte of this action, and to affirme that he departed the towne for the greate love he bare to me.

Other speches concerninge the attempt of the Queene's person then before mentioned, I doe not remember; how be it, it is not vnlike but that we at sondrye tymes discoursed of the same matter, but euer to that effecte aforesaide.

Ballard tolde me amongest other motions that there was one man woulde deliver me two thowsand pounds towards the Charge of the action, what his name was I knowe not.

[§ 11, ff. 222, 223. *Correspondence with Queen Mary.*]

This is a continuation of § 9, and is further continued in Examination 4 *below*. For facility of comparison the section figures from the original letters are added, and the report will be found remarkably accurate.

I writt a lettre to the Queene of Scottes and gave it to the vnknowen boye[3]; the tenner of it was [§ ii.] That Balarde coming from Mendoza had informed me of the

---

[1] See Interrogation 12 [2] See Interrogation 13.
[3] The unknown boy was, of course, Phelippes's messenger.

purpose of the Christian princes touchinge this Countrye, and [§ iii.] that I was desirous to [do] her some service therein for hir deliuerye; [§ iv.] If there were assurance on the other side of suche things as were necessarye to this exployte, [there] woulde not fayle of coresponden[ce] on this side; [§ viii.] that there were sixe would vndertake somewhat vppon the Quenes person, [§ vii.] and that my self with sixe[1] others would vndertake her deliuerye; [§ iv., c.] that there were portes to be found[2] for the landinge of the forces, [§ iv., b] and assistance sufficient within to ioyne with those without; [§ ix.] that rewardes were necessarye to be promissed to the cheefe actors for theire better incouradgement, and to be geven to theire posterities if they miscarye in the execution.

Vnto this lettre I receaved an answere in the same cipher by which I write vnto her, but by an other messenger, which was a homely servinge man in a blew cote. He brought a lettre from his M^r[3] vnto me, by which he promised to discouer him self by the next dispatche vnto me, subscribed no name, willed me not to be curiouse or inquisitiue vntill his owne cominge. The inclosed lettre, which he by his saide to come from the Queene of Scotts, was of this tenner:

[§ i.] Declaration of her good opinion of me and due thanks for my readines to do her service, that she woulde not fayle to corresponde in all thinges she might, that she woulde aduise me so sone as resolution should be taken herein, [§ iv.] that I woulde with all speede imparte it to Mendoza, [§ iii. 1] consideringe first what forces on foote or on horsbacke we coulde make, what place for their asemblye, what leaders in euerye shere, [§ xii.] what generall or Cheefe leaders there were named to be sounded for that purpose—the Earle of Arundell or his Brothers, the

---

[1] 'Sixe,' for ten. Mary does not mention the number ten, which may account for Babington's slip of memory.

[2] 'Found.' So the Caligula text, which gives this section 11. The Yelverton reading is 'sounded,' which is, as so often with this scribe, an inferior version. The original was 'appointed.'

[3] 'Mr.' His master was really Phelippes.

§ II. CONFESSIONS OF BABINGTON

Earle of Northumberland, and (from beyond the Sea) the Earle of Westmerlande, the L. Paget and the others banished to folow them ; [§ iii. 2] then the fittest [ports] in the west, Northe and Southe partes, to receave ayde from ffraunce flanders and Spaine, what nombers to invade, for howe longe paid,[1] [§ iii. 4] what provision of munition, armoure and money, [§ iii. 6] in what manner the Six gent[2] ment to execute theire purpose : [§ viii.] advisinge that there should be some men in readynes about the Court well horsed to bringe worde when the designement was performed, to the ende she might be taken awaye before her keeper could eyther convaye her awaye or fortifye the place, [§ xiv.] proposinge three meanes for her delyvery. The first that when she should ride abroade vnto a certaine more twixt that and Stafforde, her keeper beinge accompayned but with xviij or xx, it might be easye for fiftye or three score to take her awaye.

The seconde waye—to set fier in the barnes and Stables neare the house about midnight and when they should come to quench the fyer, we beinge nere might surprise the house and take her awaye.

The third—that before daye in a morninge a Carte comminge with provision to the house, there might be such Carters appointed that might cause the Carte to overturne when it should be iust in the gate, so that they should not possibly shut them, duringe which tyme we might enter with safety the Solders lyenge distant some halfe a myle and more from the place. [§§ ix. xv.] And so willing me to assure the gent of all that should be required of her for their good, she ended[3] requiringe to knowe the

---

[1] So *Caligula*. Y. has a blank.

[2] Babington here runs together the two occasions in which 'the six' were mentioned by Mary. The introductory phrases correctly represent § iii 6, where 'the six' were mentioned first; but he goes on, as from the second mention of the six in § 7. In Examination IV. below he is prompted to say more about the second mention of the six, and he does so quite correctly

[3] The next sentence describes the forged postscript. But *Caligula*, C ix 459, which was read in court, is brought to an end *exactly* at this point; evidently in bad faith, to prevent the forgery from being detected.

names of [the] sixe gent: that she might give her aduice therevppon.

I write for answer by the same messenger that so sone as any resolution should be taken I would informe her.

[§ 12, f. 223. *Final Plans.*]

Within three dayes after the writtinge of this lettre, Ballard was taken,[1] vppon whose apprehension, forced with the extreame daunger to be discovered and then no hope of any pardon for so hatefull an offence, the attempt vppon the Quenes person was then, and neuer till then, resolued on my parte, which I moved vnto Savadge,[2] which motion accordinge to his former vowes, he readely imbraced. I sought in the meane tyme to obtayne liberty for Ballarde vnder pretence of better service; which not takinge effecte and my selfe restrayned, I departed the Towne in hope to escape into Fraunce or to liue obscurely ells where.

Dunne,[3] as I presume was acquaynted herein by the meanes of Ballard with whome he [was] muche convarsant. I acquainted him with the invasion, but I do not remember that I tolde him of the manner of the Quenes deathe, but he had knowlidge of some thinges to be donne therein, but by whome it was to be donne, I thincke he was ignorant.

ANTHONYE BABBINGTON.

Caligula, C. ix. f. 459, has this attestation:—

Confessed before us, and by him self also written at sundrie times betweene the eighteenth and Twentieth of Auguste 1586.

THOMAS BROMLEY, Cancellar:
WILLMS DNS BURGHLEY.
CHRISTOFERUS HATTON.

---

[1] Ballard was arrested on the 4th of August, five days after the receipt of Mary's long letter, but only one day after Babington's answer to it.
[2] See Interrogation 18.
[3] MS. reads Denis.

§ II. CONFESSIONS OF BABINGTON

No. 18

SECOND EXAMINATION OF ANTHONY BABINGTON

[*Ely House*, 20 *August* 1586.]

Yelverton MS., xxxi ff 223-6. Babington's further examinations differ considerably from his first In that he aimed at telling his story fully and finally In these his veracity and the completeness of his confessions are being tested. Upon the whole he comes out well from the test, no substantial error is discovered, and no notable omission Additional information is given of course, especially on fundamental ideas of Catholic politics, etc, which had not been touched before, and there is much that is valuable and interesting, especially in Examination V After this came the commital to the Tower on the 25th of August. The delay over this was probably due to the time it took to move on prisoners previously immured there (*Cath Rec Soc.*, vol. ii. pp. 253-76). But meanwhile the government had nearly finished their quest, and after two more examinations the lawyers step in to prepare evidence for the trial.

Interrogations are extant for Examinations II, IV., V., but not for III, VI., VII, VIII., IX Though on separate pages in the MS they are here combined; questions in italics with answers, and numbers are added to both. The first set of questions is based *seriatim* on Confession I, and references are added to the passages concerned.

For Mr Babbington

(1) *Who were those that muche abiused your zeale in religion and drew yow into these courses, and how many?* [On § 1, p. 51.]

Ballard abused my zeale in religion by manye and often perswasions, drawinge me and the rest into these courses. He is able to witnes my dislike of the acction, soundrye tymes tellinge him that I woulde get me over, and the rest with me, and never meddle in matters of state againe. He reprehended muche my delayes at soundrye tymes; and vppon my could proceedinge, suspected I would discouer it, as he tolde to Henrye Dun sondrye tymes. Savadge likewise disliked the same delayes.

(2) *When and by whose meanes was the excommunication to be revived, and to what effecte, and whether it be reviued or no?* [On § 2.]

That the excommunicacion is revived I doe not vnderstand; yf it be, by the meanes of the Pope who hathe a greate regard of the reformation of this Countrye.

Ballard helde expressly that the excommunicacion did not neede to be revived, standinge in sufficient force.

Savadge had asked the opinion of some learned in france, touchinge the lawfullnes of his vowe for the deathe of the Quene, declaringe her former excommunicacion never revoked but onlie tolarated for a tyme in regarde of the subiects, who otherwise could not obaye her without mortall sinn. The opinion of that learned man was that the acte was verye lawfull and meretorious that the excommunicacion could not be revoked by the Cannon lawe without the submission of the partye.

(3) *By what meanes and when had Barnewell, Salisburye, and Tychburne first vnderstandinge of these attempts, and what moved them to enquire of yow, what yow thought therein, and when and where?* [On § 3.]

Salisburye had vnderstandinge (as he told me then) by Savadge three monethes or more before Ballard's comminge. Ticheburne and Mr Barnewell, eyther by Mr Salisbury or by Ballard, I thincke theire purpose, to concurre with me in any course then moved, then to inquire my oppinion. It was soone after [? his] comminge over, and eyether in the feldes of Grayes In or Lincolns In.

(4) *Who were those Catholiques which Ballard had sounded and founde could?* [On § 4.]

Who they were whome Ballarde had sounded I never knewe, nether whome he had founde could.

(5) *When and at what tyme did Edward Abbington moue the exposition for the surprisinge of her maiesties person, and who were then present and made acquainted with the same? At what tyme and at what place did Abbington and Tilney yeld to vndertake the exploite for destroyenge of her Maiesties person, and who were then present?* [On § 5.]

I knowe not where it was that Mr Abbington moved the

surprise of the Queene, but I thincke Mr Tilney and Mr Tuchburne were present, and but that once I never remember to have talked with Mr Tilney concerninge any parte of this action, neyether doe I remember that eyether of them did consent directlye to take awaye the Queenes life, but I did reckon them two amongest the sixe, for that they had offered for to surprise the Queene.

(6) *When and where did yow discourse with Robert Pooley touchinge these matters? What perswacions did Pooley vse vnto yow, when and where?* [On § 7.]

Concerninge these things I discoursed with Pooley nere my lodginge I thincke three weekes since. He held not lawfull the killinge of the Queene, but for the three proposed Courses he aduised me, as by my former confession is declared, which was to reforme this estate rather then to preserve it with the subversion of the Catholique religion, or to leave our Countrye standing indifferent.

(7) *Where and when were these discourses touchinge the burninge of the shippes, poisoninge of the Gonnes, takinge away of the Earle of Licester, and who and how manye were present and to geather at the same?* [On § 8.]

Where the discourse was for burninge of shippes I knowe not. It was but moved and dishked. Ballard said the Gunnes might be poysoned : I thincke in the feldes nere my lodginge.

Oneley Robin Pooley and I talked of the Erle of Leycester as I haue before confessed, in the garden or feildes of my lodginge. I told some of the others that the world would reforme very well by a tolleration, the Queene livinge, if my L. of Leycester and my L. Threasurer were taken awaye, and not any of these sixe but would be farre more readye to performe any thinge against them, as an act in theire conscience farre more lawfull, for so said, as I remember, Mr Tuchburne and Mr Barnewell. Savadge was readye to have bene imployed in that or any other daungerous parte of the enterprise.

(8) *Who were those that 'cryed out on your delaye' and how manye?* [On § 8.]

[There is no answer to this question.]

(9) *What is meant by these words, 'that some authoritye were graunted,' and who and by whome were they to be so authorised?* [See § 9.]

It was meant that the Queene of Scotts should graunte authoritie vnto some to give certaine offices and dignities necessarye for this acction; that the authoritye were graunted to whome it might please her; that suche should be advanced thereby as were founde willinge and able to doe greate service in this acction, which was to be knowen when they were sounded. But to sound them I helde not convenient vntill the verye instant of execution, and that all thinges were assuredlye in readines before, bothe on the other syde and this, and therfore I had not entered into any consideracion thereof.

(10) *When and where did yow conferre with Ed Windsore, and how often and what was that reste which yow comunicated vnto him, and which he allowed?* [See § 10.]

I conferred with Edward Windsor but onely concerninge this matter to my remembraunce, and that was at Southhampton house, at which tyme Ballard and Savadge were there. [? We] comunicated vnto him, that some thinge was to be done by sixe touchinge the Queene's person; but I doe not remember to haue named them to him. I told him of the surprise of the Queene of Scotts, in which he offered to be one. For the takinge of Killingeworthe Castell I moved him, wherin he offered to indevoure what he coulde; but the meanes I doe not remember. The inuasion wth what soeuer Ballard knew, I presume he knew before.

(11) *What direction did Mr Tichburne give for the Iland in the west, when and where?* [See § 10.]

Mr Tuchborne gave no direction concerninge the Ilande.

He onlie told Mr Barnewell, after I was departed the towne, that there was suche a convenient place, whence he hoped we might have passadge.

(12) *When and where did Charnock reporte him self to be disposed by yow in what accion?* [See § 10.]

Mr Charnocke never referred himselfe vnto my dispossition vntill the same night that Ballard was taken; then he offered to spende his life wherin I should directe him. I discoursed that Ballarde had trusted Mawde and Mawde had betrayed him, so that it behoved some thinge to be done presentlye, and that I hopped Ballard should be restored vnto his libertye, by meanes of hoppe of better service wch I had geven Mr Secretarye, the which was the effecte of our talke in Poweles Churche yarde.

(13) *When and where did yow talke with Sr Tho Gerarde and to what end, and what was the verye speeche that passed betwene yow at that tyme?* [See § 10, note 2.]

I talked with Sr Thomas Gererd, as I take it, once at [his] house at Chanon Rowe, and at my lodginge at Mr Cookes, when he came to require me to be bounde for him vnto Mr Kinnersley. I told him at the first there was a brute of an invasion, from whence and what number. And after, when I talked wth him concerninge the same, I told him theire would be an invasion, and that the Queene of Scotts should be taken awaye; in wch exployte I asked whether he would be one. He answered he woulde. I bidd him rest so vntill he heard more from me, wch he shoulde not fayle to doe so soone as any thinge was concluded. As a man necessarye for any thinge, other then his owne person and servantes for the takinge of the Queene, I did not holde him; and therefore I did not wishe him to sounde any one, neather did I thincke it convenient to imparte vnto him any of the rest of the exployte, being resolved not to have communicated to any touchinge this affayre (other then with the aforenamed who were acquaynted from the beginninge) vntill all things were in readiness and assurance both on ther syde and this, vnto which rypenes it never grewe as yet.

(14) *When and where did Ticheborne saye vnto yow that he would spende his life with yow, and wherin did he offer to spend his life with yow, and when and where did he say vnto yow that he would doe any thinge that should be honorable and famous, and vppon what occation saide he so, and what meante he thereby?*

[This and the next three questions do not seem to be founded upon Examination I.]

Since Ballardes coming, but I know not about what tyme, and as I think at my owne lodginge, Mr. Tuchburne offered to be one to undertake the dispatch of the Queene yf it were defined for lawfull, or any other thinge, much rather tendinge to the reformation of our countrie, that were honorable and meritorious of what danger so euer, though there were nether expectation of life nor rewarde for the zeale, which he did beare to the Catholique cause, I told him I would imploye his life to the best, otherwise not at all, nether without assurance of infinite fruit to our countrye, and rewarde to him and his posteritie, worthie his resolution.

(15) *When and where did yow speake with Ed. Abbington touchinge the distroyenge of her Maiestie, and when and where did he saye vnto yow that he would willingly enter into that facte and liked well of it, when where and how often did yow talke with Tilney of the saide acction against her Maiestie and what allowance did he give of it?*

With Mr. Abbington I never conferred more then as I haue before mencioned, neyther with Mr. Tylney any more then what I have before declared.

(16) *When and where was it that Barnewell saide vnto yow that he would willingly adventure his life in this acction of takinge awaye her Maiestie?*

Mr. Barnewell, as I take it at my owne lodginge, said

that he would willinglie spende his life eyther in that of the Queenes person, if it were helden lawfull and meritoryous, or muche rather in any other parte of the accion that should be profitable to the Catholique cause, without life or rewarde. I told him his honorable resolution should not fayle to be rewarded worthely, and that I woulde imploye his life to singular profit, otherwise not, which he recommended to be imployed by me whereinsoever.

(17) *Where was Robert Gage made acquainted or pryvie to the purpose of destroyenge of her Maiestie or the invasion of the realme, when, where and by whome, and what assent or allowaunce gave he to the same?*

That euer Robert Gage was acquainted with the inuasion I doe not knowe, nether with any other parte, being not holden a man of any execution, and therefore not necessary to be acquainted therewith.

(18) *Wherfore after the apprehendinge of Ballard did yow move Savadge to execute the facte for distroyenge her Maiestie with speed, without taryinge for any further ayde or expectinge the invasion, and when and where was the same?* [See § 12.]

I asked Savadge in regarde of the present daunger of discouerye wherein we remayned vppon Ballardes apprehension, what was to be don. Who said no remedy but to hasten the execution. I was of that opinion, that there was no other meanes to secure our lives but that; and therefore I willed him to be in a readines, and I would ad some of the other unto him for assistance. Mr. Tuchburn was then lame of a leg, and therefore could not assist. The hope which I had to recouer Ballard's liberty made me defer the conclusion, meaninge vppon his deliverye, eyther all to have departed, if possible we could, or otherwise for our last refuge to have performed that, our former designment, by so many of these as were in readynes, and to have sent ouer presentlye, that the Strangers should hasten, in as greate nomber as they coulde, with prouision of all things necessarye, munition, monye, and vittayle, and that the L. Padget should haue hastened his repayre in pryvate towardes Stafford Shere, the Earle of Westmerland with forces into the Northe partes, my selfe in the meane tyme would have departed the Towne post into the Counties of Stafford and Derbye and Worester, to haue moved suche the principall there of Catholiques and Schismatiques as I thought most likely to be drawen herevnto and able to drawe the rest of the Countrye so disposed in religion or for any other cause discontented, for the takinge awaye of the Queene from Charteley and for ioyninge with her vntill some forayne forces should aryve; but that euer I sounded any man in the sayde Countryes, I denye.

The talke betwixt Savadge and me was at the garden where Poly did lodge.

(19) *Whether were any of the other sixe to haue hastned the same act against the Quenes Maiestie vppon Ballarde's apprehension, and who and how manye, and what don in that behalfe?* [On § 12.]

I tolde Mr Tychborne I was much discontented his legg was so evill for that we were in daunger to be discouered, and therefore we were either to flee or performe somewhat, and that I had som †experiment† expectation of Ballards delivery, vppon which or the dispaire of which I would resolve what shoulde be convenient. So dismissed him, as I remember in Smithfielde. I talked not with any other further then I haue declared.

(20) *Wherfore did yow moue John Charnock after the apprehension of Ballarde for the speedie executinge of the distroyenge of her Maiestie, and when and where?*

What I moued John Charnock, when and wherefore I haue set downe before.

§ II. CONFESSIONS OF BABINGTON

(21) *Who were those sixe that should haue ioyned with yow for deliueringe of the Queene of Scotts?* [On § 11, p. 64.]

The sixe for takmg awaie the Queene were never named nor sounded, nor in my owne determination resolued vppon.

(22) *To how manye and to whome did yow shew the Queene of Scotts lettre of answer vnto yow?*

I know not vnto how many I shewed the Queene's lettres. Mr Tychborne did assist in the disciphringe of them, for that I coulde not mdure the paine. Ballard sawe the Copye and so did Poly. I possessed [1] no other.

(23) *What money haue yow spent in the prosequucion of these plotts, and vppon whome haue yow bestowed the same and howe muche seuerallie?*

I am not able to saye what money I haue spent m this affaire. Ballard hath had som xx^{li} or xxx^{li} and Sauadge som x^{li} or lesse. The rest I never spent any thmg vppon in regard of this actıon.

(24) *What aduise proceded from the Queene of Scotts touchinge the kindlinge of fyer in Irelande, to hold the Quenes Maiestie busied there whilest these plotts should proceede here?*

[This does not seem based upon Babington's previous statements, but on Mary's original letter, § xı]

Touchıng the kındlınge of some fire in Ireland, she expressed no meanes ; only wished that it were to th'ende †our† attention might be dıstracted from that parte whence the stroke shoulde come, which was from Fraunce Flanders and Spaıne.

---

[1] In MS 'pressed'

No. 19

THIRD EXAMINATION OF ANTHONY BABINGTON

[*No date.*]

Yelverton, xxxi. f. 227. 'Mr Gifford' in (5) will be George.

TO THE NOTES OF FARTHER EXAMINATION

(1) I thinke that Mr Tuchborne made som question of the Scottish [Q.] lettres, but I remember not in what manner.

(2) I never vsed that course to aske mens lives to be bestowed at my disposition otherwayes, nor to no other then before confessed.

(3) The Devise to destroye the Queene was doubted to be vnlawfull as well by Salisbury as Mr Barnewell, and Mr Tychborne made question thereof; but Ballard and Savadge affirmed that there was no question, and that the opinion of the best of our nation on the other side was so.

(4) That Mr Salisbury, Tychborne and Barnwell had not persevered in this action but thorough me, I do coniecture, so that they very quickly disliked Ballard's discretion and his want of authoritie and assurance; and whether the qualitie of the action or not, I can not tell.

(5) That these had knowledge of the attempt against the Queene person before they talked with me of the invasion, I never knewe; But the invasion they knewe, as I have before mentioned. The inventors of killing the Queene, it semeth, are those who set Mr Gifford, Savadge and Ballard first in hand with theire entreprise.

(6) What speache Gage had touchinge the ffrenche lettres, I remember not.

(7) I deny that ever I tolde Savadge that I knewe Tuichener would be one of the sixe, neyther that I ever saide vnto Ballard any such words; for what presumption I had of him was but an ordinarie coniecture, because I hearde him to be a forward Catholique, a valiant man and Ed. Abington's follower.

(8) I am ignorant to whome Ed. Abington imparted his

advise of the surprice of the Queene person, and what counseillers in such a case shoulde be taken awaye.'.

(9) I remember not that ever Ballard named any noble man vnto me, neither that he saide there were fowre to assist in this entreprise.

(10) The devise of association proposed by the Queene was never put in vre by me, but reiected as a thinge which I helde daungerous and not necessary in this case.

No. 20

FOURTH EXAMINATION OF ANTHONY BABINGTON

[20 *and* 21 *August* 1586.]

Yelverton, xxxi f 228. These are points which Babington had omitted in his account of Queen Mary's letter. He is now enticed into re-casting his recollections

20 August 1586

Confessed by some of the confederats [1] conteined in the Scottish Quene's Lettres omitted by Babington.

(1) That she advised that it were necessarie an association shoulde be made betwene the Catholiques in respecte of the malice of the puritaines. [=Mary's letter, § vi. *b*.]

(2) That being don it shoulde be 'time for the vj gentlemen to worke taking order for the accomplishment' of the daye for her deliuery. [=§ vii.]

(3) To deale 'carefully and vigilantly' to provide all things 'necessary for effectuating the entreprise' in suche

---

[1] It is clear that this statement is fraudulent These points are *literal* quotations from the letter, and so must have been extracted from it Otherwise some prisoner must have quoted the whole letter by heart. whereas, in fact, when the evidence of the other prisoners besides Babington about the letter was gathered, the fullest version to be found was that of Ballard, which is short (see p. 138, *below*) That of Dunne and that of Poley are more superficial still The reason for the imposition is clear The government did not want Babington to guess that they had an intercepted copy. With Curll and Nau a different deception was used to obtain the same object. *Introduction*, p clxxxix.

sorte as the same woulde take good effect 'with the grace of god.' [=§ ix.]

(4) To giue out about that the Earle of Leycester had som plott to returne home with the English forces he hath in the Low countreys and to ioyne not only with the puritaines in rooting out the Catholiques of this Realme, but also shoulde haue an intent to depriue the Queenes Maiestie. [=§ vi.]

(5) That by his last lettres unto the Queene he did aduertise that one Mawde had discovered the entreprise. [= Letter iv., p. 46.]

All this verie true.   ANTHONIE BABINGTON.

[This brief answer did not satisfy the examiners. The following tells its own story. He has been ordered to write out his own recollections of the passages, and does so quoting §§ v. vi. vii. viii. ix. and his answer of 3 August, all which are cited very accurately. What follows is also contained in *Caligula*, C. ix. 459, the readings of which are preferable.]

The Quene's letters advised that upon returne of aunswere from Mendoza with assurance that all things requisite was in a readines, then and not before it shoulde be requisite to sounde the countrie; and, to collor [1] the prouision and preparation, it shoulde be given out that what they did was not upon anie euill or disloyall disposition towardes the Quene but for the iust defence of our bodies, lives and landes against the violence of the puritaines; the principall whereof being in the Lowe countryes with the chief forces of the realme [under the E. of Leicester, he] purposed at his returne to ruin [2] not only the whole Catholiques, but also meant to deprive her Maiestie of her Crowne if she did not conforme herselfe wholy vnto his will, and that therefore this preparation was likewise for the defence of her Maiestie and her lawfull successors, not naminge her, under which pretence an association might be made.

Which being don and all things in readines both within and without the realm, it shoulde be time for to set [3] the sixe gent. to worke, taking order that presently therupon

---

[1] Y., cover.   [2] Y., remove.   [3] Cal. and Y., let.

she might be taken awaye. And because the time would be uncertaine, of[1] the exploit of her Maiestie's person, therefore she thought it convenient that there shoulde be fower well horsed gentlemen allwaies to attende to bringe worde post in the countery, and by severall wayes for feare of interceptinge. And further that it were good to cut of the ordinarie postes betwixt the Court and that place.

She advised me to deale carefully and vigilantly for effectuating the entreprize, in such sorte that it might take good effecte by the grace of God, affirminge that she shoulde dye contentedly, whensoever understanding of our delivery out of the seruitude wherein we were holden as slaves.

Vnto which long letter I made no other aunswere, then that she should understande what resolution was taken vpon her proposition, in the meane time that I suspected one Mawde (who came ouer with Ballard) had discouered the plot and indaungered us depely, which how I would repare, she shoulde understande by the next.

ANTHONY BABINGTON.

Confessed afore vs, and written by him self the 21 of August 1586.

THO. BROMLEY.	W. BURLEIGHE.
CHR̃OPHER HATTON.	F. WALSINGHAM

No. 21

FIFTH EXAMINATION OF ANTHONY BABINGTON

[*No date*]

Yelverton, xxxi ff 229-231. In this examination Babington, true to character, allows his eloquence to run away with him, and does not strictly follow the order of questions set. Sometimes he gives the fullest scope to his easy credulity. Indirectly he thereby lets us see how it was that Ballard so easily made a victim of him

(1) *What did move you after the apprehension of Ballard to hasten the resolution of Savage and to proue Charnock's readines and disposition? And if their purposes had taken no effect what other hope of likelyhoode was lefte you?*

---

[1] Y, upon

(2) *What your opinion is touching the invasion ? whether any is like to followe uppon your apprehension and discovery ?*

(3) *What your opinion is touching the k. of Scotts of his affection towards his mother, and his disposition to this estate ?*

(4) *What hope you could have had to escape had you ben able to have gotten into your countrey. what meanes you could have made to haue moved the people and how they are disposed in those partes ?*

(5) *Whether Salisbury had conceived anie matter against this estate before you broke with him of it. what his determination was and what credit and meanes he had to escape in his owne countrie ?*

(6) *What your opinion was touching the Earle of Arundell whether he was privie to these actions. what meanes you had to procure his safetie and deliuerance upon the execution of this coniuration ?*

(7) *What Barnwells opinion was concerning the faciletie of the attempt upon her maiesties person. what speeche he had with you after his returne from Richmonde when he saw her maiestie in the greene ?*

(1) After the apprehension of Ballard the imminent daunger of discovery of o^r former proceedings caused that sodden resolution to be taken against her Maties person as a last and only refuge. I pourposed so soone as they had ben gone to the court for the execution of their designe to haue sent wth all possible spede into fraunce to signifie so much, and [to] will the forraine forces to be hastened in as much expedition and as great strenght as by any meanes they coulde, directing their landing in sondry places.

The Earle of Westmerland wth som forces out of the low countries shoulde lande in the North parts, all wch countries I presumed woulde be readie and forward, som part in regarde of the loue they beare unto his house and name, others in regard of religion. the com̃ons of those partes in generall being catholiquely disposed, but all in generall

§ II. CONFESSIONS OF BABINGTON

in regard of the harmes susteined after the last rebellion, since wch time it hath ben thought those partes haue thirsted for a daye of revenge.

The rest of the forces to haue landed at Milford haven in Wales & at the Pile of Fowdrie in Lankashire, wch two countries I held universally assured to the straungers, the cause of their coming considered. All those countries beinge either catholiques Schismatiks or malcontents, of all wch we might be assured in any confusion.

Of the West contries I made no sure accompt (though sondrie partes thereof had ben this yere muche disposed to sturre), for that there wanted heads to leade the comons, and portes to arriue. For wch two things I thought to have moved Sr John Arundell to have departed the towne secretly, and to haue drawen unto him Sr William Curteney a man valiant, populer and I suspected somwhat malcontent affecting hono^r and advauncement. Of wch two if we might be assured, I woulde haue aduised that som of the straungers shoulde haue landed there. In which foure severall places [1] arriving, being everie of them farr distant from the Court and in the verie extremities of the kingdome, I made accompt that, passing towards London and the South partes, which only remayned sure unto the Queene, if she escapt with life, we shoulde dayly encrease our forces, and cut of all such as should be holden contrarie unto us; making all sure behind our backes, reforming the country as we shoulde passe, placinge Catholique magistrates to governe.

So soon as this direction had been geven with aduise, accordinge to his [?Mendoza's] promise to send armour and weapons to fournishe fowrtie thousand of our naked men, and prouision of corne and wine. I purposed presently to haue gon into the Counties of Stafford & darbie and woseter to haue conferred with so many of those partes as shoulde haue ben necessarie for the takinge of the Queene of Scotts awaye, causinge them to be in redines against assurance

---

[1] According to Savage the proposed ports were Plymouth, Scarborough, and Hartlepool (Boyd, p 612) Cf p 93.

should come either of the Queenes death, or of the straungers their arrivall, uppon either of which I purposed to haue proclaymed her, and made no doubte of desired success, holding for certain that our nation deuided into three equall partes, two of them be discontented, either in that they desire & fayle of preferment, either for the enuye of others estates and aduancements, either for extreme want ther estates wasted and consumed & no hope to recouer any thing, the state standing, either for desire of revenge of som iniuries don unto them or their houses whereof they despair the state continewinge as it is.

Or generally in regard of religion, which of all other is the most impatient and violent; and universally the commons in regard of oppression (not so much for the taxes, subsides and sondry other payments to the Queene, whereat they neuertheles repine so farr as they dare), but in regard of the extreme racking of rents, the great fines, the enclosure of Commons and sondrie other sortes of extreame dealinge, wherwith they remayne in doubt, so farr discontented as maketh them fit for every alteration or chaunge. At which time they wilbe more readie to cut the throtes of their Lords in regard of their inhumane dealinge, then as heretofore to spende their lifes in their defence and the Queene from whome the sufferance of these extorsions hathe alienated their hartes. The reformation of all which, beinge a thing verie populer, shoulde haue ben published as our chefe pretence, by meanes whereof we shoulde haue ben sure to be fellows with thousands, that respected little any religion at all.

(3) I ever helde the king of Scotts wholy devoted to his mother, though in regarde of the daunger of his person, possessed by his mother's enemies, he hath pretended the contrarye. And I do verily beleue that religion, whatsoeuer in him [is], to be Catholique, which I expect he will manifest, whensoeuer he may with securitie. I iudge his disposition to this state is, to holde any course to possesse himself of this state otherwise surely, then to serue his tourne. I cannot thinke he affecteth the present regi-

§ II. CONFESSIONS OF BABINGTON

ment, the courses holden towards his mother & his own person considered, and also in regarde of his title to the crowne, which in his mother the state present hath euer disfauoured, and therefore lesse hope they will ever sincerely allow it in him.

I purposed to have sollicited the remove of his person from those protestants that now compasse him vnto the hands of Catholiques of that realme, whereof the Queene his mother, as your honours finde, gave hope by her letters.

(2) Touchinge invasion my Lordes, I do verily beleeve there wanted not mindes in the Christian princes, your honours can best iudge if there want meanes. The resolution, no doubt, is taken, and will be put in execution, early or late, if the deaths of one of those great monarches doe not prevent it. It is holden the readie meanes to reforme all Christendome, this place being the fountainhead that feedes all others, and therefore all their abilities are to be bended this waye, by which worke the k. of Spaine shall quiet his Indies, and recover the rest of his Low countries: the protestants of Fraunce shall not be able to assist, and in fine uppon the good issue of the enterprise of this countrie the general quiet and good of all the kingdomes adjacent is holden and defended. Mendoza protested that his master had vowed upon his soule he woulde reforme this countrie or loose Spaine.

The Pope hath drawn his pensions from the banished of all countries and diminished the revenues of all the seminaries and of all countries other charges whatsoever, to employ in the reformation of all countries falne from the church, but of this especially, whereof he hath greater care and respect then of the rest. And when some of our nation, brought up in the Seminarie at Rome, came to kisse his hande before their departure, he inquired what they were, and it was aunswered they were Inglishmen that were to goe home to spend their blood for the reformation of religion in preachinge and reconcilinge. He said they do well, it is a good worke; and musing a little saide, it was a good slowe waye, but he woulde use a more spedy and violent, and make a passage of wood over the ditch that environeth it.[1]

There is no doubt amongst them of the facility of the conquest, if they could have landing, the extreame and universal discontentment of the great part of our nation being knowen unto them; only her Maiestie's strength at sea keeps peace in the house, without which ther could [be] no suer pease or quiet.

That there wilbe any invasion this yere it is not probable in regarde of the discoverie and prevention of our late practize, uppon which I suppose they presumed muche, without which or the like, I do holde their enterprise extreme difficult; and verily beleeue they will neuer enter this [kingdom] without assurance of her Maiesties death, which by anie meanes they will endevour. They will procure [it] at anie price whatever. Ballard from the mouth of Mendosa swoore that September coulde not passe without an inuasion. Charles Padget confirmed as much, and since Gilbert Gifford confirmed the same.[2]

Though there were no correspondence on this side, only that the Queenes life were taken away was their chief and only desire, and some one port where to arrive. But if all these failed, ther was no doubt of the invasion being a vowed resolution; but if before the next yere was doubted, for that there was not in readines neither men nor shipping sufficient for the enterprise without the aforesaid mean of assistance on this side.

---

[1] In Examination VIII. 21, he says that he forgets his authority for this tittle-tattle, though Mr. Abington used to tell such stories. The character of Sixtus was, even from early times, strangely liable to the fictitious adornments of romancing newsvendors. But here we have the ever-present element of romance exaggerated and poisoned by the visionary Ballard and the tempter Gifford.

[2] 'And since Gilbert Gifford confirmed the same.' Savage tells the same story in his confession of 11 or 15 August (Boyd, 612), on the authority of Gilbert Gifford and of the letters of Morgan to him. He concludes, 'But [even] if none of the above things chance, they [the Spaniards] will be in England,' said Gilbert Gifford, 'before Michaelmas day.' On the word 'since' see *Introduction*, p. cxxxv.

§ II. CONFESSIONS OF BABINGTON

I have heard [1] that the chefe banished of our nation of late being desperate of anie good from the house of Scotland, by means of the captivitie of the mother, and of the sonne thoughe in another kinde, are in regarde of the daunger, which both their persons are thought to remaine in, as being in the hands of their enemies, and withall in regard of the dissimulation of the young prince in matter of religion, or his evil affection in religion—have endeuored to lay the title upon the house of Spaine, clayming from Clarence, which shoulde be invested by the autoritie of the Sea apostolike, for confirmation thereof, and the taking away of all obiections made or to be made against the claime of that house, the which I have heard is the cause of D. Allen his long staye at Rome.[2] Which if it take effect, I presume presently some of our nacion, the most reverent unto us both for learning and vocation, shalbe sent ouer,[3] to enforme under confes-

---

[1] From Examination VIII. 22, it appears that Babington's informant here was Ballard, and Ballard probably heard it from Charles Paget. Neither of these witnesses can carry any weight, but the evidence is early. The discussion of the subject did not begin at Rome till after Mary's death in 1587, and *Dolman's Conference on the next Succession*, which gave some publicity to the speculation, did not appear till 1594. It must also be remembered that this affair never passed beyond the region of speculation. No public claim about it was ever made; no official negotiation, nor any practical steps were taken for its realisation.

Babington has evidently no real knowledge of the subject. He alleges the Spaniards to claim through the house of Clarence, who was Edward III.'s second son, whereas, in fact, they claimed through John of Gaunt, the third son; while James claimed through Clarence. But the Spanish claim had the advantage of resembling the claim of the house of 'time-honoured Lancaster.'

Besides the *Spanish Calendar*, 1587 to 1603, and T. F. Knox, *Letters of Cardinal Allen*, see also *The Month*, May 1903.

[2] Allen had been summoned to Rome by Sixtus v. in September 1585, and the Pope kept him there for the rest of his life. Babington was not wrong in supposing that Allen remained on English Catholic business, but was probably mistaken in what he understood (? from Gifford) as to what that business was. So far as our papers go they indicate that the succession was not discussed at Rome till next year.

[3] 'One of the most reverend for learning and vocation.' We easily recognise here Gilbert Gifford's little plot of getting over his cousin, Dr. William Gifford, to act as a stalking horse.

sion,[1] the chefest of our nacion, such as are able to sway the mindes and abilities of the rest, of the disposition of the Pope concerning the same, and perhaps to move something to be don against her Maiestie's person.[2] Which if they will endevor with their authoritie and persuasion, declaring the action for lawfull, meritorious, honorable before God, and the only meanes to recouer the religion of our forfathers, to redeeme our lifes and liberties, to exempt us from the imminent daunger of death wherein we hourly remaine, surely I fear me there will many be founde fitt and forward instruments to execute whatsoever [is] proposed.[3]

The discouery of our late practize will make the next

---

[1] 'To inform and move under confession.' Babington seems to have mistakenly thought that a priest could safely and secretly 'inform under confession' about invasion and assassination. This is a fallacy. The secrecy of the confessional protects the penitent, not the priest. If the penitent in confession betrays a criminal intent, the priest cannot accuse him; but if a priest should betray a criminal intent, the penitent is bound to charge him.

[2] In making this infamous suggestion, Babington was speaking under the wretched spell which the *exalté* Ballard and the traitor Gilbert had cast over him. This it was which made him oblivious of the true spirit of the missionary priests, and best explains Father Weston's words, 'If I had had an opportunity of seeing him [Babington], I should have abstained from so doing.' Weston's imprisonment prevented that Father from ever learning the truth about the plot, and he never knew Babington's guilt. But this only makes his deliberate renunciation of his quondam friend the clearer indication of Babington's deterioration under Ballard's influence. It was only the prevalence of what I have described as 'Ban fever' (*Introduction*, p. xix.) which made the present perversity of mind possible.

In reality the Church has so insuperable an objection to a priest being connected in any way with a deed of blood, that even in the case of a just execution, and even if the cleric only participates by persuasives, he becomes, in the technical sense, 'irregular' *ex defectu lenitatis*, and is debarred from any exercise of priestly functions until he has been absolved. How much more if blood be shed without the forms of law or against them, or with widespread scandal and offence. See *The Catholic Encyclopedia* under 'Irregularity,' and *above*, p. xxviii. n.

[3] It is possible that Babington, here and elsewhere, in his scaffold speech for instance, was consciously exaggerating, on purpose to frighten Elizabeth into some sort of toleration. If so, he did not perceive that the animus of the bigots, which he was sharpening, was much more effective in the long run than Elizabeth's quickly varying whims.

§ II. CONFESSIONS OF BABINGTON

better handled with more secresie and fewer conspirators [or] rather many sondry conspircies, to thend if one fayle, som other may take effect, especially without delaye in execution which hath bin the ouerthrow of us and ours.[1]

(6) I verily thinke the E. of Arundell was never priuie vnto any parte of the practise. The preservation of him was a thing whereof I had a special care in regarde of his callinge and firmnes in religion. But the meanes of his deliverance out of the tower coulde never be aduised except by the participating with many, which might overthrow the rest more important.

(5) Touching Mr. Salisbury I never knewe of any practise that he had conceived against the state except this of late. I have heard him holden for a man very much beloued in his countrie and one of whome there is amongst them a vniversall great good opinion, his antecessors hauing ben of great livinge and chefe rulers in those partes, himself a comly personage, valiant, an extreme lover of his nation, and I thinke not the lesse affected for the displeasure, which it is thought he indureth for his countrie sake of the E. of Leicester, who is a man by report so hated there, as to oppose himself against him is holden sufficient to make any man folowed of all North Wales, the most discontented part of all this lande.

(7) Mr Barnewell returning from the Courte tolde me he sawe her Maiestie vppon the greene, fewe about her and those without weapon, that he presumed himself able to haue performed whatsoeuer against her person, and therefore thought [2] the entreprise would be verie easie if she continued that custome.

At the same time he tolde me Mr Secretarie deliuered som lettre or other intelligence, whereat her Maiestie started

---

[1] 'Delay in execution' was not the cause of Babington's overthrow, but Walsingham's spies. They fostered and provoked the plot at every stage. Elizabeth was never in danger, but Babington's life had been in Walsingham's power from the first. He did not even yet suspect in what a fool's paradise he had been living.

[2] MS. sought.

and looking about her, blamed her servants present for being without weapon, saying she woulde banishe those longe cloakes that were the cause. Other talke I do not remember that he had concerning that matter, which if I did and knew it profitable vnto the state I woulde most willingly manifest it. And woulde god, my lords, it laye in my knowledge or any other abilitie by discovery of daungers present or prevention of harms to com, to repaire in som part mine offences past.

[*The copyist here repeats answers 6, 5, 7, with a few alterations and verbal variations. Presumably he had got hold of a stray sheet of Babington's draft and copied it mechanically, without noticing that the information contained had been given better before. The only additional matter is about Salisbury.* 'Neither had he medled in (this late practice) had it not been through me. *Tantum infelicem nimium dilexit amicum.*']

Thus much in answer of your Honours demands according to my knowledge and the short time to consider thereof, which, I wish to God, may be profitable to her Matie and the Commonwealth by our lives and deaths.

No. 22

SIXTH EXAMINATION OF ANTHONY BABINGTON

Yelverton, xxxi. f. 232. [*No date.*]

Babington's attendance upon the Earle of Shrewsburie in London,[1] Auguste 27. [27 Elizabeth was 1585.]

Returning out of Lanckeshire from the house of Mr. Norrice of the Peake [2] vnto my place, [whither] I went to accompany Philipp Draycott, my wife her elder brother, who had married the ladie of the late Sir Thomas Butler,

---

[1] Queen Mary had inquired about Lord Shrewsbury from Barnes (*above*, p. 15), and was answered by Phelippes (*ibid.*, p. 18).

[2] For 'Peake' the scribe should have written 'Speke' Hall in the parish of Childwall, Lancs. For the Norreys family, see *Catholic Record Society*, iv. 199. Edward and his wife, Margaret of Speke, figure in the Recusant lists (*ibid.* xviii. 173, 201). Philip Draycote is mentioned (*ibid.* xviii. 303), as ' nuper de parochia de Chedull [Cheadle] in com. Staff. armiger.' This was at Michaelmas 1593.

daughter of the said Mr. Norrice,—I understoode presently upon my coming home that the Earl of Shrewsberie was by appointment to take his iorney towards London within few days following. Whereupon for the honour and love, which, aswell myself as my predecessors did ever, and had ever borne unto his house and name, I proposed myself to attend upon his Lordship, who being sett forward from home before me, my horse newly taken from grass, I did not reach Leicester that night, the place where his lordship did lye; [but was] xii miles short; and by meanes thereof I did not overtake his lordship until it was past Welford, where finding him I delivered the end and cause of my cominge, and received many thankes of his honour for that simple testimony of my affection to him and his house.

I lefte him not vntill he came unto Otelands[1] where then this court was, having stayed there two hours or there abouts, which was the time of his honours staie with her Maiestie. I wayted [on him] to his Lodging, thence taking my leave, with many thanks for my trouble, I departed that night to kingston, thence to London, so home to my house in the countrie.

No. 23

SEVENTH EXAMINATION OF ANTHONY BABINGTON

[No date.]

Yelverton, xxxi. f. 232. Babington's letter to Nau does not seem to be extant, but Nau's answer is printed *above* (p. 24), and again Babington's recollection of it will be found very accurate.

I never writt any one lettre neither ever sent any message vnto Curle or to any other servaunt or attendant of the Queene excepting one letter vnto Mr Noe her secretarie, the tenore of it was, I informed him of Robert Polye his good partes and the free accesse which he had to Mr Secretarie that I conceyved he bare good affection vnto

---

[1] The palace of Oatlands was near Chertsey in N.W. Surrey.

the Queene, and that he was in good place to do service, if the Queene might be assured of him, willed him to write his opinion and what he thought of the man.

His aunswer was that there was great assurance given of Mr Poley his faithfull serving of her Maiestie and his owne lettres had vowed asmuch, But that her experience of him was not such that he woulde recommende him to me to be trusted, hauinge neuer written vnto the Queene but once, vnto which letters she had returned no aunswer not knowing by what meanes to sende, neither whither to direct them, in fine willed to know my opinion. I sent my letter vnto him at the same time and by the same boye that I writte vnto the Queene by, when I proposed the late practize vnto her.

I receiued his aunswer with her aunswer the last time that I heard from her by the serving man in the blew coate, which letter I aunswered not.

But that once I neuer writt vnto him nor any other of her servants.

Neither but that once in answer did I euer receyve letter or message from any of them nor at any time haue I spoken with anie one of her people, neither do I remember that euer I sawe any of them.

If their honors finde other then truth in what I affirme, let them entreate me accordingly.

No. 24

EIGHTH EXAMINATION OF ANTHONY BABINGTON

[*2 September* 1586.]

Yelverton, xxxi. ff. 233, 234. The remaining examinations are of a new class. They are conducted by the law officers of the Crown, who were so soon to prosecute Babington to the death. The bloodhounds are here endeavouring to find out more victims through the inflated language in which Babington had addressed Mary, but he maintains the accuracy of his first statements, and the lawyers gain nothing. Answers 12 to 17 have a character of their own; they are occasioned by the stories of the hysterical Tyrrell, of whom we have heard in the *Introduction, above*, p. lxviii.

Thexamination of Anthony Babington Esquier before

§ II. CONFESSIONS OF BABINGTON

John Puckeringe Esq., one of her Maiesties Seriants at the lawe and her Maiesties attorney and Solliciter generall.

2 Septembris.

(1) He saith and protesteth that he never conferred with anie touching the actions intended, saving with the persons whom he hath before named, but to thintent to move the Scottish Queene to deale the more roundely, & readily, he did write unto her that—after longe consideration and conference had with so manie of the wisest and most trustie, as with safetie he might recommend the secrecie thereof unto [1]—as is contained in his letter.

(2) The reason why he did not conferre with anie other was for that he [...] [2] of itself sufficient; and that if the Queen Maiestie were taken away, then the Scottish Queene was assured of all the Catholiques and Schismaticks in the realme; and therefore it had been nedeles to have sounded them, or to have had any conference with them in the matter.

(3) He saith that he knoweth not any nobleman that woulde be assured in this action, either at libertie, or in prison or otherwise restrained, but he saith he presumed that the E. of Arundell would have ben a fit man to have ben sounded in these actions, in respect of his earnest affection and zeale to the catholique religion, but he never knewe any thinge of him.

(4) He saith that Ballard did tell him that he had taken the fidelitie of sundry persons as well in the North as in the West parts, but named not any for ioyninge in these actions, but he knoweth not any other that have taken the fidelitie of anie persons, saving as he hath before declared, howbeit he did write so to the Scottish Queene to thintent to moue her to deale the more readily and willingly in the matter. He denieth that he did recommend any gentleman by name to the Scottish Queene to be Lieutenant,[3] but the effect of his letter in that point was, that

---

[1] These words occur in § iii. of Babington's letter. Yelverton MS. inserts *her* after unto.

[2] The sense requires, 'thought what had been done was.'

[3] See Babington's letter, § vi.

he woulde afterward recommend some vnto her, and he saith his promise was to have sounded some for that service, as he hath before declared upon returne of her aunswere.

(5) He saieth he meant to have chosen ten gents, one of the countie of Suffolk, one [of] Darby to have delivered the Scottish Queene, either of them to have ben accompanied with ten followers, but he never found any for that purpose, but Sir Thomas Gerard and Thomas Salsbury. But his intention was that the L. Paget shoulde haue returned secretly, and he also meant to have moued the L. Staff. in respect of his decay, and som hope to have been conceyved by this meanes to have been releived. He meant also Mr. John Draycote, Mr. John Gifford, Mr. Samson Oulswick, Mr. Fowler and Mr. Wolusley in Staff. shire, and in darbieshire Sir Thomas Fytcherbert and the rest of his name, and Nicholas Langfourd in worcestershire.[1] Mr John Talbot of Grafton and the Throckmortons and the L. Windsor, if by his brothers meanes he coulde be drawen vnto it.

(6) And whereas in his letter to the Scottish Queene he subscribeth your sworne servant he denied that ever he was sworne vnto her, but vowed his service by that letter, and never before, but limited and restrained with his duetie and allegiance to the Queene Maiestie.

(7) Touchinge the portes he saith that there were none assured saving, as Ballard sayde, Hartipole in the North,

---

[1] For Sir Thomas Gerard of Bryn see *Cath. Record Society*, xxi. *passim*. Thomas, third Baron Paget, has a notice in *D.N.B.* Edward, twelfth Baron Stafford, in consequence, no doubt, of this confession, was nominated one of the jury of peers to condemn Queen Mary; but he is mentioned in 1574 as a Catholic in *Cath. Rec. Soc.*, xiii. 90. John Draycote, Babington's father-in-law, of Draycote, Staffs., was a wealthy and staunch recusant, *Cath. Rec. Soc.*, xviii. 301-8. John Gifford of Chillington was the father of Gilbert Gifford. 'Samson Oulswick' I cannot identify, but take the name to be a clerical error for Sampson Erdswick of Sandon parish, Staffs. (*ibid.*, xviii. 301). Mr. Fowler seems to be Bryan Fowler, of St. Thomas, beside Stafford (*ibid.*, xiii. 128, 136, also xxii. 92). 'Mr. Wolusley in Staff.shire,' seems to be Erasmus Wolsley of Wolsley, Colwich parish, Staffs. (*ibid.*, xviii. 295). 'Nicholas Langfourd in Worcestershire,' is Nicholas Langford of Longford in Derbyshire (*ibid.*, xviii. 28, etc.).

but it was meant that Plymouth in the west should haue ben taken, if by the meanes of Sr John Arundell and Sr William Curtney it might be compassed. And in Lancashire they meant the Pyle of fowdrey and in wales Mylfurd haven; but he never resolved vpon anie speciall persons to haue ben emploied for the takinge of these hauens, but hoped of the generall disposition of the Countries in the generall confusion.

(8) He saith he was never acquainted with Sr William Curtney, but he was once at supper with him at the three tonnes in Newgate market, where this examinate and Mr Tycheborne met Sr William Curtney and diuers gent: were in his company, but knew not of their beinge there, but came thither by chaunce, and so by reason that Mr Tychborne had familiar acquaintance with Sr William Curtney they supped together, and this was since Easter last. He saith his intention was to haue sounded Sr William Curtney by Mr Tychborne, but he neuer moued Mr Tychborne to deale with Sr William Courtney in it, nor never thought good to sounde any for assisting the forraine forces at their landing; but did hold, the countries being affected as they are, woulde have performed that sufficiently, her Maiestie being taken awaie.

(9) He saith that such of the gent: aforenamed as were to vndertake the action against her Maiestie did vowe and promise to performe it, and after signification of assurance from the Scott: Queene this examinate meant they should haue received the sacrament vpon it.

(10) He saith there was no resolution of any place where the forces shoulde mete, or which way they shoulde marche, for the same was proponed by the Scottish Queene, but never resolved by reason of this examinate's trouble. He saith and protesteth vehemently that he never heard of any plot or intention for destroying her Matie other then he hath before set doune.

(11) He saith he meant to have gone himself in[to] Fraunce to have conferred with Mendoza, and to have seen assurance of that which was to be performed on their part concerning the inuasion: and not prevayling in

his suite for licence he determined to send Ballard[1] to supplie that seruice. And before his returne he thought it not necessarie nor conuenient to sounde any other concerning the havens, the mouing of the countries or transporting of the Scottish Queene's person.

(12) He denieth[2] that Ballard did tell him of his iourney to Rome or of any sute he had there to the Pope, or of any doing of Ballards at Rome, nor ever heard that Ballard was at Rome. But Ballard did always hold it to be honorable, lawfull and meritorious to undertake the action of destroying of the Queenes Maiestie; and persuaded this examinate to proceed in it, and he should lack nothing, that might serve in the effectuating of it.

(13) He denieth that he did ever knowe that Ballard had any lodging at St. Giles, or that he was there with Ballard, nor ever saw David Inglebie in Ballard's companie. But he saith he hath ben in companie of Ed. Windsore and Ballard once at the Rye Tavern without Temple Bar, and once in Windsor's lodging at Southampton House, and there discoursed with him to such effect as he hath before declared.

(14) He denieth that Ballard did ever talke of any doing that he had with Dr. Lewis at Millaine, or elsewhere, or that he ever heard that Ballard had been in Millaine. He saith that this examinate Tichborne and Salysbury did discourse together how the Lords of the Council in the Starchamber might be killed there,[3] which

---

[1] In point of fact Gilbert Gifford was sent (see *Introduction*, p. clviii.). But the original intention was to have sent Ballard.

[2] It is clear that §§ 12 to 17 were occasioned by Tyrrell's hysterical confessions, for which see *Introduction*, iv. § 3. Tyrrell had made two statements (August 30, 31) before the date of this document, 2 September. They are now printed in Boyd, viii. pp. 641-53. It is clear that the government learned all the names and events on which they now examine Babington from those papers; and it will be noticed that Babington always denies or corrects Tyrrell's statements.

[3] Tyrrell's account of 'the Star-Chamber practice' is in Boyd, p. 651. The names, Dunne, Ingleby, etc., all figure in Tyrrell's list (*ibid.*).

It may be asked how Tyrrell could possibly have heard of the 'Star Chamber Practice' by August 30; and it may be suggested that he did so through the promptings of his examiners, Lord Burghley, Justice Young,

§ II. CONFESSIONS OF BABINGTON 95

was to this effect, that six or ten gentlemen, eche one with a pistoll, might dispatch it, every one choosing one of the Lords. This was only talked of thus far walking in Crow lane, but no resolution upon it, but propounded only by this examinate. And he denieth that he had talke or conference touching that matter at a supper with any, or that seuerall, Donne, Davye Ingolby, Transome, Fortescue, and Tyrrell, or any of them, ever talked or conferred with this examinate of this attempt. And he saith that this proposition was moved to [sic? by] this examinate the last winter.

(15) He saith that in the last lent this examinate tooke his leave with Ballard at the plow without Temple Barre, the night before Ballards going; at which time there was in this examinates companie Mr. Tichborne and Mr. Barnwell, and with Barnwell there was Anthony Tunstall, Maude, Donne, and one Donnington, whom this examinate knew not, but he remembreth not that he was at dinner with Ballard at the kings head in Fish street.[1]

(16) He saith he knoweth Jacques,[2] a souldier of Ireland. He sawe him first in Fraunce in company of Mr. Cary about three yeres agoe, he saw him last a little before the same Jacques went into Ireland, which was about the last terme. He saith he never talked with him of any part of this action.

---

etc. Babington's first examination, § 8 (20 August), approached the subject nearly. Other conspirators, whose examinations are now lost, may have said still more. On the practice of examining one prisoner from the confessions of another, see Waad's *Discourse*, printed *Cath. Rec. Soc.*, xxi. 175.

[1] This was Tyrrell's statement, Boyd, viii. p. 653.

[2] This man was afterwards more widely known as Captain Jacques, his real name being Jacomo Francesco, or da Franceschi. He afterwards served in the cosmopolitan forces of the Prince of Parma in Flanders; indeed, he was himself of Flemish extraction. He was, says Dr. Jessopp (*Letters of Henry Walpole*, p. 7), 'a dangerous and violent man,' and the English spies constantly reported his injurious words, and malevolent, nay treasonable, persuasions and acts. At this time, however, he was under the protection of Hatton, and he seems to have got off with a year's imprisonment in the Fleet. He had been named by Tyrrell (Boyd, p. 654).

(17) He denieth that he knew Mr. Bold[1] or ever saw him to his knowledge.

(18) Touching the disposition of the people in the west parts to stirre this summer, He saith he meant the common people in respect of the dearth and their discontentment.

(19) He saith he sent no advertisement to Mendoza but for [*sic*, ? by] Gylbert Gyfford, as he hath before declared, but he meant to have sent Ballard with such direction as before.[2]

(20) The means of removing the Kinge of Scotts into the hands of the Catholiques he knoweth not nor ever hearde, but the Queene of Scotts would have aduertised of that.

(21) He saith he remembreth not who tolde him that the Pope woulde make a bridge over the Ditche, and so make alteration of things in England. Saving that he hath heard Abington use some speeches to that effect.[3]

(22) He saith that he hath heard that D. Allen and Charles Pagett endevor to set forth [the] title for the Kinge of Spaine to the croune of England,[4] but he remembreth not of whome he hath heard it, saving that Ballard as he remembreth hath tolde him of it.

No. 25

NINTH EXAMINATION OF ANTHONY BABINGTON

[8 *September* 1586.]

Yelverton, xxxi. f. 235.

The Examination of Anthony Babington Esq., before John Puckeringe one of her Maiesties Seriants at the lawe, and her Maiesties attorney, and solliciter generall, and Miles Sandes Esq. the viii of September, 1586.

(1) He saith that Chideock Tichborne and he have had

---

[1] Mr. Bold is mentioned by Tyrrell (*ibid.*). Richard Bold was afterwards examined in this connection (Boyd, viii. p. 698; see also Morris, *Troubles*, ii., *passim*).

[2] See Examination I. § 9, p. 69.

[3] See Examination V. p. 84.

[4] See Examination V. p. 85.

some conference and speach tegether touching the taking of Plymouth haven and that was moved by Tichborne as being thought by him to be a port of verie great importance if it could be taken, but he said that ther was neuer any course resolved upon for the taking of it saving a pourpose to have drawn Sir John Arundell and Sir William Curtney [1] to have dealt therein, if they could have ben persuaded therunto, wherin it was meant that Tychborne should have ben used.

(2) He saith that he understood by Pooley, and also by Savadge, that Yardeley was come over, but he hath had no talk with Yardeley since his coming over. He saith he willed Savadge to enquire the cause of his coming, but this examinate never understood what it was, and as he thinketh, Savadge never spoke with him of it.

(3) He saith also and protests earnestly upon salvation of his soule, that to his remembrance he never moved nor dealt with any touching the act against her Maiesties person, or the invasion of the realme, or the deliuery of the Scottish Queene, but with such and in such manner as he hath before declared. Yet he saith he must nedes confesse that his letters to the Scottish Queene do import great probabiltie to the contrary.

---

[1] Sir John Arundell of Lanherne, a zealous Catholic (*D.N.B.*, ii. p. 141) and *Cath. Rec. Soc.*, xiii. 90 n., which also quotes the corrections in *Notes and Queries*, 11th Series, iii. 415, 491. Sir William Courtenay, ancestor of the present Earls of Devon, and then High Sheriff of Devon, was to all appearances a zealous protestant. But the sanguine Ballard represented him as ready to join the invaders (Boyd, p. 612). (See § 8 of the previous examination.)

SECTION III

LETTERS OF GILBERT GIFFORD

GILBERT GIFFORD'S CORRESPONDENCE.—As Gilbert Gifford was a prime-mover in the plot, and as his movements, operations, and methods are still imperfectly known, all his letters at this period are naturally of great importance. Only nine written during the plot survive, about twenty-eight letters from him, and seventeen to or about him remain for the subsequent years. All the plot letters are printed here in full. The subsequent correspondence is treated briefly in an Appendix, in which all the correspondence is indicated, and the confessions about the plot are described more fully.

Gilbert Gifford, it will be remembered, had been educated abroad, and his English shows evident traces of this. That he was clever and intelligent in no ordinary degree will not escape the notice of the student; but the signs of instability and want of discipline are also but too clear. His signatures differ widely. In later letters such irregularities show themselves more than ever. 'The profanity of this letter is singular,' wrote Father Morris, p. 380, about one of them.

The first letter was written to Curll when Gilbert was about to start on his first journey (*above*, pp. 1, 5) to bring back his cousin, Doctor William, in order to make him a stalking-horse for the ruin of Mary's friends. He is going, we may say, on a mission for blood, but nothing of the sort appears on the surface. Thomas Barnes (here called 'my kinsman,' possibly a deceit) has been engaged to carry letters in his stead; and Gilbert is using all his arts—he is mild, unctuous, chatty, in order to flatter Mary into feeling that all is well. The student should be especially critical! Where the writer uses strong but vague terms—like 'for very necessity,' 'I fear too true,' 'Doubt not any default in my substitutes'—he will do well to think more than once. The assumption now of a pro-Spanish tone, now of one against Elizabeth, is sufficiently notable. Mary's love of news is known, and repeatedly played upon.

§ III. LETTERS OF GILBERT GIFFORD

No. 26

GILBERT GIFFORD TO GILBERT CURLL

[*London, 24 April* 1586.]

R O. *Mary Queen of Scots,* xvii. n. 55. Autograph, with Curll's interlinear decipher, which is here printed in italics. A summary of the principal parts in Boyd, viii. n 359

Sir,—According as before I signifyed my iournay to London in haste was for very necessitie, so that I could not stay for her Maiesties depesche. Here at my arryvall I receaved this packet from †+,[1] *w*^{ch} *I send by Pierre Soigne*[2] *to yow.* I deliuered the partie the some, wherof he was no little glad, and I truste it will be a meanes of his greater diligence.

Newse in these partes are not dentie. For flaunders the common reporte is, and *I feare too trewe*, that the Inglishe defaited vij hundred spaniardes by Graue,[3] and as is reported vitled the towne; the wch spaniardes were moste of them principal souldiars and capitaines. There goes greate troopes of souldiars from these partes thether dailie, albeit *this queene* is not yet determined to enter absolutlie into that course, if by anie coulor he [*sic*] can dissemble it; allthough her Maiestie of Englande, at the reporte of these newse, seemed alltogether to allowe of my lord of leicester's proceedings, yet since she beginnethe to waver, *many wayes dislykeing his absolute tytles, as is thowght wilbe changed as never approved by her*, wherat *Walsingham* and his frendes are greeued, but they knowe howe to deale wth her humor for theire purposes. In Englande is greate preparation to meete Drake at his retorne; who is arriued, as is constantlie reported, in

---

[1] This sign (as we see in MS xvii. n 58, bound next but two after this letter) means Morgan It was sufficiently familiar at Chartley to need no interpretation.

[2] Pierre Soigne must mean Barnes The 'party,' to whom Gilbert gave the 'sum' of money, may well have been the brewer, otherwise called 'the honest man'

[3] Graue was given back to the Spaniards a few weeks later. All the news that follows is coloured to please Mary.

Hispagniola. Lickwise his maiestie of Spaine preparethe for the same purpose. The kinge of france hathe a nauie, as is reported, to clenze they seaes of Englishe pirates.

A straite leage is concluded betwixte England and Scotland, the yonge prince beinge pentioned by Englande to the some of three or foure thousande l by yeare.[1] *Archibald Dowglas is in Scotland*, w^(th) all instructions for that purpose. Imediatlie at my arriuall here were executed ij seminarie preestes [2] and shortlie shall be banished greate parte of suche as are in houlte, they reste condemned to perpetuall prison. Mr Thomas Somerset [3] is latlie departed this life in Clinke after his release from the Tower briefe. All partes of Christendome are, as it seemethe, in garboile, wherof none seemethe more uncertaine then this of Englande, dependinge of womenlie humors; who to daie will, to morrowe no.

Lett not her maiestie doubt any defalt in my substitutes, whom I will leve so instructed, that they shall content yow. I doubt not the reason why these packets are devyded, yow may understand by the Ambassador, albeit I lyke not so well therof. I was present when he opened them. Yow may do well to aduertis †+ to be as briefe as he can, consideringe the wante of delyvery, I purpose the next weeke to take my voiage. Then I will informe †+ of all the course. †+ in his last perswadeth my tarying here, but I have informed him of the danger & impossibilitie therof; for that my frendes thought me gone, when I was last w^(th) yow; and I

---

[1] Her son's infidelity to her is mentioned by Nau (Labanoff, vii. 208) first among the reasons which moved Mary to agree to the Babington plot. But, of course, Mary knew of it from other sources as well as from Gilbert. The treaty of Berwick was agreed in principle July 1585.

[2] Richard Sergeant and William Thomson, both 'venerables,' were martyred at Tyburn, 20 April 1586. Their brief story will be found in Burton and Pollen, *Lives of the Martyrs*, ser. II, i. pp. 200, 201. There was no wholesale transportation of priests abroad in 1586, as there had been in 1585. The measure, however, was under discussion, because Walsingham wanted to clear the prisons in order to have room for the Babington conspirators (*Cath. Rec. Soc.*, ii. 253, 272).

[3] Thomas Somerset had been arrested on suspicion, because Morgan had got him to forward letters (see *Cath. Rec. Soc.*, xxi.; also Boyd, viii.). The name of the place where he died cannot be read with certainty.

have sent over my money long since, wch I think †+ hath now receaved. Therefore I will accept her maiesties leve the next opportunitie, thanking almightie God it hath pleased him to prosper by her maiesties poore servant the intelligence, wherin I receave no small comfort trewly. Beseechinge her Maiestie to accompt of me as one yealding to none in affection towardes her highnes, as th'effect shall shew, when [it] pleaseth her [to] command me. My kinsman will wryte, I thinke, to yow.[1] He wilbe hable to informe yow [of] the state of this consell, having good frendes in the courte, as yow shall direct him. When I shalbe in france I will imploy all my tyme & travell in her Maiesties service, in any course I shalbe directed, where I shall think me fortunat & therefore happy to be imployed. Praying yourself not to spare me, if yow have occasion in any sorte, desyring yow knew me as well as good frances[2] did. From London the xxiiijth of Aprile. [No Signature.]

Addressed, L. L.
L. L.

Endorsed, Pietro the 24 Aprile 1586. *Numbered*, 24.

[? In Phelippes's hand] 'Gilbert Gifford's lettre, decifred by Curle.'

Written across fols. 230 & 231—this decyphered/cumming from one Pietro by me/Gilbert Curll/1586.

No. 27

HEADINGS BY PHELIPPES, FOR A LETTER TO BE WRITTEN BY ? GIFFORD TO MORGAN

[*London*, 24 *May* ? 1586.]

R.O. *Domestic Elizabeth*, clxx. n. 89, Phelippes's hand, but wrongly calendared as 1584. The fairly numerous, though small alterations (here marked by small stars), show that this is a draft. The placing of this piece among Gilbert's letters is a conjecture. It is true that Gilbert was presumably still abroad at this date, but, on the other hand, he was expected back daily, and would have to write to Morgan on his arrival. Gilbert is also spoken of by his cipher name, Cornellis, which we should not expect to be communicated to another spy.

---

[1] This probably means that Gilbert had already written a draft for Barnes's letter of 28 April, p. 5, *above*.

[2] These unctuous words perhaps refer to Francis Throckmorton.

Still there are some lines, especially in § 3, which look as if Barnes might have been the intended writer. But at this date he was not yet in Phelippes's service.

The general purpose of the letter is plainly indicated in § 4, namely, to induce the communicative and imprudent Morgan into the betrayal of as many of Mary's friends as possible. Discussion of a change from Chartley, § 3, had been not uncommon in Mary's correspondence of an earlier date, and it is mentioned in Mary's letter to Babington. 'The address for Scotland,' § 5, had been mentioned by Phelippes to Walsingham (though in different terms), 19 March 1585/1586 (Morris, p. 155, 156). Mr. Bagot is probably the puritan gentleman Richard Bagot, a neighbour of Chartley, and often mentioned in Morris. E seems to be a cipher sign for Queen Mary; Thomas Germin is an *alias* of Morgan; Cornellis of Gilbert Gifford.

24 *May.* (1) Fr. Emb. advertised y^t * in case her ma^{ty} shall have more dispaches to send then one man can make viages. I will send another who shall call him selfe 'Roland.'

(2) Tho. Germin [? *Morgan*] required to send answer of the matter concerning her service sent to Nicholas Cornellis him selfe wth whome I will deale only hereafter by writing EL.

(3) I advertise ['require' *cancelled*] Nicholas Cornellis [? *Gilbert Gifford*] of the delivery of the packetts by a messenger because I am not able to goe to R. yett my selfe, my presence being necessary for establishing the intelligence in case of her remove loked for before winter.

(4) I crave to have a calender of soch persons' names as, about or in London, are servants & frendes of E * [? *Queen of Scots*], with Tho. Germin [? *Morgan*] his opinion how fare every of them * hath bene, is or may be vsed, to the ende y^t I may take my choyse according to such further judgment as I may by my experience make of him, to deliver a letter now or then or a message.

(5) I require the addresse for Scotland with the names of soch honest frendes as we may be bold to trust in y^t [*several words not legible*]. Privye tokens of creditt and addresse for both kindes of [? *papists*]. Perfett instruccions of the disposition of all the great personages & others about the court towardes E [? *Queen of Scots*].

(6) I promise to send a calender of * SS people to Tho. Germin.

(7) Touching Mr Baggott & Phellippes.

Endorsed, Written to Germin, &c.

§ III. LETTERS OF GILBERT GIFFORD

No. 28

GILBERT GIFFORD TO PHELIPPES

[? Near Chartley, 7 July 1586.]

R.O. *Mary Queen of Scots*, xviii. n. 37; Morris, p. 216; Boyd, viii. 512. Gilbert's autograph. No place named. Since the last letter Gilbert has been to Paris to see Morgan, and on his return he had regalvanised the plot into action (see *Introduction*, p. cxxxiv.). About the 4th he went down to Chartley. Assumed names like 'Honest man,' 'Second messenger,' are printed in italics.

Sire Towe principal points, wherof manie secondarlie were derived (as we discoursed at our last being together)[1] were the cause of my cominge hither[2] for the triall of the *honeste man* and the discoverie of the *seconde*.[3] In the firste we have so proceeded, that the *honest man* is totaliter ours, who is towe gladde to have thus escaped with his xx*l*, besides manie good angells, than to encurre the same danger.[4] He seeketh nothinge more then to winne credit with the Governor in this service. There was never so fortunate a knave, so that there cannot possiblie be anie thinge added to this pointe, and I thinke he is sufficiently charmed for[5] admittinge anie other but *the firste man*.

---

[1] 'At our last being together.' We do not know when this was, but perhaps only a few days back, as Gilbert will not restate the objects on which they had agreed. Perhaps then immediately on Gilbert's return, before he regalvanised the plot.

[2] 'Here.' The place is not mentioned, but the writer was within call of the Burton brewer, and from elsewhere we know he was near Chartley, and presumably lodging with 'Mr. Newport, steward to the Earl of Essex,' referred to by Poulet in Morris, pp. 196, 197.

[3] 'The seconde' is below styled 'the seconde messinger'; and we also have 'the firste man.' The latter is evidently the firste intermediary with the brewer, the same as 'the substitute' of Poulet's correspondence, who is perhaps to be identified with Mr. Hoby. The 'second messenger' was Thomas Barnes.

[4] 'Encurre the same danger.' That is, the same danger as Curll, Nau, and the other correspondents, who now seemed sure to be imprisoned for life, even supposing no actual treason was proved against them. Once a man had been hanged on a wall opposite Mary's windows at Tutbury. Mary was afterwards told that he had committed suicide, but she evidently thought he was hanged there *in terrorem* (Labanoff, vi. 152, 8 April 1585).

[5] 'Charmed for admittinge.' The sense seems to require 'from,' *i.e.* 'He is so bribed as not to admit.'

For the *seconde*, at my speakinge with *the honest man* he toulde me that *the seconde messinger*[1] was gone to London a sennight and more before, and that his appointmente with him was uncertaine.

Whereof this morninge I have onelie written to sir Amyas, declaringe the necessitie of my retorne. The conclusion of my letter is, Either this partie is at London or no; if not, he will not be longe in these parts, as well for that I have his letter, as also to finger more packetes. Besides that I will leave with *the honest man* an earneste letter for his cominge up.

If he be Allredie at London (as is probable not repairing to the honest man in so long a space), then it is likelie that I shall find him theare, coming up speedelie, whence we will dispose of him. His name is Barnes; I knowe him well, but I thinke he hathe no chamber in London, neither were it expediente you leane harder of him,[2] for the case I toulde, for that woulde spoil all: but assure your self and I promise, and undertake of my credit to cutte him clean off from this course, and to that end I have written to z[3] the coppie whereof you shall see at oure meetinge. I have no leasure but to committe you to God, this 7 of Julie.—Youre to commande,

CORNELYS.

Postscript, I truste you [d. *cancelled*] have displaied they armes of P;[4] let them be daintie at the firste, let

---

[1] See note 3 on page 103.

[2] 'Leane harder of him,' so Morris. Boyd, 'Lead hands of him.' Another case of Gilbert's faulty style (see also *below*). Gilbert is a careless, hurried writer. His English is ill-formed, perhaps because of his foreign education. His hand straggles, his letters are shapeless and changeable.

[3] This cipher is not yet interpreted. It might mean Curll.

[4] 'Displaied they armes of P.' The writing here again is very ill-formed and uncertain. Morris reads 'displayed [? delayed] the journey'; Boyd, 'displayed the arms.' 'The' and 'they' are interchanged at pp. 111, 114. Though I print 'they armes,' the reading might be 'the yarmes.' If 'arms' is the true reading, then the sense may be 'shown up in his true colours,' and P. may be Poley, of whom Phelippes was very jealous. But the reading is still unsatisfactory. Another case of careless writing.

scarse one of them be seene, I woulde gladlie deliver this Packet to 80 [1] my selfe.

Addressed, To my very lovinge frende,
Mr Thomas Philips, London.

No. 29

GILBERT GIFFORD TO SIR FRANCIS WALSINGHAM

[*London*, 11 *July* 1586.]

R.O. *Mary Queen of Scots*, xviii. 40; Hosack, ii. p. 602; Morris, p. 220, cited also in Froude. Autograph. In this important letter Gilbert is giving Walsingham more definite news of the plot or practice, though particulars are as yet few. He asks for permission to plot in Ballard's company. There are several indications that Gilbert was not at the meeting of 5 June, as charged against him in the indictment. He alleges, in fact, that this was 'the first day' he heard of the practice. See p. 107, *n.* 4; see also Boyd, p. 518.

RIGHTE HONORABLE—

Barnes hathe not yet appeared in anie of his frequented places, so that I thinke he came not as yet to towne. I knowe not whether he hathe bin with the Ambassador, for I dare not go thether, till suche time as I bringe the packet [2] with me. I am assured he shall no sooner come to the towne but I shall heare of him, and needes he must come, for I have his letters with me from ☿.

I trust Mr Philips will meete the said packet by the waie [3] and peruse it, that it neede no delaie in deliverie.

Tuchinge the practise in hande.[4] Before my laste

---

[1] 8o, Morris reads 'you.' Boyd puts stars for the cipher. The sense seems to indicate that 8o should mean 'French ambassador,' but in Phelippes's correspondence 8o means 'Berden.' See *Cath. Rec. Soc.*, xxi. p. 78; see also R.O. *Dom. Eliz.*, clvii. 3.

[2] 'The packet.' This was Post II., containing Mary's letters of 2/12 July.

[3] Phelippes picked up the packet between Shilton and Stanford. See his letter of 8 July, Morris, 218; Boyd, 514.

[4] 'The practise in hande.' Since Gifford's last letter, the plot had taken form. He had seen Morgan in Paris before 28 June, which was about the date of 'his last coming over.' Morgan then knew that Ballard had been sent over 'to solicit,' but how far the plot had progressed he could not yet have learned.

cominge over in discourse with Morgan, I smelled some thinge afar of, and he toulde me that he had sent one to sollicite matters heare, promisinge me that in time I shoulde knowe all, as occasion shoulde serve, for it is theire custome to discover thinges by litle and litle, albeit they trust one never so muche.

Now yesterdaie [1] by great inquirie, one Balart founde me oute, (I never was well acquainted with him) but he toulde me that he had saughte me greatlie, and that he knew my endeuoures thereughlie in behalfe of the cause, and that he purposed verilie to have comen to me in the contrey, for, said he, I thoughte you were there.

After great intertainementes at the lengthe he bracke with me into greate complainte of Morgan and Charles Paget sainge that they promised him intelligence verie ofte, and that he neuer harde from them since his cominge ouer: herof I gaue him some reasons of theire delaie.[2]

Then he toulde me that at his cominge ouer he was directed to me, and that findinge me not,[3] he was in greate perplexitie, thankinge God that we were met together to be an helpe one to an other. He toulde me that he was on Sattardaie nighte [4] with the Ambassador, and he expectethe letters dailie. But, saied he, if they will not

---

[1] 'Yesterdaie' was Sunday, 10 July. Gilbert does not deny some previous knowledge of Ballard, but it was clearly not intimate acquaintance. Tyrrell says that 'every gentleman called Ballard Captain Foscue, and every man that knew him thought,' etc., etc. He was a well-known man, so well known that Gilbert could hardly fail to have had some acquaintance with him. Ballard had been told, apparently by Morgan, that Gilbert carried Mary's letters. By 'the country,' the neighbourhood of Chartley seems intended; perhaps Chillington, the family home of the Giffords.

When Morgan told Gilbert that 'he had sent one to solicit matters here,' he really told him all that had yet been done on his side (see p. 96).

[2] 'I gaue him some reasons of theire delaie.' One can easily imagine how our *provocateur* improved the occasion. He had just come from Paris.

[3] 'Directed to me, and, findinge me not.' Again strong evidence that Gilbert was not at the meeting of 5 June, when the plot was resolved upon.

[4] 'Sattardaie nighte' was 9 July.

§ III. LETTERS OF GILBERT GIFFORD

perfurm that they promised, we will doe at the leaste oure partes, by which wordes I perceued that [*sic* ? he] thoughte me priuie to the course—[which indeed I, *cancelled*].¹

I asked him what was to be done on our partes; he replied, that I must needes obtain of ☉ her hande and seale to allow of all that shoulde be practised for her behalfe; Withoute the which, saied he, we laboure in vaine, and these men will not heare us.

I answered that it was a matter of greate importance, and that we shoulde expecte Morgan and Paget to do it; he saied the matter woulde groe longe, and that he was in great daunger.

Well, saied I, in my opinion this was never obtained hitherto by anie man, and the grauntinge thereof will be harde. But what persuasions and what probabilitie of successe can you leaie ² before ☉, wherby he [*sic*] maie be moved to graunte it. Saied he, I will vndetake within fortie daies to procure his [*altered from* her] libertie.³

Well, saied I, let vs thinke of it, and to-morrow I will answer you. So he parted oute of towne, and lefte his man with me for answer, which he is maruelouse erneste in.

This Balart is the onlie man used in this practise, whatever it be, which I cannot thereughlie discouer the first daie ⁴; but in time it will be easie, for he desirethe my companie and helpe therein. What youre Ho: thinketh good I shall answer him; I desire to be enformed, and

---

¹ 'He thoughte me priuie, which indeed I—' One can hardly help picturing Gilbert on the point of writing 'was,' when he checked himself, and cancelled the too-confidential phrase. But even if he had put down that word, he would not have meant that he was privy to every detail, and much less that he was privy all along, or before starting for France, when as yet no details at all had been settled.

² 'Leaie,' *i.e.* lay, Morris *reads* 'leave.'

³ Walsingham would at any time have understood these words as revealing a plot against Elizabeth's life. But now that he had read Babington's letter, he knew their significance by objective evidence.

⁴ 'Which I cannot thereughlie discouer the first daie.' Gilbert had not yet heard of Babington's letter. He had been away from town when it was written, and Phelippes, having taken it down to Chartley, was not at hand to tell the *provocateur* about it.

howe far I shall ioine with him ¹ and keepe him companie, which doinge it is vnpossible but I shall discouer all.

He complained much of Sʳ T. Tressom ² and my Cosin Talbot,³ for not onlie they woulde not heare him, but thretned to discouer him; and, saiethe he, vnlesse we obtain that from ☿, all is but winde.

I besiche yor Ho: so soone as the packet shall arriue, that it be conuoied to me by this bearer, before which time I cannot goe to the Ambass

Ballart toulde me that youre Ho: had an Inklinge of some thinges, especiallie of the Amb. intelligence with ☿. Youre Ho: hathe some verie corrupted men aboute him, wherunto greate regard is to be taken. He toulde me that Philips was gone to Chartley for the removinge of Nawe and Pio.⁴

I truste youre Ho: considereth how necessarie it is to entertaine D. G. and Gratley.⁵ For herby they be persuaded that theire is no other dealinges of myne but that onlie, otherwise it were vnpossible but I shulde be suspected.

D. G. cominge over woulde coulor me muche, as allso I can knowe his whole thoughts, and no doubte he woulde be greatlie emploied, so that by him I shoulde understande

---

[1] 'I desire to be enformed, and howe far I shall ioine with him.' According to the absolutist ideas, current in Elizabeth's government, the *provocateur* might always be punished, unless he had his permit from the tyrant. Gilbert is here asking for such a permit, as well as for directions as to the answer he is to make. But Walsingham gave no answer. It will probably be that he left this to Phelippes, who could not do what was desired, because he was staying on at Chartley. Gilbert in time got nervous at this, and refers to his fears later as one of the causes which made him fly.

[2] Sir Thomas Tresham of Rushton, Northamptonshire, one of the principal Catholics of England and a constant confessor of his faith (*D.N.B.*, etc.).

[3] 'My Cosin Talbot,' *i.e.* Mr. John Talbot of Grafton, mentioned by Babington, § vi., with Sir Thomas Tresham and others.

[4] 'Pio.' Mary's chaplain, Camille Du Préau, is intended.

[5] To entertaine, D. G. and Gratley. Phelippes, on 8 July, had made the same request (Morris, p. 219). He had suggested that Gratley's 'mad book' against the Jesuits should be 'on the press.' But this was never done.

Gilbert's suggestion is repeated in many of the following letters.

all theire courses, for he can hide nothinge from me. Thus protesting before God that nothinge shall passe my handes and hearinge but youre Ho: shall soone understand it, [I] besiche the Almightie longe to protecte your Ho: this xi of Julie.—Youre honor's faithfull scruante,

G. G.

Addressed, To the Righte Honorable Sr Frauncis Walsingham, Knighte, Her Mat^{ys} Principall Secretarie.

Endorsed, 11 July 1586.—From G. G.—Several Aduertis.

No. 30

GILBERT GIFFORD TO SIR FRANCIS WALSINGHAM

[*London*, 12 *July* 1586.]

B.M. Harleian, 286, f. 136. Autograph. Written the day after the last letter, it continued the story of the intrigue.

Ballard is still pouring out his news, his griefs, his boasts to his treacherous companion. He has found out a good many of Phelippes's treacheries; and we can see that Gilbert is alarmed at this, and urges Walsingham to use great caution. Later on we shall hear Walsingham laying the blame on Elizabeth.

R[IGHT] H[ONOURABLE]—

I talked this tuesdaie morninge the xij of Julie wth the greate practisioner, he is in a maruelous rage for that he hearethe nothinge from his compartnors.

He vauntethe muche of greate personages ioined wth him in this action, wch principallie he saiethe be scismatickes.[1] I haue not yet lerned manie of theire names, neither dare I encrotche to muche on him, but as willinglie he vtterethe by occasion geeuen him in discourse, he namethe my l. Buckhorste, my l. Morley, my l. Arrundell, my l. sturton,[2] and diuers others. I knowe not whether he dothe it vaine gloriouslie, or whether in truthe it be so.

---

[1] 'Schismatics.' This name was popularly given, at this period, to men Catholic at heart, who, yielding to force, attended heretical service.

[2] All these persons are named, in Morgan's letters, as Mary's friends, though he had probably had no communication with any of them. The Earl of Arundel, for instance, was in the Tower. It can cause little wonder, then, to find them on the lips of Ballard.

He hathe verie good intelligence of that your ho: dothe, in so muche that he toulde me that your ho: had my name, and that I had youre honors protection, wherin I satisfied him fullie, and he restethe verie contented. He toulde me againe that Philips was gone, and railed vppon him greatlie, sainge that he had commission to open and reade all letters or packets he met by the waie. Moreouer he saied that Philips shoolde saie these wordes, Thes papistes hope for a daie, but we will shewe them ⊖ [*Q. Mary*]¹ heade furthe of the windowe, as they vsed the Admirall of fraunce. He saied that Philips retornethe w^thin a fortnighte, but not to continewe heare longer, for he is to abide at Chartley saied he. He toulde me that this intelligence coosethe ² him sweetlie. Surlie it is some man neare to youre ho: Wherfore it is especiall garde to be taken of youre honr's letters, either suche as you wrighte, or as you receue, wherin allso greate charge is to be geeuen to suche as haue bin vsed in this action; otherwise it is vnpossible but that shortlie all will come furthe. I vnderstande by this practioner that manie call his name and [move] it in question and that they beeliue him not. For certain it is, he hathe nothinge to shewe them as yet but wordes, which causethe men to mistruste him.

Yea he was halfe in minde to retorne consideringe the slacknesse of M[*organ*] and P[*aget*] but at length he resolued to attende theire letters.

He is very erneste wth me to write for ⊖ [*Q. Mary*] approbation of his actions, wherin I promised him to presume what I coulde.

In fine it is certaine he hathe determined no certaine

---

¹ The sign for Queen Mary is here, and in the last letter, a crossed bar on an O. In the next letter a crossed cross on an O. It is characteristic of Gilbert at this period to be always varying. His signature is never the same; in fact, every detail of diplomatique, signet, folding, etc., is unsettled. See also *below*, 'it is special guard' for 'there is.'

'The admiral of France,' *i.e.* Coligny, at the massacre of St. Barthélemy.

² 'Coosethe.' Though there is a verb 'to couse,' or 'cose,' from French *causer*, meaning 'to have a chat,' this will not suit the sense, which requires 'comforts' or 'gratifies.' Perhaps it is a verb formed from 'cosy,' *i.e.* comfortable; but I cannot find a precedent for it.

course, onlie he hathe felte the disposition of mens mindes, wch he hathe written to M[*organ*] and P[*aget*] the answer wherof when he shall receue I will immediatlie informe youre ho:

D. G[*ifford's*] cominge is most necessarie, for M[*organ*] and P[*aget*] with they reste will imparte all thinges to him, wch I am towe assured I shall knowe, for he can hide nothing from me ; wherfore the sooner he were sente for, the better leasure we shall haue to prouide for theire diulishe deisier ; and if youre ho: thinke expediente my selfe will goe for him. Or, if my abode heare will be necessarie, fearinge leste ballart shoulde seeke him selfe to occupie my place wth ♁ [*Q. Mary*] in my absence, then I truste youre honor will provoide for his moste speedie cominge, as a thinge wherof greate and vnspeakable good dothe depende. Thus comittinge youre ho: to Allmightie god this xij of Julie.—Youre ho: seruante to commande,

GG.

Endorsed, 'Secret Aduertisements' from G. G.

No. 31

NOTES FROM THREE LETTERS BY GILBERT GIFFORD TO WALSINGHAM

[*London*, ? 14, ? 15, ? 16 *July* 1586.]

B.M. Harleian MS. 360, f. 27. The same hand appears at f. 10.

On 9 September Walsingham wrote to ask Phelippes for 'such secret advertisements as you have received from Ber[den], G.G[ifford] and Cat[lyn],' Boyd, p. 704. During the critical days of July Phelippes had been at Chartley, and so Gilbert's notes to Walsingham may have been sent on to the decipherer there ; perhaps they went there directly (Phelippes's letter of 19 July, Morris, p. 235, seems to contain a report of one of the notes below). Our paper of notes, endorsed 10 September, is clearly a consequence of Walsingham's letter, probably drawn up by some secretary of Walsingham's from the papers sent in by Phelippes. (There is also a summary of letters from Berden, Boyd, p. 123, but they were of an earlier date, so probably made on a different occasion.) Of the letters here summarised, the second, called B, is preserved, and will be given at No. 33.

There seems to have been no date, signature, or address on the letters of Gifford, only the mark ⚥. This is characteristic of Gilbert in these anxious moments. It will be noticed in the headlines that the scribe took 'A' as the indication of the writer's name, not ☩. This makes one suspect that this *copy* was not revised by Phelippes. A evidently means letter 1, and B letter 2.

As to the dates, it is clear that the letters came after the 12th, while the third letter was cited by Phelippes on 19 July.

The contents of 2 lr̃es receaued by Ball[ard] from M[organ] and communicated to this Aduertiser named A.

In margin, A ☩.

ffirst. That after his [*Morgan's*] accustomed greeting in propounding of honn^or and Credit, he told him that C[*harles*] P[*aget*] had left order wth him to open all such lettres as came to him, amongest wch there had bene two of Ballards, to wch he answeared thus :—

1. That he requested him & charged him straightly nether by himselfe nor any other directly or indirectly to intangle ⊕ [*Q. Mary*] wth his proceedinges, saying, *Non est tutum*, etc.[1]

2. That it was a thing impossible to have that authoritye from ⊕ [*Q. Mary*] for him to dispose of men : but, said he, Wryte to me the names of ye personages & I will preferre them to ⊕ [*Q. Mary*] so y^t they shall lacke no comfort nor hono^r.

3. That he animated him to go forward promising him both ayde and preferment.

4. That he told him of 2. Jesuits Southwell & Garnet lately come into Engl[and].[2]

That vppon the receapt of the Lettres aforesaid, he wth weeping said he was vtterly discredited, that thousands wold be vndone for his sake: ffor he trusting vppon Mendoza & C[*harles*] P[*aget*] had dealt wth many : and that they sought all hono^r for them selues & gave him but words.

---

[1] For the cipher sign for Mary, see last letter. Morgan had sent similar messages out to Mary on 24 June/4 July, 29 June/9 July; to Gilbert on 4/14 July. See *Hatfield Calendar*, p. 147 ; Boyd, pp. 499-501.

[2] The news about Garnet and Southwell was sent out by Morgan 3/13 July. Walsingham had spoken to Poley in consequence about 25 July. See *Introduction*, p. cliv. The Jesuits themselves soon heard of this. See *The Month*, March, 1912.

§ III. LETTERS OF GILBERT GIFFORD

The heddes of a conference betweene Ball[ard], Babington & this Aduertiser

ffirst. That Bab[ington] after other discourse of those matters declared the many daungers and difficultyes touching a Cheefe man for a head and for authoritye in this Cause : for that the noblemen wold do nothing before they sawe some Certaintye ; & yt the rest being all equall, wold bring Confusion. That M[organ] sought nothing but honor to him selfe, & yt he wold seeke honor for them yt better deserued it. That him selfe wold go and to sollicitt these matters. That Bab[ington's] discourse tended to make him selfe Cheefe, wherin he was backed by Ball[ard] who highly Comended him.

The answeare yt Ball[ard] returned to M[organ] is this in effecte.

That his demaund is farre vnreasonable to request the naming of the personnags ; as also to seeke all to his owne hand, being but a seruant to ⊕ no more then they, &c. That they all concluded that one shold go over for solliciting of matters.

Extract of another lettre [1]

In margin, B ✝.

Wherin the partyes aforsaid having resolued to send this Aduertiser ouer, the only Chardge they shold Comitt vnto him by word of mouth was, 'To knowe whither the King of Spayne intended any thing or no ; &, at what tyme,' wch he was to demaund in the name of such personags whose names & hands shold be Conveyed by the Ambr wth many Circumstances not fitt to be knowen of any man till he was saefe, wch they promised this Aduertiser shold receaue wth all expedicon.

In margin, In other lettres of ✝.

That one Gage was to go ouer & to receaue his directions th[ere] [2]

---

[1] This letter B, as will be seen, will be the letter printed in full next page *below*

[2] Robert Gage, though not one of the conspirators, was executed with the others, 21 September 1586 (Boyd, ix. p. 38)

That one Barnes shold Come out of the Countrey & wa[s to] receaue Certaine Packets.

That one appoynted to go ouer, shold passe vnder the name of Thoroughgood.[1]

Endorsements, 10 Sept. 1586./Extract of Secret Aduert./ Receaued from ☧./A: B:

No. 32

GILBERT GIFFORD TO SIR FRANCIS WALSINGHAM

[*London*, ? 16 *July* 1586.]

R.O. *Domestic Elizabeth*, cxci. n. 36. Autograph. This is letter B in the previous summary. No date, but it seems to have been written a few days before 19 July, when Phelippes, then at Chartley, appears to cite it in his letter of that date, printed in Morris, pp. 235-236. The parts omitted in the summary, as we now see, were considerable, but to Walsingham they were of little moment at the time the summary was made.

R[IGHT] H[ONORABLE].

Since the writinge of my other lettere,[2] theese men have conferred with me, sainge that they find no man so fit as my selfe, consideringe my credit on the other side, my dealinges and knoledge in these matters, my langige and experience, whom better they may use and truste in this case, with manie persuasions. 'In so muche,' saie they, 'that, if you will not doe it, we muste needes saie you are not so carfull of the case, as you are taken to be.' The [they] proffer me a licence, wch Ballart hathe this daie procured for him selfe, under a nother name.[3] I

---

[1] Phelippes, writing 19 July to Walsingham, says, 'Great mean was made unto me at my coming away for one Thorwood to pass the sea, &c. ... It was whispered unto me that it should be Ballard to pass under that feigned name. I have had an inkling, even in this country, it should be he or as bad a man.'

[2] The 'other lettere' will be that containing the summary of Morgan's to Ballard, No. A, above. 'These men' will mean Ballard, Babington, and their companions.

[3] The passport which Ballard 'this day' procured 'under a nother name' is not preserved. But from Phelippes's letter, in Morris, p. 235, we see that the 'other name' was 'Thoroughgood,' as also appears in the previous extract.

toulde them that I would consider of it this nighte, as so wightie a matter requierethe, and to morrowe woulde answer them.

Nowe youre honor is to consider whether this be expedient for me or no. Sure it is they will get some one or other over, by whom we can neuer come to the lighte of thinges so soundlie and speedelie, if I goe not.

I vowe before God to declare to youre honor wth all speede all theire answer in generall and particular, wth all circumstances.

The charge they committe unto me by worde of mouthe, is onlie *to knowe whether the K. of Spaine intendethe anie thinge or not, and at what time,* wch I must demande in the name of suche personages, saie they, whose names and [? handes] shall be convoied by the Amb[assador], wth manie Circumstances not fit to be knowen of anie man, till he be saufe, wch they promise I shall have wth all expedition. In my opinion we shall so certenlie knowe oure enemies on this side, [and] their designmentes on the other, by this course, that herafter we shall be voide of care.

And for more speedie sendinge to youre honor, it would not be amisse that I had some course directed how to hasten the poste; for I will send all thinges to youre honor, as soone as they shall be deliuered me. This course will auoide all suspicion of my dealinge wth youre honor.

If this course please youre honor, I desier answer wth all possible speede. I will tell D. G.[1] that I slipped ouer, and that for so shorte a time I canot be missed, for that I craved leave of youre honor to goe to the countrey, wth all I will see him set for owte[2] before I departe. Therfore suche money as shall be imparted to them by youre honor I woulde reqeste the deliuerie of it my selfe to my uncle Hughe Offley, before my departure, wch they woulde have

---

[1] 'D. G.' is, of course, Doctor William Gifford.

[2] 'Set for owte.' Evidently a combination, due to preoccupation, of 'set forward,' and 'set out.'

to morrowe nighte.[1] Thus besichinge youre honor to give me information herof wth all speede.

Youre honor's seruante,
♆.

Signet, Small, of red wax, with device of triple blossom on a shield. Endorsed, (1) July 1586. (2) from ♆ secret aduerts. (3) Sc[ottish] Q[ueen]. (4) B. ♆.

No. 33

GILBERT GIFFORD TO SIR FRANCIS WALSINGHAM

[London, ? 19 July 1586.]

R.O. *Mary Queen of Scots*, xix. 1. Boyd gives a full summary, but mistakenly gives 2 August as date, and expands D. G., *i.e.* Dr. Gifford, into Duke of Guise.

The last three letters before the flight are all of the same tenor, and one cannot tell which of the two last was the earlier. In reality the nervousness manifested on 12 July was growing steadily stronger. As has been explained in the *Introduction*, the *provocateur* eventually fled without obtaining licence, out of fear lest he should be called up as a witness against Mary, *below*, p. 120, and for this he apologises in his letter of 3/13 September.

These letters, however, profess a different sentiment. Here he never tires of describing his readiness to assist in capturing his former friends; and so far as malice went, his words were true.

Still there remains an obscurity which I am unable to clear up. In the letters of 3 August Walsingham is found to be quite surprised and vexed at Gilbert not being at hand. 'I marvel greatly how this humour of estranging himself cometh upon him' (*below*, p. 132). But here, in three different letters to Walsingham, Gilbert not only speaks quite urgently about going abroad to his uncle Hugh Offley at Rouen, and to his cousin William at Rheims, he also seems to have received some sort of sanction for it, and, moreover, even promises of a money provision.

I can only suppose that between Walsingham, who was constantly called down to see the Queen at Windsor, and Phelippes, who was all this time at Chartley, some fault occurred in the staff work, some misunderstanding took place, though we do not know where. I do not think we need suppose any further sharp practice on either side.

R. H.—I purpose immediatlie after the receite of youre ho: letters to goe downe to the contrey, and withall to

---

[1] 'They woulde have to morrowe nighte.' 'They' will mean Babington, Ballard, etc. Gilbert did, in fact, set out, so Chateauneuf says, on the 21st. But he may easily have delayed the instant departure which the conspirators at first desired.

leaue suche meanes with this bearer [1] for the takinge of Ballart, that easlie he shall compasse it without anie suspicion of my parte. He toulde me this daie of his dealinge with Rowe concerninge youre ho: He asked my aduise therin. He knowethe not what to conceue. I toulde him that youre ho: had shewed greate coartesy of late to chatholikes, and that it moughte be your ho: mente friendelie, and so he is persuaded. But what your ho: will appointe concerninge the man I can execute it. My uncle Offley [2] is verie apte to be used in this pointe, but I would not haue him know D[octor] G[ifford] [3] his name, therefore if youre ho: onlie signifie him to deliuer suche money to those persons I shall name, it will be sufficient. I will name them by other names. I desier to knowe howe youre ho: will sende for him by letter or otherwise, that I myselfe may wright. Thus desiringe youre ho: to vse me in this service tuchinge the takinge of anie of these practisers, according as I am reddie to performe, wch I dobte not but will redounde to the service of my soueraigne and contentment of youre ho: to whom my service is auoued,   Youre ho: Seruante,

g. [4]

No. 34

GILBERT GIFFORD TO SIR FRANCIS WALSINGHAM

[*London, 19 or 20 July 1586.*]

R.O. *Mary Queen of Scots*, xix. 5.

R. H.—I desire you will write by this bearer, what is determined concerning the money to be sent, that I may repare to my vncle accordinglie. Concerning their names in my opinion, nothing is to be sed, but that I shall directe

---

[1] This was probably Phelippes's boy Casey.

[2] Mr. Hugh Offley was a merchant trading with Rouen. See *Addenda Calendar*, xxix. 63.

[3] Dr. William Gifford was a professor at the English College, Rheims, at this time.

[4] The subscribing sign is contrived to look rather like the sign † of previous letters. *Endorsed*, Secret advertisements from G.

their, or at the leste wise other names [? are not] to be used for auoidinge of suspicion; for to conuoie the money I can well direct hit by supposed names.

Ballart hath changed his opinion in goinge downe with me. So if your ho: liste to take him, I desire to vnderstande by this bearer.   Your ho: Seruante,
.*g*¹

English Pot Paper, no address, signet of two letters L, back to back.

APPENDIX TO SECTION III

GILBERT GIFFORD'S CORRESPONDENCE AFTER THE PLOT, 1586 TO 1590

As has been explained in the *Introduction*, Gilbert Gifford outlived the other conspirators by five years, in which time he underwent great changes of fortune, and died in the bishop's prison at Paris. Under these circumstances he made certain statements which have survived, in which he endeavoured to excuse or justify himself now to Walsingham, now to the Catholics. It belongs to our subject to inquire what light was thrown back on Mary and the Babington plot by these disclosures. But in the end we shall find that little, if any, positive evidence transpired. Gilbert never repented or recanted, he never told much to his prosecutors. Of excuses, of blame for his former colleagues, he was prolific enough: but of Queen Mary never a word. Nothing was said of the dealings with Mendoza (3/13 August): of the conspiracy proper only very, very little. The period falls into four episodes.

§ 1. THE NEW UNDERSTANDING, August to October 1586.

CORRESPONDENCE.—We have eight letters from Gilbert, all in R.O. volumes—
M.Q.S., xix. 8, 45, 46, 70, 71, 82, 118, and *Dom. Eliz.*, cxcviii. 85. Unfortunately we have not one from Phelippes, and only two clauses in Walsingham's notes, *M.Q.S.*, xix. 63 and 80. All but *Dom. Eliz.*, cxcviii. 85, are in Boyd, viii.

Gilbert's flight at first quite puzzled and disconcerted Mr Secretary. 'I marvel greatly how this humour of estranging of himself cometh upon him.' In reality Gilbert had spoken more than once of 'going into the country,' but without specifying where, and he had asked to

---

[1] The subscribing sign is again different, having a second cross-bar, and a full point to the left.

§ III. LETTERS OF GILBERT GIFFORD

have money sent to his uncle Offley at Rouen. But Walsingham evidently did not dream that he would have left England without getting his permission. It may also be that Gilbert's letters got sent on to Phelippes without coming into his chief's hands at all; and so Walsingham may have been quite unwarned.

When the departure was known, a bad interpretation was put upon it. Walsingham not unnaturally thought that he meant to tell secrets, and Gilbert was eventually indicted, 7 September, as a prime-mover of the plot.

We do not know the circumstances which led to this sweeping accusation being made. It is not made good by any known manuscript evidence, and, on the contrary, appears to be inconsistent with Gilbert's letters printed above. But a different line was soon taken, and Gilbert's name was kept back from publicity.

These changes agree with our documents. The earliest of these are letters from Gilbert written at Paris, and protesting his innocence from Walsingham's point of view, but we do not know what Gilbert had yet heard of the progress of events in England. His first dated papers are of 15/25 August, and crave Walsingham's favour and assure him that 'common compagnons' who 'have endeavoured to discredit him' will be found 'but chats of parasites.' The subsequent letters speak in even stronger terms.

This letter of 15/25 August may have reached London in ten days, that is about 26th Old Style, and so have given the occasion to Walsingham to tell Phelippes on the 28th. 'It shall now suffice to assure G.G. that both he and I have been greatly abused. . . . *He must be content that we both write and speak bitterly against him.*' In other words, Walsingham owns that Gilbert is not guilty (from Walsingham's point of view), but he says that he must submit to being indicted as if guilty. One of Gilbert's undated letters to Walsingham (xix. 8) is in a tone of sulky submission, which may represent his 'contentment' under this treatment.

But to Phelippes Gilbert adopted a bolder line of defence. He never ceases to declare (1) that he keeps absolute faith with his principals, and (2) that he has never failed in that faith. No threat, no dismissal, no rejection on Walsingham's part shall move him, and he hints that the Catholic side are already (though vainly) making him good offers. He can do much more than others, let Phelippes try him again.

One or other of these notes seems to have reached Walsingham early in September, and on the 3rd we find a still more benignant phrase, 'It touches my poor credit, how hardly soever I am dealt withal, to see our friend beyond the seas comforted' (Boyd, viii. p. 666). Unfortunately this is all we know on Walsingham's side right down to the end of the year, but it is enough to mark the turn of the tide in Gilbert's favour.

It would seem, however, from Gilbert's letters of this period, that Phelippes went rather beyond his chief in defending or even justifying the policy of the indictment. Gilbert in reply bids him stop joking on this matter, and protests with various oaths his absolute innocence. Phelippes in his later letters always lays it down that the subordinate must bear the blame for mistakes; but it seems clear that Gilbert's resentment against this also made a good impression.

Upon the whole the indictment was to Gilbert's advantage from a worldly point of view. It shielded him from the eyes of incurious observers in either camp, enabling the deceiver to pose as a martyr before simple souls abroad, while at home the prevalent submission to the Crown would always tolerate the pardon of an evident traitor, if the Queen's secretary wished it.

At first Gilbert easily kept up appearances with Morgan and Paget, though he was closely examined by the former especially about Barnes, of whom Ballard and Savage appear to have spoken openly in court, and who was also mentioned in the examinations. But as time went on, and as Morgan's and Paget's share in the plot became better known, they became more alert and suspicious, and Grately also became inquisitive. At this moment Phelippes, probably meaning to do Gilbert a service, wrote him a letter, which for the moment had the opposite effect. Phelippes's too well known 'boy' pressed a ciphered paper into the hand of Cordaillot, the French secretary and a quondam friend of Gilbert, just as he was starting with dispatches for Paris, Cordaillot became 'jealous,' and on arrival handed the letter to Gilbert openly in the presence of Grately, and perhaps also of Morgan and Paget. Every one was on pins and needles, and Gilbert only saved himself by consummate coolness. He handed the letter on to Grately, saying that he did not know the cipher, or the hand. Could any one read it? No. So for the moment the situation was saved; 'but,' adds Gilbert in his next letter, 'I am in great disgrace with them.' No wonder, there was ground for suspicion that he was still in confidential correspondence with the enemy.

This adventure appears to have taken place early in September. Gilbert sent the cipher to Stafford, the English ambassador at Paris, asking him to return it to Walsingham with a note, that the addressee had no cipher-key wherewith to interpret it.

In regard to the history of the plot the only passages of importance in these letters to Phelippes and Walsingham are Gilbert's excuses for his flight.

To Walsingham he wrote 3/13 September:—

'As for my departure, your Ho: may perceive what just cause I had, dealing by your Ho: consent, with so impious members, practisers of the ruine of my dear country. I say, to deal with such treacherous, youthful companions, without any warrant or discharge, in how dangerous a practice . . . I beseech your Ho: to know this to have been the only cause of my departure, as also fearing to be brought face to face in witness of some dealings' (*M.Q.S.*, xix. 82, see Boyd, viii. p. 672).

To Phelippes he wrote a little later, in December or January:—

'Know that whatsoever report be or shalbe made unto you against

&c¹ [? me], either proceedeth of malice or ignorance, as in like cases of dealing with ii parties, you know, cannot but chance, pretending as you know I always did by your advice. But I fear no backbiter in the world, so that [it] may please, &c, that I may come to my answer. And for your ii vehement suspicions, which methinks yet sound in my ears, the one of writing the cipher with b. [the name is given as "Morgan" in a parallel passage in xx. 45, Boyd ix. 222], the other of departure. The first was only to satisfy w. [?], which otherwise was impossible. Your self may prove by my letter to n., that I meant sincerely to remove Ja. [? Barnes].

'For the other [*i.e.* my departure] the chiefest motive, as I told you, was I feared to be brought for witness &c. And I feared not knowing the state of those men whom I dealt with. I knew they were entered into some great matters (I knew not what) and shortlie to be taken. I feared lest I [*sic*] mought have been suspected to have concealed that which I never knew, or to have been accused by them either for the hearing of some speech, which happily [*i.e.* by some chance] I had forgotten, [or had] not related to his Honour. Or for malice to have been accused by them, or at least all the world would have condemned me seeing I had escaped. These and many other points being in my head carefully, ever after I understood of your going to c. [? Chartley], after my voyage to l [? Paris], and withal talking to &c [? Ballard], whom I neither knew nor ever spake with in my life before that time nor his confederates, and then I straight acquainted him [Walsingham] with it.

'Judge you now whether I be not innocent, and what I deserved . . ., and whether it imported me not to depart, if ever I meant hereafter to serve &c. Or had I not been mad, seeing the bountifulness of his Ho:, and the sweetness of service, the l [?] of my [?] father &c, if I would have undone myself to join with those men, [whom] I knew were to be taken and could not scape; and that their drift was discovered. Or would I not have advised them to flee, if ever I had dealt with them otherwise than I informed? Which I not only did not, but kept them together. I doubt not but his Ho: will consider of my sincere heart, which is now composed & sure settled to serve my &c to the confusion of all' (*D.E.*, cxcviii. 85).

To return to the position which followed the presentation of the letter by Cordaillot. If Gilbert was now 'in disgrace,' he did not stand alone. The outcry against Morgan and Paget was general as their participation and imprudence gradually came more and more under the public eye with the trials of September and October. Paget was glad enough to slip away from Paris for the time, and now he did not disdain

---

¹ The cipher sign used here and elsewhere below is something like a 5, ~, or &, and the reader must judge of its various meanings as it appears. I think it means a hint to Phelippes to surmise the right name, as our 'You know whom (or what) I mean.' I add my private interpretation in square brackets.

to take Gilbert in his company. They went together to call upon the Duke of Guise at Châlons. Gilbert, who relates the fact, gives no dates or further details, except that Guise declared his grief, and promised to remain true to Mary's cause (Boyd, ix. 220).

§ 2. Ordination, 14 March 1587.

Correspondence.—There are a few almost illegible questions by Phelippes, *M.Q.S.*, xviii. 25; Boyd, viii. 489; Gilbert answers them: R.O. *M.Q.S.*, xx. 45; Boyd, ix. pp. 219-25. Both pieces undated.

Gilbert did not at once return to Paris. He wanted (alas for the sacrilege!) to be ordained a priest, in order to keep the confidence of Catholics. On the other hand, he did not like to tell Phelippes this in writing, as it was punishable by death according to the recent Act of 27 Elizabeth. So he says that he is 'going into Germany,' a strange phrase, for which I can give no certain explanation. There were examples of more extreme reformers going to Germany or Switzerland to prepare for the Protestant ministry; perhaps Gilbert takes his simile from them. Possibly, as German was spoken in parts of Lorraine, Gilbert used this phrase to disguise the fact that he was really going into a Guise country, Pont-à-Mousson, in order to attend the divinity lectures at the Jesuit University there as a preliminary to orders. He thought of going afterwards to Rome and trying to obtain a tutorship at the Sapienza (Foley H., *Records, S.J.*, vi. 16). This he hoped to do through the favour of Cardinal Allen; for Allen, it will be remembered, had been most forgiving after his early escapades.

This confirms what had been noted before, that Gilbert did not await orders from England; but, knowing what Walsingham would like, struck out lines for himself in hopes of future approval. Nor was he disappointed.

His plans for ordination proved but too effective. He was ordained on Saturday (14 March 1587) without being detected. He would presumably have obtained from Pont-à-Mousson the necessary certificates of competence for ordination. He had, in fact, already spent many years in priestly education, and had been a 'repetitore' (tutor) in philosophy. The ordination is registered in the *Douay Diaries* (T. F. Knox), p. 214.

We do not now know enough about the circumstances to blame the superiors at Rheims for allowing this. Though his early record was not a good one, they had no inkling of his later malpractices; all seemed fair and above board.

In secret, however, he was carrying on correspondence with Phelippes, in which we see the two scoundrels in their true colours. Phelippes's draft questions are indeed illegible in great part; still they clearly contain the suggestions which Gilbert in his answer elaborates, *e.g.* Phelippes asks, 'What meane to cause Paget to come over?'—*i.e.* how could he be decoyed within the reach of Walsingham's *agents*? Gifford shakes his head over this question, but says there 'is no remedy but *lex talionis*' (*i.e.* assassination), and if I were assured that the Queen would 'take it gratefully, we would have, one way or another, all the crew.' The suggestion is repeated on next page (Boyd, ix. 222, 223).

I do not think we ought to take these suggestions quite seriously. But they give a test for the morality of Walsingham and of Phelippes, as well as of our *provocateur*. And if Gifford could propose such things to Elizabeth's underlings, how much more to his dupes like Savage and the rest.

His suggestions about Barnes are especially significant.

'If you have Barnes, keep him close. If you have him not, I would you had him in your hands. However it be, either bring him by promise or fear to write to Morgan, or if you have him not feign his hand to me. His name was Pietro Maria. Write by the name of Pietro Maria, discoursing of the whole success, and yet as chance was your name never came in question, and now is time to begin again, which they desire beyond measure and no doubt they will take hold of it, for they are about another practice, I assure you' (*M.Q.S.*, xx. 45; Boyd, ix. p. 220).

This is 'provocation' pure and simple, to be procured if necessary by forging Barnes's name. Eventually Phelippes got hold of Barnes, and acted on Gifford's suggestion until the end of Elizabeth's reign (see *above*, pp. 2-5). Moreover, Phelippes took Gifford's alternative hint and wrote a letter in Barnes's name. But, when it came, Gilbert had changed his mind, and declared that Morgan probably had a letter of Barnes's, so that he dared not present Phelippes's forgery. It was so unlike the real thing.

Gilbert's letter, which is very long, may be considered as his *apologia* from the point of view of the government. It travels over all the points on which suspicion might arise in the minds of Elizabeth and Walsingham, which he did doubtless at Phelippes's suggestion. Gilbert's line is to say that his intentions were always admirable, but he was 'forced' to talk treason with the traitors, and so there are things which he does not defend. 'Look not for a mathematical satisfaction at my hands.' Sometimes he had 'to beguile' Morgan, and Phelippes must 'interpret' all his doings for the best.

§ 3. Spy Life in Paris, 11/21 April to 3/13 December 1587.

Correspondence.—The pieces are almost all in R.O. *Domestic Elizabeth*. From Gifford, March, cxcix. 20; April, cc. 48, 49, 50, 65; May, cci. 42; October, *Addenda MS.*, xxx. 55, vi. vii. From Phelippes, April, cxcix. 96; June, ccii. 38; September, cciii. 36.

With this letter in hand Phelippes was satisfied, and succeeded in pleasing both Walsingham and Elizabeth. It is remarkable that she should have been interested in Gilbert's fortunes. But Phelippes says so, and in such a matter he would not have knowingly exaggerated. The 'minute' of his note (*D.E.*, cxcix. 96) informs Gifford that 'Her Majesty has promised you 100 *li.* pension by the year for your service.' This pension, continues Phelippes, together with your father's allowance, will royally maintain you. The advice I gave you ' to be a good husband grew from a friend upon complaints in a former letter that you were bare.' Finally he was to become a spy and informer, and was to write to Walsingham, to Phelippes, and also on selected topics for the Queen's own eye. This letter would have been written about 15 April, and when it reached Gilbert he had been in Paris since the 21st.

On its receipt Gifford was quite carried off his legs with delight. Being unable at first to distinguish what would please the English Queen, he sent a 'rhapsody' of everything he could think of, with offers of murder, kidnapping, and thievery. (1, 7, or 10 May, the original is *D.E.*, cc. 48; a selection from it by Phelippes is in Harleian MS. 290, printed by Boyd, p. 411. See also *below*, p. 174.)

What Phelippes selected from this for the Queen, we do not know. None of Gilbert's letters at this period seem to be so clever as those which were intended to deceive Mary, but only few are preserved.

There was a reason too for his want of news, as the execution of Mary had robbed the English Catholics of all romance and almost all hope of liberty, except through Spain, which was distant, slow, inactive. On 25 May Gilbert writes that the best thing to do would be to get some spy established near the Prince of Parma, Philip II.'s commander-in-chief, while he rather quaintly promises 'neither will I let anything pass so sliberly as heretofore.' Phelippes in his emended edition writes the word 'slipperly.'

If this refers to others, the sense will be disparaging, and 'sliberly' may be akin to 'slipshod' : if, however, it refers to himself, the meaning will be laudatory, and the word will mean 'deftly,' as Dutch ' slim.'

After this there are only letters to him from Phelippes in June and September. From the last of these we learn that our spy has found a lodging in the same house as Morgan. Phelippes suggests that, if Morgan wants to go to Rome, Gilbert might offer to be his correspondent at Paris. But in the meantime he is to be very much indeed upon his guard against the *rusé* Welshman, and he is always to keep his cipher key sewn up in his doublet. For the present Gilbert should employ himself in unravelling the case of Roger Walton, whom Sir Edward Stafford, the English ambassador at Paris, had commended, but whom Walsingham had clapped into prison on his arrival (*D.E.*, cciii. 36).

This reminds one of the commissions Gilbert used to receive to test ' the honest man' and other instruments. But now the result of the trial verified the proverb, 'set a thief to catch a thief, and you have them both.' The rival sharper against whom Gilbert Gifford was now pitted by Phelippes was Lilly *alias* Mr Ambodester, who stood to the ambassador in much the same relation as Phelippes did to Walsingham

Of course, it was a gross fault against *étiquette* for Phelippes to set Gilbert to spy on Lilly and by consequence on Stafford himself.

Hitherto Lilly had been, or had affected to be, the friend of Gilbert; but when he perceived the change of part, he got in his blow, which proved fatal, before his adversary could strike. We do not know the details, but there is a letter in the *Addenda* series (*Calendar*, p. 259, Morris, p. 385), dated 9 December 1588, written by Henry Caesar, who, though a Catholic priest in exile, had gone over to the Protestant side, and was in sympathy with Gifford, so far as he understood his case. We have also a letter, in Gifford's own hand, which affords Lilly's side much justification. It is dated 26 October, printed (so far as it is legible) in *Addenda Calendar*, p 230, the original is MS. *Addenda*, xxx. 55, vii. In this Gilbert appears to be charging Sir Edward with having sent Lilly to tempt Gilbert to assassinate the Queen.

A reader not used to judging spy-correspondence will be puzzled So grave a charge, he would imagine, would not be brought without some good ground, and yet the idea of one of our ambassadors soliciting by his servant the assassination of his sovereign seems too wildly improbable for credence In those days, however, when Elizabeth and her ministers were always fussing about alarms of this nature, they obtained any number of them. Spies knew by experience how highly such stories were welcomed The inference is that Gilbert was preparing for some *grand coup* against his rivals. Unfortunately for him, however, his letter found its way into Lilly's hands, and even if it had stood alone it would have explained all that follows

But there was much more Gifford was spending his time in writing an answer to Allen's *Defence of Stanley for the rendering up of Deventer*,[1] and when finished gave it to Lilly to send to England Caesar, who tells us this, adds that Lilly gave it to Sir Charles Arundell instead, the most zealous of the Catholic party then in Paris. Lilly also procured from Phelippes for Sir Charles the book, which Gifford and Grately together had written against the Jesuits.

It is doubtful, however, whether Lilly would have obtained his object by any of these means, if Gifford had not been arrested one night (13 December) in a brothel He was at first taken to the Bastille, and when it was known that he was a priest, he was transferred (19 December) to the Bishop's prison, where he lay till his death

NOTE —Too much stress must not be laid on Gifford's charge against Stafford of solicitation The text is obscure, though Stafford would

---

[1] It is not impossible that a fragment of this may survive in an extract made by Fr Chr. Grene, printed in the *Letters of Cardinal Allen*, ed Knox, pp 299-301 The date, 23 October, would agree.

certainly have read it in the worst sense. The critical passage in Gifford's letter runs as follows:—

'|| (*The Amb.*) by 5927 (*Lilly*) exhorted greatly H (? the present writer) to u (? *kill*) δ (*the Queen of England*) with great promises. X (*Gifford*) answered that he would never offend her.'

1. The ciphers are not facsimiles, but roughly represent their shapes.
2. Phelippes's decipherment of *u* is very obscure; he has none of H; but the rest are clear.
3. It is strange that this document, which is supposed to have been sent by Stafford to Walsingham against Phelippes, should have decipherments in Phelippes's hand.
4. Of course the whole document *might* be a forgery by Lilly against Gilbert.
5. As the evidence now stands, Stafford sent in the document, and says he was furnished with the key to read it. No doubt therefore that (though he treats the insult as unmentionable), he knew it well, and took it in the worst sense.

§ 4. IN PRISON, 3/13 December 1587 to [? November] 1591.

CORRESPONDENCE.—The pieces are again mostly in *Domestic Elizabeth*. From Gifford [? December 1587], ccviii. 90; January 1588, ccviii. 4, 5, 11, 20, 21; February, ccviii. 48, 57, *Addenda MS.*, xxx. 78; July, ccxii. 54; August, *Hatfield Calendar*, iii. 346; September, ccxv. 69 [? 1588]; ccxvii. 81; December, ccxix. 13. From Phelippes, ccviii. 54; July, ccxii. 72.

All Gilbert's papers were now seized, including his alphabet, which he was using in order to write to Phelippes. One or two earlier letters had been intercepted before: Paget and Morgan knew that he had proposed to kidnap or murder them, and the Ambassador was infuriated at seeing that Gifford had probably charged him with plotting against the Queen's life, and that Phelippes had certainly employed such a 'double treble villain' to watch him. He wrote:

'His confession (for I see he will confess anything that is, and more than is) may give subject to the enemies of her Majesty to procure a scandalous opinion to be conceived of her and of her Council. For they mean to turn a letter or two, but especially one of Phelippes to him to prove that he was the setter on of the gentlemen, that were executed for that enterprise of the Queen of Scots, and then to discover them. Also that he was practised to this by you and Phelippes, and withal they would fain have it,—with her Majesty's knowledge. . . .

'He hath showed himself the most notable double treble villain that ever lived, for he hath played upon all the hands in the world. I have sent you the copy of his answers, whereby you may see how vilely he dealt with me,' etc. etc. (*Addenda Calendar*, p. 233).

The letter of his to Phelippes 'proving that he was the setter on of the gentlemen that were executed for the enterprise of the Queen of

§ III. LETTERS OF GILBERT GIFFORD

Scots' is not in our hands. Later on Stafford alludes to it again as 'dated 11 June 1586' (*Addenda Calendar*, p. 227). This date agrees exactly with the time Gilbert was starting for Paris, after the first conferences of the conspirators. No definite plans had as yet been formed, and Gilbert was not then (it would seem) familiar with all the conspirators. But the connection had begun, and according to the indictment Gilbert was then in the very thick of the conspiracy.

Four letters of Stafford, printed in the *Addenda Calendar*, give some account of the first proceedings against Gifford. Then in the absence of English church authorities who could prosecute, the papal nuncio, Mgr. Moresino, Bishop of Brescia, called the case before his tribunal. Lord Paget stood as his accuser; Thomas Fitzherbert and Thomas Throckmorton had their places in the court. But the incriminating evidence was not very conclusive. There were some cipher letters, but Gilbert would not, perhaps could not explain them. Curll and Nau had been freed from prison in England, but nothing very conclusive could be drawn from them. They had no conception how the plot was really discovered, and had been told in England that the actually fatal papers had been seized on the persons of the conspirators. They never realised that they had been read, while in the custody of Gilbert Gifford. Curll, while in England at least, remained under the impression that Gilbert had been a trusty servant of Mary, and with touching fidelity, kept Gilbert's name out of all his confessions. Phelippes noticed this, and gave Gifford word of his security on this side (R.O. *Dom. Eliz.* cxcix. n. 96, f. 218). Morgan and Charles Paget knew little or nothing of what had happened in England, and what they knew about the intrigue in France made them tongue-tied. The same thing may be said of Mendoza. It does not seem to have been known in Paris that Gifford had been indicted in the English courts; for (as has been explained in the *Introduction*) Gifford's name was carefully kept out of all the published accounts of the trial.

For these reasons the evidence against Gilbert could hardly justify a strong verdict against him, so far as the treason against Mary was concerned, however vehement the suspicions might be. It seems to have been known beforehand that this would happen: for the letter from Rome, 18 February 1588, giving directions to the nuncio for the trial, adds that 'efforts should be made to keep Gifford in prison' (Vatican Archives *Let. di Principi*, cli. f. 108).

On 14 March, Mgr. Moresino sent in his report on the trial, viz. that nothing material could be found against the accused except ciphers, which no one could read. But now a Jesuit father has persuaded him to confess, and he promises to reveal all (R.O. *Roman Transcripts*, Bliss, bundle 83). We hear nothing of the verdict; and if Gilbert was still kept in captivity, it will have been partly on suspicion, partly on other charges, as the libel on the Jesuits, and the arrest in the house of ill-fame, partly because his promised confession was slow in coming.

We have heard Stafford say, 'I see he will confess anything.' But this did not prove true. He did indeed make so-called confessions, but these were in fact charges against others.

The first of Gifford's extant confessions was addressed, says Stafford, to Throckmorton, but more probably to his *procureur*, Thomas Fitzherbert, perhaps in January 1588. He begins by saying that his employment commenced with Cardinal Allen's full approval. Allen was really at Rome, when Gilbert was asked for by Morgan. Still it may be true that Allen allowed Morgan the service of some of his young men from time to time, and that the college authorities in Allen's absence continued his policy and let him go. Gilbert represents this as an approbation of his dealing with English officials in hope of some little alleviations in good time.

Then he goes on to speak of his second visit to England in June-July 1586, during which he says he became so frightened by the rage of the persecution, that he fled back to France. The conspiracy was discovered immediately after, and Savage (quite unjustly of course) then accused him of having helped the conspiracy. Thereupon Gilbert's father became endangered, and it was to save his father that he had to go on corresponding with the persecutors, which correspondence had now been discovered, etc., etc. (R.O. *Addenda MS.*, vol xxx. no. 78).

So long as the prosecution had not evidence sufficient to analyse and expose excuses and misstatements such as the above, it was clear that our miscreant could never be convicted by ordinary legal proceedings. A note from him, dated 8/18 February, is extant, in which he tells Phelippes that he 'expects to be freed daily.' But we have also a note from Charles Paget written two days later, in which he says, 'Gifford remaineth where he did, and is like to do so a good while for anything I know. He deserveth to have lost his life, and if he were in Rome or Spaine, I am sure he should' (R.O. *Dom. Eliz.*, ccviii. nn. 57, 63, February, 1588).

The second and third confessions have perished. We hear that on 2 and 25 April Gilbert wrote to Allen and to Father Persons. But Father Christopher Grene, who has mentioned this fact among the notes he prepared for Bartoli's *Inghilterra*, gives no further details, except that, in the apologia to Persons, some description was given of the book against the Society.

The fourth confession was on 14 August, 1588, and a complete copy of it is preserved among the Hatfield MSS. (printed in the *Hatfield Calendar*, iii. 346). Father Grene gives the date and a short abstract which confirms but adds nothing to the Hatfield document. In substance, the whole paper is an accusation of Morgan, and it charges him with responsibility for many details not mentioned elsewhere.

There does not appear to be any reason for doubting its general tenor, and one sentence is especially important. For there, contrary to his own interests, Gilbert lets out, what he nowhere else admits, that

§ III. LETTERS OF GILBERT GIFFORD

he was the chief *provocateur* of the conspiracy. This passage is quoted in its proper place in the *Introduction*, p. cxx.

The last extant confession is in French, dated 16 December 1588. Like the preceding, it is mainly an indictment of Morgan, and gives no details about the entrapping of Mary. Phelippes, to whom Gilbert had managed to send a copy, endorsed it—'G. Gifford, confession to the knaves on the other side,' a pregnant phrase indicating Phelippes's contempt for law and veracity (*Dom. Eliz.*, ccxix. 13).

Next we should cite a report by Phelippes's own servant Casey, which was sent in by 'Cousin Barnes,' and is dated conjecturally the end of September 1588.

'He of Bishops Gate Street (*i.e.* the French ambassador, see *Add. Cal.*, xxx. p. 200) has been carefully sounded by me about Gylbert Gifford. Also your man Casey in his drink (but there is often *in vino veritas*) he told me thus much of my cousin Gylbert—that he was first the practicioner with the gentlemen executed, and after the discoverer &c. That he was indicted here, and priested there colourably. And lastly, that as yet, whether in prison or delivered over to D. Darbishire, the Jesuit (as some say) doth deale still underhand, and is an intelligencer for this state' (R.O. *Dom. Eliz.*, ccxvi. n. 53).

It will be seen from this that though Gifford's secret was in one way well kept, in another the truth was not unknown in general terms. Though no authentic document against him became public, Stafford and Paget were talking of the facts in Paris, and Casey in London. In Antwerp too the news was known, for the report which Morris quotes from the Stonyhurst MSS., is really by Verstegan, who lived there (*Sir A. Poulet*, pp. 386-8, from MS. *Anglia*, i. n. 70; see also Paget's letter of 31 January/10 February 1588, R.O. *Dom. Eliz.*, ccviii. n. 39).

'Gilbert Gifford doth still deal underhand, and is an intelligencer for this state,' said Casey, and so in truth he was. Ten letters of this period survive, and show that, so long at least as we can watch him, this perversity of will continued. His ambition is to deceive, to mislead, to betray, and he died as he lived. Some of the contrasts in his letters are not unamusing. On 16 July (*Dom. Eliz.*, ccxii. n. 54), we find a letter very different from his ordinary style. He praises Stafford and Lilly, regrets that he has not been able to write since his imprisonment, and ends with the pious wish that England may make peace with Spain before the Armada sails. But on the margins he has scribbled in invisible ink, that all this was written while his enemies were at his shoulder, and that they were letting him write to see what Phelippes would answer. In reality, of course, Lilly was an arch rascal, and Walton, whom Stafford had commended, was a suspicious character, &c., &c.

Phelippes has also preserved a few of his own 'minutes' or drafts. They are very much corrected, very hard to read, and show us a character even more repulsive than that of Gifford, more cynical, more hypocritical, a stronger hater. The most remarkable perhaps is that of

20/30 July, which possibly answers Gilbert's of the 6/16th. He here reappoints him to his old trade of news-writer, and again he grossly exceeds in his confidences towards so unreliable a person.

He tells him, for instance, that Lord Burghley had been compromised in his proceedings against Mary, by his partiality towards her. Not only was this false, but the false impression was due to Phelippes himself in great measure. It is true that Burghley was not quite so bitter a hater as Walsingham; but a mortal enemy for all that, who took the lead in all the proceedings for Mary's death. The indiscreet Morgan having, in his exaggerated letters to Mary, overstated Burghley's considerateness, Phelippes by his deciphers had brought this to Walsingham's knowledge, perhaps also to Elizabeth's. And here we find this 'customs-collector' repeating the gross indiscretions which he made in setting Gifford to inform upon Stafford, only here the quiet hint is given in regard to the first minister of the crown. It must be remembered, however, that this 'minute' was not necessarily followed in the dispatch; indeed, it is lightly scored through, in such a way that *might* mean either 'Done,' or 'Omitted.'

In any case, however, it is truly remarkable that Phelippes should again appoint Gifford his correspondent, while still fast in prison. Walsingham, and probably Elizabeth too, must have liked either his manner, or his matter. But no later news-letters survive to justify or condemn their choice. In December 1588 we hear from Gerard Gifford (a brother whom Phelippes employed as an intermediary) that the decipherer intended to drop Gilbert altogether. What that exactly meant we cannot tell. There is still a letter from Bacot, Gilbert's former servant in Paris, saying that with money something might be done (*Addenda Calendar*, p. 279, ? August 1589).

Then the Wars of Religion broke out again in France, and Paris was beleaguered by Huguenot-Loyalist forces. We can easily imagine that a poor prisoner had a good deal to bear at such a crisis. Next a sentence is found in a note from Sir Francis Englefield, saying that Gilbert had been importunate to have his case re-opened amid such untoward circumstances (3 Feb. 1590, *Addenda Calendar*, p. 297). Finally a casual announcement in a letter from Henry Walpole, S.J., dated 29 November 1591, tells us that, 'Gilbert Gifford is dead in prison in Paris' (Augustus Jessopp, *Letters of Father H. Walpole, S.J.*, 1873, p. 23).

SECTION IV

VARIOUS WRITERS

I.—FOUR LETTERS FROM SIR FRANCIS WALSINGHAM

No. 35

WALSINGHAM TO PHELIPPES

[? *Richmond, 2 August* 1586.]

B.M. Cottonian, Appendix L, 140, ff 140, 144, 141, 143 These letters appear to have slipped out from *Caligula*, C ix. In them we see Walsingham in the act of pulling down the nets on the conspirators and nervously excited during those critical moments At every hitch he is agitated, and complains about matters, like the postscript, the responsibility for which he here inadvertently admits. There are three letters on 3 August

The enclosed I receyved this [MS. perished] Sr Amias Pavlet. Yt is more carelesly made up then others y^t heretofor have passed my hands. Whether yt be don *De industria* or no, I knowe not.[1] So soone as you shall have decyphred the letter, so earnestly looked for by her ma^{tye},[2] I praye you bryng yt wth you [*erasure*; ? safely down] for y^t I thinke meet you shoold delyver yt your selve.

I dyrected ffra. Mylls to confer w^t you abowt the appryehensyon of Bal[lard], wch I wyshe now execvted owt of hande, vnless you shall see cavse vppon the decyphrye of the letter to the contrarye. Yt shall be meet

---

[1] For the 'make up' of the packets see *Introduction*, p lviii.

[2] The 'letter so earnestly looked for by her Majesty' would be either Mary to Mendoza in Post III , which did not come out till 7 August, or it might also be Babington's answer, and this seems certainly to be the letter alluded to four lines lower down.

also to apprehend Bab[ington] and sooche as are noted to be his famylyars. Sorry I am that G. G[ifford] is absent. I mervayle greatly howe this hvmor of estrayngyng of him selve commethe vppon him.

I praye you thinke [? of a] man to apprehende Bab[ington] and consyder also of the manner.

I meane bothe he and Bal[lard] shall be kept in my howse vntyll they shall be thorrowghely examyned.

I hope you have thowght on the articles [1] that are to be ministred vnto them bothe, as also cavsed Barden to set downe the names of the pryncypall practysers as well Clergye men as temporall.[2] I woold be glad to vnderstand whoe doe accompagnye s^r G. Peckham [3] for I take him to be a great practycor and his compagnyon s^r Tho: Gerard. And so I comyt you to god; in hast at the coorte the second of Avgvst 1586.

Y^r Loveng frend,
FRA: WALSYNGHAM.

No. 36

THE SAME TO THE SAME

[? *Richmond, 3 August* 1586.]

The order of the following letters is decided, firstly, by the allusions to Poley. In the first two letters he is expected, in the third he has called. Secondly, the directions given in No. 36, about the apprehension of Ballard, are approved in No. 37, and this settles their order.

S^r at the Causting vp . . . [*MS. perished* ? of accounts] . . . I am sorry the event favlethe [owt so] yll. I dowbt

---

[1] The articles drawn up by Phelippes for Ballard are extant. See Boyd, viii. pp. 591, 592; *cf.* p. 510.

[2] Nicholas Berden, previously, and perhaps truly, known as Thomas Rogers, see *Introduction*, p. xl. Twenty-six of his informations will be found (partly *in extenso*, partly in abstract) in *Cath. Rec. Soc.*, xxi. pp. 66-73, with a commentary. Similarly his proposals for dealing with Catholic prisoners are printed (*ibid.*, ii. 253, 272-276). As Walsingham seems to think that he has already set down 'the names of the principal practysers, as well Clergymen as Temporal,' this paper very probably did, and possibly does still exist, though I am not able to point it out.

[3] For Sir Geo. Peckham of Denham (see *Introduction*, p. lxviii. n.). He

greatly her ma^{tye} hathe not vsed the matter w^t that secreacye that apperteynethe. The cyrcomestavnces shewethe y^t he is departed vppon somme dowbt of apprehensyon. I feare he hathe come to some knowledg by Dunne. I have dyspatched a letter vnto Sr Amias Pavlet and have acquaynted him w^t Bab[ington's] departvre and desyered him to geve somme secreat order for his apprehensyon. But I dowbt he wyll not repayre in thos partes. Towching your going downe I thinke yt not necessarye. Owre waye wyll be to dyscover here what is the cavse of his departvre, wherin great secreacye woold be vsed. I looke for Pooley from whom I hope to receyve some lyght. Ballarde woold be taken, but w^t no other coorse of proceading then w^t an ordenarye Iesveste; accordingly as I have dyrected ffra: mylls, w^t whome you may confer, whoe is most secreat and he . . . [*MS. perished*] . . . You wyll not beleve howe myche I am greved w^t the event of this cavse. I feare the addytyon of the postscrypt hathe bread the ielousie. And so prayeing god to send vs better svccesse then I looke for, I comyt you to his protectyon. At the coorte the 3 of this present 1586.

Y^r Loveng frend,
Fra: Walsyngham.

I praye you learne of M^r. H. Ofeley what is become of G. G., whos streyng manner of w^tdrawing him selve I knowe not whatt to thinke of. Let the messenger repayre this daye to Bab[ington] to sollycyt awntswer.

---

and Sir Thomas Gerard were no conspirators. Peckham died almost immediately after this, but Gerard remained a prisoner in the Tower until he was persuaded to bear evidence against the Earl of Arundel (*Cath. Rec. Soc.*, xxi., *passim*).

No. 37

THE SAME TO THE SAME

[*Richmond, 3 August* 1586.]

... [*MS. injured*] ... your Latten lettre ... comforted me. I thinke [yf your] messenger receyve not awntswer this daye at Bab[ington's] handes, then were yt not good to dyffer the apprehension of him, least he shoold escape. yf you hope by geving of tyme [*erasure*] that an awntswere wyll be drawen from him: then wyshe I the staye. yt may be y^t the dyfferring of the awntswere proceadethe vppon cōference, wch yf yt be so, then were yt a great hyndravnce of the servyce to procead over hastely to the arrest. Thes cavses are svbiect to so many dyfficvltyes as yt is a hard matter to resolve. Only this I conclvde yt were better to lacke the awntswer then to lacke the man. I doe not meane to speake w^t him for many cavses. And therefor yf pooley repayre hether I wyll pvtt off the meetyng vntyll saterdaye, to the ende he may in the mean tyme be apprehended. I lyke well that Bal[lard] shoold be apprehended in sooche sorte as is agreed on. ... [*MS. injured*] have dyspatched ... Sr Amyas to ... then of the former dyrections.

I mean to acquaynt her ma^{tye} w^t the contents of youre letters. In the mean tyme I woold the messenger you vsed myght be dyrected to sollycyt awntswere, vnles you shall see some cavse to the contrarye. And so in hast I commyt you to god. At the coorte the thirde of Avgvst 1586.   Y^r Loving frend,
            FRA: WALSYNGHAM.

I send you two blankes sygned to be converted into warrants.

Addressed, To his servaunt, Thomas Phillips.

Endorsed in Phelippes's hand, '3 August, from Sr Fra. Walsingham.'

No. 38

THE SAME TO THE SAME

[*Same day.*]

Pooley[1] hathe ben w^t [me and] hathe geven me great [assvr]ravnce of Bab[ington's] devotyon bothe to my selve and the pvblycke servyce: and to strengthen my opynyon and good conceypt towards him he hathe towld me from Bab[ington] that there is one Bal[lard] a great practycer in this realme w^t the catholyques to styrr vp rebellyon w^{t}in the realme, being set on by the Imb[assador] of Spayne and Charles Paget. I wylled him to geve him great thankes for this advertycement and to requyre him in my name to drawe from Ballarde what he coold towching sooch partyes as he hathe dealt w^{t}all: and to meet me at my howse on saterdaye next. Thowghe I doe not fynde but that Pooley hathe dealt honestly w^t me: yet I am lothe [to] laye my selve any waye open vnto him: but have only delyvered sooche speeches as might worke. . . . [*MS. perished*] . . . in Bab[ington] I doe not thinke good notw^{t}standyng, to dyffer the apprehensyon of Bab[ington] longer then ffrydaye.[2] *Ne forte.* I lyke well therfore that you hasten the ffr[ench] Imb[assador's] dyspatche. And yet can I not thinke that he shoold vse his helep in the matter: but doe rather ivdge y^t he dowbtethe what to awntswere. I long to heare of Bal[lard's] apprehensyon wch I have cavsed to be don by a warrant sygned by the L. Admyrall for that I woold not be seen in the matter. Sorrye I am that I heare not of G[yfford] whoe myght at this present have gyven good assysteavnce. And so

---

[1] Walsingham's story corresponds exactly with that of Poley himself, printed in Boyd, viii pp 601, 602.

[2] Babington in the event fled on Friday, 5 August, and was not arrested till a week later. Ballard was seized on 4 August, in virtue of the Lord Admiral's warrant mentioned in the postscript

prayeing god to blesse you w^t all happye successe I end, at the coorte the third of Avgvste 1586.

Y^r Loving frend,
FRA: WALSYNGHAM.

The L. Admyrall warrant is in ffra: myll hands.

Endorsed by Phelippes, 3 August 1586, fro Sr ffra Walsingham.

II.—EXTRACTS FROM THE OFFICIAL RECORD
OF THE EVIDENCE READ AT MARY'S TRIAL

This record by Edward Barker and Thomas Wheeler has not yet been printed, or used methodically. Two abbreviated versions of it, however, have been made and printed. The one is widely known because it appears in all editions of *State Trials*. The other is somewhat more full and explicit, and has been printed in *Hardwicke State Papers*, the full title of which runs '*Miscellaneous State Papers from* 1501 *to* 1726, London, 1778, largely from papers in the library of the Earl of Hardwicke,' i. 224-251. This has been reprinted with a commentary by B. Sepp, *Process gegen Maria Stuart*, Munich, 1886.

Though some description has already been given of this official statement by Barker and Wheeler, p. 36, *above*, further details must be given of our copy. This appears to have been made by one of Cotton's clerks, writing early in the 17th century, with great care and accuracy. That Barker and Wheeler were the notaries employed does not seem to be affirmed in the MS. itself, but the fact is asserted in *State Trials*, p. 148.

The Cottonian possesses two copies, (1) A draft now *Caligula*, B. v. ff. 371-413, which contains all the formalities, rubrics, etc., written in full, but not all the documents, which are generally represented by blanks. In the Catalogue the title is 'Commission for and examination of Mary Queen of Scots at Fotheringay—the end wanting, 1586.'

(2) The completed copy, now *Caligula*, C. ix. ff. 340-405, is thus described in the catalogue. 'A full account of the whole proceedings against the Queen of Scots, containing several letters from her and to her, her sentence at the end, ff. 340 to 405.' In the course of various rebindings the pages now bear no less than five different paginations (340=436=477=580). I am here following that used in the catalogue.

As has already been noticed in connection with Mary's letter to Babington, this source is one of the fullest and most trustworthy guides, even in the matters of literary minutiae. I have therefore

§ IV. VARIOUS WRITERS

extracted from it several confessions of importance, hitherto unknown, or only known in faulty, and possibly garbled versions. These faulty copies come to us through the so-called *Hardwicke Papers* (reprinted also by Sepp), but no critique of this text has yet appeared. In compiling one, use should be made of a contemporary or sub-contemporary copy, *Caligula*, C. ix. f. 494, endorsed 'A brief summary of proceedings against the Scottish Queen,' and had previously been entitled, 'Sommaries of the proceedings,' etc. In this MS. we see that some paragraphs have shorter lines than others. As will appear in No. 45, the editing of these short lines is in some cases not only faulty, but fraudulent. Hence it is very desirable that the whole series of examinations should be examined critically, because in the *Hardwicke Papers* the not very palpable distinction between the short lines and the long has been neglected, with the result that in the printed version there is no distinction at all between the record of the trial and the handiwork of the deceitful abbreviator.

The MS. is written in court style, with hardly any breaks. A few are here introduced for the reader's convenience; especially as paragraphs were used in the style of original examinations.

No. 39

EXAMINATION OF JOHN BALLARD

[16 *and* 18 *August* 1586.]

Caligula, C. ix. 363-364 (=460, etc.). The *Summary* only gives three lines to this confession, Hardwicke, p. 228; Sepp, p. 35; MS. *Caligula*, C. ix., 495*b*. The heads of evidence in Boyd, viii. 682, also refers frequently to this paper.

It will be found that Ballard recollects §§ iii. iv. viii. ix. of Babington's letter, and §§ ii. iv. vi. iii. of Mary's to Babington.

Et ulterius adtunc et ibidem ex parte domine nostre Regine in presencia dicte Marie, allegatum fuit quod decimo sexto et decimo octavo diebus Augusti ultimi praeteriti, predictus Johannes Ballard examinatus fuit coram Joanne Puckering, uno servientium ad legem, Francisco Bacon armigero, et predictis Thoma Egerton. [Francisco Bacon *cancelled*] et Edwardo Barker, Quodquidem predicte examinationes prefati Johannis Ballard, in scriptum reducte, et per eundem Johannem Ballarde pro verificatione inde manu sua propria coram prefatis Johanne Puckering, Thoma Egerton, et Francisco Bacon et Edwardo Barker subscripte fuerunt, quarum quidem examinationum predicti Johannis Ballarde quedam partes coram eisdem commissionariis in presentia dicte Marie lecte fuerunt, Quarum quidem partium tenores sequuntur in hec verba.

EXAMINED what letters he is privie to, hath passed to or from the Queen of Scotts, he sayeth he is only acquaynted that Babinton wrote once unto her and receaved another from her. The contents of Babington's (as he remembreth) was this.

A significacion of foreine princes care and his, and his freindes for the preservation and deliuerie of [? of the Scottish Queen, and for] the plot layed for the performance thereof, vidẽt, of the invasion and (as he remembreth) of the attempte against her Majesty's person. And lastley he required from her to geve her lyking and auctoritie thereunto.

The coppie of this letter he sayeth he reade abowte five or six weeks since [1] in the Chamber of Babington, who then lay in his bed, and told him that he had sent the letter in cypher, but he cannot tell by whom, nor how, adding that it was needful the Queene of Scotts sholde geve her lyking and aucthoritie, otherwise men wolde be loathe to enter into the action.

Towching the letter from the Queene of Scottes to Babington he sayeth that about three weeks after [2] the shewe and reading of Babington's letter aforesaid, Babington shewed and read to this examinate a parte of a letter, the whole not being then (as he sayed) disciphered, which he sayed came from the Queene of Scotts, the contents whereof (as he remembreth) weare theis:

First she accepted his service verie well, and gave him greate thanks for the same, lyking his course and referring him for all things necessary to be supplied unto Mendoza, prescribing this order unto him, that he sholde not make her name appeare herein, but sholde make showe that all was done for the Catholickes safetie, bycause if the Erle of Leicester shold retourne, they sholde hereafter lyve

---

[1] This date would be 5 to 12 July.
[2] This date would be 26 July to 2 August.

in greater daunger then before, bycause he was stronger, Further she appoynted Babington to consider what number of horsemen and footemen he cold provide, or procure and furnishe, and that for their wants he sholde have repaire to Mendoza, and that she wolde allow whatsoever shold be done therein by Babington.[1] And further he sayeth that (as he remembreth) it was conteyned in that letter thus, vidēlt. That towching the great accion he must be very circumspect, and more of the said letter, he doth not presently remember.

He also sayeth that he had of Charles Pagett twentie poundes before his coming out of Fraunce, and since his coming over he hath had of Babington twentie pounds, and of Edward Windsor twentie pounds.

JOHN BALLARDE.

No. 40

ATTESTATIONS OF BABINGTON, NAU, AND CURLL TO QUEEN MARY'S LETTER III

[? 1, 5, *and* 6 *September* 1586.]

B M Cotton. *Caligula*, C. ix 376 (473 v.): *Caligula*, B v 433; Boyd, viii 679. On 1 September Babington attested his cipher-key, *Dom Eliz* cxciii. 54 His attestation here is probably of the same date.

This is the verie trewe coppie of the Queenes letter laste sente vnto me. Anthony Babington.

Je pense que cest la litere escripte per sa Ma^{te} a Babington Comme il ne [me] peult souuenir, Sexto Septembris 1586. Nau.

The lyke I thinke of this was written in frenche by Mr Nau, and translated and ciphered by me, as I have mencioned in the ende of a coppie of Mr Babingtons letter where Mr Naw hath firste subscribed, Gilbert Curll, Quinto Septembris 1586.

---

[1] This seems to be Ballard's only error, a very natural one for him to fall into

No. 41

HEADINGS FOR THE BLOODY LETTER

Caligula, C. ix. f. 377 (474); *Caligula*, B. v. 433. The latter omits the French document.

The document is to be compared with R.O., *M.Q.S.*, xix. 90; in Morris, 230; Boyd, viii. 679, 680. It follows from note 1 to this text and from note 1 to the next that the R.O. version may be interpolated in a sense hostile to Mary.

Et vlterius ad probandam informacionem predictam adtunc & ibidem ex parte dicte domine nostre Regine nunc in presencia predicte Marie allegatum fuit quod predictus Jacobus Nau scripsisset in quodam papiro quasdam notulas, siue capita, in lingua Gallica predicte vltime litere per predictam Mariam ad prefatum Anthonium Babington vt prefertur misse. Quodque eedem notule siue Capita sic scripta apud Chartley in Com. Staff. in conclavi, Anglice *the Cabonett*, predicte Marie sub custodia eiusdem Marie inter alia scripta et munimenta sua invente fuerunt, ac per prefatum Jacobum Nau manu sua propria, ex predicta vltima litera per prefatam Mariam ad prefatum Anthonium Babington vt prefertur missa, scripta et extracta, Ac quod idem Jacobus Nau manu sua propria sub eisdem notulis et capitibus declarabat ad quem finem et propositum eedem notule sive capita sic per ipsum scripta et extracta fuerunt. Et super sacramentum suum vt prefertur prestitum affirmabat notulas et capita predicta esse per eum scripta; ac ad quem finem & propositum eedem notule sive capita sic scripta et extracta fuerunt. Que quidem notule, declaracoes et subscripioes, adtunc et ibidem coram eisdem Comissionarijs in presencia predicte Marie publice lecte ac eidem Marie ostense fuerunt, et superinde eadem Maria respondebat se credere easdem notulas declaracoes et subscripcoes esse scriptas manu propria predicti Jacobi Nau,

Quarum quidem notularum declaracionum & subscripcionum tenores sequntur in hijs verbis.

'Sicours dehors: forces dans le pais. Armee d'Esp. au retour des Indes; Armee de france au mesme temps, la pais se faisant. Guise sil ne passe, tiendra la france occupée, de flanders de mesme, Escosse au mesme temps, Irland ainsy, Coup, Sortie' et 'Cecy sont les pointes qu'en presence de la Royne ma maitresse et par son commandement. Je tiray pur fair la despeche en france ascauoir L'Archeuesque de Glasco, et l'Ambassadeur d'espaigne et Charles Pagett. Quant a la lettre escripte a Babington [1] Jenay rien faict ny escripte comme Jay proteste sans son expres commandement, e speciallement touchant le pointe de son eschape en mettant le feu aux granges pres de la maison. v^{to} Septembr: 1586. Nau.

'Il [2] me souuient que dans la lettre de la Royne a Babington sa Ma^{te} le renuoyoit a l'Ambassadeur d'espaigne pour le support qu'ilz demandoient. Et que sur ceste occasion si tost qu'ilz seroient sousleues du coste de deca, Ilz luy pouruenssent pour l'enleuer hors de Chartley en surprenant la maison comme il est ia dict cy dessus Et le tout fut par le commandement expres de la Royne qui Je m'asseure le tesmoignera et aduouera.

'v^{to} Septemb: 1586. Nau. Je depose que dessus par mon serment.'

No. 42

CONFESSION OF JACQUES NAU

[6 *September* 1586.]

Caligula, C. ix. 378; *Caligula*, B. v. 435v. The latter omits the document. In *M.Q.S.*, xix. 90, this is prefixed to No. 41 *above*; Boyd, viii. 680.

Et Vlterius adtunc et ibidem in presencia predicte Marie ex parte dicte domine nostre Regine ostensa fuit in evidencia eisdem Commissionarijs quedam declaracio dicti Jacobi Nau, manu sua propria scripta et per sacramentum suum similiter vt prefertur prestita, testificat tam concernens scripcionem literarum predictarum per predictam Mariam ad prefatum Anthonium Babington vt prefertur

---

[1] *M.Q.S.*, xix. 90, here adds: Sa Ma^{te} me la bailla pour la plus part escripte de sa main, et . . .

[2] This paragraph is omitted in *M.Q.S.*, xix. 90.

vltime missarum, quam concernens modum per eandem in scribendis et recipiendis alijs literis importancie communiter vsitatum et observatum. Quam quidem declaracionem et subscripcionem predicte Marie ostensam, eadem Maria respondebat se credere esse scriptam manu propria predicti Jacobi Nau. Cuius quidem declaracionis et subscripcionis tenor sequitur in his verbis.

'Pour la lettre escripte par la Royne ma maistresse a Babington Je l'ay escript [1] par son expresse direction et commandement,[1] comme J'ay depose pour les aultres lettres, comme tousiours sa maieste a accoustume elle mesmes seant a table, et Curll et moy deuant elle, sa maieste me commande particulierment et de poinct en poinct tout ce quil luy plaist estre escript. Et [2] soubz elle [2] J'en tiré les poinctez aussi particulierement et amplement [3] qu'il se peult [3] faire, puis les lui monstre et relis. Et selon cela ne restant plus que la disposition de la matiere, Jay escript les dictes lettres, et a elle monstrees et deliueres, pour en estre faicte comme il luy plaist ordonner. Car sa maieste ne veult permettre qu'on escripue pour [? pas] lettres d'Importance et secrettes hors de son Cabinet. Et ne se ferme mesmes aulcune despeche qu'elle ny soit present. Et relist tousiours toutes les lettres auant qu'elles sont mises en Chiffre et translates, Ce qui se fait par Curll, mesmement de la lettre escripte a Babington.

'vj^{to} Septembr: 1586. Nau. Je le depose par mon serment.'

---

[1] *M.Q.S.*, xix. 90, adds: Sus une minute de la main de Sa Ma^{te}.
[2] *M.Q.S.*, xix. 90, *reads* sur cela.
[3] *M.Q.S.*, xix. 90, *reads* que je puis.

§ IV. VARIOUS WRITERS

No. 43

EXAMINATION OF GILBERT CURLL

[23 *September* 1586.]

Caligula, C ix. f 379 (=476); *Caligula*, B. v f 437.

Et vlterius ad tunc et ibidem ex parte eiusdem domine Regine ac in presencia predicte Marie ostense fuerunt in evidencia eisdem Commissionarijs separales declaraciones predictorum Jacobi Nau et Gilberti Curll specialiter pertinentes tam predicte litere per prefatum Anthonium Babington ad prefatam Mariam misse, quam predicte littere per eandem Mariam superinde ad eundem Anthonium Babington similiter directe et misse sub manibus et per sacramentum predictorum Jacobi Nau et Gilberti Curll separatim et seorsim vt prefertur prestite declarate et testificate. Quas quidem declaraciones predictas Jacobi Nau predicti ostensas eadem Maria respondebat se credere esse scriptas manu propria eiusdem Jacobi, Ad quas quidem declaraciones predicti Gilberti Curll predicte Marie similiter ostensas eadem Maria respondebat se credere esse subscriptas manu propria eiusdem Gilberti, quarum tenores sequntur in hijs verbis.

'Certains poinctes qui m'ont este bailles en langage Anglois par monseigneur le grand Tresorier par ordonnance du Conseil, a ce qu'ils fussent par moy translatees en francois, et que sur ce Je deposasse s'il ne me souuient pas Iceulx auoir escriptz par Babington en sa lettre a la Royne ma maistresse. Il ma este addresse' and so forthe as by the seuerall lettres before written may appeare in the Englishe tounge.

Vpon the sighte and pervsall of the copie of the letter written by Babington to the Queenes Matie my mistres, I doo remember well that the Clauses hereafter written were conteyned in the same letter diciphered att her Ma^{ts} commandement.

By me Gilbert Curll the three and twentith of September 1586.

There was addressed vnto me from the partes beyonde the seas one Ballarde a man of vertue and learning and of singuler zeale to the Catholick cawse and yor Maties service. This man enformed me of greate preparacions by the Christian princes yor Maties Allies for the delyeraunce of o^r Contrie from the extreme and miserable estate wherein it hath so longe remayned, my especiall desire was to advise by what meanes wth the hazarde of my lyfe and my freinds in generall I might doo yor sacred Matie one good dayes service, And so reoiteth allmoste all Babingtons lettre to the queene of Scotts wch is here before sett downe as it was geven in evidence and subscribeth his name therevnto. Then he setteth downe all the poynts of the Queen of Scotts lettre to Babington in self same wordes that it is heere formerly sett downe to be geven in evidence againste her, and subscribeth also therevnto. By me Gilbert Curll, and affirmeth as before that the said lettres weare firste written in frenche by Mr Nau and translated in Englishe and ciphered by him by the Queene his mistres commandement, the xxiijth of September 1586.

No. 44

EXAMINATION OF JACQUES NAU

[21 *September* 1586.]

Caligula, C. ix. f. 380 (477); *Caligula*, B. v. 438. The latter omits the document. A summary of this paper is given in *M.Q.S.*, xix. 107. (?) Not in Boyd.

Et vlterius ad tunc et ibidem ex parte eiusdem domine Nostre Regine ac in presencia predicte Marie ostense sunt in evidencia eisdem Commissionarijs separales examinacões predictorum Jacobi Nau et Gilberti Curll per prefatos Thomam Bromley, Willum dominum Burghley et Chrõferum Hatton vicesimo primo die Septembris vltimo preteriti separatim et seorsim capt ac manibus proprijs predictorum Jacobi Nau et Gilberti Curll subscript et per eosdem Jacobum Nau et Gilbertum Curll per sacramentum sua similiter vt prefertur prestitum testificatione et affirmatione: quibus quidem subscriptionibus predicte Marie ostensis existentibus, eadem Maria respondebat se credere easdem esse scriptas manibus proprijs eorundem Jacobi Nau et Gilberti Curll. Quarum quidem separalium examinacionum et subscripcionum tenores sequntur in hec verba.

The Examynacōn of Mr James Nau taken by the Lorde Chancellor the Lorde Treasuror and Sr Xpofer Hatton knighte vice Chamberleyne to her Matie the xxjth of September 1586.

He sayeth, That he tooke the pointes of the lettre written by the Scottishe Queene vnto Anthony Babington of the date of the xxvijth of Julye laste paste, of the delyuerie, of the Scottishe Queenes owne mowthe from pointe to poynte in the verie same fashion and manner as him self did putt the same in writing wch letter therevpon was drawen in frenche by this Examinate, after wch the Scottishe Queene did correcte the same letter so drawne by this Examinate in suche sorte as the same was after putt into Englishe by Curll and after putt into Cipher, by the same Curll in suche sorte as it was sent vnto Anthony Babington. He sayeth that the Scottishe Queene gave her direccion vnto this Examinate for drawing the same letter in her Cabynett att Chartley, Curll being present thereat & none ells. He sayeth theis points conteyned in the Scottish Queenes lettre to Babington weare firste delyuered by the same Queene vnto this Examinate by her owne speeche vpon consideracon of Babingtons lettre written to her, wherein the same pointes weare conteyned and in answeare of the same letter, That is to saye, first That Babington sholde examyn deepely what forces as well on foote as on horsebacke they mighte raise amongest them all, The second what Townes portes and havens they might assuer themselves of as well in the Northe west as Sowthe, And so through, as it is before sett downe att large in the Scottish Queenes letter to Babington & concludeth or signeth his examination wth theis wordes in french.

Je certefie les choses dessus dictes estre vrayes et par moy deposes xxj^{mo} Septemb: 1586. Nau.

No. 45

EXAMINATION OF GILBERT CURLL

[21 *September* 1586.]

Caligula, C. ix. 381. Not in *Caligula*, B. v. Compared with R.O. *M.Q.S.*, xix. 107.

The examinacõn of Gilbert Curll taken by the Lorde Chancellor the Lorde Treasuror and Sr Chrõfer Hatton knight vice Chamberleyne to her Matie the xxjth daye of September 1586. He saieth that him self did discipher the letter written in July laste paste to the Scottishe Queene by Anthony Babington. He sayeth that the intelligence that the Scottishe Queene had wth ffrancis Throckmorton was for conveying of letters, and advertising of occurrents vnto the Scottishe Queene. He sayeth that when he this Examinate had disciphered the said letter written from Anthony Babington, he delyvered the same so disciphered vnto Mr Nau whoe read it, and therevpon did delyver it to the Scottishe Queene in her Closett att Chartley. He sayeth that the daye after the same letters weare disciphered Mr Nau read the same letter vnto the Scottishe Queene in her Closett in the presence of this Examinate. He sayeth that herevpon the Scottishe Queene directed Nau to drawe an answeare to the same letter, the wch Nau drewe in frenche, and that doone, Nau read it vnto her, and that doone, the Scottish Queene willed this Examynate to putt it into English wch this Examinate did accordinglie, and when he had so doone, this Examinate did reade the same so Englished vnto Mr Nau, wch doone the Scottish Queene willed this Examinate to putt the same letter so Englished into Cipher, wch this Examinate did. He sayeth the lettre directed by the Scottishe Queene to Babington, had amongest others theis partes in it.

The firste that Babington sholde deepely examyne what forcs on foote and horse : ' and so reciteth the cheife pointes of her letter in the verie same wordes as you haue allreadie read them heretofore, and concludeth ' :

§ IV. VARIOUS WRITERS

All theis things above rehearsed I doo well remember and confesse them to be trewe. By me Gilbert Curll the xxjth of September 1586.

He sayeth that the letters wch weare written in July laste, anon after the said letter written to Babington aswell vnto S^r ffrauncis Inglefield, as vnto the Lo: Pagett and Charles Pagett, weare firste written by the Queene of Scotts herself in french and delyvered to her by [? by her to] this Examinat to be translated into Englishe, wch this Examinat did, and delyvered the letters written in frenche by the Scottishe Queene vnto the same Queene againe, and did putt that wch himself had englished into cipher by the Scottishe Queenes commaundement, and that wch was englished by this Examinate this Examinate did putt into a trunke that was in the Scottishe Queenes Cabynett vnder locke and key. Theis things abovesaid I have confessed and are true. By me Gilberte Curll this one and twentith of Septemb: 1586.

Et insuper &c. [The transition to the letter to Charles Paget.]

The last five lines of the last number are entirely misrepresented in Hardwicke, and in Sepp. Barker and Wheeler had given the strong evidence for *the preservation* of the minutes. 'That which was Englished . . . this examinate did put into a trunk under lock and key.' In the published version we read for this, 'She willed him to burn the English copy of the letters sent to Babington.'

This seems like a falsification of the *record*, but possibly (as mentioned before) the passage was originally intended as a gloss,—a false gloss, not a forged record. In MS. *Caligula*, C. ix. 499, this passage is introduced by the words, 'It is to be noted,' and the lines are 'indented' (as printers would say). Possibly these little signs are meant to indicate that the editor was now speaking. When, however, as in Hardwicke, the distinction between short lines and long was not observed, students were naturally deceived, as is seen in the case of Sepp. and others.

The same fraud was repeated twice in subsequent paragraphs (*Caligula*, C. ix. ff. 499, 502, 503, *Hardwicke Papers*, 237, 249, 250, or Sepp. 50, 68, 69), in each of which the order to burn the minutes is substituted for the record of the preservation.

It seems impossible to give with certainty the motive for this falsification. Mary was already dead. Perhaps her adversaries were endeavouring to maintain the defence of some of their points. We know that they told Nau and Curll, that they had seized copies or minutes of the most compromising letters. Nau, deceived by this, had told his examiners that they had the minutes; perhaps others were similarly imposed upon. The present fraud may be meant to balance the earlier deceit; and to explain why the all-important minute was not found, because (so they now falsely allege) Mary herself ordered it to be burnt.

No. 46

NAU'S REGRETS AND CURLL'S DISSUASIONS

[Given in Evidence, 25 October 1586.]

Caligula, C. ix. ff. 398 (=495b); *Caligula*, B. v. 415.

Nau *[after renewing his acknowledgment of the letters]*—quod quanquam non sine magno animi sui dolore contra Dominam suam ista protulisset, tamen veritate rei coram Deo magis commotus confitebatur se vere, sincere, et iuste in omnibus examinationibus, declarationibus, scriptis et subscriptionibus suis praedictis dixisse et subscripsisse. *[Nau retires, Curll comes in, renews his attestations.]*

Ac ulterius expressis verbis voluntarie adiunxit quod super lectionem eidem Marie dicte litere predicti Anthonii Babington ad dictam Mariam misse et tradite, ipse idem Gilbertus dixit et declaravit eidem Marie in predicto conclavi dicte domine sue ubi predictus Jacobus Nau adtunc etiam presens fuit, quod attempt articuli et proposita in predicta litera predicti Anthonii Babington specificati fuere valde periculosa (*sic*), rogans eamdem Mariam dominam suam, quatenus eadem Maria ad attempt articulos & proposita illa nec auscultaret nec consentiret aut responderet. Ad quod eadem Maria respondebat quod ipsa agere vellet in negotiis illis prout sibi placeret, precipiens eidem Gilberto ut obedientiam suam prestaret et faceret prout sibi per eandem Mariam in ea parte mandatum est.

[On which he makes oath, 25 October, etc.]

III.—AN ORDER FROM QUEEN ELIZABETH AND LORD BURGHLEY'S ANSWER

The original creators of the situation which issued in the Babington Plot had been Queen Elizabeth and Lord Burghley, and the following letters, written during the trial of Mary, give vivid examples of their ways of action. Elizabeth, imperious but changeable, gives orders the day after the hearing for an immediate *and unanimous adverse* verdict, as well as sentence and execution against her cousin, though she had given different commands just before. What tyranny could be more stark?

Lord Burghley and his fellows naturally resented this. Walsingham had groaned to Burghley a few days earlier, 'I would to God her Majesty would consent to refer these things to them that are best judges of them, as other princes do' (*Dom. Eliz*, cxciv. 14). Walsingham was a ministerialist, Lord Burghley followed a different line. He pleads that his mistress's orders are 'unpossible,' as well as dishonourable, and 'an error in law,' and he thus induced her to relent in her capricious despotism. By informing his confrères of the line he had taken, he ensured their support for his policy, which prevailed, as it so often did on other occasions

No. 47

ELIZABETH'S SECRETARY TO LORD BURGHLEY

[15 *October* 1586.]

Oxford, Bodleian Library, Tanner MS. lxxviii f 173 An office copy with several slips; the writer has become unrecognisable, but from the rest of the correspondence it may be by Davison.

My verie good L. her Maiestie findinge by your Lordship's letter, together with others from Mr. Secretarie of the deferinge to pronounce the sentence theare uppon hearinge of the cause against that Q:, wilbe a matter subject both to slaunder and confusion,—bicause the voices, given as theie ought to be publicquelie, must necessarelie be followed with the sentence bothe pronounced and recorded, and that the Commission do [1] determine—hath comaunded me to signifie unto you, albehit by her frind she gave you other direction (not thinkinge it cold have

---

[1] MS to.

proved in anie sort prejiudiciall to her honor and service) yet is she nowe verie well pleased; and so hathe comaunded me expresselie to signifie unto your Lordship, Mr. Secretarie and Mr. Vicechamberlaine, that [1] you should againe convene the rest of the Lords and others in Comission so soone as you maie possiblie after the receipt hereof, to the place appointed for this purpose and there to proceede to votinge and finishinge of this acte with the sentence accordinge to the comission in that bequest. Whereat neuertheles she thinketh it needed that good heede be taken: that in gatheringe the opinions and proceedinge to the said sentence ther fall out no difference or contrarietie amongst you that be in Comission prejiudiciall to her H. said service, besides that for the maner she thinketh it meete, that at the pronouncinge thereof none be admitted but such onlie as are in Comission and are of necessitie to be present. Herewith her H. hath comaunded me to dispatche this messenger expresselie whom I beseech your Lordship to return with your answer so soone as you maie possiblie, bicause you have such direct comaundment from her Majestie. And so in hast most humblie take my leave. At the Corte, etc., xvth October.

Endorsed [? *Mruulſutre* = ? *Mr. und'ſectre* = ? Mr. Undersecretarie] to my L. Tres.

No. 48

LORD BURGHLEY TO SIR F. WALSINGHAM

[*Burghley*, 16 *October* 1586.]

<small>Dom. Eliz., cxciv. n. 45. Autograph, hastily written, the termination elliptical.</small>

SIR,—Even now I have receaved these included, the lyk wherof I thynk you have. I have answered that by this accident hir Maiesty may se the Inconvenience to have had this commission to be executed so far distant from hir: and for the matter conteaned therin I have shewed how unpossible it is to Conveane vs to gether afor the xxvth, both because it should be an error in law the

---

[1] MS. if.

commissioners being arrived and almost in fact vnpossible to come sonar than on [the] day appoynted. I have gyven hope that the matter will tak a good end, and honorable for such a cause; which wold not vpon .2. only dayes, or rather but vppon 1. day and a half hearyng be also judged. For so we might verefy ye scott: Qu. allegation, that we cam thyther with a preiudgment, and that, as she sayd, it was so reported comenly.

I tak my leave of Mr. vicech[amberlain] and your self, wishyng my self [? with you], seing I cold have nether [? of you] wth me. from my hows at burley, xvi^th Octr. vii^a hor. Yours ass., W. BURGHLEY.

IV.—FATHER CRICHTON'S MEMOIR, 1582-1587

No. 49

DE MISSIONE SCOTICA PUNCTA QUÆDAM NOTANDA HISTORIÆ SOCIETATIS SERVIENDA

[*Chambery*, 1611.]

From codex *Scotia Historica*, 1566-1637, ff. 12-15. A volume in the possession of the Order and made up of reports, memoirs, and other historical pieces. It was put together for or by N. Orlandini, F. Sacchini, and other writers of the *Historia Societatis Jesu*, in six volumes, folio. The volumes covering Fr. Crichton's period, by F. Sacchini, came out in 1661, but I cannot make sure that he has really used this memoir. There is a biography of Father William Crichton in *D.N.B.*, in G. Oliver's *Collectanea*, and in H. Foley's *Records S.J.*, vol. vii. Crichton's Memoir falls into two parts. The first half is a narrative of his own adventures from 1582 to 1587. The second part, which is very short, gives dates for the deeds of his fellow Jesuits during a later period. This part is for the present held over.

Scotia ab anno Christi 203, quo sub Victore summo pontifice suscepit Donaldus Rex Scotiæ et regnum eius fidem catholicam, permansit per successionem continuam octoginta regum constans in fide catholica vsque ad hunc regem qui nunc regnis Angliæ Scotiæ et Hiberniæ dominatur, qui anno primo nativitatis suæ e gremio Reginæ matris suæ ab hereticis ereptus in heresi est educatus, et omni fraude et industria instructus vt fidem catholicam detestaretur, quam instructionem hactenus est amplexatus et secutus.

Anno Christi 1583 [1] R. P. Claudius Aquauiua Generalis Societatis Jesu misit in Scotiam Gulielmum Creittonum sacerdotem eiusdem Societatis Scotum, vt dispiceret quid auxilij posset Societas illi regno iam ab hæreticis occupato adferre, et imprimis vt ageret cum nobilibus a quibus tota vis regni dependet. Cum P. Creitton in Scotiam venit solus fuit inter nobiles (qui sunt consilij Status regni) inuentus constans in religione catholica Dominus lord seu Vicecomes de Seton, qui P. Crittonem libenter hospitio suscepit ac humaniter tractauit. Cœteri omnes tyrannidem eorum qui regnum Gubernabant præsertim Ministrorum hæreticorum predicantium metuentes hæresibus subscripserant. Gubernabat tunc regem adhuc sub tutela viuentem Dux Lenoxiæ regis consanguineus, cum quo existimabat P. Creittonus imprimis tractandum, quippe quod corde nouerat eum esse catholicum, quamuis in exterioribus satisfaciebat Ministris in omnibus.

Post multas difficultates obtinuit P. Crittonus colloquium [2] cum duce; noctu in palatium regis introductus et per biduum in secreto cubiculo absconditus obtinuit a duce vt regem in fide catholica curaret instruj, vel (cum tempore) extra regnum educi, vt posset liberius fidem catholicam amplecti; et hæc sub quibusdam conditionibus tantummodo pecuniarijs et multo minoribus quam videbatur res tanti momenti mereri. Articulos huius rei curauit P. Crittonus confici et manu ducis subsignari, vt rei certa adhiberetur fides, et vt Summus pontifex, qui tunc fuit Gregorius 13 pie memorie non verbis P. Critton sed scriptis ipsius ducis fidem adhiberet.

---

[1] Crichton got his commission in Rome, 23 December 1581. He passed through Paris in February 1582 and reached Scotland before the end of that month, and was received by George, Baron Seton, who died in 1585. It was the next lord who was advanced to the title of Earl of Wintoun.

[2] The interview with Esme Stuart, Seigneur d'Aubigny, and Duke of Lennox, took place at Dalkeith; the articles mentioned below were dated there on the 7th of April. The original, in French, and signed by Lennox, is still preserved in the Vatican Archives (*Inghilterra*, i. f. 219 and 224), printed by I. Kretschmar, *Invasionsprojecte*, Leipzig, 1892, pp. 123-128. Crichton rightly says that the articles stipulated for a subsidy; though he was forgetful when he adds that this was all. A strong body of troops was also bargained for.

His obtentis a duce discessit statim P. Critton et in Galliam traiecit. Vbi Parisios venit dux Guysius, Regis cognatus, Archiepiscopus Glasguensis, P. Tyrius et Scoti existimarunt causam catholicam iam obtinuisse,[1] et effecerunt vt P. Critton summa diligentia Romam ad summum pontificem contenderet, quod fecit. Fuit negotium Pontifici gratissimum, et pollicebatur se omnia subministraturum ; sed rex Hispaniæ voluit huius rei et contributionis pecuniæ esse particeps. Conuentio facta est quantum quis contribueret, et vt deponeretur pecunia in manibus R^{mi} Archiepiscopi Glasguensis Scoti, Parisijs legati Regis Scotiæ apud Regem Galliæ. Stetit summus Pontifex promissis, sed vbi spacio duorum mensium rem confici oportuit procrastinata est in duos annos : interim res detecta est a ministris et nobilibus hæreticis, a quibus rex ereptus est e manibus ducis [2]; qui vix manus hæreticorum et mortem euasit, et in Galliam aufugiens in itinere Londinj datum fuit ei venenum (vt fertur) et vbi Parisios venit, post paucos dies e vita migrauit, et sic tota illa spes et negotiatio concidit.

Anno postea 1585 [3] missus est in Scotiam P. Iacobus Gordon vna cum patre Critton, sed inter nauigandum capta est nauis ab holandis hæreticis rebellibus a suo Rege, qui cum bellum non haberent cum Scotis, nauis demissa est libera, sed a mercatore qui nauem conduxerat detecti sunt P. Gordon et P. Critton et accusati tanquam

---

[1] The meetings in Paris took place in April 1582, and Crichton reached Rome early in June Crichton's memory is again faulty in regard to King Philip's action It was the Pope who urged acceptance Philip, his hands full with the war in Portugal, would not accept till his fleet was free. It did not return till after the Raid of Ruthven

[2] The Raid of Ruthven took place 23 August 1582 Lennox then retired to Paris and died 26 May 1583. The plan, which fell to the ground in August 1582, was revived in a modified form when James recovered his liberty in July 1583 Spain soon after definitely refused to act, the exiles, however, continued to hope that she would till 1584 This is what Crichton means by ' procrastinata est in duos annos '

[3] Fathers James Gordon and Crichton left Paris early in August 1584 Patrick Ady, who was imprisoned with Crichton in the Tower and tortured there (Hart, *Diarium Turris*, p 361), seems also to have been set free with him in May 1587.

hostes suæ sectæ in Scotia, et propterea ab holandis detenti, sed mercator timens ne a Comite Huntleo nepote patris Gordonj occideretur, ob detectum et accusatum eius patruum curauit vt liberaretur P. Gordonus et in eius locum substitueretur dominus Ady sacerdos secularis in Scotiam proficiscens, qui vna cum patre Critton ductus est Ostendam, vbi cognitus P. Critton esse Societatis Iesu addictus fuit morti ob necem principis Auriaci, quem dicebant interfectum consilio Iesuitarum, et ideo omnes Iesuitas qui in eorum manus inciderent esse suspendendos,[1] et in hunc finem fuit furca erecta ad P. Critton suspendendum. Interim tractabatur in Anglia fœdus inter holandos et Reginam Angliæ, quæ quidem intelligens p. Crittonem captiuum esse Ostendæ, petijt ab ijs qui fœdus tractabant eum sibi donari, et misit nauem expressam qui [*sic*] eum in Angliam deduceret; et sic fuit P. Crittonus dono datus Reginæ Angliæ, et ita euasit crucem sibi Ostendæ præparatam.

Sistitur [2] coram consilio in Anglia, petunt qui vocetur; respondit se vocari Gulielmum Critton, se esse Scotum, catholicum, sacerdotem, Iesuitam, 'si hæc' (inquit) 'sunt crimina,' non opus est multis interrogationibus vt ea fateatur, se nihil commisisse contra Reginam aut regnum Angliæ, si quid sit in quo esset accusandus, vt eum in Scotiam ad suum regem remitterent iudicandum, Anglis enim non erat subiectus, nec propria voluntate venit in Angliam. Responderunt se habere in quo eum accusarent, Et proferunt litteras quasdam eius interceptas, in quibus continebatur se quorumdam catholicorum confessiones audiuisse Lugdunj, et inter ceteros Dñi Thomæ Arundel, cognati Reginæ, Ostendunt ei litteras; petunt num agnosceret illos caractheres: subito ei in mentem venit nec fateri nec negare cognitionem caractherum. Respondit igitur se non posse discernere vere inter illos caractheres

---

[1] The Prince of Orange had been assassinated 30 June/10 July 1584. For the cruelties in England consequent on his murder, see *Introduction*, p. xxiv.

[2] Crichton's examinations in *Dom. Eliz.*, clxxiii. nos. 2, 3, 4, are dated 3 and 4 September 1584, printed from other sources in Knox, *Letters of Cardinal Allen*, pp. 425-434.

et suos; sed quia alias per confictos caractheres fuit deceptus Lugdunj cum amissione 40 aureorum se nolle facile fidere caractheribus. Respondent; 'si vis ignorare caractheres, non potes ignorare sensum litterarum; lege.' Legit et videns rem vergi in dispendium nobilium respondit, caractheres non confingi nisi vt tegatur, et artificiosius fungatur materia; iam duos annos elapsos esse a data litterarum, et ideo se non habere memoriam rerum ad se parum pertinentium. Responderunt; 'tu putas euadere, sed te habebimus.' Dimiserunt illum in cubiculum et conficiunt plurimas cautelosas interrogationes, quas mittunt ad eum per subsecretarium, quibus scripto ei erat respondendum. Subsecretarius hic habebat patruum in Societate P. Laurentium Fant[1]: prima igitur eius verba ad P. Critton fuerunt; ' Vix,' inquit, 'poteris euadere inconueniens in tuis responsionibus, sed iuues me apud patruum meum Iesuitam, vt mihi cedat bona sua, et ego te iuvabo vt respondeas omnibus his articulis sine vllo tuo præiudicio': et sic fecit. Putabat igitur P. Critton se tunc demittendum; sed e domo Dñi Valsingam secreto missus est ad carcerem in turri Londinensj.

Agebatur tunc temporis a Regina et consilio Anglicano de Regina Scotiæ morte plectenda, pro cuius defensione missus fuit a Rege Scotiæ eius filio Dñs Grayus Scotus,[2]

---

[1] There is a letter from 'Nicholas Fante' in *Dom. Eliz.*, clxxiii. n. 14, in which he reports to Walsingham his version of Crichton's conversation. He professes to disparage him, and dwells on weak points. The letter, however, is not at all inconsistent with Crichton's story of ministerialist dishonesty, so characteristic of Elizabeth's reign. Father Arthur Lawrence Faunt, born at Foston, Leicester, was of Merton College, Oxford; then of Louvain, then of Munich, and Rome, afterwards Rector of various colleges in Poland (Foley, *Records S.J.*, vii. p. 247). Both Faunts are mentioned in *D.N.B.*

[2] Queen Mary wrote, 9 November 1584, to Sir F. Englefield at Madrid: 'My son ... is about to dispatch ... Gray to the Court of England, and I hope to God they will allow him to speak to me.' On 7 February Mendoza writes: 'Mr. Gray ... has returned, having given little satisfaction to the English Catholics, and the adherents of the Queen of Scots' (*Spanish Calendar*, pp. 529, 531). Englefield's letter in English, dated 5 January 1585, is in *Caligula*, C. viii. (decipher), and Harl. MSS. 4651, fol. 212, a copy.

cui misit Regina captiua instructiones inter quas fuit articulus vt de liberatione patris Critton ageret, quj eum reddidit suspectum de intelligentia cum regina. Huic dño Grayo scripsit ex carcere litteras P. Critton,[1] quem summum putabat amicum, sed fuit proditor et Reginæ et patris Critton; nam reginæ instruciones et litteras Crittonj ostendit Reginæ Angliæ et eius consilio, dicebatur quoque in mortem Reginæ Dñæ suæ consensisse;[2] sed cum litteræ Crittonij nil continerent vnde possent eum accusare, tamen accusabatur quod per litteras scripserit et per litteras cum alijs communicauerit, quod captiuis negabatur.

Volebant[3] Crittonem e medio tollere, vt esset [dispositio][4] ad mortem Reginæ, quæ paulo postea secuta est. Quare accusarunt eum tanquam conscium et consentientem in mortem Reginæ Angliæ per conspirationem D. Caroli Paget, qui in Angliam venit et nobiles subornarat, vt cum eo in mortem reginæ Elizabethæ insurgerent. Et quamuis conspiratio hæc facta fuerit Parisijs, et P. Critton Lugduni tunc maneret, habitus est tamen particeps conspiracionis, et die lunæ proximo debebat condemnari. Interim die sabbati[5] diem illum præcedente captus est D. Gulielmus

---

[1] There is a good deal of illustrative matter in *Foreign Calendar*, 1584-1585, and *Cath. Rec. Soc.*, xxi. n. 20. Hence it appears that Walsingham, warned by Gray, examined Crichton about his letter-carriers, but Crichton declined to commit himself or them, and afterwards transmitted an account of his answers to the Archbishop of Glasgow at Paris. But this was seen by a spy (? Bruce), who reported it fully to the English ambassador, who passed this round to Walsingham again (1 March 1585). Berden was then set to watch Crichton, and (6 April) sent in many details about Crichton's intermediaries. From Berden we learn that Crichton was at first in the Martin Tower (which still stands at the N.E. angle of the ballium); he was afterwards in Coldharbour (on the site of the modern guard-room).

[2] Gray consented to Mary's death, but not on this embassy.

[3] The trial of Crichton, as to which he is not likely to have been mistaken, appears to be hitherto unknown. Perhaps it was abandoned without any legal settlement.

[4] 'Dispositio,' in MS. dispo°. The death of Mary was, in reality, a year later than Crichton's trial. The *conspiratio* here described seems to be that attributed to Francis Throckmorton, who was executed 10 July 1584. Neither he, nor as yet Paget, intended Elizabeth's death.

[5] The true date of Parry's arrest was Monday, 8 February 1585 (Holinshed, *Chronicles*, iv. 562).

Parry Anglus doctor Iuris, nobilis, ob conspirationem in mortem Reginæ, qui P. Crittonem purgauit et e morte liberauit.

Is enim agentem et exploratorem agebat Venetijs pro Regina Angliæ, cum tamen esset catholicus et contra catholicos inseruiret hæreticis: pecunia ductus[1] promisit se interfecturum Reginam, et ita satisfactionem facturum malorum quæ perpetrauit contra Catholicos, quos hoc facto putabat se liberaturum a persecutione hæreticorum, et Reginam Scotiæ captiuam catholicam in regnum successuram. Vt hoc exequeretur Venetijs venit Lugdunum, vbi P. Crittonem consuluit, an hoc tuta conscientia posset facere. Respondit P. Critton quod non; 'quia, vt quis occidat, duo debent concurrere, causa et potestas'; causam posset habere, sed potestatem non habet, cum sit vir particularis. Respondit se id posse facere propter ingentia bona quæ sequerentur. Respondit P. Critton, ad hoc respondere D. Paulum, *non facienda mala vt veniant bona*. At ille; 'non est' (inquit) 'facere malum, sed bonum': respondit P. Critton, esse sophisma; posse quidem esse bonum in effectu, sed non in modo; vnde ait Sanctus Augustinus Deum magis amare aduerbia quam nomina, quia bonum non amat nisi bene fiat: bonum est occidere latronem, sed si sine potestate, peccatum est. Addidit ille; 'licet occidere tyrannum.' Respondit P. Critton; 'Nec tyrannum quidem, sine potestate legitima.' Replicat ille; 'Papa factum haberet ratum et gratum.' Respondit Critton; 'Hoc verum esse potest, sed erras in quæstione: Quæstio enim est, an sub spe ratihabitionis papæ, possis occidere?: dico quod non.' Petijt; 'Quis mihi potest potestatem dare?' Respondit Critton;

---

[1] The story of Parry, drawn from first-hand evidence, is in the *Introduction*, § 1, 5. Here Crichton is reporting from prejudiced stories heard in the Tower. There seems no ground to believe that he was *bribed* to dirk Elizabeth, or that he would have done so if he had had his dagger by him. On the other hand, Crichton's account of the interview at Lyons shows in Parry all the characteristics of a *provocateur*. Crichton, 20 Feb. 1585, wrote to Walsingham, giving an account of the meeting, which agrees well enough with this, except as to the last clause. (Holinshed, as *above*.)

'Papa, qui potest infectam pecudem e grege separare.' Iuit igitur Parisios et mediante Nuntio Apostolico R^{mo} Episcopo Bergamotensi obtinuit licentiam[1] signatam manu et sigillo Ill^{mi} Cardinalis Comensis, Secretarij Gregorij 13, quam secum tulit in Angliam. Conuenit Reginam, cui persuasit vt in remotum cubiculum se reciperet et eum audiret; et ita factum est, sed cum manum admoueret ad pugionem percepit eum pugionem in cubiculo suo relinquisse, quem si habuisset certo Reginam confodisset. Postea, similem non inueniens occasionem, rem suo cognato[2] detexit; is rem Reginæ aperuit, vnde captus est, et in carcere dum examinaretur dixit se omnia declaraturum, modo non torqueretur, se non petere vllam gratiam, morte se dignum iudicans. Petitum est ab eo num Crittonem nosceret, et num eius consilij fuerit conscius. Respondit et declarauit, omnes eius petitiones et responsiones superscriptas Patris Critton, et consilia P. Critton semper sibi hæsisse in mente, ne occideret Reginam. Sic ille mortem subijt, et ab ea Crittonem liberauit.

Habuit P. Critton commoditatem in carcere quotidie dicendi missam et singulis diebus dominicis audiendj confessiones et communicandi plures nobiles captiuos, qui per ingeniosam aperitionem ostiorum aut pauimentorum cubiculorum noctu poterant conuenire, non sine ingenti consolatione nobilium.[3] Cum Dñs de Chasteauneuf legatione pro Rege Franciæ fungeretur in Anglia et per falsos testes

---

[1] Crichton is again in error when he calls the cardinal's letter a licence to kill. There is nothing at all about killing in it. It was an indulgence for performing some good work not specified. In view, however, of the whole correspondence, there is no doubt that the cardinal was here badly infected by the 'ban' epidemic, which was at its height. Parry, when the letter came (he did not bring it with him), at once sent it in to Elizabeth, and was well rewarded for his cleverness (Holinshed, iv. 568). The Cardinal's letter is among the Lansdowne MSS., and has been often printed.

[2] Edmund Neville, who claimed to be Lord Latimer. They called each other 'cousin,' but in what degree is uncertain.

[3] Much information on this subject may be found in *Cath. Rec. Soc.*, xxi.; also in Morris, *Troubles*, ii. 195, etc.

accusaretur de conspiratione contra vitam Reginæ, misit Dñm de trapes eques [*sic*] expedite in Galliam, vt Regem suum de re tota informaret. Sed captus est in itinere, et fassiculus litterarum et informationes ad Regem missæ, et in carcerem coniectus prope patrem Crittonem, ad quem scripsit legatus rogans vt litteras quas misit curaret dari Dño de trappes, et responsum quam primum haberi. Effecit P. Critton vt eodem die darentur et responsum haberetur, quamuis ipsemet locumtenens Reginæ nunquam claues cubiculj vbi D. de trappes custodiebatur e manibus deponeret, et hoc per famulum quemdam ipsius locumtenentis, responsumque misit ad legatum, qui celeri nuntio admonuit suum Regem, qui curauit legatum extraordinarium quem misit Regina Angliæ Parisijs [1] detineri captiuum sine audientia, donec de trappes liberaretur et Parisios veniret pro defensione sui legati, ob quod obsequium legatus misit P. Crittono eleemosinam plurium aureorum, eique gratias egit quasi honori et vitæ suæ consuluisset.

Sed supra omnia obsequia quæ in hac vita fecit P. Critton pro seruitio diuino illud existimauit primum et præcipuum, quod multorum nobilium Anglorum vitas saluauerit. Inierunt consilium catholici quidam Angli liberandi Reginam Scotiæ catholicam e carcere et restituendi religionem catholicam; cuius consilij Regina Angliæ et eius consilium non fuerunt ignari, imo huius consilij habebantur inuentores et instigatores, et immiserunt catholicum furtim, qui feruentius cœteris rem urgeret,[2] vt ita caperentur catholicj, et inter eos fuit sacerdos dictus Joannes Balard, vir bonus et sincerus, qui totum

---

[1] The arrest of des Trappes was the result of the so-called plot of Moody and Stafford, perhaps the most disgraceful of all the ministerial malpractices of this period. The French ambassador describes the arrest and the dispatch of Waade, 28 January, and repeats it, 7 February 1587. He reports on 17 June that Waade had 'at length' had his audience, and had apologised in the Queen's name for this 'pure calumny' (*Scottish Calendar*, ix. pp. 249, 267, 445). These intercepted letters are in the British Museum; but being without references, I have found only one of the originals.

[2] The parts of Gilbert Gifford and of Pooley are here blended.

regnum circumijt et plurimos nobiles comites vicecomites seu lords et Barones in eam sententiam induxit, sed nunquam ei suam mentem aperuerunt nisi in confessione sacramentali. Proditor nomine **Pouly** numerum aliquem horum catholicorum vocauit ad cœnam et Reginam admonuit, qui in eius cubiculo capti sunt et in vincula coniecti, et inter eos Joannes Balard sacerdos, cui promisit Regina et consilium honores et vitam si omnes detegeret, factum non poterat negare, complices enim eius tulerunt contra eum testimonium. Promisit miser se omnes detecturum, quod erat facturus.

Interim confluunt omnes catholici Londinum qui in confessione tantum mentem Balardo aperuerant trepidi, nescientes an fuga vitæ consulerent, an manerent confisi constantia D. Balard ne proderet sigillum confessionis. Interim scribunt ad P. Crittonum, sub cuius cubiculo fuit in carcere Balard, vt intelligeret quosnam accusauerit Balard, qui ne cum vllo communicaret duos habebat inclusos custodes, qui noctu dieque vigilarent ne per litteras aut verbo cum vllo haberet communicationem. P. Critton aliud non inueniens remedium, curauit fieri fissuram paruam supra sellam vbi D. Ballard exonerabat aluum, et per eam reliquit cadere super genua Ballard dum super sellam sederet folium subtile [1] obductum colore qui expungi poterat, in quo scripsit et petijt quomodo valeret et in quo ei poterat prodesse. Accepit folium et deleto colore rescripsit se confessum multa digna morte, sed Reginam et consilium ei vitam et multa promissos, si omnes detegeret qui ei sunt confessi, et quia vita ei erat chara, ideo vt ei condonarent si omnes detegeret,[2] quamuis ei fuisset durum comites et alios nobiles accusare. Ascendit postea super sellam et per eandem fissuram porrigit P. Critton illud folium. Subito Critton delens quæ scripsit ille, rescripsit accusans eum de scelere hoc et infamia, et

---

[1] A sheet of vellum or paper, rubbed over with ashes or dust, and on which letters could be traced with the finger, would perhaps suit the circumstances here narrated.

[2] The reading is clear, but the sense required 'se omnes detecturum.'

quia ita non saluaret vitam temporalem et amitteret æternam. Accepta hac P. Crittonj admonitione ei gratias egit et iussit vt admoneret omnes qui ei erant confessi se nunquam manifestaturum quempiam eorum ob vlla tormenta huius vitæ, et se malle millies mori quam hoc facere, et se ex animo pœnitere quod vllos detexerit, et eos quos detexit nominauit. Passus est postea sæpius grauissima tormenta, sed perstitit constans et passus [est] mortem crudelem cum 14 juuenibus nobilissimis in vigilia et die Sancti Matthei 1587 [*sic* for 1586].

[*From margin.*] Diligentiam qua vsi sunt multi pro liberatione P. Critonj multum ei obfuit. Missus enim fuit nobilis e Scotia in hunc finem. Missus fuit Parisijs pastor Sancti Germanj doctor sorbonicus. Archiepiscopus Lugduncnsis tunc preses consilij regij curauit litteras Regis sui frequentes ad Reginam et Consilium Angliæ, quæ omnia persuaserunt P. Crittonum virum esse magni momenti, et ideo ne ejs posset imposterum nocere, expedire vt moreretur. Quare vt eum caperent, fingunt Reginam ei libertatem concessisse, et propterea vt litteras daret ad reginam quibus ei gratias ageret. Has litteras habuit P. Critton suspectas, quare cauit ne quid in eis esset quod ipsi posset nocere. Cum secretarius litteras vidit et nil tale esse, quod voluit ille, remisit litteras rogans P. Crittonum hæc verba adijcere: 'Et quamuis iure potuerit Vestra Maiestas mihi vitam adimere, placuit tamen eius clementiæ mihi omnia condonare.' Renuit P. Critton allegans prouerbium: 'Turdus sibi malum creat'; quia ex eius stercore fit viscus quo capitur: se nolle turdum imitari.

Egit tandem P. Critton per litteras cum D. Christophoro Haton consiliario et omnium familiarissimo Reginæ, quem sciuit corde esse catholicum, eius humori se accommodans; qui ei a Regina libertatem obtinuit et humanissime tractauit: quare, cum ad aulam et suam domum vocarat, petijt a P. Crittono quid de eo sentirent principes et viri catholici, respondit eos idem de eo sentire quod sentiunt mathematici de motu orbium cælestium, quj cum motum habeant naturalem ab occidente in orientem rapiuntur tamen a primo mobili, motu raptus in occidentem. Ille, vt fuit doctus, statim intellexit P. Crittonum velle dicere quod amplectatur heresim, vt placeret Reginæ ; et protulit crumenam, et dedit P. Crittono 20 Angelotos [1] ac dimisit.

[*TRANSLATION. Some dates are introduced in square brackets ; * denotes that a note will be found here in the latin text.*]

Of the Scottish Mission: Certain Points to be Noted to Serve for the History of the Society

Scotland, from the year of Christ 203, when under Pope Victor the Scottish King Donald and his realm embraced the Catholic faith, has through an unbroken succession of eighty sovereigns remained constant to the same faith up to the present king, who now rules over the kingdoms of England, Scotland, and Ireland. He, snatched by the heretics in the first year after his birth from the bosom of the Queen his mother, was brought up in heresy and taught by every fraudulent device to hold the Catholic faith in abhorrence, which teaching he has till now accepted and obeyed.

In the year of our Lord 1583 [1582]* the Rev. Father Claudio Aquaviva, General of the Society of Jesus, sent into Scotland William Crichton, a Scottish priest of the same Society, to find out what help the Society could afford to that realm then already occupied by the heretics, and especially to deal with the nobility, from whom all the power of the kingdom is derived. When Fr. Crichton came to Scotland, among the nobles, who form the council of their state, the only one found steadfast in the Catholic faith was my lord the Lord or Viscount Seton, who gladly received Fr. Crichton as his guest and treated him with courtesy : all the others, going in fear of the tyranny of those who ruled the kingdom, and especially of the ranting heretic ministers, had made their submission to heresy. Acting then as guardian of the king, who was still in a state of pupilage, was his kinsman the Duke of Lennox, with whom Fr. Crichton deemed it necessary in the first place to deal, inasmuch as he knew that Lennox was at heart a Catholic, though in all external matters it was his wont to humour the ministers.

After many hindrances Fr. Crichton gained an audience [Dalkeith, 7 April 1582]* with the Duke ; for, after being smuggled in by night into the royal palace and lying hid for two days in a secret chamber, he got from the Duke a promise that he would see either that the king should be instructed in the Catholic faith, or should after a time be taken out of the kingdom, so that he might be at greater liberty to

---

[1] The 'angel' (French *angelot*, a diminutive) was at first 6s. 8d., and rose to 10s. before it ceased to be coined by Charles I.

embrace the faith—and this merely on certain money considerations, much smaller than the importance of the matter would seem to warrant. Fr. Crichton took care to have the details of this agreement drawn up, and witnessed with the Duke's signature, so that absolute reliance might be placed on the scheme, and the supreme Pontiff (who at that time was Gregory XIII. of blessed memory) might ground his trust not on the words of Fr. Crichton, but on the Duke's own handwriting.

With this concession from the Duke Fr. Crichton departed at once and crossed over to France. When Crichton got to Paris [April 1582]* the Duke of Guise (cousin to the king), the Archbishop of Glasgow, Father Tyrie, and all Scotsmen were convinced that the Father had made good the Catholic cause, and caused Fr. Crichton to hasten away with all speed to the Pope at Rome, which he did. The project was most acceptable to the Pontiff, and he promised to back it in every possible way; but the King of Spain wanted to have a finger in the matter and to contribute to the funds. An agreement was made as to the amount each was to contribute, and for the money to be entrusted to the hands of the Most Reverend Archbishop of Glasgow, a Scotsman, ambassador at Paris to the French king for the King of Scotland. The sovereign Pontiff was true to his word, but whereas the affair ought to have been concluded within the space of two months, it dragged on for two years: in the meantime it was discovered by the heretic ministers and nobles, by whom the king was wrested from the custody of the Duke of Lennox [23 August 1582]*. He barely escaped death at the hands of the sectaries, and fleeing away to France, in the course of his journey (as is reported) poison was administered to him at London; a few days after his arrival at Paris he passed from this life [26 May 1583]*—and so all the hope that centred in that scheme came to naught.

In the following year, to wit 1585 [August 1584]*, Fr. James Gordon was sent into Scotland along with Fr. Crichton, but on the voyage their ship was captured by the heretic Hollanders, who were up in arms against their king. As they were not at war with the Scots, the ship was freed from embargo; but, as Fr. Gordon and Fr. Crichton were recognised by the merchant who had chartered the ship, and accused of being enemies of his sect in Scotland, they were for that reason kept in durance by the Hollanders. The merchant, however, fearing lest he should be slain by the Earl of Huntly, Fr. Gordon's nephew, for his spying accusations against the uncle, took care that Fr. Gordon should go free, and that in his room should be substituted Master Ady, a secular priest, who was on his way to Scotland. So Ady, along with Fr. Crichton, was taken to Ostend. Here Fr. Crichton, being known to belong to the Society of Jesus, was condemned to death on account of the assassination of the Prince of Orange, who they declared had been slain by the machinations of the Jesuits, and that therefore all Jesuits who fell into their hands were to be hanged, and to that end a gallows had been erected on which Fr.

Crichton was to be hanged. In the meantime there was being negotiated in England a treaty between the Hollanders and the Queen of England, and she, learning that Fr. Crichton was a prisoner at Ostend, asked of those who were arranging the treaty, that he should be handed over to her, and sent a ship expressly to carry him off to England. So Fr. Crichton was made a gift to the English Queen, and thus escaped the gibbet prepared for him at Ostend.

He is brought before the (Privy) Council in England [Sept. 1584]*; they ask him by what name he is called; he answered that he is called William Crichton, that he is a Scotsman, a catholic, a priest and a Jesuit, 'If these things,' quoth he, 'are crimes,' that there was no need of many questions to make him confess them; that he had done nothing against the Queen and realm of England; that, if there was anything for which he was to be accused, they should send him back to Scotland to his own Sovereign to be tried, that he was not subject to the English, nor had come of his own accord to England. They answered that they had grounds of accusation against him, and they produce certain letters of his that had been intercepted. In the course of which letters it appeared that at Lyons he had heard the confessions of certain catholics, and among them that of Mr. Thomas Arundell, a kinsman of the Queen. They show him the letters and ask him if he recognises the handwriting. It suddenly occurred to him neither to acknowledge nor to deny recognition of the handwriting. So he answered that he could not be quite sure as to the difference between that handwriting and his own; for inasmuch as on another occasion at Lyons he had been deceived by a forged script with a loss of 40 gold pieces, he did not like to be over-confident as to handwriting. They reply, 'If it's your whim not to know the hand, you cannot but acknowledge the drift of the letter; read.' He read, and seeing that the matter tended to the undoing of the gentlemen, he replied that the characters had been formed for no other end than that the matter might be kept secret and more craftily performed; that two years had gone by since the date of the letters, and so he had no recollection about matters that had so little reference to himself. They made answer, 'You hope to go scot-free, but we will catch you.' They sent him back to his room, and drew up several crafty questions, to which he had to answer in writing, and these they sent to him through an under-secretary. This under-secretary [Nicholas Faunt]* had an uncle in the Society, Fr. Laurence Faunt: and so his first words to Fr. Crichton were, 'Hardly' quoth he, 'will you be able to avoid trouble in your replies; but do you befriend me with my uncle the Jesuit, so that he bequeath his possessions to me, and I will help you to answer all these articles without any hurt to yourself'; and so he did. Then Fr. Crichton thought that he was now going to be released, but from Master Walsingham's house he was secretly dispatched to prison in the Tower of London [16 September 1585].

At that time efforts were being made by the Queen and Council of England to put to death the Queen of Scots, for whose defence the

Master of Gray, a Scotsman, had been sent by her son, the Scottish king [November] *. To Gray the captive Queen sent instructions, among which was a clause that he should treat for the liberation of Fr Crichton, which caused Crichton to be suspected of holding communication with Mary. Fr. Crichton wrote from prison a letter to the Master of Gray *, whom he deemed a very trusty friend, but Gray proved false both to the Queen and to Fr. Crichton; for he showed Mary's instructions and Crichton's letter to the Queen of England and her Council. Gray was also said to have been a consenting party to the death of the Queen his Sovereign *. However, although Crichton's letter contained nothing which they could bring as a charge against him, yet was he accused of writing letters and of communicating with others by letter (a thing forbidden to prisoners)

They wished to remove Fr. Crichton, so that he might be a [preparative] for the death of the [Scottish] Queen, which shortly after ensued. And so they accused him of having a knowledge of and consenting to the murder of the English Queen by the plot * of Mr. Charles Paget, who came to England and had instigated the gentry to rise with him to compass the death of Queen Elizabeth [1584]. Although this plot was hatched at Paris, and Fr. Crichton was then staying at Lyons, yet was he judged a party to the scheme and was to be condemned on the following Monday: meanwhile on the Saturday preceding Dr. William Parry, an English gentleman and doctor of law, was seized * on account of his conspiracy against the life of the Queen; and he cleared Fr. Crichton and saved him from death.

For Parry was acting at Venice as agent and spy for the Queen of England, and although a catholic was serving heretics against catholics: won over by money, he promised to murder the English Queen * and so [hoped] to atone for the wrongs he had done to catholics, whom by this enterprise he thought that he would free from persecution at the hands of heretics, and that the captive Queen of Scots, a catholic, would succeed to the kingdom. In pursuit of this project he came from Venice to Lyons, where he asked counsel of Fr. Crichton whether he could do this with a safe conscience. Fr Crichton answered that he could not, 'Because, that one may put to death, two things must concur, a [good] cause and [legitimate] power; that perhaps Parry had a [good] cause, but that he had not [legitimate] power, as he was only a private individual Parry replied that he might do it on account of the immense good that would follow. Fr. Crichton replied that St Paul's answer to this was, *Evil is not to be done that good may ensue.* But Parry said, 'That is not to do evil, but good.' Fr. Crichton replied that this was a sophism; that it might be good in effect, but not in the manner, wherefore says St. Augustine that God loves adverbs rather than nouns, because He loves not the good unless it be done well. It is good to slay a robber, but (if done) without [legitimate] power, it is a sin. Parry went on, 'It is lawful to kill a tyrant' Fr Crichton answered, 'Not even a tyrant without lawful authority' He retorts, 'The Pope would hold the deed as rightly and kindly done.' Crichton answers, 'This can be true, but you are wrong in the [preliminary] question. For the question is whether you can kill in the hope of ratification by the Pope. I say you cannot.' He asked, 'Who can give me this power?' Crichton answered, 'The Pope, who can separate an infected sheep from the flock.'

Parry went to Paris, and by means of the Apostolic nuncio, the Most Rev. Bp. of Bergamo, he obtained a licence signed and sealed by the Cardinal of Como, secretary of Pope Gregory xiii., which he took with him into England*. He met the Queen and persuaded her to betake herself into a remote room to give him audience. So it was done, but when he moved his hand to his dagger, he perceived he had left it in his room; if he had had it, he would certainly have stabbed the Queen. Not finding a similar occasion afterwards he opened the matter to his relative [Neville]*, and he to the Queen. So Parry was captured, and while he was examined in prison, he said he would declare all, if only he was not tortured; he would not ask for any favour, judging himself worthy of death. He was asked whether he knew Crichton, and whether he [*i.e.* Crichton] was aware of his plot. In answer he declared all his questions and the answers of Fr. Crichton noted above, and that Crichton's counsel against killing the Queen always stuck in his mind. So he suffered death, and from it freed Fr. Crichton.

In his prison Fr. Crichton had the opportunity every day of saying mass, and every Sunday of hearing the confessions of many prisoners of gentle birth, and of giving them communion. By the ingenious opening of doors, and [? lifting] of paving stones in the cells, they were able to meet at night, not without their intense consolation*.

When M. de Chateauneuf, ambassador in England for the King of France, was accused by false witnesses of conspiracy against the life of the Queen, he sent M. des Trappes to France, riding express, to inform his King of the whole affair. But he was made prisoner *en route*, with his packet of letters, and informations for the King, and he was thrown into a prison cell close by Fr. Crichton. The ambassador wrote to him, begging that he would take care that the letters he sent should be given to M. des Trappes, and an answer obtained as soon as possible. Fr. Crichton caused the letter to be delivered the same day and an answer to be obtained, although the Queen's Lieutenant [of the Tower] never let out of his hands the keys of the cell, where M. des Trappes was guarded: and this was done through a servant of the Lieutenant himself. Crichton sent the answer to the ambassador, who sent a messenger post-haste to warn his sovereign, who in turn took good care that the ambassador extraordinary [Sir William Waade]*, whom the Queen of England had sent to Paris, should be held captive without audience, until des Trappes should be freed, and came there to defend de Chateauneuf. For this service the ambassador sent to Fr. Crichton a large alms in gold, and thanked him, as though he had been the protector of his honour and of his life.

But above all other services which Fr. Crichton did in this life for God's cause, he thought that the first and the chief was that he saved the lives of many English lords [and gentlemen]. Some English Catholics had made a plan for liberating the Catholic Queen of Scotland from prison, and of restoring the Catholic religion. Of this plan the English Queen and her Council were not ignorant: indeed, they were held to be its inventors and instigators. They stealthily introduced a Catholic, who should urge the affair, with special fervour, and so deceive the Catholics*. Amongst these was a priest called John Ballard, a good and sincere man, who went round the whole kingdom and induced very many nobles—earls, viscounts, or Lords and Barons—to [favour] this opinion [project], though they never spoke their minds except in sacramental confession. The traitor, by name Poley, had invited a number of these Catholics to supper, and informed the Queen; so that they were taken in his rooms and cast into prison, and amongst them this priest John Ballard. The Queen and the Council promised him life and honours if he would betray all. He could not deny the fact, for his accomplices had given testimony against him. So the poor wretch promised to betray all, and this he was about to do.

Meantime those who had spoken to Ballard in confession only, flocked to London, not knowing whether they should protect their lives by flight, or remain trusting to the constancy with which Mr. Ballard would maintain the seal of confession. Meanwhile they write to Fr. Crichton, because Ballard was in the cell under his, begging him to let them know whom the English priest had accused. Now there were two warders locked up with him, who were on the watch night and day to prevent any one communicating with him by word or letter. Fr. Crichton therefore not finding any other means, carefully made a small cleft over the closet which Ballard used, and let slip through it a thin leaf covered with coloured matter, which could be brushed off. On this he wrote asking how he was, and how he could help him. Ballard, having rubbed the colouring matter, wrote back that he had confessed many things worthy of death, but that the Queen and Council had promised him life and many other things if he would but reveal all those who had been to confession to him. So, as life was dear to him, he hoped that all whom he named would forgive him, hard though he found it to accuse the earls and others. Then standing on the seat he handed back the leaf through the cleft. Crichton immediately rubbed out what he had written, and answered accusing him of crime and infamy: that he would not save temporal life, and would lose life eternal. Having received this admonition from Fr. Crichton, he returned him thanks, and told him to inform all his penitents, that he would never reveal one of them for any torments in this life; and that he would rather die a thousand times than do so: that he regretted from his heart that he had named any, and he mentioned their names. He afterwards suffered the most grievous tortures, but stood firm and constant, and underwent a cruel death with fourteen other young gentlemen of family on the vigil and on the feast of St. Matthew [20, 21 September 1586].

The diligence which was used by many for his liberation did Fr. Crichton much harm. One of noble house was sent from Scotland for this purpose; from Paris was sent the Curé of St. Germain, a doctor of the Sorbonne[1]; the Archbishop of Lyons, then president of the Royal Council, took care that a number of Royal letters should be dispatched to the Queen and Council of England: but all this persuaded them that Fr. Crichton was a man of great importance, and so, lest he should be able to injure them at some future time, it was expedient that he should die. Wherefore, in order to entrap him, they pretend that the Queen has granted him liberty, 'so let him write a letter to the Queen, and return her thanks.' Fr. Crichton being suspicious of these letters, took care lest there should be anything in them which might do him injury. When the Secretary saw the letter and that it was not such as he desired, he sent it back, asking Fr. Crichton to add these words, 'and though your Majesty might by rights take away my life, yet it has pleased your clemency to pardon me everything.' Fr. Crichton demurred, quoting the proverb, 'The thrush makes ill for itself,' *i.e.* because from its dung is made the bird-lime by which it is caught.

Fr. Crichton dealt by letter with Sir Christopher Hatton, the councillor, and the most familiar of all with the Queen. He knew him to be a Catholic at heart, and he accommodated himself to his humour. Hatton obtained liberty for him from the Queen, and used him with very great humanity. He asked Crichton what princes and Catholics thought about himself. Crichton answered that they felt about him, what mathematicians think about the motion of the heavenly bodies. They have a natural motion from west to east, but still they are drawn by the primum mobile, and carried by motion to the west. Being a learned man, he at once understood that Crichton would have liked to say, that he had embraced heresy to please the Queen; and taking out his purse he gave him 20 angels [about £10] and let him go. [? May 1587.]

---

[1] Fr. Alexandre Georges, S.J., wrote to Rome, 22 June 1586, that M. de Cueilly, of the Sorbonne, had taken the King's letter to the ambassador in London, and that he had interceded with much effect. Elizabeth had commended Crichton and promised his release. 'I pray God this may not be hindered by her dishonest ministers.' Jesuit MSS. *Galliæ Epistolæ*, xv. 42.

APPENDIX

GEORGE GIFFORD'S PLOT, 1583-1586

George Gifford's plot was so intimately connected with that of Babington, that it seems worth while to give all the accessible documents about it in calendar form. Documents *A, C, D* will be found conveniently printed in T. F. Knox, *Letters of Cardinal Allen*, 1882, pp. xlviii, 412, 413, 414; also in Kretschmar, *Invasionsprojekte der katholischen Mächte gegen England*, Leipzig, 1892, Nos. 24, 25. The Spanish documents *B, E, F* are in A. Teulet, *Relations Politiques*, v 276, and *Spanish Calendar*, pp. 464, 479. Pieces *H* to *M* are unpublished.

A. THE NUNCIO CASTELLI TO THE CARDINAL OF COMO

[*Paris, 2 May* 1583.]

The Dukes of Guise and of Maine tell me that they have a plan (*maneggio*) for killing the Queen of England. One of her household who conceals his catholicism, hates the Queen because she has executed some of his relations He made proposals to the Queen of Scotland, who would not listen to them. He was sent here, and it has been agreed that the Duke of Guise shall give him a bond for 50,000 francs (£5000),[1] and that he shall see 50,000 francs deposited with the Archbishop of Glasgow. The Duke does not ask the Pope to aid him in this matter, but to have money ready for an expedition to England, if the plot is successful.

I, the Nuncio, answered that, 'I believed the Pope would be glad that God should chastise that enemy of his in any way; but it would not become him to procure her punishment by those means.' I would not write to the Pope about it, nor do I say this to make you report it It will be sufficient if the subsidies, which may amount to 80,000 scudi, are ready to be paid later.

B. JOHN BAPTIST TAXIS TO KING PHILIP II.

[*Paris, 4 May* 1583.]

The Duke of Guise is making active preparations for the

---

[1] 'The piece of silver called Franke, . . . is worth two shillings English' (Fynes Moryson, *Itinerary*, ii. p. 294).

enterprise of England. We ought to have our contributions ready to give him in case his plans succeed, 'especially one which I dare not set down here, because of the danger. It will be well enough known, if it succeeds, and if it does not, news may be sent some day with safety, and the delay will not matter.'

C. The Cardinal of Como to the Nuncio Castelli.

[*Rome, 23 May* 1583.]

'I have told the Pope what you wrote home, about the affairs of England, and he cannot but think well that the country should be freed by any means from oppression, and restored to God and to our holy religion. He says that in case the business takes effect, the 80,000 scudi will be very well spent.'

D. The Nuncio Castelli to the Cardinal of Como.

[*Paris, 30 May* 1583.]

'Father Robert [Persons] has returned from Spain, having left Madrid on the last day of the past month of April. . . .

[*What follows is on a separate sheet.*] The design against the Queen of England will, I believe, come to nothing.'

E. Taxis to Philip II.

[*Paris, 24 June* 1583.]

'The project on which the Duke of Guise had embarked, and upon which I wrote on the 4th of May, *was a violent attempt against that lady, from whom some one (perhaps for private interests) was to have relieved him.* I see that at present it is entirely lost sight of; there is no further dealing with it. The provision which was asked on this account will therefore be no longer required.'

[*The words in italics above were underlined by the King, who notes in the margin,* 'So I think we understood it here. If they had done so, it would not have been wrong; but they should have provided certain things beforehand.']

[With these letters our first-hand evidence ceases: there are half a dozen later pieces, but their value is not very great.]

F. The Ambassador Mendoza to Secretary Idiaquez.

[*London, 19 August* 1583.]

The person, whom I mentioned in my former letters, has been

APPENDIX 171

ordered, in consequence of an accidental circumstance, not to go where the other person is. For this reason he has come to give [me] that which was entrusted to him, saying that he would deceive no one, for the occasion was gone. This shows that he proceeds with sincerity, and that God does not wish that the business should be done in this way.'

[*The King wrote in the margin,* 'I do not understand what this circumstance can be, if the matter had been well arranged.'[1]]

[This might indeed be a new endeavour of the same scoundrel that attempted to get money from the Duke of Guise; but, *pace* Mr. Froude, the words would suit a thousand other hypotheses. We cannot gather anything for certain from this, as it now stands.]

G. THE NUNCIO RAGAZZONI TO THE CARDINAL OF COMO.

[*Paris, 10 March* 1585.]

The father Provincial of the Jesuits told me to-day that Father Crichton has been asked in England, whether he knows that the Pope deposited 12,000 scudi in the keeping of Father Claude [Matthieu] to procure the assassination of the Queen of England. This question was put to him after the imprisonment of William Parry.[2]

[Neither the names, nor the sum, nor any other detail precisely corresponds with the story of George Gifford. Nothing of the sort occurs in Parry's extant letters or confessions. The question put to Crichton may have been a mere *ruse de guerre*. But Pope Gregory had in the past sent money to English suitors through Père Claude Matthieu.]

[A few years later Father Jasper Heywood, S.J., who was then old and odd, and had developed a wonderful animus against Father Persons, wrote a long complaint to Father Aquaviva, in which the following occurs, Jesuit MSS. *Anglia Historica*, i. 118]:

H. FATHER JASPER HEYWOOD, S.J., TO FATHER GENERAL AQUAVIVA.

[*No place or date, but probably after* 1586.]

'George Gifford, a prodigal dissolute young man, lived at the court of Queen Elizabeth. Father Robert [Persons] dealt with

---

[1] Spanish text in Froude, xi. 379: an English translation in *Spanish Calendar*, p. 502.
[2] T. F. Knox, *Letters of Cardinal Allen*, p. 434.

him about the slaughter of the Queen, and the whole matter was entrusted to him to kill her by himself. This he undertook, and then betrayed the whole affair. Whether the Queen may be killed or no, it is not for me to judge. The Father General will decide what is becoming for the Society.'

[Here we see a considerable error about Father Persons, who did not in reality return from Spain until the plot was abandoned (so *D*). This error occurs in *I*: so that they probably both came from the same source—possibly Morgan. It seems also to be erroneous to say that George Gifford 'betrayed the whole affair.' If he had, he would not have been imprisoned in 1586, nor have answered as we shall see under *K*. See also *M*.]

I. The Confession of John Savage, taken 11 August 1586 (*extract*).[1]

'Also that George Gifford promised to have slain her Majesty, for the futherance whereof he receaved 800 crownes or pounds (I know not whether) sent him by the D. of Guise, *all which Gilbert Gifford affirmed unto me,* saying that the D. of Guise protested, if ever he caught him, he should die for it, for that he performed not before this.

'Item, that George Gifford (as far as I could learn) was first and specially moved to this attempt by Parsons the Jesuite. Notwithstanding lately sollicited to the same out of France, by the letters of D. Gifford, his brother [*in*] *the presence of Gilbert Gifford.*

'Item, that Gilbert Gifford had often conference with Richard Gifford, brother to George Gifford, and that the said Richard was privy to this vowed attempt by his brother George against her Majesty, *as Gilbert Gifford told me.*'

In the Official Summaries of Examinations to be used in court, the references to Gilbert's solicitation (here in italics) are generally omitted. In the *State Trials* they altogether disappear. This solicitation took place in June 1585. In this account again all the details are altered. In the original the sum was 50,000 francs, or £5000; here £800. In reality the money was to be given *after* the crime; here before. In reality Persons was in Spain since Midsummer 1582, and only returned after the plot was given up in 1583; here he was the first to move the conspirator.

---

[1] R.O. *M.Q.S.* xix., n. 38; B.M. *Caligula,* C. ix. f. 292=408. Cf. Boyd, viii. 613.

APPENDIX

K. OFFICIAL SUMMARY OF THE EXAMINATIONS OF THE CONSPIRATORS.[1]

[*6 September* 1586.]

[*After giving an abstract of Savage's examination just quoted, the summary thus alludes to other examinations now lost*]

Ballard (examined) 8 August, 'as he hard, and that George Gifford had sworn it to Persons.'

Ballard, 12 August, sayth, ' he hard it of Gilbert Gifforde.'

Ballard, 19 August, 'that he told it to Babington and Donne.

Tichburne, 29 August, 'Babington told him that George Gifford had received money of the Duke of Guise for undertaking to kill the Queen'

GEORGE GIFFORDE himself herupon examined 23 August,
> utterly denieth that ever he knew Persons or Ballard,
>> that ever he had any intelligence from the Duke of Guise,
>>> or from any other from beyond the seas,
>> or ever received any mony from the Duke of Guise,
>>> or from any beyond the seas.'

[This professes to be evidence for and against believing that George Gifford was a conspirator. It really shows how the virus of Gilbert Gifford's story spread. Having previously infected Savage, it contaminates Ballard. From Ballard it passes to Babington and Dunne, from Babington to Tichborne, and probably to Poley. At all events Poley says that George was 'practised by Persons, and had received 800*l* or 900*l*. at several times for the attempt' (Boyd, viii 600). George Gifford's statements may in themselves be true.]

L ARTICLES BY RICHARD YOUNG AGAINST GEORGE GIFFORD.[1]

R. O. *Domestic Elizabeth*, cxcv 58, f 142

[*London,* 13 *December* 1586.]

'Item. Item, it was confessed by Ballarde that he had talked with Mr Gifford, and told him that he had been in France, and brought him letters from his brother William, wherein the said Gifford was entreated and persuaded to leave the court and to go over into France, where order was taken for his maintenance. 'Nay,' said he, 'sith that I have consumed and spent myself in the Courte, I will take another course.' Ballard did also confess that divers times he had speech and conference with him.'

The message confessed by Ballard tallies exactly with that brought by Gilbert Gifford in October 1585. But there is nothing suspicious in this.

---

[1] R.O. *M.Q.S.* xix. 91. Another copy, B.M. *Caligula,* C. ix, fol. 295 Boyd, viii 680

M. GILBERT GIFFORD TO PHELIPPES (*extract*).

[7 May 1587.]

After Gilbert Gifford had received Elizabeth's promise of £100 a year as a reward for his treacheries, he wrote to Phelippes a letter (R.O. *Dom. Eliz.*, cc., no. 48, fol. 101, cipher with a decipher by Phelippes (*ibid.*, no. 50), in which, however, there are several omissions), dated 1 or 7 May 1587 N.S. I copy the paragraph relating to George Gifford. The names in italics are in cipher. Gilbert, as will be seen from the conclusion, is now boldly acting the part of a trickster. See *above*, p. 124.

'And for *George Gifford* it were a long circumstance to declare how cunningly *I* was brought into the matter, which as I said, so will I answer at the day of judgment, I knew nothing but by mere conjectures at my first coming over [Dec. 1585], and *I* brought him only this message from *D. Gifford*, that he would devise a course for him to live honourably, the state standing as it doth. These were the formal words, which I delivered him from D. Gifford, Marie, that he requested him to come over. At my return [June 1586] I had a further light in the matter; but having delivered this message and perceiving it tended to this effect, which when I had not at first discovered, I feared lest it might cause jealousy in *Mr. Secretary's* head, considering my green acquaintance with him, as also that I knew *him (Gifford)* a man unresolved, and unfit of whom to build of. But since I have understoode the matter a thousand waies. It is certaine that such a devise there was in hand: *Nau* had the handling of it, and *delivered money* for the purpose in *Throgmorton's* time, and Ch. Arundel laid it forth. This is the sum and substance and is most sure.[1]

'Now give me leave to insinuate how you may salve all sores; which you may do either in laying the discovery of matters past upon him [George Gifford], for in truth all men think he uttered it *a principio*. Or in laying it upon *Nau*, or else that *Heywood* uttered it, for he hath spoken it to divers in these parts. *Guise* would give nothing beforehand. Look well to it, lest it renew an evil opinion of *me*, who am clear now: this would hinder the *Queen's* and Mr. *Secretary's* good service in these points. Look not for mathematical satisfaction at my hands.'

---

[1] It will be noticed that this story is *entirely different* from that which Gilbert told in *I*, above. He is acting as a bold, slippery rogue, telling Phelippes 'not to look for mathematical satisfaction at his hands.'

APPENDIX

N. FATHER PERSONS TO DON JUAN DE IDIAQUEZ.

M. A. Tierney, *Dodd's Church History*, 1840, iii. p. lxv. prints both the Spanish and the English text.

[*Rome, 30 June* 1597.]

The Queen of Scotland wrote to the Duke of Guise in the year 1585 reprehending the said Duke and the Archbishop of Glasgow, because they had not helped, at the petition of Morgan and Paget, to deliver a certain sum of money to a certain young *cavallero* in England, who promised the said pair to kill the Queen of England for the said sum of money, as they made the Queen of Scotland believe.

But [it was] because the Duke and Archbishop had learnt that the said *cavallero* was a reprobate (*un perdito*), who would do nothing, as the effect proved (his name is not given as he is still alive) that they would not deliver the money. For this the pair obtained for them a scolding, as has been said.

[*In the margin opposite to the words* 'young cavallero' *are written the initials* 'J. G.,' *which correspond with* Jorge Gifford, *the form one would expect in a Spanish paper.*]

In this version Father Persons may be frankly telling all that he knew, but he omits all the original story, and dwells solely on what will redound to the blame of Morgan. It is therefore a partisan story, and must not be accepted without due caution.

INDEX

ABINGTON, EDWARD, cxvi, cxxi, clxxiii, clxxx, 68, 72, 76, 84 *n*, 96; proposes to seize Queen Elizabeth, 57 and *n*, 58; suggests a successor in the event of Mary's death, 62.

Act of Association, xlix, cxciii.

Ady, Patrick, a secular priest, 153 *n*, 154, 163.

Aldred, Solomon, one of Walsingham's spies, lxxxviii, lxxxix; attempts to gain over Dr. Gifford and Edward Grately, xc-xcii.

Alfield, Thomas, priest and martyr, xiv *n*, lxxiii *n*.

Allen, William, cardinal, xxxiii, xliii-xlv, lxxiii, lxxiv, lxxvi, lxxix and *n*, xcii, cxi, cc, 8 *n*, 85 and *n*, 96, 128; his *Defence of Stanley*, 125.

Aquaviva, Claudio, general of the Society of Jesus, lxxvi, 152, 162.

Aray, Martin, priest, cli.

Arundel or Arundell, Sir Charles, 125.

—— Sir John, of Lanherne, 58, 81, 93, 97 and *n*.

—— Philip Howard, Earl of, xl, lxxiii and *n*, 43, 64, 80, 87, 91, 133 *n*; in the Tower, 109 and *n*.

—— Thomas, 154, 164.

Assassination, proposed, of Queen Elizabeth finds favour in high places, xx and *n*.

Aston, Sir Walter, 6 *n*.

BABINGTON, ANTHONY, of Dethwick, parentage, civ and *n*; his mistaken belief that the Catholic princes were ready to invade England, xvii-xviii, cviii-cix; the conditions which made the Babington plot a possibility, xix-xxx, xxxix; Gilbert Gifford the real originator of the plot, xli; a double conspiracy, lxxxvii; Babington plot, May-June, 1586, civ; interview with Ballard, cvii, 19, 52; hesitates to involve himself in the conspiracy, cix; the counts in the indictment against Ballard and Gifford, cxii; list of the conspirators, cxvi; Babington's activities, cxx; interviews with Walsingham, cxxiv, cxxvi, cxxvii and *n*, cxxix, clxiv, 56 *n*, 134; consults with Poley, cxxv, 58; Mary writes to Babington, cxxix, clxvi, 15, and receives in return the plan of the conspiracy, cxxxvi, 18, 63; Mary's letter of acceptance of the proposals, cxlii-cl, clxxxiv; the history of the letter, 26-37; the *textus receptus*, 38-45; the conspirators to be apprehended, 132-135; Babington's last interview with Walsingham, clxi; offers of service, clxii; shadowed by Poley, clx-clxiv, clxvii-clxviii; alarmed by the arrest of Ballard and Poley, clxix; resolves on the murder of Elizabeth, clxx; a prisoner in the Tower, clxxiii; confessions and examinations of Babington, clxxxiv-clxxxv—

    First examination, 49.
    Second examination, 67.
    Third examination, 76.
    Fourth examination, 77.
    Fifth examination, 79.
    Sixth examination, 88.
    Seventh examination, 89.
    Eighth examination, 90.
    Ninth examination, 96.

Babington, Anthony, letter to, from Nau, as to Poley, 24; execution of the conspirators, clxxxii; confiscation of their property, ccv and *n*.

—— Richard, 62.

Bacon, Francis, 137.

Bagot, Richard, 6 *n*, 102.

Bagshaw, Christopher, xlviii, lxxvii.

Ballard, John, priest and conspirator, xxxi, xxxii, xxxix, xlvii, xlix, lxxii, lxxvi, lxxvii, lxxx, lxxxvi, lxxxvii, cii, cxvi, cxxi, cxxxvi,

ccvi n, ccxii, 19, 21 n, 46, 59, 63, 67, 75, 94, 95, 106 and n, 109, 110, 114 and n; sketch of his career prior to the conspiracy, lxvi; Ballard as described by Tyrrell and Babington, lxxviii; accused by Tyrrell of plotting against Elizabeth, lxxiv, 94; interview with Morgan and Paget in Paris, lxxvii, lxxx; his character under the influence of Morgan, lxxix; first steps in politics, lxxxi; endeavours to discover the plans of the Scottish Catholics, lxxxii; involved in the conspiracy of Savage and George Gifford; on the certainty of an invasion, lxxxiii, xcvii, cvii, cxxxv, 52-54, 56; accompanied by Mawde he travels north in search of information as to the strength of the rising, cxvii, clii; contradictory accounts of the expedition, cliii; insists on having Mary's authority for the rising, cliii-clv; offers to turn Queen's evidence, clxv; warrant issued for his arrest, clxviii, 131-135 and n; a prisoner in the Tower, clxix, clxxii, 160, 167; his examination, 137; put to the torture, lxxx, clxxx; executed, 161, 167; letters to, from Morgan, 112.
Ban against William the Silent, xix, xx, xxiii.
Band of Association for the Safety of Queen Elizabeth, xxiv-xxv, xlix.
Barker, Edward, notary, 36; his record of the evidence at the trial of Queen Mary, 136, 137.
Barlow, William, priest, lxix.
Barnes, *alias* Barnaby Thomas, agent in carrying correspondence to and from the French ambassador, ci, cxxx-cxxxiii, cxxxviii, cciv, 1, 99 n, 103 n-105, 120, 123; note on, 2; letter to Queen Mary with offer of service and enclosing a packet of letters, 8; the queen's reply, 13; his confession, 3-5; letters to Gilbert Curll, 5 and n, 10, 17; letters to, from Curll, 8, 11, 14, 16, 23, 25, 47.
Barnewell, Robert, conspirator, lxxxiv, cix, cxvi, cxx, clxxii, clxxix, clxxx, 54, 57, 58, 62, 63, 68, 71, 72, 76, 80, 87, 95.

Beale, Robert, clerk of the Privy Council, 49.
Beaton, James, archbishop of Glasgow, liii, cxlvii, cxlviii, 8 n, 49, 141, 153, 156 n, 163, 175; letter to, from Queen Mary, cxcvi.
Bellamy, Bartholomew, conspirator, clxxii and n.
—— Elizabeth, conspirator, cxvii.
—— Jeremy, conspirator, cxvii.
Berden, Nicholas, *alias* of Thomas Rogers, q.v.
Birkhead, George, D.D., ccii.
Blount, Sir Christopher, xxxvii.
Bold, Richard, 96 and n.
Boste, John, priest and martyr, lxxxi, lxxxii.
Bray, Mrs., in Sheffield, 50.
Brewer, the, at Burton-on-Trent, 'the honest man,' carries correspondence, cii and n, ciii, cxxxii, cxxxix, 3, 4 and n, 6 n, 99 n, 103 and n, 104.
Bromley, Thomas, chancellor, 66, 144.
Bruce, Robert, one of Walsingham's spies, xxxv.
Buckhurst, Lord, 109.
Bull, executioner of Queen Mary, cc.
Burghley, William, Lord, xiv n, xxiv, xxxviii, clxxxii, clxxxiii, clxxxvi, 28, 66, 94 n, 130, 144, 151; letter to Walsingham on the trial of Queen Mary, 150; letter of instructions from Elizabeth regarding the trial of Mary, 149; the reply, 150.
Butler, Sir Thomas, 88.

CAESAR, HENRY, Catholic priest in exile, 125.
Campion, Edmund, S.J., accompanies Persons to England, xv.
Carter, William, xxiv.
Casey, a servant of Phelippes, 129.
Castelli, papal nuncio, writes to the Cardinal of Como on the plot to murder Queen Elizabeth, 169-170.
Catesby, Sir W., 58.
Catholic League, xv, 52 and n, 77.
—— priests liable to torture and death, xxv and n.
—— revival of 1581, xxix, 52 and n.
Catholics, severe laws against, in 1584, xxvi; familiarised with the defence of regicide, xxix.
Cecil, William. *See* Burghley, Lord.

Charnock, John, conspirator, cxvii, xliv, clxv, clxxi, clxxii, 4, 58, 63, 71, 74.

Châteauneuf de l'Aubespine, M., French ambassador to England, lii, liii, lix, lxiii, lxiv, cl, clix, clx, 6, 8, 17 and *n*, 44, 129, 158, 166.

Clenog, Maurice, rector of the English college at Rome, xlii.

Colderin, Mr., an *alias* of Gilbert Gifford, *q.v.*

Como, cardinal of, xxiii, xxix, 169-171.

Cordaillot, M., secretary to the French ambassador, liii, lvi, 120, 121.

Cornellis, Nicholas, an *alias* of Gilbert Gifford, *q.v.*

Courcelles, secretary, 50.

Courtenay (Curteney), Sir William, high sheriff of Devon, 81, 93, 97 and *n*.

Creagh, Richard, archbishop of Armagh, ccv.

Crichton, William, S.J., xv, xxii; his mission to Scotland to help the old religion, xv, 151-153, 162-163; a prisoner in Ostend and narrowly escapes a hanging, 153, 163; tried before the Privy Council, 154, 164; opposed to the murder of Elizabeth, xxviii and *n*, 157, 165; a prisoner in the Tower, clxxx, 155, 159-160, 164-167; efforts for his liberation, 161, 168.

Curll, Gilbert, secretary to Queen Mary, cxxxi, cxxxii, cxxxix, cxl, cxlvi, cxlvii and *n*, cxlviii and *n*, ccx, 1, 28, 77 *n*, 127, 139, 142; his examination, clxxxvi and *n*, clxxxviii, cxc and *n*, cxci, cxcvi, 143, 146; his dissuasions, 148; letters from, to Barnaby, 11, 14, 16, 23, 25, 47; letter from, to Barnes, 8; letter to, from Barnes, 5 and *n*; letter to, from Barnaby [Phelippes], 17; letter to, from Gilbert Gifford, 99.

Daniel, Richard, li and *n*.

Darbishire, D., S.J., 129.

Defence of the . . . sentence and execution of the Queen of Scots, 30, 36.

De missione Scotica puncta quaedam Notanda historiae Societatis servienda, 151; translation, 162.

Des Trappes, M. de, messenger of the French ambassador, arrested, and imprisoned in the Tower, 159 and *n*, 166.

Dethick, or Dethwick, 15 *n*.

Dolman, Alban, xlviii.

Dolman's Conference on the next Succession, 85 *n*.

Donne. See Dunne.

Donnington, Mr., 95.

Douglas, (?) a Scottish Jesuit, clxiii.

―― Archibald, 100.

Draycote, John, of Draycote, 92 and *n*.

―― Philip, 88 and *n*.

Driland, Christopher, priest, xxviii.

Dunne or Donne, Henry, cxvi, cxxi, clxxii, 58, 59, 66, 67, 77, 94 *n*, 95, 133; his examination, clxvi.

Du Préau (Pio), Camille, chaplain of Queen Mary, 108 and *n*.

Du Ruisseau, M., 8 *n*.

Egerton, Sir Thomas, solicitor-general, clxxxi, 91, 96, 137.

Elizabeth, Queen, her excommunication, xviii-xix and *n*, clxxvi *n*, 53 and *n*, 67-68; causes Thomas Morgan to be thrown into the Bastille, xxx-xxxi; furnishes French Huguenot rebels with money, liv; informs the French ambassador that she is aware of the secret correspondence with Mary, lxiv; proposal for her seizure, 57 and *n*; plots for her assassination, xx-xxi and *n*, xxxviii, xlv-xlvii, lxxiv-lxxxv, cviii, cix, cxxi, cxxxiv, cxxxvi, cxliii, clvi, clxii, clxx, ccxii, 66, 68, 72-73, 80, 84, 156-158, 165-166, 169, 175; measures taken for her safety, xxiv-xxv, 88; Mary refuses to consent to her murder, 33-34; Babington's letter to Mary on the proposed assassination, 21-22; orders the arrest of the conspirators, cl; the indictment of Ballard, Babington, and Gilbert Gifford, cxii and *n*; her wrath against Mary, clxxx, cxciii; insists that extra torture be inflicted on the prisoners, clxxxii; instructions to Burghley as to Mary's trial, 149; Burghley's reply, 150; Mary denies complicity in the murder plot, cxcv-cxcviii.

Ely, Humphrey, D.C.L., xxi.
Englefield, Sir Francis, cxlviii, cxlix, cxc, 8 n, 130, 147, 155 n.
Erdswick, Sampson, of Sandon, Staffordshire, 92 n.
Evidence against the Queen of Scots, cxlviii n.
Exorcisms and witch-hunting, lxviii and n.

FAUNT, LAWRENCE, S.J., rector in Poland, 155 n.
—— Nicholas, 155 and n, 164.
Fitton, Sir Edward, cxxii, 51 and n.
Fitzherbert (Fytcherbert), Sir Thomas, li n, 92, 127, 128.
Fletcher, Richard, dean of Peterborough, cxcviii, cxcix, cc.
Foljambe, Godfrey, 7, 8 n.
Fontenay, M. de, advises Mary to get into touch with Babington, cxxx and n.
Foscue, captain, *alias* of John Ballard, q.v.
Fowler, Bryan, of St. Thomas, 92 and n.
Francisci, Jacomo, soldier of fortune, lxxxvi and n, 95 and n.

GAGE, ROBERT, involved in Babington's plot, cxvii, clxxi, 73, 76; a prisoner in the Tower, clxxii; executed, 113 and n.
Garnet, a Jesuit, clxiii, 112 and n.
Gerard, Sir Thomas, of Bryn, cxvii, 63, 71, 92 and n; a prisoner in the Tower, 132 and n.
Germin, Thomas, an *alias* of Morgan, q.v.
Gifford, Sir George, of Itchell, conspirator, lxxxiii, c, cxi, clxxx, 4, 54 n; his disreputable career, xxxvii; his plot to assassinate Queen Elizabeth, xxi, xxxviii, 169-175; gentleman pensioner at the English Court, xxxix.
—— Gerard, 130.
—— Gilbert, spy of Walsingham, xxxix-xli; his family connections, xli; expelled from the English College at Rome, xlii; plotting against Queen Elizabeth, xliii-xlvii; recommended to Queen Mary by Morgan, xlix, lvii; arrives in London with letters from Beaton, Morgan, and Paget, liii; in Walsingham's secret service as *provocateur*, l, 128-129; with Phelippes at Chartley, lvi and n; offers his services to convey letters to and from Mary, lvii; on trial, lviii-lx; his offer accepted, lx; the method adopted for the conveyance of the correspondence, lxi and n-lxiv, cxxxi; the beginnings of the conspiracy, lxvi; assures Walsingham of his hostility towards the Jesuits, lxxxviii; desirous of gaining over Dr. William Gifford, lxxxviii, lxxxix, xc, cxxviii; 85 n, 108 and n; plotting in Paris, c; returns to Chartley, cii-ciii; sent to Paris to obtain an authoritative deliverance as to the lawfulness of the conspiracy, cxviii-cxix, clviii, clxxiii; writes a book against the Jesuits, cxix, cxx, cxxxiv, cciii and n-ccvii, 125, 128; confesses that the real purpose of his journey from Paris was the plot for the assassination of Queen Elizabeth, cxx, cxxxiv; returns to London, cxx, cxxix; his interviews with Ballard, cliii-cliv and n, 106 and n; prepares for flight, clix-clx, 108, 111, 114-118; his interview with Mendoza in Paris, clxxiii, 114, 115; obtains his approval of the plot to murder Elizabeth, clxxiv; surprised in a brothel and taken to the archbishop's prison where he dies, ccii, 118, 125, 127, 130; note on his letters, 98; note on his confession, 128; his correspondence after the plot, 1586-1590, 118-130; letter from, to Gilbert Curll, 99 and n; letters to Phelippes, 2, 103 and n, 123, 174; letters to Walsingham, 105 and n, 109-114 and n, 116-117 and n.
—— John, of Chillington, xlii, lvi and n, 92 and n.
—— Richard, 172.
—— William, archbishop of Rheims, xxxvii, xlii, xlv and n, xlvi and n, xlviii, lxxiv, lxxxviii-xci, c, 108 and n, 111, 115-117 and n.
Gordon, James, S.J., 153 and n, 163.
Grately, Edward, a priest, xlviii, lxxxix, xc, xcii, ci, cxix, clxxvi n, clxxvii, 108 and n, 120, 125; dies in prison, cciii.
Gray, the Master of, his mission to England, 155 and n, 156 n, 165.

Gregory XIII., pope, xvi, 152, 163; his alleged approval of the plot for the assassination of Queen Elizabeth, lxxv, 170.
Gregory, Arthur, a writing expert, lviii and n, clxvi.
Grene, Christopher, S.J., 128.
Guise, Francis, duke of, his assassination, xxxviii.
—— Henry, duke of, xv, xvi, 53, 122, 153, 163, 169, 172-173, 175.

HAMILTON, ALEXANDER, a Scotch Catholic, lxxi.
—— Lord Claude, lxxxii.
Hanmer, Meredith, xlviii.
Hartlepool, 81 n.
Hatton, Sir Christopher, xxvii, clvii and n, 66, 144-146, 161, 168.
Henri III., King of France, at the instigation of Queen Elizabeth, throws Thomas Morgan into the Bastille, xxx-xxxi.
Hervies' Rents, London, 52 and n.
Heywood, Jasper, S.J., letter to Aquaviva, on George Gifford's plot to kill Queen Elizabeth, 171.
Hodgson, Christopher, a reader in philosophy at Rheims, xlv and n.
Hurt or Hourt, Richard, mercer in Nottingham, cxxxi, 15 and n.

INGLEBY, DAVID, lxxxi, 94 and n, 95.
Ive, Mark, 49.

JACQUES, CAPTAIN. *See* Francisci, Jacomo.
James VI., xv, xvi, ccx, ccxi, 56, 80, 82, 96, 100 and n, 151-153, 162-163; deserts his mother and accepts a pension from her enemies, cxli.
Jones, Edward, cxvi; discusses plans for the Welsh rising, cxxi; taken prisoner, clxxiii.

KENILWORTH CASTLE, 62 and n, 70.
Kent, Henry, Earl of, cxcviii-cc.
Kyffin, Maurice, supposed author of *A Defence . . . of the execution of the Queen of Scots*, 30, 36.

LANGFORD, NICHOLAS, of Longford, 92 and n.
Leicester, Earl of, 60, 69, 78, 87, 99, 138.
Lennox, Esmé Stuart, Duke of, xv-xvii, 152 and n, 153 n, 162-163.

Lesley, John, bishop of Ross, xviii, 8 n.
Lewis, Owen, bishop of Cassano, xxii, xxiii, lxxiv, ccvii, ccviii.
Liggons or Lingens, (?) Ralph, 8 n.
Lilly, *alias* Ambodester, 124-125, 129.

MAINE, DUC DE, 53.
Mary Queen of Scots, the Council of Elizabeth determined on her death, xiii-xiv and n; the Catholic revival in England raises the hopes of her adherents, xvi; the Band of Association and its threat to Mary, xxiv-xxv, xlix; events leading up to Babington's plot, xxix; unfortunate in her choice of agents, xxxiv, ccix; Walsingham's intrigues against her, xli, lxvi, lxxxvii, xc; the beginnings of the Babington plot for her liberation, xli, 62-63, 70; at Chartley, lii; Paget writes to Mary on Ballard's proposals for a rising, xcv; Morgan and de Fontenay suggest that she should get into touch with Babington, cxxx and n; writes to Babington, cxxxi; receives Babington's letter on the plans of the conspirators, cxl; accepts his offer of service, cxlii-cxlvi; methods adopted for the conveyance of letters, li, lvii-lxiv; requests Babington to forward letters, 15; letter from Babington on the proposed invasion of England and the assassination of Elizabeth, 18, 23; her approval of Babington's plans refer to her liberation and not to the proposed murder, cxlii-cxliv, 33; Babington informs her that her friends 'will performe or die,' 46; the forged postscript asking the names of the six conspirators, clxvi, 45, 133; realises the necessity of foreign aid, cxlvii-cxlviii; misled by the extravagant assertions of Ballard, and the false statements of Gilbert Gifford, cxlviii; despatches the fatal letter to Babington, cxlix, cli; the authentic text, 26-27; the *textus receptus* and its history, 29-46; Ballard's examination on the correspondence between Mary and Babington, 137; Babington's

INDEX

confession as to the receipt of Mary's letter and his reply, cxxxvi, 63; the deception practised upon her secretaries, clxxxix-cxcii; their evidence becomes her death warrant, cxcii; the trial, cxciii-cxcv; Barker and Wheeler's official record of the evidence at the trial, 136; her execution, cxcviii-cc; her death a source of strength to the Church, cci; notes on her friends and servants, ccvi. *See also under* Babington, Ballard, Gifford (Gilbert), etc.

Matthieu, Claude, S.J., 171.

Mauvissière, Michel de Castelnau de, French ambassador, 50.

Mawde, Bernard, one of Walsingham's spies, lxxxiv-lxxxvii and *n*, lxxxviii, cii, cxvii, cxlvii; clii and *n*, cliii, ccv, 46, 71, 78, 79, 95.

Mendoza, Bernardino de, Spanish ambassador in France, xvi, xciii, xcvii-xcix, cviii, cxii, cxvii, cxliv, cxlviii, 8 *n*, 39, 112, 127, 135, 141; interview with Gilbert Gifford, li, clxxiii; interview with Ballard, xciv, xcviii, cviii; deceived by Gifford he writes to England approving of Elizabeth's murder, clxxiv; letter to, from Queen Mary, after her death sentence, cxcvi; pays a tribute to Queen Mary's courage, cci; his character outlined, ccxi; letter from, to Idiaquez, 170.

Montalto, *alias* of Mawde, *q.v.*

Moresino, Mgr., bishop of Brescia, Nuncio in Paris, 127.

Morgan, Thomas, xxvii, xl-xli, li, cliv, clv, 4, 49, 50 and *n*, 51, 99, 100 and *n*, 106-112 and *n*, 120, 121, 127, 128; plots the assassination of Queen Elizabeth, xxii; thrown into the Bastille, xxx; his activities on behalf of Queen Mary, xxxiii-xxxiv, xxxvii, xlviii; recommends Gilbert Gifford to Queen Mary, xlix; her anxiety for his welfare, lvii; feud with Allen and Persons, lxxix and *n*; deceived by Gifford, lxxxviii; writes to Queen Mary on the fidelity of Dr. Gifford and Grately, xcii and *n*; requests Savage to support the plot, ci; warns Gilbert Gifford as to Ballard, cxix; advises Mary to get into touch with Babington, cxxx and *n*; veiled warnings to Mary on the proposed assassination of Elizabeth, clvi; his indiscretions partly responsible for Mary's death, ccvi; his after career, ccviii-ccix and *n*; letter to, from Gilbert Gifford, 101.

Morley, Lord, 109.

Morton, James Douglas, Earl of, xv.

Mylls, Francis, clxix, 131, 133, 136.

NAU DE LA BOISSELIÈRE, JACQUES (? CLAUDE), secretary to Queen Mary, cxxxix, cxl, cxlii, cxlvi and *n*-cxlviii and *n*, clxxxiii, ccx, 77 *n*, 89, 108, 127, 139-140; his examination, clxxxv-clxxxvi and *n*, clxxxix, cxci, cxcvi, 27-28, 141, 144; his regrets, 148; letter to Babington, on Poley, 24.

Neville, Edmund, lodges an information against Dr. Parry, xxvii.

Newport, Mr., steward to the Earl of Essex, ciii, 103 *n*.

Nix, a highwayman, xxxviii.

Norreys of Speke Hall, 88 and *n*.

Northumberland, Earl of, 65.

OATLANDS, 89 and *n*.

Offley, Hugh, in Rouen, 115-117 and *n*.

Old and new style in dates, lxiv.

Oulswick, Samson, 92 and *n*.

PAGE, CATHERINE, clxxii.

Paget, Charles, conspirator, xxxiv, xxxvii, xli, xlv *n*, xlviii, xc, xciii, cxii, cxvii, cxxxv and *n*, cxlviii, cxlix, cliv, cxc, cciv, ccvii, ccix, ccx, 5, 8 *n*, 43, 84, 85 *n*, 96, 106, 107, 110-112, 120-122, 127, 128, 135, 139, 141, 147, 156, 165; letter to Mary on Ballard's proposals for a Catholic rising, xcv; mistaken in by Ballard, xcix.

—— Thomas, lord, cxc, 43, 65, 74, 92 and *n*, 127, 147.

Papal league rumours, xvii-xviii and *n*.

Parma, Prince of, xvii, xix, xcviii, cviii, 53.

Parry, William, his bogus plot for the assassination of Queen Elizabeth, xxii and *n*, xxiii, xxxiv, ccvi; receives from Pope Gregory an indulgence for an enterprise for the liberation of Queen Mary, xxiii; his accusations cause Morgan to be thrown into the Bastille, xxx; arrested and executed, xxvii and *n*, xxviii, 156 and *n*, 158, 165-166.

Parsons. *See* Persons.

Pauncefote, John, Catholic exile, lxxxvii.

Peckham, Edmund, exorcist, lxviii *n*, lxix *n*.

—— Sir George, of Denham, 132 and *n*.

Persons or Parsons, Robert, S.J., xv, xxxiii, xxxiv, xlviii, lxxvi, xciii, cxi, cciii and *n*, 128, 170-172; letter to Don John de Idiaquez, on the proposed murder of Queen Elizabeth, 175.

Phelippes, Thomas, one of Walsingham's spies, l, liii, lvi and *n*, lxiii, lxxxiii, cxxxii, cxxxiii, cxxxviii, cxxxix and *n*, cxli, cxlix, cl, clx, clxv, clxvii-clxviii, clxxxiii, 1, 2, 5, 7 *n*, 26-27, 47 *n*, 101, 105 *n*, 109-111, 114, 116; explains to Elizabeth the significance of the intercepted letters, clxxix; in possession of Mary's correspondence, clxxxiv; determined on the death of the conspirators, clxxxix; his copy of Mary's letter to Babington untrustworthy, 29-32; defends the indictment of Gilbert Gifford, 119-120; Gifford defends himself against Phelippes's suspicions, 120; his loyalty to Walsingham his chief virtue, cciii-cciv and *n*; a repulsive character, 129; Queen Mary's description of his personal appearance, liv; letters to Curll, 10, 17; letter to, from Gilbert Gifford, 103 and *n*; extract of letter from Gilbert Gifford, concerning George Gifford, 174; letters to Phelippes from Walsingham, 131-135.

Philip II. of Spain, xvi, xvii, 153, 163; sets a price on the head of William, Prince of Orange, xx; appoints Mendoza ambassador to Paris, xciii; letter from Mendoza giving an account of his interview with Ballard, xciv; approves of the proposal to assassinate Queen Elizabeth, clxxv and *n*, 170; resolved on the conversion of England, 83.

Pierce, William, D.D., ccii.

Pius V., 21 *n*.

Plymouth, selected as one of the landing-places for the invading troops, 81 *n*, 93, 97.

Poley or Pooley, Robert, a spy in the service of Walsingham, xxxvi, cxxii-cxxiv, cxxxix, clii, cliii, clx-clxii, cxc, 22, 24, 27, 56 and *n*, 75, 77 *n*, 89, 97, 104 *n*, 112 *n*, 133-135, 160, 167, 173; informs Walsingham of the plot against Elizabeth, clxii; confidential talks with Babington, clxiv, 58, 69; on guard over Babington, clxvii-clxviii; letter to, from Babington, clxx; his later years, ccv.

Poulet or Paulet, Sir Amias, custodian of Mary Queen of Scots, liv, lvi-lxiii, ciii, cxxxii, cxxxix, cxli-cxlii, ccvii, 7, 37, 104, 131, 133.

Priests held to be synonymous with traitors, xxv *n*; opposed to regicide, xxviii and *n*.

Puckering, John, law officer of the Crown, 91, 96, 137.

RAGAZZONI, papal nuncio, letter from, to the cardinal of Como, 171.

Raid of Ruthven, xvi, 153 and *n*.

Raleigh, Sir Walter, ccv, 54 and *n*, 61.

Rheims College, xliii-xlv.

Rogers, Thomas, *alias* Nicholas Berden, one of Walsingham's spies, xl and *n*, xli, li, lii, cl, clxvii, 132 and *n*, 156 *n*.

Rolston, Anthony, cxxx, 50.

Rowsham, Stephen, martyr-priest, 2, 4 and *n*.

SADLEIR, SIR RALPH, 50 *n*.

Salisbury, Thomas, conspirator, c, cix, cxvi, 57, 68, 76, 80, 87, 92, 94; consultation with Babington, 54; to effect a rising in Denbigh, cxx; discusses plans for the Welsh rising, cxxi; a prisoner, clxxii.

Sandes, Miles, 96.

Sandys, Edwin, protestant archbishop of York, lxxxiv.

Savage, John, conspirator, xxxiv, xxxix, lxvi, lxvii, c, ci, cxv-cxvi, cxxxiv, cxxxv and *n*, clxix, 3, 4, 97, 128; his antecedents prior to the murder plot, xliii;

undertakes to assassinate Queen Elizabeth, xlv and *n*-xlvii, cviii-cix, clxxi, 54 and *n*; joins Babington's conspiracy, cx; ready for any dangerous work, 69, 73; holds it to be lawful to murder Elizabeth, 68, 76; discusses details of her assassination, cxx-cxxi; his delay in the accomplishment of his vow, clxxi, 57, 58, 60; a prisoner in the Tower, clxxii; extract from his confession, 172.

Scarborough selected as a landing-place for the invaders, 81 *n*.

Schismatics, 109 and *n*.

Scudamore, one of Walsingham's spies, clxxi.

Sega, Mgr., papal nuncio, xxi and *n*.

Sergeant, Richard, priest, executed at Tyburn, 100 and *n*.

Seton, George, Lord, 152 and *n*, 162.

Shrewsbury, George Talbot, Earl of, cxcix, cc, 15 and *n*, 18, 50 and *n*, 88 and *n*, 89.

Sixtus v., pope, xx, 83-84 and *n*, 85 *n*, 96.

Soigne, Pierre, *alias* of Thomas Barnes, *q.v.*

Somerset, Thomas, 100 and *n*.

Somerville, John, threatens Queen Elizabeth, xxiii.

Southwell, Robert, 112 and *n*; his *Humble Supplication to Her Majesty*, cli and *n*, clxiii and *n*.

Spanish claim to the throne of England, 85 and *n*, 96.

Speke Hall, Lancashire, 88 and *n*.

Spies and dupes, 1584-1585, xxx.

Stafford, Sir Edward, English ambassador in Paris, xxxv, xc, xci, 92 and *n*, 120, 125-126, 129; letter on the employment of Robert Bruce as a spy, xxxv-xxxvi.

'Star-Chamber practice,' 94 and *n*.

Statute of Silence, xiii and *n*, xiv.

Strancham, Edward, a priest and martyr, xli.

Strange, Lord, 62.

Stuart, Esmé, Sieur d'Aubigny. *See* Lennox, Duke of.

Sturton, Lord, 109.

TALBOT, JOHN, of Grafton, cliv, 58, 92, 108 and *n*.

Taxis, Don Juan Bautista de, Spanish ambassador in Paris, xvi, xciii; writes to Philip II. on a plot against the life of Elizabeth, 169-170.

Thomson, William, priest, executed at Tyburn, 100 and *n*.

Thoroughgood, an *alias* of John Ballard, *q.v.*

Throckmorton, Francis, 7, 101 *n*, 127, 128, 146; his execution, xxiv.

Tichborne, Chidiock, conspirator, lxxxiv, c, cix, cxvi, cxxi, clxvii, 27, 49, 62, 68, 70, 73-76, 93-97; consultation with Babington, 54, 58; offer of service, 72; a prisoner in the Tower, clxxii; his confession, clxxx, 34 and *n*.

Tilney or Tylney, Charles, conspirator, lxxvii, lxxxiii and *n*, cxvi, cxxi, clxxx, 57-58, 68-69, 72; a prisoner in the Tower, clxxii.

Topcliffe, Richard, a persecutor of Catholics, clxxii *n*.

Transome, 95.

Transportation of priests, 100 and *n*.

Traves, John, cxvi.

Tresham, Sir Thomas, of Rushton, cliv, 58, 108 and *n*.

Tunstall, Anthony, lxxxiv, 95.

Tylney. *See* Tilney.

Tymperley, Nicholas, lxxvii.

Typping, John, cliii.

Tyrannicide, theories of. Always illicit if on private authority only, 35, 61, 72, 157, 165; no authority for, given by the bull of excommunication, xix, xxi *n*, 21 *n*; erroneous views on this, xxi, 21, 61, 67, 68; authority for, to be solicited by Gilbert Gifford, clviii, 61 *n*. Mary will not encourage explicitly, cxliii, 33; but does so implicitly, cxliv, 34, 35; her authority asked for appointments to offices, 67, 70. Lax views on, result from the Ban, from the wars of religion, and do much harm, xix, xx, xxi, xxviii, xxix. Comparisons, with English intentions against Mary, xiv; with murder by state trial, xxxix; with the Band of Association, xxv. Bogus plots of, and bogus charges of, *see* Carter, George Gifford, Parry, Somerville, Tyrrell; *provocateurs* to, *see* Gilbert Gifford; *see also* Babington, Ballard, Como,

Crichton, and Mendoza, xciv, clxxiv, clxxvi.
Tyrrell, Anthony, subject to hysteria, lxxvii, 90, 94 n, 95 and n, 153, 163; sketch of his career, lxvii-lxxi; the value of his evidence, lxxii; the pilgrimage to Rome, lxxiii; his unreliability, lxxvi; on Ballard's character, lxxviii.
—— Gertrude, a Bridgettine nun, lxxi, lxxiii.

VERSTEGAN, RICHARD, ccii, ccx n.

WAADE, SIR WILLIAM, 159 and n, 166.
Walpole, Henry, S.J., 130.
Walsingham, Sir Francis, xiv, xxiv, 85; his hatred of Queen Mary, xxx; his political morality, xxx; his spies, xxxv; endeavours to enlist agents for his conspiracy against Mary, xc-xci; actively assists in furthering the Babington plot, cxxxiv-cxxxv, clxxii n, clxxviii, ccv, ccxii, 87 n; interviews with Babington, cxxiv-cxxviii and n, cxxix, clxi, clxiv, 56 n, 134; receives Poley's report on interviews with Babington, clxiv, 134; disturbed by the flight of Gilbert Gifford, 116-119, 132-133, 135; gives instructions for the arrest of the conspirators, cl, clxviii, 131-135; letter to Queen Elizabeth, lxxxvi; letters to Walsingham from Gilbert Gifford, 105 and n, 109-114 and n, 116-117; letter from Burghley on Queen Mary's trial, 150.
Walton, Roger, commended by Sir Edward Stafford, but imprisoned by Walsingham, 124.
Watts, or Waytes, William, a secular priest, xxviii.
Westmorland, Earl of, 65, 74, 80.
Weston, William, S.J., lxviii n, lxix n, 86 n; his description of Babington, cv and n, cvi, and of Poley, cxxii; his account of Babington's interviews with Walsingham, cxxvi and n-cxxviii.
Wheeler, Thomas, notary, 36; his record of the evidence at the trial of Queen Mary, 136.
White, Richard, a Catholic martyr, xxiv and n.
William the Silent, Prince of Orange, his assassination, xix, xxiv and n.
Williamson, a spy, lxxxvii n.
Windsor, the L., 92.
—— Dorothy, lxxxvii.
—— Edward, conspirator, lxxxi, lxxxii, lxxxiii n, lxxxvi, lxxxvii, c, cxvi, cxviii, cxxi, cliii, clxxx, 62, 70, 94, 139.
Witch-hunting and exorcisms, lxviii n.
Wolsley, Erasmus, of Wolsley, 92 and n.
Worseley, Thomas, 49.
Wotton, Sir Edward, 30.

YARDLEY, ROGER, a suspect, xl n, clxiii, 97; a 'prisoner in the Clynke,' 5 and n.
Young, Richard, magistrate, clxxi, 173.
Younger, James, priest, lxxix n.

ZOUCHE, LORD, qualified verdict on Queen Mary, cxciv and n.

REPORT OF THE THIRTY-FIFTH ANNUAL MEETING OF THE SCOTTISH HISTORY SOCIETY.

The Thirty-Fifth Annual Meeting of the Society was held on Saturday, 12th December 1921, in Dowell's Rooms, George Street, Edinburgh,—Sir James Balfour Paul, C.V.O., LL.D., in the Chair.

The Report of the Council was as follows:—

During the past year forty-six members have died or resigned. Thirty-five new members have joined the Society, and the number now on the roll, exclusive of libraries, is 370.

Since the last General Meeting the first volume of the Third Series, viz. *Consultations of the Ministers of Edinburgh*, 1652-1657, has been issued, and owing to the expense of printing is the sole volume for 1919-20. This book took precedence of the *St. Andrews Graduation and Matriculation Roll*, 1413-1579, which is assigned to 1920-21 and is almost ready. For 1921-22 the *Diary of George Ridpath*, 1755-1761, is well advanced. The Council has arranged for a volume by Father Pollen relating to Mary and the Babington Plot. Its issue as a second volume for 1921-22 or its postponement to 1922-23 will depend upon the funds available and the expense of printing.

The Members of Council retiring by rotation are Dr. William MacKay, Sir George M. Paul, and Dr. J. Maitland Thomson. They are recommended for re-election.

The accounts of the Hon. Treasurer appended in Abstract show a credit balance of £282, 14s. 10d. on 11th November 1921.

The Annual Subscription of One Guinea is now due and should be paid *at the George Street branch of the Bank of Scotland, Edinburgh.*

The motion for the adoption of the Report was moved by the Chairman and seconded by Mr. James Curle, W.S.

Mr. George Lorimer moved that it be remitted to the Council to consider the question of publication of the Edinburgh Burgh Records, and if necessary to approach the Town Council on the matter, and to report to next General Meeting.

Mr. William Cowan moved a vote of thanks to the Chairman.

ABSTRACT of the INTROMISSIONS of HONORARY TREASURER of the SCOTTISH HISTORY SOCIETY for the year ending 11th November 1921.

CHARGE.

Funds and Effects at close of last Account,	£261	15	0
Subscriptions received from Members,	360	3	0
Libraries,	61	19	0
Publications sold,	3	3	0
Interest on Deposit Receipts,	34	15	8
SUM OF CHARGE,	£721	15	8

DISCHARGE.

Printing, Binding, and Issue of Publications—

1. *Register of Consultations of Ministers,* £333 4 8
2. *Early Records of the University of St. Andrews*—
    Cost to date, £185 17 3
    Less previously paid to account, 99 17 2
    — 86 0 1
3. General Printing Account, 9 14 8

Miscellaneous Payments, 10 1 5

£439 0 10

Funds and Effects at close of this Account—

1. On Deposit Receipt with Bank of Scotland, dated 28th Oct. 1921, £100 0 0
2. Do. 22nd June 1921, 60 0 0
3. On Account Current with Bank of Scotland, 523 4 2

£683 4 2
Less due to Honorary Treasurer, 400 9 4

282 14 10

SUM OF DISCHARGE, £721 15 8

EDINBURGH, 30*th November* 1921.—Having examined the Accounts of the Honorary Treasurer of the Scottish History Society for the year ending 11th November 1921 [of which the foregoing is an Abstract] we find the accounts to be correctly stated and sufficiently vouched, closing with sums on Deposit Receipt with the Bank of Scotland of One hundred and sixty pounds (£160): Balance at credit of the Account Current with the said Bank of Five hundred and twenty-three pounds, four shillings and twopence: and a balance due to the Honorary Treasurer of Four hundred pounds, nine shillings and fourpence (£400, 9s. 4d.) arising through a cheque issued to the Printers not having been presented at the Bank until after the closing date of the Account.

WM. TRAQUAIR DICKSON.
RALPH RICHARDSON.

RULES

1. The object of the Society is the discovery and printing, under selected editorship, of unpublished documents illustrative of the civil, religious, and social history of Scotland. The Society will also undertake, in exceptional cases, to issue translations of printed works of a similar nature, which have not hitherto been accessible in English.

2. The affairs of the Society shall be managed by a Council, consisting of a Chairman, Treasurer, Secretary, and twelve elected Members, five to make a quorum. Three of the twelve elected Members shall retire annually by ballot, but they shall be eligible for re-election.

3. The Annual Subscription to the Society shall be One Guinea. The publications of the Society shall not be delivered to any Member whose Subscription is in arrear, and no Member shall be permitted to receive more than one copy of the Society's publications.

4. The Society will undertake the issue of its own publications, *i.e.* without the intervention of a publisher or any other paid agent.

5. The Society normally issues yearly two octavo volumes of about 320 pages each.

6. An Annual General Meeting of the Society shall be held at the end of October, or at an approximate date to be determined by the Council.

7. Two stated Meetings of the Council shall be held each year, one on the last Tuesday of May, the other on the Tuesday preceding the day upon which the Annual General Meeting shall be held. The Secretary, on the request of three Members of the Council, shall call a special meeting of the Council.

8. Editors shall receive 20 copies of each volume they edit for the Society.

9. The owners of Manuscripts published by the Society will also be presented with a certain number of copies.

10. The Annual Balance-Sheet, Rules, and List of Members shall be printed.

11. No alteration shall be made in these Rules except at a General Meeting of the Society. A fortnight's notice of any alteration to be proposed shall be given to the Members of the Council.

PUBLICATIONS

OF THE

SCOTTISH HISTORY SOCIETY

For the year 1886-1887.

1. BISHOP POCOCKE'S TOURS IN SCOTLAND, 1747-1760. Edited by D. W. KEMP.
2. DIARY AND ACCOUNT BOOK OF WILLIAM CUNNINGHAM OF CRAIGENDS, 1673-1680. Edited by the Rev. JAMES DODDS, D.D.

For the year 1887-1888.

3. GRAMEIDOS LIBRI SEX: an heroic poem on the Campaign of 1689, by JAMES PHILIP of Almerieclose. Translated and edited by the Rev. A. D. MURDOCH.
4. THE REGISTER OF THE KIRK-SESSION OF ST. ANDREWS. Part I. 1559-1582. Edited by D. HAY FLEMING.

For the year 1888-1889.

5. DIARY OF THE REV. JOHN MILL, Minister in Shetland, 1740-1803. Edited by GILBERT GOUDIE.
6. NARRATIVE OF MR. JAMES NIMMO, A COVENANTER, 1654-1709. Edited by W. G. SCOTT-MONCRIEFF.
7. THE REGISTER OF THE KIRK-SESSION OF ST. ANDREWS. Part II. 1583-1600. Edited by D. HAY FLEMING.

For the year 1889-1890.

8. A LIST OF PERSONS CONCERNED IN THE REBELLION (1745). With a Preface by the EARL OF ROSEBERY.
    Presented to the Society by the Earl of Rosebery.
9. GLAMIS PAPERS: The 'BOOK OF RECORD,' a Diary written by PATRICK, FIRST EARL OF STRATHMORE, and other documents (1684-89). Edited by A. H. MILLAR.
10. JOHN MAJOR'S HISTORY OF GREATER BRITAIN (1521). Translated and edited by ARCHIBALD CONSTABLE.

For the year 1890-1891.

11. THE RECORDS OF THE COMMISSIONS OF THE GENERAL ASSEMBLIES, 1646-47. Edited by the Rev. Professor MITCHELL, D.D., and the Rev. JAMES CHRISTIE, D.D.
12. COURT-BOOK OF THE BARONY OF URIE, 1604-1747. Edited by the Rev. D. G. BARRON.

PUBLICATIONS

For the year 1891-1892.

13. MEMOIRS OF SIR JOHN CLERK OF PENICUIK, Baronet. Extracted by himself from his own Journals, 1676-1755. Edited by JOHN M. GRAY.
14. DIARY OF COL. THE HON. JOHN ERSKINE OF CARNOCK, 1683-1687. Edited by the Rev. WALTER MACLEOD.

For the year 1892-1893.

15. MISCELLANY OF THE SCOTTISH HISTORY SOCIETY. Vol. I.
16. ACCOUNT BOOK OF SIR JOHN FOULIS OF RAVELSTON (1671-1707). Edited by the Rev. A. W. CORNELIUS HALLEN.

For the year 1893-1894.

17. LETTERS AND PAPERS ILLUSTRATING THE RELATIONS BETWEEN CHARLES II. AND SCOTLAND IN 1650. Edited by SAMUEL RAWSON GARDINER, D.C.L., etc.
18. SCOTLAND AND THE COMMONWEALTH. LETTERS AND PAPERS RELATING TO THE MILITARY GOVERNMENT OF SCOTLAND, Aug. 1651-Dec. 1653. Edited by C. H. FIRTH, M.A.

For the year 1894-1895.

19. THE JACOBITE ATTEMPT OF 1719. LETTERS OF JAMES, SECOND DUKE OF ORMONDE. Edited by W. K. DICKSON.
20, 21. THE LYON IN MOURNING, OR A COLLECTION OF SPEECHES, LETTERS, JOURNALS, ETC., RELATIVE TO THE AFFAIRS OF PRINCE CHARLES EDWARD STUART, by BISHOP FORBES. 1746-1775. Edited by HENRY PATON. Vols. I. and II.

For the year 1895-1896.

22. THE LYON IN MOURNING. Vol. III.
23. ITINERARY OF PRINCE CHARLES EDWARD (Supplement to the Lyon in Mourning). Compiled by W. B. BLAIKIE.
24. EXTRACTS FROM THE PRESBYTERY RECORDS OF INVERNESS AND DINGWALL FROM 1638 TO 1688. Edited by WILLIAM MACKAY.
25. RECORDS OF THE COMMISSIONS OF THE GENERAL ASSEMBLIES (*continued*) for the years 1648 and 1649. Edited by the Rev. Professor MITCHELL, D.D., and Rev. JAMES CHRISTIE, D.D.

For the year 1896-1897.

26. WARISTON'S DIARY AND OTHER PAPERS—
    JOHNSTON OF WARISTON'S DIARY, 1639. Edited by G. M. Paul.—THE HONOURS OF SCOTLAND, 1651-52. C. R. A. Howden.—THE EARL OF MAR'S LEGACIES, 1722, 1726. Hon. S. Erskine.—LETTERS BY MRS. GRANT OF LAGGAN. J. R. N. Macphail.
    Presented to the Society by Messrs. T. and A. Constable.

27. MEMORIALS OF JOHN MURRAY OF BROUGHTON, 1740-1747. Edited by R. FITZROY BELL.

28. THE COMPT BUIK OF DAVID WEDDERBURNE, MERCHANT OF DUNDEE, 1587-1630. Edited by A. H. MILLAR.

For the year 1897-1898.

29, 30. THE CORRESPONDENCE OF DE MONTEREUL AND THE BROTHERS DE BELLIÈVRE, FRENCH AMBASSADORS IN ENGLAND AND SCOTLAND, 1645-1648. Edited, with Translation, by J. G. FOTHERINGHAM. 2 vols.

For the year 1898-1899.

31. SCOTLAND AND THE PROTECTORATE. LETTERS AND PAPERS RELATING TO THE MILITARY GOVERNMENT OF SCOTLAND, FROM JANUARY 1654 TO JUNE 1659. Edited by C. H. FIRTH, M.A.
32. PAPERS ILLUSTRATING THE HISTORY OF THE SCOTS BRIGADE IN THE SERVICE OF THE UNITED NETHERLANDS, 1572-1782. Edited by JAMES FERGUSON. Vol. I. 1572-1697.
33. 34. MACFARLANE'S GENEALOGICAL COLLECTIONS CONCERNING FAMILIES IN SCOTLAND; Manuscripts in the Advocates' Library. 2 vols. Edited by J. T. CLARK, Keeper of the Library.

Presented to the Society by the Trustees of the late Sir William Fraser, K.C.B.

For the year 1899-1900.

35. PAPERS ON THE SCOTS BRIGADE IN HOLLAND, 1572-1782. Edited by JAMES FERGUSON. Vol. II. 1698-1782.
36. JOURNAL OF A FOREIGN TOUR IN 1665 AND 1666, ETC., BY SIR JOHN LAUDER, LORD FOUNTAINHALL. Edited by DONALD CRAWFORD.
37. PAPAL NEGOTIATIONS WITH MARY QUEEN OF SCOTS DURING HER REIGN IN SCOTLAND. Chiefly from the Vatican Archives. Edited by the Rev. J. HUNGERFORD POLLEN, S.J.

For the year 1900-1901.

38. PAPERS ON THE SCOTS BRIGADE IN HOLLAND, 1572-1782. Edited by JAMES FERGUSON. Vol. III.
39. THE DIARY OF ANDREW HAY OF CRAIGNETHAN, 1659-60. Edited by A. G. REID, F.S.A.Scot.

For the year 1901-1902.

40. NEGOTIATIONS FOR THE UNION OF ENGLAND AND SCOTLAND IN 1651-53. Edited by C. SANFORD TERRY.
41. THE LOYALL DISSUASIVE. Written in 1703 by Sir ÆNEAS MACPHERSON. Edited by the Rev. A. D. MURDOCH.

For the year 1902-1903.

42. THE CHARTULARY OF LINDORES, 1195-1479. Edited by the Right Rev. JOHN DOWDEN, D.D., Bishop of Edinburgh.
43. A LETTER FROM MARY QUEEN OF SCOTS TO THE DUKE OF GUISE, Jan. 1562. Reproduced in Facsimile. Edited by the Rev. J. HUNGERFORD POLLEN, S.J.

Presented to the Society by the family of the late Mr. Scott, of Halkshill.

44. MISCELLANY OF THE SCOTTISH HISTORY SOCIETY. Vol. II.
45. LETTERS OF JOHN COCKBURN OF ORMISTOUN TO HIS GARDENER, 1727-1743. Edited by JAMES COLVILLE, D.Sc.

For the year 1903-1904.

46. MINUTE BOOK OF THE MANAGERS OF THE NEW MILLS CLOTH MANUFACTORY, 1681-1690. Edited by W. R. SCOTT.
47. CHRONICLES OF THE FRASERS; being the Wardlaw Manuscript entitled 'Polichronicon seu Policratica Temporum, or, the true Genealogy of the Frasers.' By Master JAMES FRASER. Edited by WILLIAM MACKAY.
48. PROCEEDINGS OF THE JUSTICIARY COURT FROM 1661 TO 1678. Vol. I. 1661-1669. Edited by Sheriff SCOTT-MONCRIEFF.

For the year 1904-1905.

49. PROCEEDINGS OF THE JUSTICIARY COURT FROM 1661 TO 1678. Vol. II. 1669-1678. Edited by Sheriff SCOTT-MONCRIEFF.
50. RECORDS OF THE BARON COURT OF STITCHILL, 1655-1807. Edited by CLEMENT B. GUNN, M.D., Peebles.
51. MACFARLANE'S GEOGRAPHICAL COLLECTIONS. Vol. I. Edited by Sir ARTHUR MITCHELL, K.C.B.

For the year 1905-1906.

52, 53. MACFARLANE'S GEOGRAPHICAL COLLECTIONS. Vols. II. and III. Edited by Sir ARTHUR MITCHELL, K.C.B.
54. STATUTA ECCLESIÆ SCOTICANÆ, 1225-1559. Translated and edited by DAVID PATRICK, LL.D.

For the year 1906-1907.

55. THE HOUSE BOOKE OF ACCOMPS, OCHTERTYRE, 1737-39. Edited by JAMES COLVILLE, D.Sc.
56. THE CHARTERS OF THE ABBEY OF INCHAFFRAY. Edited by W. A. LINDSAY, K.C., the Right Rev. Bishop DOWDEN, D.D., and J. MAITLAND THOMSON, LL.D.
57. A SELECTION OF THE FORFEITED ESTATES PAPERS PRESERVED IN H.M. GENERAL REGISTER HOUSE AND ELSEWHERE. Edited by A. H. MILLAR, LL.D.

For the year 1907-1908.

58. RECORDS OF THE COMMISSIONS OF THE GENERAL ASSEMBLIES (*continued*), for the years 1650-52. Edited by the Rev. JAMES CHRISTIE, D.D.
59. PAPERS RELATING TO THE SCOTS IN POLAND. Edited by A. FRANCIS STEUART.

For the year 1908-1909.

60. SIR THOMAS CRAIG'S DE UNIONE REGNORUM BRITANNIÆ TRACTATUS. Edited, with an English Translation, by C. SANFORD TERRY.
61. JOHNSTON OF WARISTON'S MEMENTO QUAMDIU VIVAS, AND DIARY FROM 1632 TO 1639. Edited by G. M. PAUL, LL.D., D.K.S.

PUBLICATIONS

Second Series.

For the year 1909-1910.

1. THE HOUSEHOLD BOOK OF LADY GRISELL BAILLIE, 1692-1733. Edited by R. SCOTT-MONCRIEFF, W.S.
2. ORIGINS OF THE '45 AND OTHER NARRATIVES. Edited by W. B. BLAIKIE, LL.D.
3. CORRESPONDENCE OF JAMES, FOURTH EARL OF FINDLATER AND FIRST EARL OF SEAFIELD, LORD CHANCELLOR OF SCOTLAND. Edited by JAMES GRANT, M.A., LL.B.

For the year 1910-1911.

4. RENTALE SANCTI ANDREE; BEING CHAMBERLAIN AND GRANITAR ACCOUNTS OF THE ARCHBISHOPRIC IN THE TIME OF CARDINAL BETOUN, 1538-1546. Translated and edited by ROBERT KERR HANNAY.
5. HIGHLAND PAPERS. Vol. I. Edited by J. R. N. MACPHAIL, K.C.

For the year 1911-1912.

6. SELECTIONS FROM THE RECORDS OF THE REGALITY OF MELROSE. Vol. I. Edited by C. S. ROMANES, C.A.
7. RECORDS OF THE EARLDOM OF ORKNEY. Edited by J. S. CLOUSTON.

For the year 1912-1913.

8. SELECTIONS FROM THE RECORDS OF THE REGALITY OF MELROSE. Vol. II. Edited by C. S. ROMANES, C.A.
9. SELECTIONS FROM THE LETTER BOOKS OF JOHN STEUART, BAILIE OF INVERNESS. Edited by WILLIAM MACKAY, LL.D.

For the year 1913-1914.

10. RENTALE DUNKELDENSE; BEING THE ACCOUNTS OF THE CHAMBERLAIN OF THE BISHOPRIC OF DUNKELD, A.D. 1506-1517. Edited by R. K. HANNAY.
11. LETTERS OF THE EARL OF SEAFIELD AND OTHERS, ILLUSTRATIVE OF THE HISTORY OF SCOTLAND DURING THE REIGN OF QUEEN ANNE. Edited by Professor HUME BROWN.

For the year 1914-1915.

12. HIGHLAND PAPERS. Vol. II. Edited by J. R. N. MACPHAIL, K.C. (March 1916.)

(*Note.*—ORIGINS OF THE '45, issued for 1909-1910, is issued also for 1914-1915.)

For the year 1915-1916.

13. SELECTIONS FROM THE RECORDS OF THE REGALITY OF MELROSE. Vol. III. Edited by C. S. ROMANES, C.A. (February 1917.)
14. A CONTRIBUTION TO THE BIBLIOGRAPHY OF SCOTTISH TOPOGRAPHY. Edited by the late Sir ARTHUR MITCHELL and C. G. CASH. Vol. I. (March 1917.)

PUBLICATIONS

For the year 1916-1917.

15. BIBLIOGRAPHY OF SCOTTISH TOPOGRAPHY. Vol. II. (May 1917.)
16. PAPERS RELATING TO THE ARMY OF THE SOLEMN LEAGUE AND COVENANT, 1643-1647. Vol. I. Edited by Professor C. SANFORD TERRY. (October 1917.)

For the year 1917-1918.

17. PAPERS RELATING TO THE ARMY OF THE SOLEMN LEAGUE AND COVENANT, 1643-1647. Vol. II. (December 1917.)
18. WARISTON'S DIARY. Vol. II. Edited by D. HAY FLEMING, LL.D. (February 1919.)

For the year 1918-1919.

19. MISCELLANY OF THE SCOTTISH HISTORY SOCIETY. Third Volume.
20. PAPERS RELATING TO THE HIGHLANDS. Vol. II. Edited by J. R. N. MACPHAIL, K.C.

THIRD SERIES.

For the year 1919-1920.

1. REGISTER OF THE CONSULTATIONS OF THE MINISTERS OF EDINBURGH, 1652-1657. Vol. I. Edited by the Rev. W. STEPHEN, B.D.

For the year 1920-1921.

2. DIARY OF GEORGE RIDPATH, MINISTER OF STITCHEL, 1755-1761. Edited by Sir JAMES BALFOUR PAUL, C.V.O., LL.D.

For the year 1921-1922.

THE CONFESSIONS OF BABINGTON AND OTHER PAPERS RELATING TO THE LAST DAYS OF MARY QUEEN OF SCOTS. Edited by the Rev. J. H. POLLEN, S.J.

In preparation.

THE EARLY RECORDS OF THE UNIVERSITY OF ST. ANDREWS, 1413-1579. Edited by J. MAITLAND ANDERSON, LL.D.

REGISTER OF THE CONSULTATIONS OF THE MINISTERS OF EDINBURGH, WITH OTHER PAPERS OF PUBLIC CONCERNMENT. Vol. II. Edited by the Rev. W. STEPHEN, B.D.

Projected.

A TRANSLATION OF THE HISTORIA ABBATUM DE KYNLOS OF FERRERIUS.

PAPERS RELATING TO THE REBELLIONS OF 1715 AND 1745, WITH OTHER DOCUMENTS FROM THE MUNICIPAL ARCHIVES OF THE CITY OF PERTH.

THE BALCARRES PAPERS.

A VOLUME OF DARIEN PAPERS. Edited by G. P. INSH, D.Litt.

Lightning Source UK Ltd.
Milton Keynes UK
UKOW07f1914190715

255408UK00012B/201/P